GUARDED WORDS

£6

GUARDED WORDS

Writing from Prison:
England, France, Russia

ERIC de BELLAIGUE

||||||||||||||||||||||||||||||||||||||||||||||||||||||||||||||||||||||||||||||||||||

UNICORN PRESS

First published in 2020 by

Unicorn Press
60 Bracondale
Norwich NR1 2BE

www.unicornpublishing.org

ISBN 978 1 916495 78 4
A Catalogue record of this book is available from the British Library

Set in Adobe Caslon Pro
Designed by Andrew Barker www.andrewbarker.co.uk
Index by Christine Shuttleworth
Printed and bound in the UK
by TJ International Ltd, Padstow, Cornwall

In Memory of my Brother
GEOFFREY

Contents

Seventeenth Century – Eighteenth Century

(B)
INCARCERATION
IN FRANCE

The French Revolution

(C)
INCARCERATION
IN RUSSIA

(D)
CONVICTED
MURDERERS

Preface

Can prison writing lay claim to a distinctive chapter in histories of literature? Is there a thread linking prisoners' output across the centuries and between countries? Can confinement provide the ideal environment for literary creativity? Is there common ground as to the subjects treated? Alternatively, does diversity ride rough-shod over the shared experience of imprisonment?

These are the kind of questions that the free pose when studying the writings of the incarcerated – a case of outsiders looking inwards. But what if they were to try to take up a position inside so as to look beyond prison walls? I have attempted to offer readers both options.

My own curiosity was stirred when I read Isaac D'Israeli's short essay "Imprisonment of Learned", to be found embedded in his *Curiosities of Literature*. His observation "Imprisonment has not always disturbed the man of letters, but often unquestionably promoted them" led him to choose some 20 prison authors ranging from Boethius through Cervantes to Defoe and Voltaire.

Such a listing underlines one of the major challenges facing anybody embarking on an enquiry into prison writing, namely that of choice. If Boethius were to be chosen, why not St Paul? How wide should the geographic coverage be? Is prison writing in translation acceptable? The answers to such questions are bound to be idiosyncratic, but at the same time, the selection process once made should be rigorous.

Under my self-imposed restrictions, texts need to have been composed within the prisons themselves, memoirs written after release being excluded. With three exceptions, the writings are in English or French. They have the year 1500 as a starting point. In two chapters, the contrasts and occasional similarities between the English and French legal systems are exposed, with particular reference to the operations of debtors' laws in England and the *lettre de cachet* (sealed writ) in France. Throughout, importance has been given to placing the prison authors within an historical setting. The chapter on Totalitarian Incarceration breaks new ground with a geographic switch and an acceptance of writings in translation. The choice of Alexander Solzhenitsyn, Lev Mishchenko and Irina Ratushinskaya has furthermore presented the opportunity of tracing in part the evolution of imprisonment of dissidents from the Stalin era to the post-Stalin era. It also serves to illustrate some of the diversity that was an aspect of the whole camp system. It is salutary to be reminded that the Gulag was still in operation little more than 30 years ago.

A recurrent feature, to which considerable attention has been given, concerns prison conditions, essential information for those wishing to come anywhere near entering the skin of the victims. The variations were indeed wide, ranging from something akin to house arrest for Charles I to slave labour for Solzhenitsyn, and often having a decisive bearing on the form their writings took. Access to writing materials, contacts with the world outside and within prisons, the rewards or the dangers of committing thoughts to paper were some of the variables that give to prison literature its rich patchwork character. This is matched by widely different ways that prison texts were transmitted. Where publication occurs, the business practices of the day call for elaboration and this leads at times to some bibliographical analysis.

The writers who make their appearance in this book are happily a mixed bag. Where some common ground is most apparent is at the personal level, notably in the causes of imprisonment.

- For religious views: John Bunyan preaching without a licence; Clément Marot for his leanings towards Protestant reform; Anne Askew for her denial of the real presence; Thomas More for his refusal to accept Henry VIII as head of the church; John Hart for his role as a Catholic priest.
- For reasons of state: Walter Ralegh tainted with conspiracy; William Prynne for his diverse political/religious views; Antoine Lavoisier for his association with the *ancien* régime; Madame Roland, André Chénier and Jean-Antoine Roucher for falling foul of the Jacobins; Surrey for posing a threat to the succession of Henry VIII; Richard Lovelace and Charles I for finding themselves on the losing side of a civil war.

- As victims of civil action: William Combe and Theodore von Neuhoff, King of Corsica, being serial debtors; Mirabeau for bringing "dishonour" to his family; Voltaire for protection from his own actions.
- For murder: Pierre François Lacenaire and William Chester Minor.
- As a nest for radical writing: Newgate Prison
- For dissidence in Russia: Alexander Solzhenitsyn; Lev Mishchenko; Irina Ratushinskaya.

This leaves unanswered the motivation that pushed them into becoming prison authors.

Antoine Lavoisier and William Combe were "working writers". The day after entering the Port Royal prison, Lavoisier was to be seen continuing with the *Mémoires de Chimie* on which he had been labouring for more than a year. From the start of his incarceration in King's Bench Prison, Combe secured commissions for translations and thereafter for the supply of verses to accompany aquatint prints – all with a view to earning money, some of it intended to pay off his creditors.

For Bunyan to have written in Bedford County Gaol *Grace Abounding*, the account of his spiritual development, and Thomas More *A Dialogue of Comfort against Tribulation*, described as his ultimate spiritual testament, in the Tower of London, may be said to point to the encouragement that solitude in a deeply solemn setting can give to meditation and introspection – something that Isaac D'Israeli sensed. For a diametrically different response, one turns to the prison love letters of Mirabeau to Sophie and those of Lev Mishchenko to Sveta, in both cases aimed at conquering that very isolation and solitude by smuggling as it were the girls they loved into their cells.

The prison autobiography has two sides to it. One, in the spirit of Rousseau's *Confessions*, being an intimate account of the author's life, as exemplified in the second half of Madame Roland's *Memoirs*. The other, is more akin to a court room summation, where the opportunity is taken "to set the record straight". Charles I's *Eikon Basilike* is an extreme example of its kind: a royal vindication that successfully functioned as a powerful posthumous political tool. By contrast, Lacenaire's own memoirs are unusual for being an extended celebration of a life of crime.

Among seventeenth-century polemical writers, William Prynne occupies a prominent place, with lengthy volumes and countless pamphlets to his name. Throughout his spells in prison, which added up to some ten years, he still succeeded in maintaining his literary flow. For radical thinkers in the eighteenth century and early nineteenth, who found themselves in Newgate Prison, incarceration was also to prove no great obstacle to writing – and indeed a club-like atmosphere may have even acted as a spur.

Walter Ralegh is the outstanding figure as a prison historian with his 1570-page *History of the World*, which takes one no further than the end of the second Punic War. His motivation will no doubt have been complex. The wish to fill his days with an intellectual challenge, the fear of otherwise being lost sight of, the satisfaction he may have derived from stimulating political thought among his contemporaries, the sheer love of literature. In common with Bunyan's *Pilgrim's Progress*, Ralegh's *History of the World* secured its place in the influential British Museum exhibition of July, 1963, "Printing and the Mind of Man" – an impressive prison testimonial. Among my prison writers, Mirabeau also features as an historian with his two-volume work *Des Lettres de Cachet et des Prisons d'Etat*, a powerful indictment written by a victim when serving his sentence.

The incarcerated have often turned to verse. For many this will have represented a continuation of an existing literary form that they had practised when free and then exercised from within prison walls. Marot, Chénier, Lovelace, Surrey carry the flag for poetry. The lyrical verse, however, quite quickly gives way: in Surrey's case to poetic paraphrases of psalms and translations of Vergil, in that of Chénier to fierce denunciations of the injustices inflicted by the despots. The correspondence of the poet, Roucher, a lifeline for him and his family, was also seen by Roucher as offering for future use a lesson in morality for his young son. This leads on to those Russian dissidents, whose prime motivation is "to bear witness to truth". With the illicit "writings", often committed to memory, the courage displayed is humbling. And if one needed evidence of the flourishing state of intolerance in modern Russia, there was the announcement in October 2014 that the Kremlin was looking to liquidate "Memorial", the country's oldest human rights organisation. In the absence of Memorial, the remarkable love letters of Lev Mishchenko and Svetlana might never have been preserved. To this day, Memorial remains under heavy political and financial pressure.

And, as an epilogue to this canter through the reasons that move the imprisoned to write, William Chester Minor stands indebted to the lunatic asylum near Crowthorne for having given him 20 productive years by enabling him to contribute to the creation of the *Oxford English Dictionary*.

The horrors — or endurances — of a prison existence varied widely. Setting aside the physical challenges, the psychological pressures will have weighed with particular intensity on those facing near-certain death – Madame Roland, Jean-Antoine Roucher, Thomas More, Antoine Lavoisier and Walter Ralegh (twice). Lacenaire, on the other hand, found the prospect appealing. More generally, the test of character posed by sentences, some with terminal dates attached, others of indefinite duration, that might yet stretch into decades, was huge. Occasionally, however, imprisonment became a way of life, not devoid of certain amenities, as experienced by William Combe, for whom King's Bench Prison was home for 24 years.

Finally, within the list of prisoners cited in this book, unusual classifications occasionally surface, as with three English "martyrs": two secured external nomination, one for the Catholic cause, Thomas More, one for the Protestant cause, Anne Askew, while Charles I stands as a "constitutional" martyr, self-proclaimed from the scaffold – though subsequently his martyrdom was embraced by the Established Church. France provides two instances of prisoners securing cult status. Throughout much of his life Lacenaire might be said to have had this as an objective, the achievement being given special impetus by a theatrical court case and a well-publicised execution. Forty-five years later, a disaffected young man, turned murderer, claimed Lacenaire as his inspiration. One hundred and five years on, Lacenaire was the subject of Marcel Carné's epic film, *Les Enfants du Paradis* ("Children of the Gods"), issued within months of the end of the war in Europe. The cult status of André Chénier was in no way of his own making. Widespread recognition of his lyrical poetic gifts had to await posthumous publication of his poems, at which point he was promptly enlisted in the ranks of the romantic movement. He then experienced two forms of identity theft, one benign, being Umberto Giordano's fictionalised operatic production, *Andrea Chenier* of 1898. The other amounted to a case of character assassination 150 years after his death, when the fascist Robert Brasillach claimed him as his mentor ahead of his own execution as a traitor. This also fell in 1945.

In the course of my research, I am indebted to the London Metropolitan Archives, the National Archives in Kew, the Parliamentary Archives in the

House of Lords, as well as to Lambeth Palace Library on numerous occasions. The London Library, with its infinitely precious borrowing facilities, requires special mention. The British Library's extraordinary resources were happily mined. A research facility that was unusual and depended on urban exploration chiefly in London and Paris, took me to prisons with their graffiti, to churches with their memorial tablets and the pious records on tombstones, to historical plaques attached to buildings and to a pillar box in Oxford. Occasionally, no amount of on-the-ground research produced the desired result.

In the writing of this book, the joys of research have been considerable. Being introduced to historians and biographers who would otherwise have remained unknown proved thoroughly rewarding. The direction given thereby to further reading has moreover encompassed the diversified output from prison of a group of talented men and women. Teasing out curiosities, such as the remnants of Minor's library held in the Bodleian, and piecing together a picture of the undocumented Peterhouse Prison, has also had its rewards. And for a bibliophile, the purchase of a copy of the speech Madame Roland will have largely composed for her husband to deliver to the Assemblée Nationale in denunciation of the prison massacres is hard to better.

Structure

The sequence of chapters is primarily governed by geography – England, France, Russia, each in its historical setting. A second influence is chronological, with coverage that starts at the beginning of the sixteenth century and extends in some instances to the end of the twentieth century. At times, however, this order is overridden when recognition is given to the prolonged role as a source of prison literature by the likes of Newgate Prison and The Tower of London. A fourth determinant affecting the structure of the book relates to the causes of imprisonment, as illustrated with the French Revolution, which takes in four prison writers, and Incarceration in Russia, which takes in three; the final chapters carry this classification one step further through the selection of two authors imprisoned for murder.

Where similarities or contrasts in the experience of the imprisoned are noted, attention is frequently drawn to them, thereby acting as a gentle form of adhesive to an account that otherwise makes a virtue of diversity.

(A)
INCARCERATION
IN ENGLAND

CHAPTER I

Historical Background

The major prisons served a number of purposes. There was the custodial role, covering the safe custody of suspects or those awaiting execution, as in the case of traitors. Then came their function as penal institutions, where imprisonment was an instrument of punishment. In third place, the coercive purpose related to the detention of debtors.

From the later medieval period the number of prison-worthy offences increased steadily.[1] On W. B. Carnochan's calculations, by 1550 there were 180 such offences under common law, vagrancy being one fruitful addition. The definition in itself of a criminal act was for many centuries extremely broad and the punishments imposed were often of the utmost severity. Capital offences were legion, with thieves, guilty of the smallest thefts, being ranged alongside murderers, fraudsters, pirates, swindlers, poachers ... Clarification, of sorts, came with a decree in 1699 under which theft only joined the ranks of capital offences when it amounted to more than one shilling when taken from an individual and more than five shillings from a shop.

The full rigour of the law could, however, be relaxed. To cite one instance: the eighteenth-century bookseller/publisher, Edmund Curll, took to court his fifteen-year-old servant, Sarah Beeston, who had stolen a number of valuable antiquarian books and sold them to a nearby bookstall for 12 shillings and 6 pence, well below their true worth. This did not deter the jury from knocking down the value of the stolen books to a mere 10 pence, thereby "saving" Sarah Beeston from the gallows and "earning" her deportation.[2]

One valuable legal loophole had its origins when literacy was largely confined to men in holy orders –their being able to invoke "benefit of clergy" and thereby have their cases placed within the more conciliatory bishops' jurisdiction. Such recognition given to literacy persisted well beyond the Middle Ages, with convicted criminals escaping the death sentence in secular courts if they could prove their literacy through reading a passage from the Bible. The outstanding instance of English literature profiting from this simple reading test arises with Ben Jonson. As a 25-year-old he had killed a fellow actor, Gabriel Spencer, in a duel. On conviction of murder, he had pleaded – as a first offender might – "benefit of clergy", had passed the reading test, suffered confiscation of his possessions and was duly branded with the letter "T" on the base of the left thumb, a precaution against any attempt at obtaining another such reprieve in the future. In this way, Jonson's prolific literary output over the ensuing 40 years was protected from extinction for posterity.

Subsequently, the application of this get-out gained in flexibility, but very much at the whim of the magistrate. Andrew Coltée Ducarel, Lambeth Palace librarian in the 1760s, wrote in his Commonplace Book that the criminal "was to have a Latin Bible in black Gothic letter delivered to him and if he could read on a Place which the judge appointed, which was generally in the Psalms . . . , the Criminal was saved as being a man of Learning, and as such might be of use to the Publick. Otherwise he was sure to be hanged".[3] The psalm normally chosen was Psalm 51, the first verse becoming known as "the neck verse"; this gave the more alert malefactors the incentive to familiarise themselves with this particular psalm – and if reading was a problem to commit it to memory. Ducarel mentions that some were even ready to sing it. Branding had ceased, a considerable help to recidivists.

From Norman times, those who owed money to the Crown faced imprisonment pending the discharge of their debt. But in the thirteenth century provision was already being made for the needs of the merchant class, leading to the Statute of Merchants of 1285, which authorised the immediate imprisonment of a debtor on the day of default. What the historian Ralph B. Pugh describes as the piece of medieval legislation which had the greatest impact on the whole history of imprisonment is contained in the 17th clause of the Statute of 1352: this placed the common creditor – whether or not a member of the merchant class – in the same position as the Crown and gave him the power of imprisoning his debtor's body until the debt in dispute should have been settled. Ralph Pugh goes on to write: "From this statute sprang all the imprisonment for debt, all the debtors' prisons or debtors' wards and all the lamentations which they brought in their train."[4]

In any account of imprisonment in London, the Fleet deserves early mention, being already designated by the year 1130 as "the gaol of London"

Fleet Prison c. 1808 by T. Rowlandson and A. C. Pugin

and from 1189 being referred to specifically as the Fleet Prison, to distinguish it from Newgate Prison, established the previous year. At an early stage, the Fleet was singled out as the prison for the king's debtors.[5] At around the same time Newgate came to be seen as the country's leading criminal penal prison. By the start of the sixteenth century the Fleet, named after its proximity to the City river of that name, acted not only as the prison for the courts of Chancery and Exchequer, but also of the Star Chamber. The latter's abolition in 1641 helped to push it towards a specialisation for which it is best known as one of the three principal London debtor prisons of the seventeenth and eighteenth centuries. The others were King's Bench and Marshalsea, both in Southwark. The build-up in the demand for prison accommodation during this period also witnessed the intensive use of local gaols for petty offenders and debtors, those falling under the jurisdiction of the City's London and Middlesex sheriffs being known as Compters; they took the names of the City streets in which they were established, as with

Bread Street, Poultry, Wood Street, Giltspur Street. Furthermore, the eighteenth century saw a proliferation of lock-ups linked to public houses.

The numbers of those imprisoned in England and Wales, let alone any breakdown as between debtors, criminals and state prisoners, are hard to come by. William Leach, a barrister, estimated in 1651 that between 12,000 and 20,000 people were in gaol, as quoted by D. Veald.[6] The spread serves as a warning against attaching great importance to such totals. Another wide-ranging assessment, this time limited to London, by Richard Byrne is that from the fourteenth to the nineteenth centuries "at least as many Londoners were locked up for debt as for crime".[7]

It is when one comes to John Howard, the great prison reformer, that the statistics start to carry conviction. The following table lists the numbers of prisoners in England and Wales, based on his prison visits in 1779 and 1782.[8]

	1779	*1782*
Men debtors	1,959	2,058
Women debtors	119	139
Felons etc.	798	991
Petty offenders	917	1,017
Prisoners in hulks	526	204
Supposed omitted	60	30
TOTAL	4,379	4,439

Some of the discomforts endured by Howard are vividly illustrated by Sean McConville: "When Howard made his extensive visitations in the 1770's, he was obliged to travel on horseback because the smell given off by his clothes, just from a few hours contact, did not permit of coach travel."[9]

Private lodgings, known as sponging houses, in the neighbourhood of debtors' prisons – frequently taverns kept by prison officers – could also be places where debtors might be held; at their best, they formed a gentle preliminary to incarceration and also supplied the delay that could be put to use by the debtor seeking to settle his affairs.[10] This was the case on March 16, 1756, when Samuel Johnson was arrested for a debt of 5 pounds and 13 shillings and taken to a sponging house; from there he sent an urgent note to Samuel Richardson, whose loan of six guineas secured his release two days later. A mere eleven months earlier, Johnson was being fêted on the publication of his great *Dictionary*.[11]

A special regime applied to the Fleet and King's Bench, where an area outside each prison was defined as the "Rules"; prisoners with means could take up residence there, providing they met certain conditions and respected various regulations. At times the "Rules" could account for 20 per cent or more of those imprisoned. Also in Southwark, "The Mint", an area 200 yards square close to King's Bench Prison, acted as a sanctuary.[12] It was a self-governing no-go area for bailiffs and constables, which gave refuge mainly to debtors. This medieval relic was annulled by law in 1697, but lingered on as a haven until 1723.

Hulks, which enter Howard's prison table, were decommissioned men of war. They acted at various times as staging posts for convicts destined to be transported to America (notably Virginia and Maryland) up to the American War of Independence in 1775, and to Australia from 1787 until 1840; fluctuations in the numbers had much to do with the timing of outward sailings. Debtors were at no time involved.

Imprisoned for Debt

In his *Biography of the Marshalsea Debtors' Prison*, Jerry White's introduction includes a timely reminder that in the eighteenth and nineteenth centuries everyone for a time was almost certain to be a debtor. Where bank facilities, often by way of a loan or an agreed overdraft limit, will now meet many individual purchasers' needs, then the more well-to-do might have occasional recourse to bills of exchange and letters of credit and the impoverished might find the pawnbroker to be a short term but expensive solution. Generally, however, credit was secured via the build-up of bilateral obligations between customers and their often numerous suppliers. A supremely practical contributing factor was the scarcity of small-denomination coins, which hindered any prompt settlement of accounts, particularly relevant to the circumstances of the man of the street.[13] The consequences of postponed budgeting and the opportunities for dishonest dealing are reflected in the prison population statistics.

In both of the years observed by Howard, close to half of the 4,400 prisoners were accounted for by debtors – 47.5per cent in 1779 and 49.5per cent in 1782. Recognition needs also to be given to the fact that on average debtors

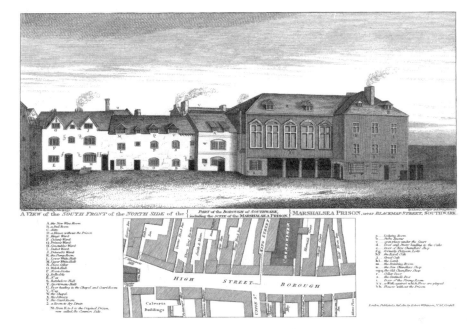

The Marshalsea Prison, mainly for debtors,
in Borough High Street, Southwark, 1773

were longer-term residents – perhaps three years or more – whereas for felons the gaol delivery before either release or execution will have often been less than a year. And when petty offenders in compters and lock-ups are considered, the length of stay will have been very short indeed, though a sophisticated analysis would need to consider repeat offenders. A much more significant adjustment would arise if allowance for the presence of debtors' families in gaols were to be made, as a way of representing the "debtor population" in prisons rather than simply the bodies over which creditors exercised their control. In 1776 Howard found that the Fleet was housing 475 wives and children.[14] At one point in 1801, of the 36 debtors in the Poultry Compter, 11 were accompanied by their wives and 17 children.[15] Any measure of the economic consequences of debtors' incarceration, taking into account length of stay, family disruption, exclusion from commercial activity would reveal the economic burden that this law put on the country as a whole.

One other statistical record was supplied in 1800 by the treasurer of the Society for the Discharge and Relief of Small Debtors (successor of the

Thatched House Society), which undertook a survey by correspondence of debtor prisons throughout the land. In addition to tabulating the returns as at mid-year, a number of entries are enriched by comments.[16] For Penzance, "This prison is in a back yard, about fourteen feet square, with one iron-barred window and a small necessary room in one corner. It belongs to Lord Arundel whose hog-stye it is said is a palace to it." Fortunately, at the time of the survey it contained only one prisoner. A happier note was struck with respect to the Poultry Compter, where the common side debtors benefited from "a collection of broken victuals from different taverns and eating houses about the Exchange, of which the London Tavern, the George and Vulture, the Cock eating house etc".[17] It is gratifying to be able to report that the George and Vulture continues to flourish; "broken victuals", however, have fallen victim to refrigeration.

This 1800 survey listed 1,982 debtors within prisons in England and Wales, the highest numbers being in the Fleet (230), King's Bench (400), Newgate (213), Lancaster Castle (87) and York Castle (73). The surprisingly low figure of 30 recorded for the Marshalsea (down from 234 in mid-May 1776) may reflect passage of the Act of 1778 protecting small debtors from frivolous or vindictive imprisonment. But why this should have had a disproportionate impact on the prison population of the Marshalsea is unclear. To the distress of the Society's treasurer, James Neild, some 25 prisons had never heard of the Society, despite its 28 years of existence. As a corrective, he promptly supplied them with the Society's painted Boards of Instructions.

The circumstances of the great bulk of debtors who are genuinely impoverished and imprisoned under the warrants of creditors who themselves may only be marginally better off, deserve elaboration. Most imprisonments were brought about by "mesne process", the creditor having sworn an affidavit quantifying the sum owed before a judge (without there being a hearing from the debtor).[18] It was only when the creditor took the decisive step of a writ of execution by way of a formal declaration as a preliminary to a trial that he was obliged by the law of 1759 to provide maintenance to the imprisoned debtor; this was initially at a rate of four pence per week, increased in 1797 to six pence per week. (Failure to keep up payments rendered the debtor supersedable, whereby he was discharged). Such a declaration could be delayed for months at a time, leaving the debtor in suspense and out of pocket.

The sums involved, at a casual glance, will often have been modest, though appearances can be deceptive. Robert Twigger, in his House of Commons research paper, estimated that today's decimal penny in 1750 would have had a purchasing power somewhat in excess of one pound in 1998. Imprisonment of itself created obligations that could mount up rapidly. The experience of John Allen is a case in point: he entered Newgate on February 7, 1797, owing three shillings five pence; he was freed in mid-1800, by which time his prison debts at eight shillings and eight pence were more than twice the sum for which he had been imprisoned in the first place and this had lifted the total that he owed to 12 shillings and one penny.[19] For a debtor on the common (disadvantaged) side, prison obligations covered outlays on food/drink – over and above any charitable or municipal allocations – plus any additional supplies for heating, for drink and assorted fees levied by the keeper and the turnkey. Allen was fortunate. In the absence of charitable support, it is easy to see him condemned to indefinite incarceration, burdened with ever-increasing obligations and unable to pay his exit dues.

The better-off debtor, who secured a place on what was known as the master's side or the state side, had by definition resources that the others did not. He also had additional costs covering rent and the conveniences of life. Against which, the big debtors were those who were best positioned to take advantage of the law. A popular perfectly legal move by the end of the eighteenth century was to secure a writ of habeas corpus, thereby permitting a change of prison. While this landed the debtor with additional legal fees, the transfer could be achieved on very little notice and a re-location to say King's Bench Prison was viewed by many as a significant upgrade. By contrast, the insolvency laws that James Pearce considers in his *A Treatise on the Abuses of the Law* of 1814, gave scope for exploitation: an incentive existed for the unscrupulous to borrow to the hilt and then enter prison so as to spend the money in tranquillity. Others might elect to remain prisoners for life in order to enable their estates to descend intact to their heirs.

From early days, the hardships that the vulnerable in society suffered were recognised, and imprisonment attracted considerable charitable giving of an ongoing nature as well as via legacies. From the fourteenth century, wills included provisions for the redemption of debtors and, as Ralph Pugh writes, by the start of Queen Elizabeth's reign this had become hugely popular.[20] Confirmation comes in numerous memorial inscriptions and in the researches made by Ian Archer into London wills covering the period from 1528 to 1638.

Among the private initiatives in the eighteenth century, one of the most important – already mentioned in connection with prison numbers – is the Thatched House Society, named after the Thatched House Tavern in St James's Street, where it held its meetings in its early years. The minutes dated Sunday February 23, 1772, read: "At Charlotte Chapel Dr. Dodd preached a Sermon for the Benefit and Relief of Persons confined for Small Debts and there was collected sixty eight pounds sixteen shillings which with twelve pounds five shillings collected before at Bedford Chapel amounted to the sum of eighty-one pounds one shilling." To this initial fund the Society set out to attract legacies, donations and apply any rental income that might come its way for the release of debtors providing they were not already beneficiaries under the Benefit of the Insolvent Act going through Parliament.

From the outset, the Committee had as its aim small debtors, with preference being given to "the most useful artists and manufacturers and those who have the largest families". The Committee undertook to visit regularly the more prominent debtors' prisons.[21] As an example of an impressive legacy, Henrietta Maria Tomlinson, whose will was proved on 30 May 1775, bequeathed to the poor debtors in the prison of Whitechapel the considerable sum of 100 pounds; to the poor prisoners (a wider definition) in the Poultry Compter and those in the Fleet Prison also 100 pounds in each case and to those in the Marshalsea 100 guineas. The will elaborates "The money I have left to Poor Prisoners I would have laid out in Food, Fireing and cloaths for such as are in want unless my Executrix and Executor find it more useful to discharge any of them by payment of small debts, and give them two or three pounds to begin the world again." These generous provisions also highlight the challenges facing executors and charities in their dealings with prison keepers or those within prisons who might have the task of administering these monies. All too often, donations will have suffered shrinkage before they reached the intended beneficiaries – if at all.

The Society got off to a strong start and made a point of stimulating interest through frequent entries in the *Westminster Journal* and other newssheets, itemising receipts and disbursements. As early as May 20, 1772, they were able to announce that they had "already discharged 104 Persons (many of whom are useful Manufacturers, and have large families) for £263.14.2" – an economical outlay of some £2.10.0. per head. Edward Farley, in his powerful indictment of the incarceration of debtors, dated 1788, credits the Society with having discharged about 12,000 debtors from prison over 14 years.[22]

The progress of the Society can be followed on a detailed basis at the London Metropolitan Archives, which holds the legacy books from the Society's inception and the Minutes Books, with the startling exception of the nine years 1818 to 1826 "during which period the minutes of the Society were destroyed by Mr. John Camden Neild, the late Treasurer". He is not to be confused with his father, James Neild, celebrated philanthropist and one of the Society's original backers, as well as author of the report quoted earlier. As an aside, there is a certain irony in that when the Thatched House Society moved from St James's Street to Craven Street and changed its name, the tavern in St James's Street became the meeting place of the Society of Dilettanti, known for a while as the Thatched House Club. On a much more solemn note, the Society, which owed its start in 1772 to the preaching of the Reverend William Dodd, had to come to terms with the fact that some five years later its benefactor was hanged for having forged the name of Lord Chesterfield for a bond of £4,200. In the chapter on Newgate he is remembered for his prison writings.

At various times in the seventeenth and eighteenth centuries pamphlets emphasising the miseries of the very impoverished made their appearance. These include: William Fennor's 1616 description of the conditions in the Wood Street Compter and the subversion of charitable donations;[23] *The Piercing Cryes of the Poor Miserable Prisoners for Debt* of 1714 addressed by the anonymous author to Queen Anne, with particular reference to the Marshalsea, where for the most part prisoners are "without those Necessaries, which are required only for the bare support of Life, two or three commonly perishing in one day"; also Edward Farley's *Emprisonment for Debt Unconstitutional and Oppressive proved from Fundamental Principles of the British Constitution and the Rights of Nature* of 1788.

For a detailed official exposé into the conditions of the Marshalsea one can turn to the 1729 Report from the Committee appointed by the House of Commons.[24] Interestingly, it serves as a major indictment of the practice of "farming" prison management.[25] William Acton, a butcher, had undertaken to pay the licensee, John Darby, on a seven-year lease £140 a year, as well as £260 representing rental income secured on the master's side. As the report succinctly puts it, "to make profit of the Prison to arise to answer the said exorbitant Rents no kind of Artifice or Oppression has been unpracticed".[26] This covered extortion on the state side – except for those in the governor's good books – and on the common side, where grinding poverty reigned supreme, appropriation of charitable donations. Ultimately, the governor was charged on four counts with murder, but escaped conviction thanks to the difficulty of linking his brutal rule to the frequent prison deaths from fever and starvation.

The King of Corsica
(1694–1756)

To conclude this chapter, the memorial tablet of London's highest-ranking victim of the debtors' laws deserves to be noticed. It survives attached to an outer wall of the tower of St Anne's, Soho, which is all that remains of this London church after heavy bombing during World War II. It reads:

> Near this place is interred / Theodore King of Corsica / who died in this parish Dec. 11, 1756 / immediately after leaving / the King's Bench Prison / by the benefit of the Act of Insolvency / in consequence of which / he registered his Kingdom of Corsica / for the use of his creditors

Born in 1694 in Cologne, Theodore von Neuhoff was brought up in the French court, served on various occasions in the French, Swedish and Spanish armies and found time to be involved in the financial speculations of John Law, to indulge his enthusiasm for the card table and to engage in the sport of dodging creditors, widely practised in aristocratic circles of the day. His encounter, however, with the rebels and exiles from Corsica, then under Genoese rule, gave him the cause – freedom for Corsica – which was to govern the rest of his life and an opportunity that no adventurer of his stamp could pass by. In 1736, having skilfully secured financial and material backing from a variety of sources, he led an expedition aimed at releasing the Corsicans from under this yoke. The force landed on March 21. The grateful islanders then proceeded to elect him king, his coronation taking place on April 15, following which he issued edicts under the name of King Theodore, created an order of chivalry and battled with the Genoese. Sadly for the Corsicans, the uprising proved unsuccessful and on November 14 Theodore's reign of seven months ended with his retreat to Livorno and then to Holland. There he suffered the immediate inconvenience of incarceration for debt; within a month he was bailed out by one of his backers. Nothing daunted, he resumed his diplomatic and financial efforts. In 1738, he was to be found gathering support for an armada and in 1743 he was once more in the island, but the foreign occupation force could not be dislodged.

By 1749 he was in London seeking as ever funds and support for the Corsican cause, but with declining success. His own financial situation remained precarious. In late December 1749 a creditor managed to serve him a writ for £400 and he was duly lodged in King's Bench prison. News of his arrest then brought into the open other creditors so that his total obligations exceeded £1,500, against which his assets were negligible.[27] He was to spend four and a half years in the King's Bench, during which time he had experience of both the master's side and the common side. For a while, he was able to trade on his royal status, the curiosity of a crowned head in a London gaol attracting visitors, some of whom became benefactors. Horace Walpole sponsored a subscription in his favour. David Garrick gave him a benefit night.[28] And Theodore generated some income himself by occasionally bestowing knighthoods under the "Order of Liberation" – for a moderate fee. Theodore von Neuhoff's prison writings are confined to a sustained correspondence directed to his partisans as well as to potential backers. The novelty of his situation was as it were a wasting asset, however, and his circumstances in prison became more constrained as the months passed. Release came in May 1755, when he was able to take prompt advantage of the recent Act under which a bankrupt could be freed provided he signed over his assets to his creditors.[29] In the document duly signed by Theodore at the Old Bailey on June 24, 1755, he stated, under the heading Schedule of Effects, "that he is entitled to the kingdom of Corsica, and hath no other estates or effects but in right of that Kingdom".

Theodor Stephan von Neuhoff, King Theodore I of Corsica (1694–1756), from a posthumous engraving

This proved all too accurate. As a free man, he was in effect destitute and this resulted in his being re-incarcerated as a debtor in King's Bench, where he spent much of the last year of his life. His final release, which came on December 5, 1756, was followed by his death on December 11; he had been taken in by a charitable tailor.[30] His funeral on December 15 was generously paid for by an oil merchant in nearby Compton Street, attracted perhaps also by the exceptional opportunity from a publicity angle to which this royal death gave rise, and he was buried in the pauper's section of St Anne's churchyard. It is to Horace Walpole that we owe the inscription, honouring the life of a man who was king, albeit for only seven months, and king in exile for the ensuing 20 years.

Some 70 years after his death Theodore was joined, so to speak, in St Anne's graveyard by William Hazlitt, who died in 1830. The latter's essay *On the Want of Money* is a comprehensive and engaging account of the indignities and hardships of such a condition, rendered all the more convincing

by Hazlitt's own experiences. Theodore had also much suffered the consequences of what Hazlitt terms "that uncertain, casual, precarious mode of existence, in which temptation to spend remains after the means are exhausted". If shades can be said to have commerce one with the other, Hazlitt, that
lifelong champion of individual liberty against the oppression of tyrants,
would have looked with additional favour on Theodore's attempt to free the
Corsicans from under the heel of their oppressors – one awkwardness, however: Hazlitt's profound admiration for the arch-imperialist and the greatest
of all Corsicans, Napoleon Bonaparte.

Abolition of Imprisonment for Debt

The abolition of imprisonment for debt was a gradual process, as was the dis-
mantling of the prison scenery. It was in part a reflection of public opinion,
increasingly shaped by the work of societies such as the Thatched House,
exposures by victims, the emergence into prominence of such reformers as
John Howard, James Neild and Elizabeth Fry, the dissemination of official
reports in the wake of epidemics and/or scandals, plus the passage of legislation, however variable in its impact. In 1673 an Act for the Relief of Insolvent
Debtors came into force; 1729 saw an Act for the Regulation of Sponging
Houses, the modest outcome of the damning report on the Marshalsea
Prison; in 1752 a parliamentary committee was set up with the aim of distinguishing between fraudulent and insolvent debtors; this gave birth in early
1755 to the Act for the Relief of Insolvent Debtors under which Theodore,
having forfeited all rights to any assets, was freed; in 1813, in a further lib-
eralisation, prisoners of three months' standing were able to apply to a special court for their discharge as insolvent debtors, while those seeking relief
through the Insolvent Debtors' Act were permitted bail, thereby reducing
imprisonment to a matter of a few days; in 1835 a bill for the Abolition of
Imprisonment for Debt was sponsored by Sir John Campbell; this had the
support of Lord Melbourne and was an accurate reflection of changing opinions. In 1842, the collapse in demand for accommodation led to the closures
of the Fleet and Marshalsea prisons and the consolidation of debtors in the
King's Bench.[31] Finally, in 1869 the Bankruptcy Act came into force, under
which debtors' prisons were abolished and imprisonment for debt outlawed,

except in cases of fraud. On the eve of its enactment, facilities across the country were stretched to the utmost in the rush of people wishing to be committed to prison, since by having served a few days behind bars they would be freed of their debts.[32]

IIIIIIIIIIIIIIIIIIIIIIIIIIIIIIIIIIIIIIIIIIIIIIIIIIIIIIIIIIIIIIIIIIIIIIIIIIIIIIIIIIIIII

CHAPTER II

Newgate Prison

In any consideration of prison writing, Newgate Prison occupies an exceptional position, having given its name to *The Newgate Calendar* and the "Newgate Novel". More to the point, its literary credentials are solidly based on the extensive list of its published authors.

Notoriety is the other distinguishing feature, making Newgate a byword for inhumane conditions of incarceration, where vice and filth vied for primacy. A dramatic instance of the latter came in 1750 with what became known as the "Black Session of Newgate", when four of the six judges on the bench caught gaol fever (typhus) and died, and so did 40 jurymen and officials of the court. The number of prisoners who also expired is not known.[1]

The Prison Ordinary

From the middle ages Newgate was recognised as a leading criminal prison. Over time, in addition to state prisoners it also accommodated religious prisoners, felons of all hues, and debtors. Landmarks in its history of particular relevance to the subject of this work include the first appointment in 1544 of a prison clergyman, then known as the "Visitor of Newgate", whose tasks included persuading prisoners to return stolen property and inducing them to disclose their accomplices.[2] In 1620 a full-time chaplain was appointed, to be known as the "Ordinary". His role was both more specific and wider. Those condemned to death were his particular responsibility: encouraging them to repent of their sins and, on the day preceding their execution, preaching the condemned sermon in Newgate Chapel. That evening, the prisoners in their cells will have benefited from the attentions of the bell- ringer from the nearby church of St Sepulchre reminding them of their fate; the small bell is displayed to this day in the church.[3]

In St Botolph, Aldgate, there is a fine monument to Robert Dow, who died in 1612, erected by the Guild of Merchant Taylors, of which he had been Master. Dow was a wealthy man and a remarkable philanthropist, having made, as the memorial tablet records, charitable bequests in the course of a long life, amounting to the considerable sum of 3,528 pounds, 10 shillings and 8 pence. Recipients of his benefactions included St Sepulchre and Newgate – with 26 shillings and 8 pence being reserved for the capital cost of the bell and the annual reward of the bellman.

On the morning of the execution, the Ordinary was required to accompany the condemned to the gallows – to Tyburn (near today's Marble Arch) up to 1783 and thereafter to a point close to the prison itself. Furthermore, the Ordinary was required to publish an account of the execution. Their exposure to gaol fever, proximity to the hangman and the whiff of the informer that stuck to them helps to explain Sean McConville's statement that Newgate Ordinaries were recruited from the lower fringes of the Church and that "this was one of the most ill-famed prison posts of all times".[4]

One striking exception to this harsh judgment is provided by Paul Lorrain. Little is known of his background other than the fact that he was a Huguenot immigrant. By the beginning of 1678, however, he was in the employ of Samuel Pepys, as copyist and secretary, a role he loyally filled for the ensuing 22 years.[5] Lorrain helped Pepys marshal the evidence against the accusation of treason levelled at him in the aftermath of the "Popish Plot", which survives in two massive manuscript volumes, partly in Lorrain's beautiful scribal hand. In a quieter vein, he helped Pepys catalogue and arrange his library, happily preserved in Magdalene College, Cambridge. In 1682 he dedicated to Pepys his translation of a work entitled *Funeral Rites*, and over the years was the author of a number of religious tracts. His deepening religious convictions led him to enter the Church in 1690, with the full support of Pepys, who praised his "sobriety, diligence and integrity". It was not until 1700 that his employment by Pepys came to an end, though more informal links were subsequently maintained up to Pepys's death in 1703. As late as October 12, 1700 we find him remonstrating gently with an impatient Pepys:

"But I find, by your Honour's expecting a further progress, that you did not take notice that much time has been spent by me in perusing, improving and preparing for a fair transcription not only the several chapters of this Appendix already written, but those that yet remain unwritten fair."[6]

In 1700, the Reverend Paul Lorrain was appointed Ordinary of Newgate by the Court of Aldermen, the post being in the gift of the City Sheriff and by extension of the Lord Mayor. In a letter to a friend dated November 7 Lorrain writes: "I (who all along have endeavoured to live blameless and suitable to my Holy Profession) was by order of that Court committed to New Gate."

This was a full-time job, which carried a salary of £35 a year; in addition, the incumbent benefited from a bequest of long standing worth £6 per year, as well as an annual allocation of a freedom of the city worth on sale about £25.[7] The Ordinary also had the use of a house in Newgate Street. All told, the post then carried with it direct remuneration of some £56. This, however, ignores variable revenues from the publication of accounts of executions.

A predecessor in the post, Samuel Smith, was Ordinary from 1676. In 1684 he had begun to produce, in conjunction with the printer George Croom, accounts of executions under the title "The True Account of the Behaviour, Confession of . . . . ." The commonplace book of the Lambeth Palace librarian, Andrew Coltée Ducarel (1713–1785), includes a poem on Samuel Smith, Ordinary of Newgate, the first verse of which reads:

> Under this Stone
> Lies Reverend Drone
> To Tyburn well known
> Who preach'd against Sin
> With a terrible Grin
> In which some may think he acted but oddly,
> Since he lived by the wicked and not by the Godly[8]

Samuel Smith claimed that his work was undertaken at the request of the prisoners themselves. Be that as it may, a certain John Allen was subsequently dismissed from this post, one reason being "his frequent prevarications in the printing and Publishing the pretended Confessions of the respective Criminals that are executed at Tybourne". The Ordinary's account became indeed a semi-official publication the production of which 24 hours after the execution was an obligation on the incumbent. At the same time, the editorial, printing and distribution were his responsibility and what profits might accrue, were his to enjoy. Under Lorrain's management, these could amount to £200 a year, almost four times the official remuneration.

During Lorrain's tenure, the typical format was one folio-size broadsheet leaf, giving therefore two pages of text, bearing a standardised introduction: "The Ordinary of Newgate, His Account of the Behaviour, Confessions and Last Speeches of . . . . . executed on . . . .". This was then followed by (a) a description of the crime, (b) a biographical sketch of the criminal(s), (c) a recital of the prison confession, if made, and (d) most important of all a report on his/her state of mind preceding the execution and of any speech made on the scaffold. Such speeches were often penitential and carried fervent exhortations to their audience to avoid following their example. A wit of the day was moved to describe these criminals as "Lorrain's saints". Each broadsheet was firmly signed P. Lorrain; he also warned readers against counterfeit productions, the only authentic accounts being his, which became available at his printers at 8am on the day following the execution.

This was a slick, business-like operation. It necessitated close contact with the printers. In a portfolio of 25 broadsheets and six pamphlets held in the British Library, extending from May 15, 1706 to March 17, 1718, four printers were used, one of whom on being replaced complained of the hard bargain driven by Lorrain.[9] The commercial aspect is also illustrated in the inclusion at the bottom of the account, below Lorrain's signature, of advertisements in a number of issues. Some of these announced the publication of works of piety – occasionally those of Lorrain himself – and others carried promises of earthly bliss: readers of the execution of William Paul and of John Hall for high treason on July 13, 1716, were also directed to the Red Ball in Queen Street, Cheapside, near Three Cranes Landing Place, where "liveth a gentlewoman that has a most incomparable wash to beautify the face which far exceedeth all that are extant . . . It takes out all manner of wrinkles, Freckles, Pimples, Redness, Morphew, Sunburn . . . It also plumps and softens the skin, making it as smooth and tender as a sucking Child's."

On the two-page broadsheets in this particular portfolio, no sales price is indicated, but the presumption is that it will have been well below the two pence or three half-pence charged for the six-page pamphlets in the

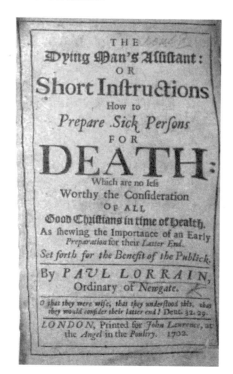

The title page of The Dying Man's Assistant: *or, short instructions how to prepare sick persons for death by Paul Lorrain, Ordinary of Newgate, published London, 1702*

portfolio, of which there are four. These relate to the execution of traitors. They are a much more considered analysis than the broadsheets, introduced with the term "Narrative" and published some two days after the date of the execution. The title is also flanked by two small woodcuts, one of the gate and one of the gibbet. The case of James Sheppard is instructive, an 18-year-old who, after reading various pamphlets and books, "concluded that King George was not the rightful heir to the throne and as a result had a mighty Impulse upon his heart that he must be the Person that should do the Deed, and by this means make way for the right Heir, as he called the Pretender". Paul Lorrain goes into great detail, recording his attempt to persuade James Sheppard of the errors of his way – thereby saving his soul – and the latter's defiant conviction that he had committed no sin in entertaining this objective, a view he held even to the scaffold.

It should come as no surprise that High Treason warrants a six-page brochure, while murder, rapine, forgery can get by with a two-page broadsheet. As a semi-official publication, any threat to the state must rank much higher than can any offence to morality. But they both offer great opportunities for uplifting comment: punishment was exemplary, penitence was inspiring and obduracy was inexcusable. It is in this spirit that one should be encouraged to view public executions in the seventeeth and eighteenth centuries. After all, J. S. Bach was occasionally to be seen directing the boys from St Thomas's School in Leipzig, singing hymns while accompanying prisoners on their way to the scaffold.[10] From Newgate this involved processions to the gallows at Tyburn, perhaps as frequently as every six weeks, attracting huge crowds along the route. The victims themselves contributed to the theatrical character of the occasion, sometimes exuberantly, with their final speeches. When the gallows were moved to a place outside Newgate itself, this change of location did nothing to detract from the spectacular attraction of executions, with crowds forming hours beforehand. It also enabled the prison keeper to hold court, giving favoured guests lavish breakfasts ahead of the event. One critic was Samuel Johnson, who lamented that "Tyburn itself was not safe from the fury of innovation".[11]

Deterrence underlay the authorities' thinking and was also behind the accounts of the Newgate Ordinaries, which had considerable publicity value. The measured ring to Lorrain's own writing – whether in reporting the statements and confessions of the prisoners or his failures at persuasion – added weight to these publications. His use of the first person singular was by way of a further guarantee of authenticity. Lorrain's writings in his capacity as Ordinary form a significant part of Newgate's literary heritage.

Lorrain died in 1719. His successors as Ordinary of Newgate faced increasing competition with publishing rivals seeking to steal a march on them. In 1745 we find the Ordinary, the Rev. James Guthrie, complaining to the Court of Aldermen that one, John Applebee, had infringed his copyright by printing his own versions of speeches and confessions.[12] Thirty-two years later, the Rev. John Villette was to give a masterly demonstration of how best to crowd out potential competition, the occasion being when the Rev. William Dodd came under his spiritual care, having been convicted of forging the name of Lord Chesterfield (who as Philip Stanhope had been his pupil) for a bond of £4,200. He entered Newgate early in February 1777, ahead of his execution some four months later. The crime of fraud, committed by a man of the cloth on a scion of nobility for whom he had acted as tutor, had all the makings of

William Dodd by John Russell, 1769

a publishing bestseller. It also justified ample coverage: the two-page broadsheet to which forgers were entitled in the past was replaced by a 24-page pamphlet, while still adhering to the traditional opening format: "A genuine Account of the Behaviour and Dying Words of William Dodd, who was executed at Tyburn for forgery on Friday the 27th of June, 1777. By the Reverend John Villette, Ordinary of Newgate".[13] The text was expansive, ending with the condemned man's "last Solemn Declaration which he intended should have been read by me at the place of execution", judged impractical because of the press of spectators at Tyburn. The price was set at six pence – no longer one and a half pence as earlier – and the link with the Ordinary was underlined by the pamphlet being made available both at J. Bew, the printers at 28 Paternoster Row, and at the author's own house, No. 1 Newgate Street. The pamphlet ran to four editions in rapid sucession, all bearing the date, June 27, 1777, and authenticated by Villette's signature on the title page.

Widespread publicity given to Samuel Johnson's efforts to spare Dodd from the gallows, together with the presentation of a petition "signed by twenty thousand hands", made for an exceptional publishing opportunity that gave rise to an exceptional response. It can also be seen, however, as marking the end of the traditional role of the Newgate Ordinary, who was coming under more and more stress to match rivals' often lurid accounts of executions with similarly doctored texts. And what had been a semi-official document increasingly joined the ranks of chapbooks, ballads and straight counterfeits. It is significant that when John Howard visited Newgate in 1780 during Villette's tenure, he made no mention of any publishing income in his breakdown of the revenues and perks that the Newgate Ordinary enjoyed.

Strong competition was already coming from *The Newgate Calendar*, which had started in 1773 as a simple record of those entering the gaol. Subsequently it was embellished with accounts of trials, to the point where *The Newgate Calendar or Malefactor's Bloody Register* had ballooned six years later into five sumptuous volumes, greatly enhanced by 46 vigorous engravings; this purported to contain the authentic lives, trials and accounts of executions of the most notorious criminals in England, Scotland and Wales from 1700 to 1779 – and obviously spread its net well beyond Newgate. The complete break from past documentary standards is marked by the "professed intention of the compilers of this work to exert their utmost endeavours to let entertainment and improvement go hand in hand".[14]

The Prison

The early prison was housed in the gateway – as was the case with the Fleet prison, located in Ludgate. In the mid-fifteenth century the prison element was greatly enlarged. Its destruction in the Great Fire of 1666 led to the prison being weaned as it were from the gate through the construction of a separate building completed by 1675. This in turn was burnt down in the Gordon Riots in 1780. Rebuilt three years later, it survived until it was dismantled in 1902. From the start, provision needed to be made for a mix of prisoners, male and female, that included felons of all ages and those incarcerated for state reasons, whether as traitors, seditious libellers, religious non-conformists, political troublemakers. Debtors formed a separate category; this was overwhelmingly male, in recognition of the fact that married women were not legally responsible for their debts. (In the eighteenth

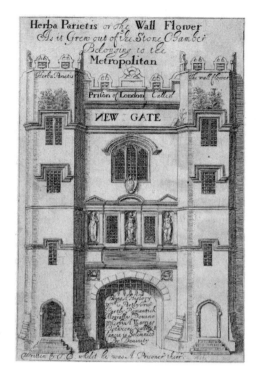

Frontispiece to Thomas Bayly, Herba Parietis, or the Wall Flower as it Grew out of the Stone-Chamber belonging to the Metropolitan Prison of London, called Newgate *London, 1650; view of the front of Newgate prison. Etching*

century, Members of Parliament were also immune from being arrested for debt.)

It had been recognised at an early stage that there should be segregation, with the state prisoners shielded from the hardened criminals and the debtors from all the others. This was even enshrined in legislation passed in 1784 and again in 1791. With each rebuilding, improvements were made in the physical separation of the prisoners, different categories being assigned different quarters. This achieved its apogee in the 1783 building that followed the Gordon Riots with the creation of clearly defined quadrangles, living accommodation and shared spaces.

In practice, however, demarcation proved hard to achieve for two reasons. One was the recurrent problem of overcrowding.[15] The rebuilt Newgate had a capacity for 490 prisoners and yet at times was called upon to accommodate many more. In this respect the new building had an early baptism of fire. The end of the American War of Independence in 1783 saw a predictable surge in crime as thousands of soldiers returned to England to no occupations and

25

often without back pay. Already, considerable upwards pressure had been exerted on prison numbers when Virginia and Maryland, the traditional destination for deportees, ceased to fulfil that function from the start of the rebellion in 1775.[16] For many years, deportation had not only provided a somewhat more humane alternative to "letting the law run its course" – by way of execution – for the most trivial offences. It had also served to hold the prison population in check. It was only in 1788 that a replacement was found, judged to be satisfactory at the time, with the establishment of a penal colony in Botany Bay, New South Wales. The prison numbers could as a result fluctuate widely. J. C. Lettson, commissioned to prepare a report on an outbreak of typhus, which incidentally had proved fatal to Lord George Gordon, noted that in October 1793 there were 200 women on the felons' side; this had fallen to 95 by early 1794, following a transfer to Woolwich that preceded transportation to Botany Bay.

A more insidious explanation for fluid demarcation lines between classes of prisoners lay in the administrative basis underlying prisons. Construction costs apart, they were largely expected to pay their way. This was achieved by making the head keepership a post of profit. As the direct representative of the Sheriffs of London and Middlesex, the keeper of Newgate was responsible for the safe keeping of the prisoners. While he received a modest salary (£200 at John Howard's visitation in 1779) the bulk of his rewards came from entrance fees, room rental charges, profits from the drinking cellars, catering charges, fines and discharge fees. The turnkeys in turn made money from releasing prisoners from their irons, visitors' entrance fees and sundry services. Opportunities for enhancing profits could come from accommodating say five people in a room meant for two, transferring those felons who had the funds to the expensive state side, economising on any services that did not lend themselves to extortion.

A glaring and persistent feature was the vulnerability of debtors.[17] As John Strype wrote of Newgate in the 1720 edition of Stow's *Survey of London*, "It is a large prison, and made very strong, the better to secure such sort of criminals which too much fills it. Insomuch that the debtors are crowded amongst them, except they have large purses to be in the Press Yard, which is a place for the better sort, or such as can gratify the keeper's extravagant demands. And 'tis a great pity that many an honest man, that through misfortunes of the world, contracted debts more than he can pay, be confined to such a place." The Press Yard got its name from the nearby cells where condemned prisoners chose to suffer death by means of oppression and privation having refused to plead – with a view to protecting for the benefit of their heirs such assets that they possessed from being forfeited to the Crown. Occasionally, relief for some debtors may have been close to hand: attached to the nearby tower of Christchurch Newgate, the memorial tablet for Thomas Firmin, who died in 1697, records his numerous charitable activities including the redemption of debtors out of prison.

Throughout the system, the profit motive served to breach physical barriers and undermine prison regulations. The decisive distinction was between those on the "state side" who had money and those on the "common or felons side" who were largely or totally bereft: at its most basic, this broke down between those who paid the keeper for their accommodation and those whose quarters were supplied free. As is occasionally the case, exceptions do occur: William Dodd, whose evidence carries weight, attributed the evils of Newgate to "the immediate consequences of promiscuous confinement and no way chargeable to Mr. Akerman's account", the keeper of the day, whose kindness and humanity was felt by many inmates.[18] Already as a free man, Dodd had been an advocate for the reform of imprisonment and in his *Thoughts in Prison* had crisply declared "Debt's not guilt".

At all times, conditions were fertile ground for denunciations.[19] Thomas Lloyd, an American incarcerated for a libel, produced in 1794 his *Impositions and Abuses in the management of the Jail of Newgate; pointed out and exposed, in a letter addressed to the late Grand Juries of the City of London and County of Middlesex.* 1813 saw the publication of Daniel Isaac Eaton's *Abuses of Newgate exhibited in a Memorial and Explanation, presented to the Lord Mayor.* Quite apart from multiple cases of peculation and exploitation, sanitary conditions left much to be desired. Thomas Lloyd brings the situation into sharp focus in his letter: "Cisterns and pipes for supplying the water closets were put on thorough repair a few months hence, yet it frequently happens for several days together there is not a drop of water to wash off the excrement and filth: how dangerous such putrid scents are."[20] This applied to both the felons' side – described by him as "in every point of view, a mansion of misery and wretchedness" – and the state side where the better sort/the more affluent resided. In his official report, J. C. Lettsom offers a comprehensive view of conditions throughout the prison.[21]

And for an atmospheric portrayal of life in Newgate, one can turn again to Dodd's *Thoughts in Prison*:

> . . . The din increases round:
> Rough voices rage discordant; dreadful shrieks!
> Hoarse imprecations dare the Thunderer's ire,
> And call down swift damnation. Thousand chains
> In dismal notes clink, mirthful* Roaring bursts   * The rattling of fetters
> Of loud obstreperous laughter, and strange choirs   was an amusement
> Of gutturals, dissonant and rueful, vex   to some offenders.
> E'en the dull ear of midnight![22]

Newgate and Radical Writing

Newgate's literary distinctiveness has a more powerful claim to attention than is provided by the reports of the Ordinaries, prisoners' indignant pamphlets and the prison thoughts of the Reverend William Dodd. This hinges on the active polemical role the prison came to play over the period covering the French Revolution and the French wars – as demonstrated in the anthology of radical prison literature published in 2005 under the title *Newgate in Revolution*. To the British administration, with memories still fresh of the successful revolt of the American colonists, the sight of the French Revolution as it passed through increasingly violent stages was bound to be disturbing. Jennifer Mori gives 1792 as the date when William Pitt's government turned publicly against the French Revolution.[23] Some time later came the suspension of habeas corpus in 1794–1795 and again from 1798 to 1801, thereby enabling the authorities to detain suspected traitors without trial. The Treasonable Practices Act and the Seditious Meeting Act, both of 1795 – known as the "gagging" acts – added to the regulatory armoury of the government and were reflected in an increased flow of political arrests of radicals, defined to include republicans, religious dissenters, democratic idealists and those believed to be traitors in the making. It has to be said, however, that, where this led to prosecutions, juries were by no means certain to render guilty verdicts.

The experience of William Hodgson is instructive.[24] On September 30, 1793, he dined with his friend Charles Piggott, after which both men went on to the London Coffee-house on Ludgate Hill to read the newspapers. These reported on a retreat from Dunkirk, with many casualties, and on the King's decision that morning to go stag hunting. Their observations on the impropriety of the King's action were overheard by others in the coffee house, one of whom "rose up in a great passion, called for a glass of punch, came running towards the box in which we were seated and . . . insisted on our drinking the King's Health . . . I did not choose to have a toast thus impudently forced down my throat and accordingly gave 'The French Republic and may she triumph over all her enemies'". Mr Leach, the master of the Coffee-house, immediately sent for the constables, and Hodgson and Piggott were taken to the compter (town gaol) in Giltspur Street. At the Old Bailey trial some weeks later, Charles Piggott was found not guilty of sedition, while William Hodgson was sentenced to two years' imprisonment in Newgate and fined 200 pounds.[25] On arrival, and presumably having secured a room to himself on the state side, he set to work on a clutch of publications, the first being *The Commonwealth of Reason by William Hodgson now confined in the Prison of Newgate*. He devoted the preface to an account of his arrest and conviction. It appeared in 1795 as being "printed for and Sold by the Author", as well as being obtainable from, among others, J. Ridgway and H. D. Symonds. These two gentlemen were themselves prisoners in Newgate. Furthermore, they were singled out for praise by Dr Lettsom in his 1794 report on the outbreak of typhus: "Some of the prisoners, who resided on the ground floor, and who were exposed to this cause of the disease, [proximity to the women's felons' side] escaped infection; but I observed that all of these, not only enjoyed the hope of emancipation, but used much exercise, or were otherwise very busily employed, as Ridgway and Symonds in the sale of books, & which not only diverted the melancholy of confinement, but afforded continual employment of body and mind."

The year 1792 had seen the publication of Part II of Thomas Paine's *Rights of Man*. Part I had already appeared in 1791, the two being his considered response to Edmund Burke's highly critical *Reflections on the French Revolution*, published in 1790. Within a week of Part II's appearance in February 1792, it was officially condemned as a seditious libel, while its publisher, James Ridgway, , was later sentenced to four years in Newgate. His charge sheet also included publication in 1792 of *The Jockey Club; or a Sketch of the Manners of the Age*, a caustic satire on British and European nobility, including among its targets the Prince of Wales, William Pitt and Queen Marie Antoinette; this was somewhat in the spirit of many of the scurrilous pamphlets of the day in France. It also earned Symonds, as joint publisher with Ridgway, a two year sentence in Newgate. The author, Charles Piggott – William Hodgson's Ludgate coffee house companion – was able to hide behind the screen of anonymity.

Ridgway and Symonds occupy a prominent position among Paine's publishers/printers/booksellers, at a time when such demarcations were blurred, with many fulfilling several roles. Another central figure is Daniel Isaac Eaton, whose devotion to radical causes earned him eight trials, a number of spells in prison and exile in America.[26] As printer and bookseller, conveniently located in Newgate Street, he was a frequent visitor on business matters, as well as in his capacity as a close friend of many of the political prisoners. In 1811, having published Part III of Paine's *The Age of Reason*, this entitled him, aged 60, to several hours in the pillory and an 18-month prison sentence. This harsh punishment prompted Percy Bysshe Shelley, 19 years old, to address a furious open letter to Lord Ellenborough, the Lord Chief Justice, who had been the presiding judge at the trial. Once made an inmate, it comes as no surprise to learn that Eaton then became a prolific Newgate author, his first title being an exposure of prison abuses.

Other figures that flit in and out of Newgate include Clio Rickman, one of Paine's numerous publishers and the author of his first biography; Sampson Perry, who had the distinction of being imprisoned in France – without any damage to his uncritical admiration of the Revolution – as well as in Newgate, whence he wrote, from the felons' side, *Oppression*.

What emerges clearly is that association with Thomas Paine acted as a focus for repressive government action. In the judgement of Paine's biographer, John Keane, publication of the first part of *Rights of Man* made him the most controversial figure of the day, with sales of what was an expensive three-shilling book exceeding 50,000 within four months.[27] This was compounded a year later with the publication of the second part, which was shortly followed by a cheap edition at six pence, thereby fomenting discussion , as John Keane notes, of citizens' rights across the whole country, from crofters in Scotland,

Thomas Paine by Laurent Dabos c. 1791

to tin miners in Cornwall, to shoemakers in Norwich ... More specifically, it was a further stimulus to making Newgate a centre of "insurgent public discourse, one where a vibrant radical subculture flourished".[28] As a state prison it had experienced an influx of those convicted under the greatly expanded sedition laws. Such political prisoners were typically articulate, disputative and much given to pamphleteering. Housed for the most part in the section of the prison that was occupied by the better off, they were able to profit from the "freedoms" won by all those inmates who had been incarcerated for a wide range of offences other than sedition. As a result, Newgate was in some respects remarkably open both viewed from the outside and from within. Visiting hours for those on the state side were from 8am to 9pm.

The prison diary kept by Thomas Lloyd, first published in 2005, is a full record of the busy daily existence of a prisoner with a wide range of contacts and interests. It has already been shown how imprisoned publishers and booksellers could continue to do business and how resident authors would often supply them with the copy they needed. Quite aside from accessibility, there was also considerable freedom of communication within. This stands in sharp contrast to state prisons in France, a prime example being the Château de Vincennes, where inmates could occupy nearby cells for several years and never meet. Without stretching the evidence to breaking point, one can visualise a club-like atmosphere developing among the colony of radicals.

And if one were to look for further evidence of Newgate's position as an editorial hub, there is the case of Sampson Perry's radical weekly newspaper, the *Argus*, which he continued to edit in the 1790s throughout his seven years in Newgate.[29] William Cobbett, convicted of sedition in 1810 for having publicly criticised the flogging of several militiamen, did not allow his two years' incarceration to interrupt his weekly editorial in the *Political Register*. And in the two years 1824 to 1826, the *Newgate Monthly Magazine* was produced by eight dissenters – freethinkers who had contributed to the publication and sale of the many "blasphemous" titles originating from Richard Carlile's publishing business and bookshop in Fleet Street.[30]

The question arises: Was all of this literary activity an instance of unintended consequences arising out of a repressive policy that was being negated by Newgate's remarkably open structure? Or was it a subtle way the authorities had of implementing the harsh legislation judged necessary to protect the country from those who would destroy the whole fabric of our constitution – in William Pitt's words[31] – while at the same time protecting the individual rights of Englishmen – by in effect sanctioning freedom of expression from within prison walls?

Newgate's Reputation

This leaves for consideration Newgate's enduring reputation. In print this is exemplified in the label *Newgate Calendar*, which had achieved popular recognition at precisely the time when the connection with the prison was being weakened by the dual pursuit of geographic spread and entertaining writing. The links were further strained in a work such as Andrew Knapp's *Criminal Chronology of the Newgate Calendar* of 1809 and subsequent versions in 1824–26 extending to *The Complete Newgate Calendar* of 1926.

The expressions "Newgate Fiction" and "Newgate Novel" came into use during the first half of the nineteenth century as somewhat disparaging labels applied to works where one or more of the characters had a criminal background. Any Newgate connection was incidental. In time, they embraced productions of such writers as Edward Bulwer Lytton, Thomas Gaspey, William Harrison Ainsworth and, of course, Charles Dickens, whose lifelong interest in crime coloured so much of his writing, and who had as background his father's confinement in the Marshalsea debtors'prison. William Thackeray, a severe critic of Newgate Novels as glorifiers of crime, wrote *Catherine* (1834) as a parody and had the mortification to find that it was avidly read by the trusting public.

Newgate can take some direct credit for the characterisation of Moll Flanders, given Daniel Defoe's personal experience of incarceration in the prison, happily brief. Beyond this, the many fiction writers invoking scenes or characters linked to Newgate have had for the most part to dig into their own imagination, with some visual support, however, from the likes of William Hogarth. John Gay's *Beggar's Opera* of 1726 famously has as its main character MacHeath, inspired by Newgate's most renowned felon, Jonathan Wild. This is now best known for its reincarnation 200 years later in 1928 through Bertolt Brecht's and Kurt Weill's *Threepenny Opera*. But for enduring literary fame one needs to go back to the start of the seventeenth century:

> I am the common bellman
> That usually is sent to condemned prisoners
> The night before they die
> (Webster's *Duchess of Malfi*)

> It was the owl that shrieked, the fatal bellman
> Which gives the stern'st good night
> (Shakespeare's *Macbeth*)

Sixteenth Century

||||||||||||||||||||||||||||||||||||||||||||||||||||||||||||||||||||||||||||||||||||||||||||||

CHAPTER III

The Tower of London

Historical Background

As a prison, the Tower of London is exceptional on numerous counts, fulfilling military, penal, palatial, archival, monetary, entertainment, fictional and even scientific roles. It started life as a fortress with a massive keep (the White Tower, the earliest stone keep in Britain), built by William the Conqueror as a guarantor of London's subjection. Its position, overshadowing the capital, promptly gave it a strategic importance, which it retained into the seventeenth century and beyond. Militarily, this called for recurrent expenditure on fortifications and armouries; the impact of the introduction of gunpowder in the fourteenth century being gradual, it was only in the sixteenth century that the musket fully replaced the bow in warfare. Jousting, however, served to prolong briefly the demand for the skills of the armourers, while Henry VIII had a particular interest in parade armour for display purposes. Well before then the cannon had taken prime position in siege warfare, and the Tower's holdings of ordnance became central to its military strengths.

From its early origins, the Tower of London functioned as a prison, notably a state prison for incarceration at the behest of the Crown. In this respect it has something in common with the Bastille in Paris, which served much of the time as the king's private gaol. But in terms of social standing, the Tower's inmates came to eclipse those of the Bastille.

The first recorded prisoner was Ranulph Flambard, Bishop of London, who, as chief tax gatherer, was accused of extortion in 1100 by the newly crowned Henry I. The first sovereign to be imprisoned was the king of France, Jean II (known as Jean le Bon – meaning the Brave rather than the

Jean II, King of France c. *1359*

Good),[1] captured together with his younger son at the Battle of Poitiers in 1356 by Edward, Prince of Wales (the Black Prince). After being held in a number of locations, he entered the Tower in 1360 with a huge retinue, some having to be housed in the town; these included his organist, who came with a man to work the bellows, two servants and a separate wagon for his instruments. The treatment given to Jean II was in recognition of his royal status. Indeed, as a general rule, conditions for prisoners were adjusted according to their social position. A ransom having been agreed, the king returned to France to raise the money, leaving his son as hostage in Calais. When the son escaped, the king stood by his word, going back to gaol in England, where he died in 1364. It was also in the Tower that Richard II renounced the throne in favour of Henry IV and that Henry VI died of unnatural causes.

The Tower owes its role as a principal royal residence to Henry III, whose reign extended from 1216 to 1272.[2] Starting in 1220, he set about a major building programme, which included construction of royal apartments away from the keep, and as a pious action the embellishment of St Peter ad

Vincula; by extending the Tower's walls, it became incorporated within the precinct and ceased to serve as a parish church. In 1230 the king ordered that the core of the Crown jewels be kept securely within the Tower, and in 1248 the minting of the coins of the realm was centralised in the Tower.[3] Both of these decisions can be seen as the prudent measures of a sovereign wishing as it were to keep his ready wealth easily and safely to hand. The appointment in the fourteenth century of a royal clerk – after whom the Wakefield Tower was named – as the archivist of state papers was later to mark a further stage in the administrative importance of the Tower.

For Henry III the Tower proved a convenient place for him to hold court. Also on several occasions he called on Parliament to meet there. Two further instances of Henry leaving a deep impression on life and practices in the Tower: firstly, his acquisition of a lion in 1240 was the start of what was to become the extensive Tower Menagerie. Secondly, he instituted the custom that the sovereign of the day lodge in the Tower ahead of his or her coronation in Westminster Abbey, thereby further underlining the Tower's unique position. The tradition persisted down to the reign of James II, two interruptions being the coronations of James I and Charles I, which fell, in the words of the eighteenth-century historian, Laurence Echard, "in a Pestilential season". James II was said by Echard to have finally broken the tradition for reasons of economy, not wishing to incur the costs of the cavalcade along the richly decorated route from the Tower to the Abbey.[4]

The complex role that the Tower was called upon to play in the country's history is perhaps best illustrated in the juxtaposition of enthronement and confinement. Henry VIII managed famously to confuse the Tower's palatial and custodial functions. After secretly marrying Anne Boleyn in January 1533 (made public in May), the king and Anne spent several months, ahead of her coronation, in the royal apartments in the Tower.[5] From there they went in procession to Westminster Abbey on June 1, 1533. Three years later she was once again in the Tower, occupying the same royal apartments, but this time facing a trial rather than a coronation. Her execution took place on May 19, 1536.

In the case of Lady Jane Grey, her proclamation on July 6, 1553, as queen – in line with the deathbed wishes of Edward VI – was effectively endorsed by her taking up residence in the Tower. Incidentally, this had the support of Archbishop Cranmer. Her reign was to last no more than a fortnight, however, with the counter-proclamations of Mary as queen gaining wide support, a rare instance where London was to fall into step with the country, and for her the Tower was converted from a palace into a place of confinement. With Elizabeth, the sequence was reversed. Suspected of being party to Sir John Wyatt's rebellion, the avowed purpose of which was to replace Queen Mary, she was summoned to London and after a short time imprisoned on March 17, 1554, in the Tower – not apparently entering through the Traitor's Gate, an embellishment of later historians. She was housed in the royal apartments to the south of the White Tower, in a suite of four rooms with access to servants and to the outdoor spaces within the Tower; one of these will have contained the scaffold erected for the execution on February 15, 1554, of Lady Jane Grey, little more than one month earlier.[6] After Wyatt's execution in April 1554 and also having been subjected to intensive interrogation she was released, going to Woodstock under what amounted to house detention. On Queen Mary's death, it was as Queen that she returned to the Tower – whence she duly rode in procession on January 14, 1559 to Westminster Abbey for her coronation.

The frequency of real and suspected plots to overthrow the established order – pride of place has to go to the Gunpowder Plot of 1605 – did indeed lead to numerous incarcerations in the Tower, sometimes of short duration for purposes of investigation, sometimes over long periods, Sir Walter Ralegh and the Earl of Northumberland being prime instances. The Elizabethan equation of priesthood and treason also led to a rich harvest of Catholic priests. The Reformation had given birth to the Counter-Reformation, at the sharp end of which was to be found the Society of Jesus, established in 1535 by Ignatius de Loyola. By the 1570s the situation in England was attracting increasing attention in Rome, and this gave rise to an inflow of priests from the Continent intent on catering to the English Catholics' spiritual needs. This was naturally hazardous, all the more so for the atmosphere having been further poisoned by the action of militant Catholics. John Felton had affixed to the door of the Bishop of London's palace on May 20, 1570, between two and three o'clock in the morning, Pope Pius V's Bull, under which the queen was excommunicated, proclaiming in the strongest terms that the queen was "a servant of wickedness".[7] Felton, who had received a copy in Calais, was "dealt withal to undertake the business of publishing it one way or the other about the city of London".[8] After three months in the Tower, during which time he was put on the rack three times, he was executed on August 8, 1570, at St Paul's Churchyard. Another inflammatory action was that of the Jesuit priest, Nicholas Sander: he had composed in 1576 a scathing attack against the Reformation which included the claim that Anne Boleyn was Henry VIII's illegitimate daughter, thereby adding incest to his list of failings.[9]

The person who gave structure to this priestly inflow was William Allen, a Lancastrian, born into a devout conservative family. After gaining his degree in 1547 at Oriel College, he taught for several years in Oxford before joining the exodus of academics, going in the first instance to Malines.[10] He was ordained and published his book on Purgatory. It was in 1568 that Allen set up in Douai, which had gained its university charter in 1559, a college specifically designed to meet the needs of English exiles seeking to enter the priesthood at a time of religious turmoil. His young pupils were trained in religious controversy and alerted to the dangers facing them. At an early stage the college received financial support from Philip of Spain and from some English sources, William Roper, Thomas More's son-in-law being one.[11] Five years later, the seminary was obliged to move to Rheims owing to Calvinist pressures, and at the same time – testimony to the success it was enjoying – an overflow college was established in Rome. This fell under the aegis of the Jesuits, for whom Allen had the greatest admiration. To start with, it had been thought that these priests might exercise their ministry on the Continent or working among the heathen in the New World, but soon the emphasis switched to England. This was given additional impetus with the establishment by the Jesuits of their English Mission. By 1580 there were already some 100 missionary priests, as they were called[12] – many of them old boys from William Allen's seminaries – working to fill the gap created by the demise of the regular clergy. One distinctive aspect of their ministry was a peripatetic existence, as they moved from one "safe" house to another.

William Allen in his *Apologie*, published in the Low Countries in 1581, states roundly that the priests, whether Jesuits or other, do not have "any commission to move sedition or to move against the temporal government" and are not traitors.[13] He goes on to suggest that they might possibly be seen as heretics, a label that did not have attached to it an automatic death penalty in Elizabethan England, but he does not carry the argument much further. Instead, he extols the merits of martyrdom: "And therefore where God giveth the grace of martyrdom it is a joyful sign of mercie",[14] and declares that "the reward so incomparable succeedeth immediately all paines: but a moment betwixt man's momentous punishment and God's everlasting payment".[15] He also tells his readers that a subsidiary benefit – citing St Cyprian – is that a sinner's slate is thereby wiped clean. In effect, William Allen may be said to have been largely running these two "Nourseries for the Church of our Countrie" as an academy for Catholic martyrs.[16]

John Hart
(1540–1586)

The Tower   *December 24, 1580 – June 7, 1585*

The year 1580 saw Father John Hart incarcerated in the Tower for what was to amount to four years and seven months of custody. Born in Oxfordshire, Hart had attended Oriel College, Oxford University, and it was as a student that he converted to Catholicism. In 1569 he left England for the Low Countries, where he took minor orders in 1575 and was ordained three years later; in 1580 he joined from Rheims the contingent of priests, one being Edmund Campion, on its way to England in support of the Jesuits' English Mission. Shortly after their arrival in June, Hart was arrested and sent to Oxford for three months of Protestant indoctrination under Dr John Reynolds.[17] In the face of his continued religious obduracy, he was again arrested and imprisoned briefly in the Marshalsea Prison before being transferred to the Tower on December 24, 1580.

John Hart is now the recognised author of *A Tudor Journal, Diary of a Priest in the Tower 1580–1585*. Published in a scholarly edition in 2000, it comes with an English translation from the Latin and extensive notes and commentaries by the editor, Brian Harrison. The journal gives valuable backing to the graffiti preserved on cell walls in the Tower and also opens a rare window onto life in the 1580s in the Tower for one particular category of prisoners: Catholic priests.

In a preface to the Diary, written when Hart was in exile in the

John Hart, woodcut after unknown artist, late 16th-century

Netherlands, he describes the conditions in the Tower.[18] Each prisoner was given his own cell and his own prison guard under whose observation he remained, thereby greatly reducing the possibility of communicating with other prisoners. On feast days and Sundays prisoners were regularly "dragooned" into attending church and hearing uplifting sermons. This did not prevent the Lieutenant of the Tower, Owen Hopton, declaring "that there was no one in his fortress who did not go willingly to the Protestant church". With the prisoners lacking means of their own, Hopton paid their expenses and every three months claimed back the money from the Exchequer, submitting Tower bills.[19] For the thirteen-week period December 24, 1581, to March 25, 1582 "the diette and charges" of Richard Craighe, Archbishop of Armagh, at 13s 4d per week came to £8 13s 4d, to which was added the charge at 5s a week for one keeper amounting to a further £3 5s and "fewell and candell" at 4s a week an extra £2 12s. The quarterly total came to £14 10s 4d.[20] In the case of Hart, the Lieutenant's quarterly claim at £5 19s 2d was considerably lower, reflecting the priest's inferior status. These bills are a remarkable historical resource, the accuracy of which is endorsed by the financial interest of the Lieutenant of the Tower.

The diary entries, numbering 91, are typically short, many relating to torture and recording executions. Torture required authorisation by the Privy Council and was applicable only to crimes carrying the death penalty. Its greatest use occurred in the sixteenth and seventeenth centuries and the rack was the instrument chiefly employed. The main purpose was to elicit information – names of fellow priests, details of other conspirators, confessions. One should not, however, ignore the objective of conversion, to which mandatory church attendance might be seen as contributing.

John Hart's imprisonment coincided with that of Edmund Campion, author of the widely distributed *Decem Rationes*, ten arguments against the validity of the Anglican Church, printed clandestinely in June 1581 at Stonor Park, Henley, 400 copies of which were on one occasion placed on the seats of St Mary's University Church, Oxford.[21] Campion was one of those surprised celebrating mass in Lyford Grange, Berkshire, belonging to Francis Yate. George Eliot, the spy responsible for this capture, gives a graphic account "of the time {and} manner of taking of Edmund Campion and his Associates "holed up in the Yates house in Lyford, Berks".[22] He managed to gain access having known the cook from earlier days: "Then said the Cook to me 'Will you go up?' By which speech, I knew he would bring me to a Mass. And I answered him and said 'Yea, for God's sake, that let me do: for seems I must tarry, let me take something with me that is good'". He was guided into "a fair large chamber where there was at the same instant one Priest called Satwell saying Mass, two other priests kneeling by, whereof was Campion and the other called Peters alias Collington; three nuns and thirty-seven other people".

Several weeks later, four priests, six gentlemen and two husbandmen were shepherded to the Tower. Hart's July 22, 1581, entry reads "Edmund Campion, Society of Jesus priest, betrayed by the same Eliot, captured and brought to the Tower in grand procession: inscribed above his head 'Campion Seditious Jesuit.'"

August 31, 1581: "Edmund Campion, secretly tortured twice".

October 31, 1581: "Edmund Campion tortured for the third time on the rack after being questioned, this was altogether more severe".

November 21, 1581: "Edmund Campion and seven others sentenced to death".

December 1, 1581: "Edmund Campion of the Society of Jesus, Ralph Sherwin of the College of Rome, Alexander Bryant of the Seminary of Rheims, priests, by Royal command taken from the Tower and dragged on wicker hurdles to the pillory at Tyburn to end their lives in glorious martyrdom". Brian Harrison notes that Sherwin "benefited" by being allowed to hang until all sign of life had gone, before being cut down for the other barbarities.[23]

A major omission in the Diary entry is that Hart himself started the day sharing the same hurdle as Campion.[24] But at the last minute, before the horses pulled away, he was released from his bonds having offered his conformity in exchange for his life. Back in his cell, he wrote his letter of submission to Sir Francis Walsingham, secretary of state and the creator of what was a very effective secret service network. Aside from pledging religious conformity, Hart offered to act as an informer were he to be permitted to return to Rheims, where he would be able to spy on his mentor William Allen.[25] This may have been seen as a ruse to get out of the country. In the event, he remained in the Tower for a further three and a half years, was given pen, ink and paper for use in Protestant propaganda work, was disciplined on several occasions for non-cooperation, earning spells in the "Pit", a 20-foot deep subterranean chamber in the White Tower totally devoid of light.[26] He was finally exiled to the coast of Normandy with twenty others on June 7, 1585.[27]

Within the Diary there are 85 persons named. Of these, 24 had been freed by the time of the last entry, 19 had been executed, 14 were in exile on the Continent, 9 had been transferred to other prisons, 3 had died in custody, 12 remained prisoners in the Tower and the fate of 4 was unknown. For an overall view, Brian Harrison suggests that the 'Protestant reign of terror, dating from 1577 when the first priest was 'martyred', may have led to some three hundred executions,[28] where the victims were typically hanged, drawn and quartered, and that the "Catholic reign of terror" covering the five-year reign of Queen Mary to 1558, where the victims were typically burnt at the stake, somewhat the same number succumbed – but over a much shorter period of time.[29] If the analysis is confined to seminary priests, Eamon Duffy's calculation points to 116 executions.[30]

Instances of prisoners being released include three on April 7, 1582, having the important attributes that they were not priests but lay gentlemen and that they had found men to guarantee their good behaviour. The haul of six from Lady Stonor's house where Catholic literature, including Edmund Campion's book, had been printed, might have attracted as a punishment appropriate for such an offence a spell behind bars followed by release. This was not always the case, as witness the experience of the printer William Carter, a layman but persistent offender as a source of Catholic writings, who suffered execution on January 11, 1584.[31] For Catholic priests, the only recognised way of escaping this fate was through recantation, as illustrated in John Hart's survival.

The way the Diary may have been produced, in an atmosphere rendered hostile by interrogations that were often accompanied by torture is a puzzle. There are no known manuscript versions that have survived. Its first printing came in 1588 as a supplement to the second edition of Nicholas Sander's attack on the Reformation. At that stage the Diary was attributed to Father Edward Rishton. Hart's own description of prison conditions, mentioned earlier, immediately raises the question of how a prisoner in isolation and under constant observation could secure the material for such a memorial, let alone its transcription. One answer may lie with the very person charged with his oversight – the guard. John Hart is known to have converted one guard to Catholicism, firm evidence that the prisoner/guard relationship was not necessarily grounded on silence. In addition, the fact that the prisoners were regularly marched to church may well have presented opportunities for news gathering.

As to the matter of transcription, Brian Harrison points out that from the date of Hart's recantation in December 1581 he became entitled to writing materials and indeed was required to make use of them in the Protestant cause refuting Catholic writings. Here also the picture of isolation needs adjustment. While it seems unlikely that he would have been able to make a start on a surreptitious diary from the date of his arrest, many events in the ensuing 12 to 18 months touched him closely and might well have remained firmly stuck in his mind and available for recall when the day-to-day constraints were lessened. At times, though, the accuracy of such recollections may appear suspect or the degree of isolation to which prisoners were said to be subject may be open to further question. When, reporting on one prisoner, Hart talks of hearing from his "own mouth shortly before his death (that) he felt no pain at all even when the tortures were at their cruellest and inflicting the greatest tortures on him".[32] But this entry is dated May 1, 1581, and falls at a stage when Hart was supposed to have still been closely guarded. The case of John Stonor is altogether more startling.[33] He was one of those carted off to the Tower when the illicit printing press was discovered in the family home. During the course of an imprisonment of nine months – ended by his elder brother standing bond for his good behaviour – the daughter of the Lieutenant of the Tower managed to fall in love with him, was converted to Catholicism and operated a conduit for communications between prisoners in the Marshalsea Prison and those in the Tower. So much for strict adherence to rules of incarceration. Sir Owen Hopton's position was seriously compromised, but not to the extent of losing his post.

On literary grounds, while Hart's Latin makes no claim to elegance, the terse directness of the entries has dramatic quality.

Sir Thomas More
(1478–1535)

The Tower   *April 17, 1534 – July 6, 1535*

Thomas More was committed to the Tower on a charge of treason. This followed passage of the Treason Act of 1534, effective from February 1, 1535, which encompassed any malicious words or writings that tended to deprive the king, the queen or their heirs "of the dignite title or names of their royall estates". Critically, this included the sovereign's position as "the onely supreme heed in erthe of the Church of England callyd Anglicana Ecclesia", as established by the Act of Supremacy of November 1534.

The Act of Succession, which became law in March 1534, had fixed the succession to the offspring of Henry and Anne Boleyn, thereby debarring Princess Mary and favouring Princess Elizabeth – pending of course any male birth by Anne Boleyn. More was ready to take the Oath of Allegiance to the Act of Succession as being within the purlieus of the king. However, he was not ready to take the Oath of Allegiance under the Act of Supremacy which gave effect to the displacement of the Pope as head of the Church "thereby jeoparding of my soul to perpetual damnation".[34] His 15 months of imprisonment were to be dominated by both the struggle over the oath, with the king seeking to bring More to heel, and by the spiritual preparations More started making ahead of a death that was becoming an ever stronger prospect.

More scrupulously tied his defence to his "conscience", thereby emphasising the intensely personal nature of his decision. This was accompanied by a refusal to pass judgment on those who were jurors and on those who were non-jurors. And when pressed, as on May 3 before the Privy Council by Thomas Cromwell, to declare his own position on the oath, he confined himself to declaring his loyalty to the Crown.[35] He was making use of an argument that was later blocked when such obstinate silence was taken to constitute a refusal. His wife, Mistress Alice, also had difficulty in sympathising with his position. As quoted in a celebrated passage in the *Life of More* written by his son-in-law, William Roper, she is said to have summed the situation up as so much "Tilly vally". The financial consequences of More's resolve were, of course, felt most keenly by Mistress Alice.

The stalemate was broken on June 3, 1535, with Thomas More coming before the Commission set up by the Privy Council. This had already ruled on the contemplative monks of the Charterhouse, vowed to silence and an obvious threat to the dignity of the king. Over several stages, the monks, by order of seniority, were hanged, drawn and quartered, some after attracting unbelievably inhumane treatment whether in the Tower or Newgate, the reporting of which may have come to the ears of More. This could have been behind the comment in one of More's letters to his daughter, Margaret, in which he writes "I found myself (I cry Godamercy) very sensual and my flesh much more shrinking from pain than methought it the part of a Christian man".[36] (A somewhat surprising comment given his practice of self-mortification through floggings and the hair shirt that was delivered to Margaret on his death.)[37] More directly relevant to his situation was the trial and conviction of John Fisher, Bishop of Rochester, the only bishop to be a non-juror, a fellow-prisoner in the Tower and close friend of Thomas More. Lacking More's keen legal mind, he had managed to fall into the trap of opening himself up to the accusation of denying Henry's religious supremacy.

Sir Thomas More by Hans Holbein the Younger c. 1526-7

More's own conviction had to rely on the perjury of Richard Rich, who blatantly misrepresented More's carefully worded responses; he was later to be appointed Lord Chancellor, an office that More had occupied from October 28, 1529, to his resignation on May 16, 1532. Thomas More's execution was on the block – as was that of Fisher – rather than following the normal practice reserved for traitors. Some argue that this was evidence of the king's charity, others that it was a "practical" response to the enfeebled condition of the victims, who would not have long survived protracted torture.[38]

This brings up the matter of More's own role in the suppression of Protestant heresy through the measures against the imports of unauthorised literature, most obviously William Tyndale's recently published *New Testament*; this was judged to be false and corrupt and all the more pernicious for being in English.[39] Early on, this resulted in arrests; in one instance, four German merchants were forced to do public penance. Possession of banned books carried with it a presumption of Lutheran enthusiasms – hence house searches authorised by More, which could lead to trial in the ecclesiastical courts.[40] At about this time, More's own household was affected when his son-in-law, William Roper, recently married to More's best-loved daughter, Margaret, became a Lutheran convert.[41] This apostasy was to prove of short duration, with William Roper subsequently playing a highly supportive role in the Catholic cause. He was also to be the author of the endearing first biography of Thomas More.

More, for his part, in addition to rounding up suspected Lutherans, undertook the task, given him by Cuthbert Tunstall, Bishop of London, of countering Protestant writings. His book, the *Dialogue Concerning Heresies*, was published in June 1529.[42] It took the form of master-pupil discussions aimed at opening the eyes of a young gullible man to the dangers presented by Lutheran beliefs – closely patterned perhaps on the conversations More will have had with his erring son-in-law. The *Dialogue* is in some ways a gentle lesson, with scope for humorous asides. But beneath it lies the view, as expounded by John Fisher, that heresy is the seed of the devil, the corruption of the heart, the blinding of the sight and the murder of the soul. More was also convinced that fire in this world could save a heretic's soul from eternal fire in the world to come.[43] On the other side of the religious divide, a man such as John Calvin would justify the burning at the stake of Michael Servetus along similar lines.

On October 26, 1529, four months after publication of the *Dialogue*, More was made Lord Chancellor of England in succession to Thomas Wolsey, a position he was to hold for two and a half years. With this appointment came the task of passing sentence on those declared guilty of heresy in the ecclesiastical courts; it also involved the occasional use of his Chelsea home as a place for their temporary confinement. Those condemned to the stake during Thomas More's administration were five: Thomas Hitton, Richard Bayfield, John Tewksbury, James Bainham and Thomas Bilney.[44]

Bilney's case was drawn out.[45] He was first brought before the ecclesiastical court by Wolsey in December 1527 after preaching against clerical abuses and the veneration of saints. More had attended the trial held in the chapter house at Westminster.[46] Bilney was pronounced a heretic and was obliged to carry a faggot at St Paul's Cross as a token of renunciation, followed by imprisonment. He was released in November 1528. Two and a half years later, after breaking his undertaking not to preach Lutheran doctrine, he was tried for the second time, on this occasion in the secular court. In the *Dialogue*,

A Man for All Seasons, *1960*
Photograph of Paul Scofield as
Sir Thomas More by Angus McBean

there is little evidence of the milk of human kindness in More's considered assessment: "neyther his iudges nor our selfe neyther nor I thinke his own father neyther…could have thought hym other than very gylty".[47] Convicted as a relapsed heretic he was burned at the stake in Norwich on August 19, 1531.[48] Like More himself, such men were ultimately not prepared to recant. But as the Yale editors point out, Bilney may also have been a victim of his own desire for martydom.

But More lost during his chancellorship the esteem of his great friend the now elderly Erasmus, who could not at first credit the reports coming to him from London.[49]

Prison Writings

More's lifelong commitment to literature was sustained during his incarceration, notwithstanding obstacles that were periodically placed in his way. His prison writings fall under a number of headings. Of the letters he wrote and received, 24 have survived, the greatest interest being attached to those to

and from his daughter, Margaret Roper. The accounts of his various interrogations are of particular historic value. The farewell note written on the
eve of his execution, addressed to Margaret and his family and members of
his household, includes a number of small bequests as well as the explicit
wish that Margaret's maid, Dorothy Colley, should be taken care of. More's
letter to Margaret dated May 1534 centres on the distress he felt on receiving
an earlier communication in which she apparently encouraged him to take
the oath of allegiance under the Act of Supremacy.[50] Given that all correspondence will have been studied by his gaolers, notably Thomas Cromwell,
this letter can be seen as a way of showing Margaret in a favourable light to
Cromwell with a view to protecting her precious visiting privileges. The fact
that she had right of access to him had been underscored by a note More
addressed "To all my loving friends". In William Rastell's introductory comment to the *Dialogue of Comfort* in the 1557 edition, he explicitly confirms
this interpretation, denying that Margaret had ever wished More to sign the
oath.[51] Another view is held by Nigel Jones in his history of the Tower, who
accepts the letter at face value as evidence of "More's stubborn – or saintly –
streak" before the united opposition of his family – as does Peter Ackroyd in
his *Life of Thomas More*.

Of the two books on which More worked while in the Tower, one was
De Tristitia Christi, an extended meditation on the Passion, the relevance of
which to a man himself facing death is clear. This was to be his last work, left
unfinished. The manuscript, revealing More's extensive revisions and corrections, eventually found its way to the Royal College of Corpus Christi in
Valencia, having been safely removed from his cell – doubtless surreptitiously – at about the time that he was denied the use of his books.[52] These were
packed up on Thomas Cromwell's instructions on June 12, 1535, some three
weeks ahead of his execution. The manuscript was preserved in a closet in the
Chapel of Relics and was the object of a detailed bibliographic analysis in
1903 by Geoffrey Bullogh. In 1557, a year ahead of Queen Mary's death, Mary
Basset, Margaret and William Roper's daughter, published *An exposition
of parte of the passion of our saviour Jesus Christ, made in latyne by syr Thomas
More (knight) whyle he was prisoner in the tower of London and translated into
Englishe, by mistress Marye Basset one of the gentlewomen of the queens majesties
private chamber, and nece* (sic) *of the sayde syr Thomas More.*[53]

The other book was the altogether more influential *A Dialogue of Comfort against Tribulation*, written in English and superficially linked to Boethius's fifth-century AD *Consolation of Philosophy*, both being the work of prison writers under sentence of death.[54] That of More, however, was anchored to Christianity in the way that Boethius's book, albeit also the product of a Christian writer, was not. In the opinion of the editors of the Yale edition of More's works, the *Dialogue* "bears every mark of being an ultimate spiritual testament ... displaying all the signs of More's finest literary skill both in the details of its language and in the total command of its development".[55] It is also happily where More still finds scope to give reign to his ebullient sense of humour in racy, vivid anecdotes, and to his understanding of the human condition – as when he writes that "we ought to find all our joy and comfort in talking of heaven, but somehow men seem to be easily wearied by the topic".[56] In the third and final section, there is a marked change of pace. The introduction to Chapter 16 reads: "The consideration of the paynefull deth of Christ, is sufficient to make us content to suffer deth for his sake". The reader is then taken along the path trodden by Christ, a literary equivalent of the stations of the cross present in many churches.

Scholars believe that the *Dialogue of Comfort* was largely written in 1534 and that, as was the case with the *De Tristitia*, More's manuscript will have been progressively secreted out of the Tower for safe keeping, well ahead of June 12, 1535, when he was deprived of his writing materials and suffered the confiscation of his books. There are two surviving manuscript copies, one in the Bodleian, the other in the British Library.[57] The former takes precedence, as being judged the earlier of the two and the more reliable.

The first printed edition is dated November 18, 1553, the printer being Richard Tottel "in fletestrete within Temple barre at the signe of the hand and starre". The sponsor and editor was William Rastell, nephew of Thomas More; his father, John Rastell, had married More's sister Elizabeth. At one stage, father and son were in business as printers, producing several of More's own books in the years 1528 to 1531.[58] William Rastell, however, abandoned printing as More's situation became more tense and concentrated on his legal career as a member of Lincoln's Inn, being called to the Bar in May 1539. In 1549/50 as the Edwardian regime took hold, he fled with his family to Louvain, the bolt-hole of choice for many persecuted for their beliefs. His assets in England were impounded. He then began the task to "diligently collect and gather together as many of his workes, bokes, letters and other writings printed and unprinted in the Englishe tonge, as I could come by"; he went on to explain that "in the evil yeres past he had been keeping in my hands very surely and safely the material that he was now able to publish".[59]

Richard Tottel, despite strong Catholic sympathies, had successfully navigated the Protestant shoals, largely by concentrating his work on legal titles. This had brought him into contact with Lincoln's Inn lawyers, a number of whom had been very much in the Thomas More circle.[60] He was therefore known to William Rastell, so that for Rastell, recently returned to England after a three-and-a-half-year exile and looking for a swift start in getting his uncle's prison writings into print, Richard Tottel was an obvious choice. Within five months of Queen Mary's accession, the *Dialogue of Comfort* was in circulation.[61]

The second printing came in 1557, some three and a half years into Queen Mary's reign, when the *Dialogue of Comfort* was incorporated into the *Workes of Sir Thomas More Knight, sometime Lord Chancellor of England wryten by him in the English tonge*. This massive volume ran to 1,458 folio pages, printed once again in Fleet Street at the sign of the Hand and Star, but this time "at the coste and charge" of John Cawood (the Queen's printer), John Walley and Richard Tottel. As before, the sponsor and editor was William Rastell, who also contributed the dedication to Queen Mary.[62] This was an altogether more ambitious and expensive production, involving three printers. Some of the type was provided by Cawood. The printing was in Tottel's establishment; his business had benefited significantly since 1553 when he was given exclusive rights on the publication of common law texts for a period of seven years; he typically employed four apprentices and ran two, sometimes three, presses.[63] Financially, he was well able to contribute to the costs of a major work of this kind. For somebody who was used to taking risks – beautifully expressed as "advanced expenses" – this cannot have presented a serious challenge.[64] The prison writings, whether in Latin or English, occupy 320 folio pages, of which the *Dialogue of Comfort* accounts for 125 pages. This second edition includes the humorous fiction that, as the work of a Hungarian, it was translated initially from the Latin into the French and then from the French into English.

More has indeed been well served by his editors, starting with William Rastell's great edition of 1557, which owed so much to the pious preservation of his writings and the industry of his nephew. The task was to be brought to a magnificent conclusion some four and a half centuries later in Yale University Press's 19-volume edition of *The Complete Works of St Thomas More*.

Prison Conditions

More's literary legacy relies heavily on *Utopia*, his vision of an ideal society, published in Latin in 1516, with the first English edition appearing in 1551. Of his other writings, those from prison, *The Tower Works*, have typically attracted special attention – notably *A Dialogue of Comfort*. The circumstances under which he wrote from his gaol have been the subject of much study and a fair amount of surmise. He was imprisoned in the twelfth-century Bell Tower, where his cell was on the ground floor in a high vaulted chamber, about 19 feet across. The nearness to the river made for extreme dampness, which was only partly allayed by his having the walls hung with straw mats. The floor was strewn with rushes and his bed was a straw pallet. He had the use of a small brick stove, which cannot have done much to counter the penetrating cold. His health was naturally affected; he suffered from severe chest pains and cramps, leading him at times to anticipate imminent death.[65] In his letter of May 2–3 to Margaret he confessed that he was "rather sorry when I saw the pang past".[66]

From the start, More had with him his servant, John Wood; he was illiterate and possibly as a result regarded as a harmless presence; a condition of his attending to Thomas More, however, was that he should report on any treasonous conversations he might overhear. More was normally allowed access to the Tower's gardens and to attend daily Mass. Visitors had to obtain authorisation; this was not freely given. Even in the case of his daughter Margaret, enjoying what we saw as an exceptional position, there was one four-month stretch on the calculations of John Guy when she was barred from seeing him.[67] We know from William Roper's biography of one visit from his wife who famously scolded him for his obstinacy. And there are references to Margaret's servant, Dorothy Colley, running errands for her, bringing him food and gifts; she had married More's secretary, John Harris.

The couple later left England for the Low Countries and helped to save More's papers and letters.

Financially, More suffered the fate of a traitor, with his assets forfeited. Initially Dame Alice was allowed to retain his movable goods and revenues from his lands, thereby enabling her to meet her expenses and those of her husband. Later, this concession ended, probably as part of a policy aimed at putting pressure on More. At the start of May 1535 she is to be seen selling a flock of lambs for 38 pounds and 8 pennies and having to top this up by the sale of some of her own clothes.[68] More's own prison expenses for board and wages came to 15 shillings a week and he was expected to meet these out of his own pocket. Later, in Queen Elizabeth's reign – as illustrated in the experience of the Catholic priests imprisoned in the Tower – such charges where impecunious prisoners were concerned were first settled by the Lieutenant of the Tower, who then claimed them back from the Exchequer. Little wonder that Alice More, in her eloquent letter to Henry VIII, sent over Christmas in 1534, should have presented a picture of destitution and pleaded for More's release so as to live the rest of his life quietly with his family.[69] A modest qualification to this dismal picture is the extent to which Margaret Roper was able to supplement her father's diet with food brought in from outside. Among friends, Anthony Bonvisi, merchant of Lucca, then living in London, managed to supply More with wine and food through his servants.[70] And there are occasional references to gifts between prisoners, notably to John Fisher, incarcerated in a cell above that of More, whose living conditions with no financial support of any kind were even more distressing than were those of More.

For somebody such as More whose daily existence depended on the pen, any writing restrictions were a major deprivation. During his imprisonment, there were times when he was without the use of pen and ink. In their stead he was dependant on "coals", in effect charcoal crayons, which were a very poor substitute. This was the case with his first prison letter and of the letter written on the eve of his execution. And during the course of the winter of 1534 he was also denied the use of pen and ink. In a note to Margaret in which he voices his delight over her letters, he declares that "a peck of coals would not suffice me to make the pens" that would enable him to express his appreciation.[71] However, the suggestion that his early biographer, Nicholas

Harpsfield, makes that the whole of the *Dialogue of Comfort* was written with coals is discounted by More's twentieth-century editors.[72] Evidence of his access to pen and ink at times of great stress comes, furthermore, with many ink annotations in the prayer book that he had with him when in the Tower.[73] As noted in the introduction to the facsimile reproduction, "they reflect his personal griefs and fears as he prayed his Psalter and strove to comfort his soul. Perused as a whole, the prayer book gives a moving impression of More's state of mind, torn between fear and hope, in the face of death". The prayer book is preserved in the Beineke Library at Yale University.

The Menagerie

Setting aside its functions as a prison that boasted a distinguished list of royal inmates, the Tower's role as a zoo comes foremost in the public perception. To Henry III's lion was added a polar bear in 1251. He was the custodial and financial responsibility of the sheriffs. By enabling the bear to fish in the Thames, this created a local attraction as well as constituting a useful saving on costs. The bear was followed three years later by the first elephant, for which the sheriffs were obliged to construct appropriate housing. Subsequently, accommodation for the lions gave rise to the naming of the Lion Tower. Over the years, diplomatic gifts and straight purchases swelled the collection.

The king who took the greatest interest was James I.[74] It was in the Tower that he chose to celebrate in March 1604 the first anniversary of his accession to the throne. That same month his daughter Princess Elizabeth, Electress Palatine, with her newly acquired husband, were said to have been delighted by the menagerie and duly impressed by the salute given them on the Tower guns.[75] A little later, another altogether more extensive royal visit took place as part of the Easter celebrations. It also fell soon after Walter Ralegh's incarceration. As an act of Easter mercy, all prisoners then in the Tower were freed, with the exception of the three bearing a traitor's label, Ralegh, Cobham and Grey, who were moved temporarily to Fleet Prison, where they were kept carefully apart. On returning several weeks later they made the unhappy discovery that the opening up of the Tower to the public had also introduced the plague.[76]

A regular form of entertainment for the king, with his twisted enthusiasms, was the staging of contests between different species, for the greater enjoyment of which he spent money on improving spectator facilities.
One bizarre "trial" organised by the king in 1609 was of a huge bear that had
killed an all too trusting little girl.[77] The bear was judged guilty and duly condemned to death. A fee paying public then came to see the sentence fulfilled
by several mastiffs, rather than the three timorous lions that had been given
a first option. Some 40 years later Oliver Cromwell was to ban bull- and
bear-baiting – but whether this was influenced by humanitarian considerations or was merely an extension of the ban on theatrical performances is
unclear. By the eighteenth century the menagerie was open to the public on
a regular basis; the entrance fee might be satisfied by handing over dogs and
cats for the sustenance of the carnivorous animals in the menagerie.

Inevitably, the population of the menagerie fluctuated, whether for financial reasons or as a result of disease. It so happened that 1828, the year that
saw the establishment of the London Zoo in Regent's Park, also coincided
with a peak in the Menagerie's holdings at the Tower, comprising over 280
animals distributed across over 60 species.[78] Two years earlier, the Duke of
Wellington had been appointed Constable of the Tower. He saw this as a
great opportunity of ridding a military castle of a frivolous tourist attraction. The progressive transfer of the animals and birds duly took place, largely
benefiting the Regent's Park zoo.

The Tower's contributions to anatomical, technological and astronomical knowledge deserve a brief mention. The seventeenth-century surgeon
John Hunter secured for dissection the carcases of dead animals, thereby relieving the Lieutenant of the Tower of a troublesome problem of disposal and furthering his own anatomical researches.[79] The appointment
in 1696 of Isaac Newton as Warden of the Mint heralded a major advance
in the mechanisation of coin production, and also the solution to the en-
demic problem of counterfeit coins and the clipping of genuine coins for
the silver content: this was achieved through the great re-coinage completed in 1698, a key element being the introduction of bevelled edges, thereby
killing dead clipping.[80] The Tower's contribution to astronomical knowledge was fleeting but distinguished: Charles II's appointment of John
Flamsteed as Astronomer Royal led to the establishment of an observatory

in 1675 located in the White Tower's east turret, whence the astronomer pursued his work of mapping and identifying thousands of stars. At that date, it was not coal pollution that drove him quickly to the Observatory at Greenwich, but reportedly the droppings of the Tower's ravens on the lenses of his telescopes.

Finally, the Tower can lay claim to a loose association with northern exploration. The oldest man-made rock garden in Europe is to be found in London in the Chelsea Physic Garden. It enjoys Grade 2 listed status. As explained in the Chelsea Physics Garden's guide, the rocks include basaltic lava used as a ballast on Sir Joseph Banks's ship on a voyage to Iceland in 1772, as well as "pieces of carved stone which were once part of the Tower of London".

|||||||||||||||||||||||||||||||||||||||||||||||||||||||||||||||||||||||||||||||||||||

CHAPTER IV

Henry Howard, Earl of Surrey
(1516–1547)

Incarcerations

Windsor Castle	*July – early October, 1537*
Fleet Prison	*July 15 – August 1, 1542*
Fleet Prison	*April 1 – mid April, 1543*
Ely Place, London	*December 2 – 12, 1546*
The Tower	*December 12, 1546 – January 19, 1547*

Henry Howard, Earl of Surrey, the eldest son of Thomas Howard, third Duke of Norfolk, and of Elizabeth Stafford (his second wife), daughter of the third Duke of Buckingham, was born into the highest ranks of the traditional nobility. His paternal grandfather, the second Duke of Norfolk, was the renowned victor over the Scots at the Battle of Flodden Field (1513), and his maternal grandfather, the third Duke of Buckingham, was executed for treason in 1521. Such contrasting fortunes were destined to fashion Surrey's own life, culminating in his own execution for treason, aged 31, a mere eight days before the death of Henry VIII, aged 56 – of natural causes.

Surrey's upbringing had much in common with the experience of others having the same exalted background: under his tutor, the scholarly and well travelled John Clerke, he was grounded in the classics, becoming fluent in Latin. In the humanist training of the day, French, Italian and Spanish were also mandatory subjects, all the more important if the pupil were ever likely to be called upon to play a role on the continental political stage. The relative insignificance of England as a European power at this stage can be lost sight of. Nor was English anywhere near to being a diplomatic language.

Another ingredient in an English humanistic upbringing was foreign travel. At the age of 16, he was chosen to accompany to France Henry Fitzroy, Duke of Richmond, Henry VIII's much favoured illegitimate son, born in 1519 and in many ways a young version of the father. The occasion was a visit that the king and Anne Boleyn, not yet queen, made in October 1532 to Calais for a meeting with François 1, with the aim of soliciting his help in obtaining the papal sanction for the king's divorce. Within the English entourage was Thomas Wyatt, Surrey's poetical mentor, whose son was to become a boon companion of Surrey's.[1] It is very likely that they would have met Clément Marot, then enjoying a period of untroubled service in the household of François 1 and of poetic recognition. Surrey and Richmond were to stay one year in France as pledges for the agreement signed by the two kings covering the planned approaches to be made to the Pope. The boys were much of the time with three of the French king's children. In the spring of 1533 they were in Fontainebleau and that summer they accompanied François 1 on a visit to Avignon. By the time Surrey returned to England, he had acquired the courtly manners for which he became noted, as well as fluency in French, which served him well in later life.

Surrey's direct royal connections were briefly extended in 1533 when Richmond was contracted to marry Surrey's sister, Mary. His early death in 1536 left her, however, as the Duchess of Richmond, both "a widow and a maid". Surrey's grief was deep and lasting. Surrey himself had been contracted in marriage in 1532 to Lady Frances de Vere, daughter of the Earl of Oxford; they were formally married three years later and the first of their five children was born in 1536.

In adult life, he managed to combine several roles: that of a fearless soldier; that of a poet; that of a courtier noted for his sharp wit and outstanding horsemanship, most conspicuously in the jousts that the king so loved; that of an independent spirit, thereby earning him four spells in prison. Throughout, he appears to have been governed by an inordinate pride in his ancestry, which prompted bursts of fury, leading to duelling challenges, setting him at times in opposition to his own father – for whom family pride was also not in short supply – and eventually, fatally, putting him at odds with the king.

The Howard lineage was indeed impressive. Surrey had as antecedents Edward I through both his mother and his father and Edward III through his mother. His sister's marriage to Richmond, albeit short lived, converted him into a near relative, as it were, of Henry VIII. And as a result of the skilled way in which the Howards – in common with other aristocratic families – paired off daughters, widows, nieces, this served to reinforce existing family links and open new ones. Such activity in the marriage option market could produce some startling results: Surrey's father found himself uncle – and hence Surrey found himself cousin – to two of Henry VIII's wives, Queen Anne Boleyn and Queen Catherine Howard. Both enjoyed a blaze of glory, Anne's being a lot longer than Catherine's, and both lost their heads on charges of infidelity. In his capacity as Lord High Steward, Norfolk was required to preside over the trial of Anne Boleyn on May 15, 1536, and to deliver the verdict. Catherine Howard was found guilty by an act of attainder dated February 11, 1542. The following day, no trial being called for, she asked for the block to be delivered to her cell, thereby enabling her to spend the evening "rehearsing her execution", a ghoulish image from Jessie Childs's biography. Surrey for his part, fulfilling the duties of deputy to his father, attended the execution of his two cousins.[2] Over time, Norfolk and Anne Boleyn had not seen eye to eye, largely because of her support of the progressive religious views promoted by Thomas Cromwell, which contrasted sharply with Norfolk's own religious conservatism; this divergence may have eased the pain of the final role Norfolk was called upon to play. More generally, throughout a long career in the service of the king, with frequent spells on the Privy Council, Norfolk had followed the rule of blind obedience to the king's wishes in all their twists and turns, suppressing on occasion awkward family loyalties.[3]

Henry Howard, Earl of Surrey, by unknown Italian artist, 1546

These developments did not put a halt to Norfolk's efforts to protect family interests if as and when the king were to die. In the course of 1546 Norfolk had devised a dynastic link – which secured the king's approval that June – involving a series of marriages binding the Howards and the Hertfords (Seymours). As uncle of the nine-year-old Prince Henry, Edward Seymour, the Earl of Hertford (later to become Duke of Somerset on Edward's accession), was bound to have an important position in any Protectorate during Edward VI's minority. Norfolk now revived an earlier proposal – that had run into the sand – that his widowed daughter, Mary, should marry Sir Thomas Seymour, brother of the Earl of Hertford. On this occasion, three of Howard's grandchildren should also be married off to three of Hertford's children. This scheme, concocted when Surrey was on military duty in the North, was a source of some irritation to him. But what he found totally unacceptable was that the Howards should demean themselves by any such ties with the Hertfords, "new money" as it were in Surrey's eyes. He publicly upbraided his sister for merely contemplating such a marriage. He further recommended – whether in jest or not is unclear – that, should she be in quest of power, she should set out instead to become Henry VIII's mistress.[4] This exchange put paid to his father's scheme.

Surrey's military career may be said to have started with the Pilgrimage of Grace, the uprising which had broken out in various parts of the country in 1536 and 1537, spurred by the dissolution of the lesser monastic houses – a revenue-raising scheme for the king, devised by Thomas Cromwell, which also provided further evidence of the move away from the old religion; in addition, the rebels' grievances were economic. Norfolk, whose military skills were recognised by Henry VIII, formed part of the force sent to suppress the northern rebellion. Initially, Surrey accompanied him, but on the king's orders was required to return to Kenninghall.[5] This was the family home in Norfolk to which his father had given a scale which went some way to vie with that of Cardinal Wolsey's Hampton Court. Some uncertainty as to Norfolk's reliability given his likely sympathy with the religious conservatism of the rebels may have been behind the king's decision to separate father and son.

In July 1537 Surrey had a fracas when at court leading to blows, probably in response to suggestions of family disloyalty to the Crown that were being relayed by Edward Seymour. It was seen as a serious offence against the king's peace, for which the normal penalty was the loss of a hand; instead, he had his first experience of imprisonment – in Windsor Castle – lasting some three months. The irony of this location was not lost on him: while his detention was gentle – he was given the run of the castle ground, but not permitted to pass outside the walls – this still contrasted sharply with the freedoms enjoyed by two sports-loving youngsters when he and Richmond were growing up in Windsor.

July 1542 saw him imprisoned for the second time, having challenged John a Legh, a half-brother to Catherine Howard, to a duel over a question yet again of family loyalty to the Crown. On July 15, the Warden of Fleet Prison was instructed "to receive the Earl of Surrey . . . two of his servants to attend on him and to suffer none to resort to banquet with him".[6] As was the experience of Sir Walter Ralegh, when he found himself transferred there for a short while to satisfy James I's wish to celebrate Easter in the Tower, Surrey and his attendants were accommodated on the more desirable state side – but firmly isolated from all other prisoners. The other attributes of the Fleet were shared by all prisoners, notably the noxious odours from the prison's location overlooking the Fleet River, which served as an open sewer, as well as a channel for the discharge of all manner of refuse.

Surrey promptly sent off to every member of the Privy Council furious letters demanding his release. Having been elected the previous year to the Order of the Garter, the sense of outrage at his treatment must have been further sharpened. Receiving no response, a second, but more conciliatory, letter was despatched. It included a request for transfer "into the country to some place of open air", as well as the strongly expressed desire to be in a position once again to serve the king. While not an apology, he acknowledged in a beautifully phrased passage that his earlier letters were "not sufficiently pondered nor debated with myself".[7] On August 1, he was moved to Windsor and four days later, having had three weeks of imprisonment, released on a surety of 10,000 marks. By September, he was heading to the Scottish border to do the king's will.

Throughout the winter of 1542–3 Surrey again saw service in the North. On his return to London in February 1543, he had a further brush with the law. From a base in Mistress Millicent's guest house in St Laurence Lane, off Cheapside, Surrey led a group of rowdies on a rampage, breaking windows, targeting prostitutes and generally creating mayhem. On April 1, he was had up before the Privy Council for this affray and also charged with having eaten meat on fast days and specifically on February 2, the feast of the Purification of the Virgin.[8] He was committed to the Fleet Prison, his companions – including John Hussey, treasurer of the Duke of Norfolk, his own squire, Thomas Clere, and the young Thomas Wyatt – being taken to the Tower. This hothead entertainment earned Surrey his third spell in gaol and second in the Fleet. It was to last two weeks, with Surrey being released once again on recognition of 10,000 marks.

Later in the year, in October, he was in Northern France, with a brief to support the Emperor Charles V. He gave a good account of himself. In June 1544, he was wounded in a skirmish, his life being saved by Thomas Clere, who himself received the wound that led to his death several months later. This action is commemorated in the moving epitaph to Clere. It was in 1545 that Surrey was given his first major command as Commander of Boulogne and captain general of the marches in France, thereby making him responsible for all English operations across the Channel. Notwithstanding advice from his father, who at the time was in frequent attendance in the Privy Council, to exercise caution, he bragged about his assured future successes. Instead, he suffered an embarrassing defeat on January 7, 1546 at St Etienne, an expensive encounter, entailing the loss of two hundred troops. More damagingly, it cost the lives of many of the captains and gentlemen fighting in the English front lines. Surrey was summoned home.

Once back in England, Surrey, while received again at court, devoted his time to embellishments at Kenninghall and Mount Surrey, the Norwich property on which he was in the process of building his own mansion. With this in mind he had commissioned heraldic decorations, which drew attention to his remarkable lineage as it blended the arms of Howard, Mowbray and Plantagenet, not forgetting a reference to Edward the Confessor.

As Surrey well knew, there was nothing frivolous to heraldry at the royal court. His own obsessive interest in his ancestry accounts for there being seven rolls of genealogical drawings in his possession, as reported by his sister. As evidence that heraldry embraced both birth and death, he will have noted the fate of his uncle, Lord Thomas Howard, who had effectively introduced himself unbidden into the royal line when he secretly married Lady Margaret Douglas, daughter of Henry VIII's sister, in whose veins Plantagenet blood flowed; at the time, with both her princess cousins, Mary and Elizabeth, having been declared bastards by their father, she was second or third in line to the throne.[9] The groom was promptly committed to the Tower as a traitor to the Crown, where he died of a fever in 1537, but not before exchanging some touching love poems with his bride.[10] Furthermore, royal sensitivities could not have been more clearly spelled out than in the Succession Act of 1536, whereby anybody who by deed, by design, by declaration raised the slightest question on the royal succession would be deemed guilty of high treason and dealt with accordingly.

It is hard to understand Surrey's apparent insouciance in his quest for armorials that would show off to better effect his royal lineage. The inclusion of references to Edward the Confessor was particularly provocative in the light of Henry VIII's own identification with this most revered forbear, the founder of Westminster Abbey, whose death on January 5, 1066, occurred a few days after the consecration of the Abbey and a matter of months before the Norman Conquest. His name alone signified continuity to the king. It was Richard II who took the step of assuming the mythical arms of Edward the Confessor and who then bestowed them on his kinsmen.[11] Surrey's improved armorial bearings were intended to be shown in both Kenninghall and Mount Surrey, inscribed in glass, as a relief plaque and painted on wood. At one point, Surrey had taken advice, consulting the Garter King of Arms, Sir Christopher Barker, England's chief herald.[12] Barker advised against one addition to the escutcheon in the interest of accuracy. For the rest, he would appear to have given a cautiously positive opinion as to Surrey's heraldic entitlements.

It was in November, 1546, that Surrey had an argument at court with Sir George Blagge; from being a Howard client he had become a Hertford client, this switch having been accompanied by a pronounced swing to religious reform. The dispute had to do with the Howard pretensions in the choice of a Protector should the king die before his son had come of age. This quarrel, fortunately not involving the striking of blows in the presence of the king, which would have attracted immediate punishment as a gross affront to the king, was, however, followed by an incendiary letter threatening "dire consequences should a mere knight ever insult his comital dignity again".[13] In the light of Henry's rapidly deteriorating health, there was already a jockeying for position in the composition of the prospective protectorate, with Norfolk's candidacy grounded on his being the premier peer of the realm. The Blagge letter (duly shown to the king) became linked to the provocative armorial statement, all of which was enhanced by Surrey's egregious contempt for any perceived inferior.[14] Blagge is also credited with having been one of the first to feed the rumour that Surrey was himself aiming at the role of Protector. On December 2, 1546, he was detained and taken to the house of the Lord Chancellor, Thomas Wriothesley, in Ely Place for questioning. This was the opportunity that the Hertfords seized to set in train a full enquiry before the Privy Council into the affairs of the Howards. Ten days later, Surrey was led on foot, itself a humiliation, to the Tower of London, a distance of one and a half miles, and charged with treason.[15]

It could not have been a hugely difficult task to arouse the ailing king's anxieties. Any royal accession can become a focus for rival claims

– had Henry VIII been gifted with prescience he would have noted how Edward VI's own deathbed choice of Lady Jane Grey was to be thwarted six years on. And, harking back in time, the Tudor dynasty had its origins in the successful force of arms that led to the slaughter in battle of Richard III the reigning king – not the most reassuring precedent. Consequently, assertions by the Seymours that the Howards harboured treasonous ambitions carried weight. These stood to be reinforced by a number of depositions being made to the Privy Council, for the most part by witnesses who bore a grudge against Surrey and his father or were simply intent on shifting allegiances opportunistically. One of the more telling was that of Sir Richard Southwell, a Howard cousin and a fellow soldier of Surrey's from Boulogne days. He declared to the Privy Council that "he knew certain things of the Earl of Surrey that touched his fidelity to the king".[16] The depositions of his sister, the Duchess of Richmond, which fell short of the total support that one might have expected, included reference to his possession of seven rolls of drawings of a coat of arms. The dying king's absorption in the case is graphically demonstrated in a document in the National Archives in Kew: dated December 24, 1546: it is a sheet of charges directed against Norfolk and Surrey, prepared for royal inspection by the Lord Chancellor, which Henry personally annotated in what was by then a shaky hand.[17]

This was Surrey's fourth spell in prison and the first in what was seen as the king's personal gaol. His father, being treated as an accomplice, joined him there. Once he was in the Tower, a good idea of his prison conditions can be obtained from the accounts that Sir Walter Stonor, Lieutenant of the Tower, duly submitted.[18] Surrey will have been housed much of the time in Beauchamp Tower; one awkwardness is that his sole recorded attempt at escape is said to have been made from St Thomas's Tower, which might therefore have been where he was initially lodged. Cell walls were hung with tapestries, as a counter to the cold, and the cost of sea coal for the fire in his chamber and for a dozen candles was itemised. His bedding comprised a feather bed, a bolster, pillows, blankets, sheets; clothes singled out for mention included a pair of furred shoes and four yards of satin, possibly to be made up ahead of his trial.[19] Board was provided for Surrey and for the two servants who were with him throughout his imprisonment. While falling well short of being luxurious, Surrey's accommodation was greatly superior to that of Thomas More. But the situation of both men differed fundamentally: Surrey was in receipt of exemplary punishment. As for More, Henry VIII was still intent on bending him to his will.

On January 13, 1547, Surrey was brought to trial in the Guildhall under the succession act of 1536, on the specific charge that "on October 7, 1546 at Kenninghall he had displayed in his own heraldry the royal arms and insignia, with three labels silver, thereby threatening the king's title to the throne and the prince's inheritance".[20] Surrey conducted his own defence eloquently and with some panache during the course of an eight hour trial. He was found guilty and executed on January 19 on Tower Hill. One account has him confessing his guilt. In another, he spoke a great deal in his defence until "they would not let him talk anymore".[21]

From his cell in the Tower, Surrey's father had just signed a full confession, hoping no doubt that a lifetime of past service would be taken into account. The charge sheet included a plan, that father and son were said to have had, to murder the members of the Privy Council, to depose the king, and that they had treasonable dealings with foreign ambassadors.[22] But this confession to colourful crimes was not what spared his life: as a peer of the realm, implementation of the procedures leading to an execution took up several days. It was the king's death on the night of January 27–28 that saved the situation for Norfolk.[23] He then spent six years as a prisoner in the Tower, only emerging on Edward VI's death in 1553 and the accession of Queen Mary. He died in 1554, aged 81.

In the opinion of the historian, David Head, the fall of the Howards can be almost entirely attributed to the actions of the Earl of Surrey.[24] Neville Williams's view is that the fatal weakness lay in the divisions within the Howard family.[25]

The Poet Surrey

Surrey's development as a poet goes back to his boyhood. At the age of sixteen, he could claim Thomas Wyatt as his mentor. A court environment, whether in England or France, would also have acted as a stimulus to artistic interests. The king himself was an accomplished musician, an occasional versifier and a good linguist; this did not preclude an enthusiasm for the hunt and for martial arts, including jousting – in all of which Surrey could share. On one occasion, Henry, having been thrown at the tilt, remained unconscious for two hours.

In common with the poets of the day, whether in England or France or Italy, Surrey entered wholeheartedly into the shoes of the lovelorn, when faced with the unprecedented charms of the women for whom their hearts throbbed. Such poems circulated freely in manuscript at court. In Frederic Padelford's anthology of Surrey's verse, the headings of love poems bearing such titles as "The Cruelty of Hidden Charms", "The Trammels of Love", "A Mistress Nonpareil" set the tone. The lady in question is not named – in contrast to Richard Lovelace's Lucasta a century later (who could of course have been a composite creation). Some of Surrey's biographers have worked hard on a putative inamorata called Geraldine, but this has failed to get the support of modern scholarship.[26]

In works that have a marked autobiographical content, often from a prison environment, Surrey also instinctively turned to verse. These include his three tributes to Thomas Wyatt, as well as the tributes to Thomas Clere and to Richmond. In some cases the location is specifically identified.

Surrey's detention in Windsor Castle in 1537 gave rise to the hugely nostalgic:

So cruel prison how could betide (happen), alas, As proud Windsor, where I
in lust and joy, With a king's son my childish years did passe . . . Thus I, alone,
where all my freedom grew, In prison pine with bondage and restraint

Another lament has as its first line "When Windseor walles sustained my wearied arme". In the opinion of his sister, Surrey's entrenched hatred of the newly ennobled was greatly intensified during these three months in Windsor.

Surrey's first spell in Fleet Prison produced a squall of letters, rather than any poetic outpourings. It was on his second experience in 1542 that he turned to verse with "A Satire on London. The Modern Babylon". This 68-line poem rehearses in colourful language the outlawry and sordidness of the capital – to which he and his cronies had just contributed and for which they had been duly imprisoned. It might be read as a morality tale. Some two centuries later, Samuel Johnson was to take up the same theme in "London: a Poem In Imitation of the Third Satire of Juvenal".

In the five weeks of imprisonment that preceded his execution, it is clear that Surrey found comfort and solace in poetry. In his paraphrase from the Vulgate of Psalm 54, verse 4, his text has a veritable ring of urgency to it – "The greslye feare of death envyroneth my brest", which is less evident in the Authorised Version in 1611 – "My heart is sore pained within me: and the terrors of death are fallen upon me". The paraphrases of Psalms 73 and 88 are also said to date from these last few weeks, as do his translations from Ecclesiastes. At one point in Ecclesiastes 1, a particularly happy image of the tide is conjured up:

> Ffludds that drink upp smale broks and swell by rage of rayne
> Discharge In sees which them repulse and swallowe strayte againe

Quite apart from the attractions of Surrey's verse, his translations are of considerable literary importance. In two books of the *Aeneid*, Surrey's metrical experiments led to the introduction of blank verse into English poetry. The translation of Vergil will have occupied him off and on for an extended period of time.[27] As W. A. Sessions sets out to explain, Surrey the Latinist may have viewed his life as being reflected in Aeneas's quest, the first chapters being associated with the difficult years to 1537, while the second group echoes Surrey's drive to build his own city, as it were, at Surrey House and there create an influential literary and cultural focus. The Howard family tragedy of 1547 can then be seen as fitting in with the conclusion to Vergil's epic. This entitles one to add to the catalogue of Surrey's prison writings, the final section of his translation of the *Aeneid*, the writing of which will have fallen during his five weeks in the Tower.

Surrey's position as a poet is also notable for the metrical innovations that served to bring the sonnet form to a level of perfection for the English tongue, from which Shakespeare was swift to profit. In this he shares credit with Wyatt. The existence in the British Library of the Devonshire Manuscript[28] opens a window onto literary gatherings within the Howard circle in the 1530s and 1540s; the manuscript has the appearance of a poetic common place book, made up of 160 lyrics, chosen by what amounted to a house clique that included Surrey's sister, Mary Richmond, Margaret

Douglas, the widow of Surrey's young uncle Lord Thomas Howard, and their long-standing friend, Mary Shelton, a cousin of Anne Boleyn.[29] While the bulk of the poems were transcribed by professional copyists, 15 were the work of Margaret Douglas, five of Mary Shelton and one of Mary Richmond. For the most part, the poems are anonymous, though ten have been ascribed to Wyatt and one to Surrey ("O happy dames"), appropriately in Mary's hand. Her transcription extends to two leaves and is in a somewhat rough state with a number of single word corrections and one whole line erased. As numerous manuscript annotations indicate, the lyrics were there to be read, to be copied, to be memorised, to be incorporated in musical entertainments.[30] This engaging domestic picture helps to soften the impression that Surrey himself frequently manages to project: that of a self-willed and thoughtless adolescent, at times strangely out of touch with contemporary practices – as when he offered "to be try'd by justice" so as to settle a dispute of honour with a medieval-style challenge, giving his opponent generously the advantage of armour, while he would be fighting "in his shirt".[31]

As is true of much literature of his time, Surrey's writings were transmitted in manuscript form, with the usual textual problems that this subsequently poses. Incarceration does not, however, appear to have presented any additional difficulties, whether of composition or diffusion. Publication, however, had to wait ten years. It was in 1557 that Richard Tottel's *Songs and Sonnettes written by the right honourable Lorde Henry Howard, late Earle of Surrey and other* first appeared.[32] While pride of place was given in the title to Surrey, Tottel's book was a collection of 271 poems, to which Surrey contributed 44, Wyatt 96, Nicholas Grimaldi 39, leaving a balance of 93 for "uncertain authors". – This wide-ranging collection was followed by seven further editions over the next 30 years.

The only poem printed during Surrey's lifetime was one of his tributes to Wyatt, which was included in a commemorative volume published in October 1542. In addition, there is a fragment of verse that – bizarrely – links Surrey with the Lincolnshire gentlewoman, Anne Askew, who was burned at the stake for denying the Catholic doctrine of transubstantiation relating to the real presence in the eucharist.

Anne Askew

(1521–1546)

Imprisonments 1546

City of London Compter	*12 days in March*
Newgate Prison	*10 days in June*
The Tower of London	*2 days end June*
Newgate Prison	*16 days in July*
Execution	*July 16, 1546*

"The Balade which Anne Askew made and sange whan she was in Newgate" must have been written from prison before her transfer to the Tower, where she was tortured on the rack in the vain hope that she would reveal the names of any prominent religious reformers at court. A copy of the manuscript, having been carried abroad shortly after her execution in Smithfield on July 16, 1546, was first printed in Germany by the Protestant propagandist, John Bale.[33] Two stanzas bear a close resemblance to lines from Surrey's translation from prison of Ecclesiastes (chapter 3):

> Askew: "I saw a royal throne, / Where justice should have sit, / But in her stead was one / Of moody cruel wit. Absorbed was righteousness, / As of the raging flood: / Satan, in his excess, / Sucked up the guiltless blood."

> Surrey: "I saw a royal throne wheras that Justice should have sit; Instead of whom I saw, with fierce and cruel mode, Where Wrong was set, that bloody beast, that drunk the guiltless blood."

The link between the two prisoners is hard to establish One presumption must be that Surrey will have had access to Anne Askew's ballad, whether as a manuscript or in print, when he was working on his translation in the Tower some six months after her execution. Alternatively – and less plausibly – Surrey's transcription may have been wholly or partly available as a manuscript as early as June 1546, the date that Anne entered Newgate.

Whatever the sequence, Askew and Surrey had much in common, including:

(a) Imprisonment, leading to execution at an early age (31 for Surrey, 25 for Askew).

(b) Both managed to fill their prison days writing. At this stage, the character of Surrey's own prison work can be said to have been reflective, while still leaving room for the occasional bursts of indignation. For her part, Askew secured thereby her position as a leading Protestant martyr through the circulation of her well-known ballad and of the detailed accounts of her two prison *Examinations*, edited and printed by John Bale in 1546–47. The second concludes with her racking in the Tower and reads movingly : "in my extremyte of sicknesse to Newgate Prison".[34]

These writings were then taken up in John Foxe's *Actes and monuments* in the revised and expanded edition of 1583. Widely known as *Foxe's Book of Martyrs*, it became, in Elaine Beilin's words, "the dominant popular account of the English Reformation".[35] Askew's own entry runs to over five folio pages, supported by an arresting woodcut showing Askew and three other victims before a large crowd in Smithfield, with the official dignitaries (the Duke of Norfolk included) seated on a bench by the entrance to the Church of St Bartholomew the Great. A chilling insight into the conflicting

The burning of Anne Askew at Smithfield, London. 16 July 1546.
Woodcut from John Foxe's The Book of Martyrs, *1563*

concerns of the spectators and the executioners is provided by the commentary that accompanies the woodcut. "Before the fire that should be set unto them, one on the Benche hearing that they had gunpowder about them, and being afrayde least the fagots by strength of the gunnpowder would come fliang about their eares, began to be afraid, but the Earle of Bedford declaring unto him how the gunnpowder was not laid under the fagots, but only about their bodies to rydde them out of their paine, . . . there was no danger to them of the fagottes, so diminished that fear."

(a) Both would have survived had Henry VIII died sooner than he did. In the case of Surrey, all he needed was eight days off Henry's life. In the case of Askew, she would have required a more demanding six and a half months. On the accession of Edward VI on January 28, 1547, the Act of the Six Articles of 1539, which had halted the legal spread of the Reformation by making Roman Catholic doctrine the law of the land, lapsed. Her denial of the real presence which had earned her martyrdom became Protestant doctrine overnight.

(b) Both succumbed to a king whose 1544 portrait engraving by Cornelius Matsys accords perfectly with Surrey's telling line from Psalm 73 "whose glutton cheeks sloth feeds so fat as scant their eyes be seen".[36]

|||||||||||||||||||||||||||||||||||||||||||||||||||||||||||||||||||||||||||||||||||||||||

CHAPTER V

Sir Walter Ralegh
(1552–1618)

Incarcerations

Tower of London	*August 3 – Christmas 1592*
Tower of London	*July 20, 1603 – March 19, 1616*
Tower of London	*August 10 – October 28, 1618*
Gatehouse, Westminster	*October 28 – 29, 1618*

Walter Ralegh was a risk-taker on an heroic scale. But hidden beneath the swagger of a successful privateer and of a privileged court favourite was an original mind that gave birth to verse of considerable elegance and prose – most significantly as a historian – noted for its musical diction and studied for its political messages.

Devon-born, he was the younger son of a country gentleman who worked his land as a tenant farmer. His father married three times, his mother twice, giving him upwards of 100 Devonian relations and connections (some having links at court). His upbringing left him with an enduring love of the West Country, the accent of which he never lost, and great experience of the sea.[1] Such modest origins no doubt pushed an ambitious 16-year old into volunteering to fight on the Protestant side in the French wars of religion. Four years later, having participated in a savage civil war, he returned to England first to Oriel College, Oxford, where tradition has it that he was once obliged to borrow a gown, not having one of his own – and omitted to return it to the lender.[2]

By 1575 he had joined the Inns of Court, becoming a member of the Middle Temple. In addition to the knowledge he was thereby able to acquire of the law, this had the great merit of giving him a London base, with potential access to the throne and more immediate involvement in overseas ventures. The first arose in June 1578 when Ralegh's half-brother, Sir Humphrey Gilbert, was granted letters patent to discover lands, not yet owned by a Christian prince, which might be colonised in the Queen's name. Walter Ralegh was one of the principal assistants in this scheme, the financing of which was linked to the projected capture of fishing fleets of Spain, Portugal and France off Newfoundland; if all were to go according to plan, the vessels and their cargoes would be taken to the Netherlands for sale, while the costs would be allocated and the rewards attributed to those who had put up the funds. This had to be a privateering venture since, inconveniently, England was not then at war with the three countries whose fishing vessels were being targeted. The Queen herself made a contribution in kind through the provision of her ship the *Falcon*, having a complement of eighty mariners and soldiers, the command of which was given to Walter Ralegh.[3] In the event, the weather put paid to the expedition, but not before the *Falcon* had, alone, challenged several Spanish men-of-war, confirming first the courage of the

Sir Walter Ralegh by unknown English artist, 1588

captain and then his wisdom in abandoning an unequal contest. He had, however, put the Queen to the expense of repairing her vessel.

An altogether more important assignment took him to Ireland in 1580, where the Lord Deputy of Ireland, Lord Grey, was charged with putting down a rebellion; his Assistant Secretary was Edmund Spencer, an old friend of Ralegh's. Ralegh was one of two to be given the task of repelling an invasion of "Spaniards". This was done with exemplary force, though the "Spaniards" turned out to be 800 Italian mercenaries who were put to the sword in what became known as The Massacre of Smerwick. This incident also served to illustrate a character trait that ensured Ralegh the hostility of many of his contemporaries, namely self-promotion in his account of the accomplishment of tasks in which he was involved.[4]

In explaining Ralegh's ten-year "reign", roughly dating from 1582, as one of Elizabeth's favourite courtiers, much is made of the fact that he was indeed very good company, with a sharp wit, a mind that was intellectually challenging and at a frivolous level well equipped to play the word games and contribute the finely phrased poems protesting undying devotion that the near-50-year-old queen required of her admirers. The fact that in 1582 he was a tall, handsome 30-year-old with the uninhibited and sometimes quirky views of a man of action also helped. The Queen's own assessment of Ralegh is revealed in her never having made him one of her Privy Councillors – reliant as they were on the cautious guidance of William Cecil, Lord Burghley, who was to occupy the post of the Queen's chief minister for some 40 years.

But as a sounding board Ralegh earned his keep. This was translated into the early bestowal of a succession of lavish gifts, the more material being the lease of two estates and the use of the episcopal palace on the Thames, Durham House, the memory of which still lingers in "Durham House Street", a stump of a road off the Strand. The Queen having as it were met his accommodation needs, the heavy running costs were then partly taken care of: in May, 1584 he was given the "farm" of wines (sometimes referred to as a "monopoly") under which he was empowered to charge every vintner one pound a year for the right to retail wine. As was the normal practice of recipients of such monopolies, he then subcontracted the licence to an agent, in this case one Richard Brown; it was he who bore the costs of collection but in return guaranteed Ralegh an annual income for the ensuing seven years of £700, a sizeable sum; any surplus was to be retained by Brown and any shortfall to be borne by him. Ralegh was later to be given control of the licence to export woollen broadcloths. These arrangements are similar to those in France, as described in the chapter on Antoine Lavoisier, but with one major difference: in France the guaranteed annual sum always went to the Crown, in England it could serve as a reward to a subject of the Crown. In addition, Ralegh enjoyed revenues from Cornish tin mining arising out of his appointment in 1585 as Lord Warden of the Stannaries. A year later he was made Lieutenant of the County of Cornwall.

The 1580s can be said to have been the years of Ralegh's greatest glory. He was knighted in 1584 and the same year entered Parliament. As with his half-brother, he was granted letters patent to explore the New World. His talents as an organiser and fund-raiser – over and above his own significant financial contribution – were put to good use. He also engaged for this expedition John White as artist and cartographer and Thomas Harriot, the mathematician, who was to prove one of Ralegh's most loyal friends.[5] Sadly for Ralegh, the Queen could not bring herself to release him so that he might personally lead this important expedition, comprising eight ships with a complement of 500 men. However, this first English colonial experiment at Roanoke was very much of his making. It also gave rise to Harriot's book, *A briefe and true report of the new found land of Virginia*, published in 1588, which was to be taken as a model account by later explorers. It is worth noting that Edmund Spenser's two volume edition, dated 1596, of *The Faerie Queene* includes a dedication to the Queen, where Virginia has been swiftly put to work in support of Elizabethan propaganda: the territory takes its place alongside France – and more convincingly England and Ireland – as forming part of Queen Elizabeth's empire.

Ralegh's attempted role as an undercover sleuth in the Babington conspiracy of 1586 – where a group of Catholics plotted the assassination of Queen Elizabeth and her replacement by Mary Queen of Scots – earned him the property of Anthony Babington, following his execution as a traitor.[6] In 1587 the Queen appointed him Captain of the Guard, which carried special responsibilities for her safety. This was a considerable mark of favour and meant frequent attendance on the Queen. In the build-up to the Armada of July 1588 he had been appointed to the Council of War.

The advent at court towards the end of 1588 of the youthful Earl of Essex served, however, to displace Walter Ralegh from his position as the Queen's special favourite. He for his part was to be shortly paying court to Elizabeth Throckmorton, who since 1584, as a 20-year-old, had been one of the Queen's maids of honour. Their marriage on November 19, 1591, which unwisely he chose to deny, and her pregnancy, were hugely displeasing to the Queen. Both he and Bess were bundled off to the Tower. This was to be his first experience of the Tower as a prisoner, but one to be measured in months rather than years. It was the start of a marriage that was to endure, marked by strong mutual affection, with Ralegh said to have been somewhat in awe of his wife.

On September 8, 1592, a Portuguese carrick, the *Madre de Dios*, was brought into Dartmouth by the English privateering fleet that had been organised by Ralegh. Its capture represented by far the richest prize ever achieved, and its docking sparked a frenzy of looting. Ralegh was temporarily released from the Tower as being the only person judged capable of bringing order to this chaos by reason of his detailed knowledge of the rights of the original backers, all of whom were particularly anxious to protect their investments and to realise their profits – not least the Queen. To Ralegh's chagrin, the final distribution as determined by the Queen saw him just recover his costs.[7]

He was in no position to argue. As a man in disgrace, he had no place at court and was "reduced" to going with his wife to the fine Dorset estate at Sherborne on which he had received a 99-year lease from the Crown as recently as January 1592 (subsequently enlarged by Ralegh to a freehold).[8] This had been by way of recognition for a powerful pamphlet recounting the heroic death of his cousin, Sir Richard Grenville, at the hands of the Spaniards in the Azores.[9] The capture of Grenville's vessel was the first such loss in the reign of Queen Elizabeth and a cause for great rejoicing within Spain. "The Revenge" was an effective piece of counter-propaganda. The battle was later to secure glowing mention in Winston Churchill's *A History of the English Speaking Peoples*.[10]

The rural delights of Dorset failed to satisfy Ralegh's restless ambition. A voyage of discovery in search of El Dorado was his first project, for which he obtained Letters Patent. He set about securing backers – one being Burghley's son, Robert Cecil, another his cousin, William Sanderson, who also took on at times the role of Ralegh's private banker – as well as that of enlisting the support of fellow privateers.[11] On this occasion, as a disgraced courtier, he ran no risk of the Queen denying him at the last moment permission to lead the expedition. He duly set off in February 1595 for Guiana (today's Venezuela) at the head of a fleet of five ships and a complement of 150.[12] In September he was back in England after enduring many privations, while also relishing many thrills of discovery in a foreign land. But this did not include identifying a source of gold. His backers were given instead an inspiring account of *The Discovery of the Large, Rich and Beautiful Empire of Guiana with a Relation of the Great and Golden City of Manoa*, and assurances that the rock samples they had collected were gold-bearing. The pamphlet, published within weeks of his return, sold well, as had done the earlier propaganda leaflet on "The Revenge".[13]

The next venture required the blessing of the Privy Council. Fears were being voiced that Spain might be planning a second Armada. Several argued for a pre-emptive strike, Cadiz being ultimately selected as the target. Such a prospect gained the enthusiastic support of the Earl of Essex, a privy councillor, and of Walter Ralegh, who had been enlisted into a Council of War, his privateering experience being thus given formal recognition by what amounted to a naval command. As it developed, the pre-emptive strike took on the characteristics of an invasion, with a fleet of 90 English vessels (plus a possible 20 from the Netherlands) transporting a 10,000-strong army. Ralegh's initial task was to assist in the gathering of the men and organisation of supplies. On June 3, 1596, the fleet set sail, with Ralegh commander of one of the five squadrons. The Spaniards were caught unprepared. The engagement had two aspects to it: the naval, where Ralegh, having in effect taken command at a critical moment, won the day by his seamanship and tactical skills; the military where Essex shone in the occupation of the town. An unusual vignette of the two great rivals for the Queen's attention in the role of brothers in arms. Once again the promise of plunder was unfulfilled, the rich cargo vessels having been fired and scuttled by the Spaniards. Moreover, to the distress of Ralegh, who had suffered a painful wound to the leg, he let it be known that he had missed out on the opportunities presented by the sack of the town.[14] Lady Throckmorton's Note Book, as cited by A. L. Rowse, disposes, however, of this "injustice", with Ralegh shown as having received spoils of £1,769 – more than any other naval commander.[15]

But the naval-military victory was greatly to the glory of the Crown and on June 1, 1597, Ralegh was received at court once again. He resumed his responsibilities as Captain of the Guard and found himself once more in frequent attendance on the Queen – but now as a man in his mid-40s, while the Queen was in her mid-60s.

The last six years of her reign were darkened by the friction at court, notably arising out of what Robert Lacey describes as Essex's paranoia, seeing plots against him from all sides, particularly from Ralegh.[16] Essex was the author of his own downfall: first of all, when called upon to quell a rebellion in Ireland, he mounted a campaign of signal incompetence, at one point even deserting his post; secondly by hosting a rebellious gathering in his London residence, Essex House; and thirdly by an astonishing intrusion into the Queen's bedroom. His execution as a traitor took place in March 1601.

The ensuing two years that preceded the Queen's death on March 24, 1603 were marked by huge uncertainties over the succession. Since the Queen only confirmed at a late stage her preference for James VI of Scotland, the delay alone gave rise to rumours of plots and counter plots, many parting company with any sense of plausibility.

A mere four months after the Queen's death, Walter Ralegh was confined to the Tower on a charge of high treason, under suspicion of being implicated firstly in what became known as the Bye Plot, aimed at securing greater religious toleration, primarily for the Catholics but also for Puritan adherents, through the forcible conversion of the king, and secondly the Main Plot of July 1603, a plan by a group of malcontents to replace James I with Arabella Stuart, his cousin, described in Lacey's account as "an empty headed young woman, belonging to a younger branch of the Scottish royal family". This was to be achieved with the help of Spanish arms and money.[17]

Ralegh's failure to navigate the uncertain waters of a change of sovereign owed much to his single-minded devotion to Queen Elizabeth; others at the Elizabethan court had been strengthening their connections with James, some over a long period. It also was a consequence of the hostility he had managed to generate over the years through arrogance, deviousness and stubbornness. Lord Henry Howard, for one, took care to put the future King James I on guard against a man who "in pride exceedeth all men alive" and who "ranked above the greatest Lucifer that hath lived in our age".[18] To this measured assessment has to be added James's own pre-conceptions: Ralegh's chemical experiments were not seen as evidence of an enquiring Renaissance mind but gave credence to claims that he occasionally dabbled in witchcraft. And for good measure he at times attracted the label of atheist by reason of his delight in disputation.

An outbreak of the plague in London meant that the trial, which took place on November 17, 1603, had to be moved to Winchester.[19] Ralegh defended himself eloquently in seeking to rebut five counts of treasonable involvements. A number of the more outlandish accusations failed to carry any weight. What he could not shake was evidence that he had been witness to treasonous discussions involving his fellow-courtier, Lord Cobham, and the Spanish ambassador, Count Aremberg. The weakness of his case is exposed in the letter, begging his life, that he wrote to the king shortly after being declared guilty of high treason: "Lost I am for heringe a vayne man, for heringe only, but never belevinge or accepting and so littell acompt I made of that speech of his, as the living God doth trewly wittnis, that I never remembred any such thinge til it was att my trial objected agaynst me". Not to have reported these exchanges to the Privy Council branded him a conspirator.[20]

The guilty verdict will not have come as a great surprise. What was unexpected, however, was the extent to which Ralegh's defence, extensively reported on, was to earn him the sympathy of the public: from being an object of widespread hatred, partly for his alleged role in the downfall of the popular Essex, he seemed to have won widespread popularity. This may well have influenced James's decision to commute the death sentence at the very last minute to imprisonment.

Imprisonment

The 13 years in the Tower were remarkable for the volume and range of Ralegh's literary output and for his continued involvement – admittedly at a considerable remove – in affairs touching the state and the throne. All of which was made possible by the practical circumstances of his imprisonment.

Initially he certainly had his travails. While his wife and their 11 year-old son, Walter, known as Wat, were able to be with him, as he was a convicted traitor his assets had been confiscated, his debts still needed to be settled and there were his prison expenses. His letter of February 14, 1604, addressed to the Privy Council, sets out the position: "My charges in this place for diet only is [sic] 208 li [pounds] a yeare, and if His Majesty do allow the rest of this sume (to make it 300 li) unto me for all the necessaries ther remayneth not above on (one) hundred mark [£66 13s 4d] a yeare for my poor wife and childe and their sarvants which God knowes will not geve them bread and cloathe."[21] In an earlier letter sent in December 1603/January 1604 to Lord Cecil, he had written: "I pay here 4 li [pounds] a week for my diet. I must pay it if [even] if the kinge geve me my pore estate agayne. And, my Lord Cecil, the Lord in heaven doth witness that I and my wife and child must proportion oursealves such a famely as we must live att 4 li a week for all our dietts, or else we must all go naked for it takes two parts [i.e. two-thirds] of all the rent I have in the world."[22] From such correspondence, it is clear that

Ralegh, a convicted man held at the king's pleasure, stood to receive an allowance from the Exchequer for basic necessities such as food and clothing. His goods and chattels were shortly thereafter granted by the Crown to the Cornish Member of Parliament, John Shelbury.[23] This was subject to their being used in part to cover Ralegh's prison allowance and also to help pay off his debts, amounting to some £3,000. Ralegh records ruefully the sales of his rich hangings for £500 and of his one rich bed for £300, while his plate, which was "very fayre", was "now lost or eaten out with interest at one Chenes in Lumbord Street".[24]

Ralegh's finances were then seriously compromised by his loss of the much loved Sherborne estate, which he had earlier put into his son's name. This would have had the incidental merit of shielding it from confiscation as with all his other assets, had it not been for the fact that the conveyancing had not been recognised owing to a solicitor's error. As a result, Sherborne became crown property. The impact on his wife was eventually lessened by dint of her importuning the king, when she received a one-off sum of £8,000 and an annuity of £400.

While Ralegh's financial position may well have been tight much of the time, the living conditions appear to have been generally acceptable. Ralegh and family were commodiously established in the Bloody Tower, which also housed his extensive library.[25] From his quarters he had access to a small garden adjoining the governor's apartments, where he cultivated his own plot of land and planted exotic shrubs; from some of these he derived the healing cordials for which he became known, notably his Guiana Balsam. In this garden he took over a small shed for use in his pharmaceutical and chemical experiments, to which he was later able to add a habitable extension. His second son, Carew, was born while he was in the Tower and was christened in the Chapel of St Peter ad Vincula. Few restrictions appear to have been made on visitor numbers, though in August 1605, with the arrival of a new governor, a curfew of five o'clock was imposed on visitors.

The chameleon-like character of the Tower was strikingly illustrated in the winter of 1605 when Thomas Harriot, who had earlier been confined there briefly as a suspected conspirator in the Gunpowder Plot, returned to take up voluntary residence. There are not many prisons that can have had such magnetic appeal. This brought together three Renaissance figures – Walter

The Bloody Tower: the lower chamber reconstructed as Sir Walter Ralegh's study, where his History of the World, *published in 1614, was written*

Ralegh, with a particular interest in medicine, Harriot, whose work on optics led him into correspondence with Kepler, and the eccentric ninth Earl of Northumberland, known as the "Wizard Earl" for his reported interest in the occult; he had been imprisoned on suspicion of links to the Gunpowder Plot conspirators, one of them being Thomas Percy, his cousin and personal secretary. In effect, this trio formed a nucleus of like-minded intellectual figures. It has to be added that the Earl of Northumberland suffered no financial constraints and spent lavishly on making his quarters and his daily circumstances thoroughly comfortable.[26] More to the point, this also enabled him to act as patron to Thomas Harriot, as well as to Robert Hues (whose published account of his travels with Thomas Cavendish was dedicated to Ralegh) and to Walter Warner, a mathematical colleague of Harriot's and also noted for his medical researches.[27] The Earl's prison library was extensive, but not literary. In effect, a scientific academy had taken root within a gaol.[28] The Earl's imprisonment was to last sixteen years.

Prison Writings

What are perhaps Ralegh's most widely read writings serve as prologue and postscript to his prison output – starting with the farewell letters to his wife of July 1603[29] and December 1604[30] and ending with his speech from the scaffold of October, 1618.

The impermanence of what were ephemeral communications was countered not by the printing press but by copyists. The moving letter from prison in Winchester opens with: "Receyve from thy unfortunate husband theis his last lynes, theis the last words that ever thow shalt receive from him. That I can live to thinke never to see the[e] and my child more I cannot.[31] I have desired God and disputed with my reason, but nature and compassion hath the victorie. That I can live to thinke howe you are both left a spoile to my enimies and that my name shalbe a dishonor to my child I cannot: I cannot indure the memorie thereof. Unfortunate woman, unfortunate child, comfort your selves, trust God and be contented with your poore estate. I woulde have bettered it if I had enjoyed a few (more) years". The original letter has not survived, but no fewer than 74 manuscript copies have been identified.[32]

The tone of the speech from the scaffold was one of defiance: "I come not hither either to feare or flatter kings. I am now ye subject of Death, and ye great God of Heaven is my soveraine before whose tribunal I am shortly to appeare."[33] His personal courage, testing the axe for sharpness and finding it such that it would "cure all sorrows",[34] the encouragement he gave to the executioner and above all the absence of any confession or expression of contrition served to contribute to an aura of innocence. It was after all his one opportunity to fashion his reputation without the need to respond to other considerations. His first request on being told that he would be executed had been to call for pen and ink. He spent his last hours preparing the speech, which he delivered with the help of notes, and in the expectation that there would be many who would seek to transcribe it. Indeed, one account has Ralegh encouraging the presence of additional witnesses on the scaffold. The speech achieved wide circulation – once again in manuscript form. Anna Beer examined 32 eyewitness accounts, grouping them according to textual similarities, many relating to details of Ralegh's comportment.[35]

There is, however, at least one printed document, which strikes a discordant note, a unique copy in the Pepys Library, Magdalene College, Cambridge: "Sir Walter Rauleigh his lamentation who was beheaded in the old Pallace at Westminster the 29 of October 1618."[36] This ballad, said to have been on sale that very day, presents a penitent Ralegh, weighed down with remorse, bereft of friends, recognising that he is being punished for "offences past", rather than a failed treasure hunt, dying "a Christian true" and:

> Kneeling down on my knee, willingly, willingly
> Prayed for his Maj(e)stie long to continue:
> And all his Nobles all,
> With subjects great and small,
> Let this my wofull fall be fit warning.

With a single but major exception, Ralegh's output when in prison remained unpublished until after his death. In terms of letters, the comprehensive 1999 edition extended to 228 letters (190 being originals and 38 transcriptions), of which 47 were written from gaol. The editors point out that whereas Ralegh employed clerks to write about half of his known total epistolary output, when in the Tower virtually all of his letters were in his own hand.[37]

His pamphlets fall under some three subject headings. Those concerned with the navy that included: (a) "A Discourse of the Invention of Ships' Anchors, Compass etc" (1610); (b) "Of the Art of War by Sea" (1608–1610); (c) "Excellent Observations, Notes concerning the Royall Navy and Sea Service" (1608). Political works, such as (a) "Touching a Marriage between Prince Henry of England and a daughter of Savoy" (1612); (b) "Concerning a Match propounded by the Savoyan, between Lady Elizabeth and the Prince of Piedmont" (1612); (c) "A Dialogue between a Counsellor of State and a Justice of the Peace" (1615) – intended as a guide to the king on how best to manage the Commons. More personal works: "Instructions to his Sonne and to Posterity" (1609).[38]

A striking feature is the way his writings are concentrated in the latter half of his imprisonment. (In the earlier years he may have spent much time on his chemical and pharmaceutical experiments.) And there is an arresting aspect of a convicted traitor dispensing widely his views on the appropriateness of projected royal marriages. What is beyond doubt is that Ralegh was increasingly turning over in his mind issues of governance. Nowhere is this more emphatically demonstrated than in his great *History of the World* and in the explicitly political *Dialogue*, his last prison writing.

History of the World

The *History of the World*, the only one of Ralegh's prison writings to have been published during his captivity, is some 1,570 pages long, dwarfing his pamphlet writings. Nevertheless, it was left incomplete: a "world" history that starts with the Biblical creation and gets no further than the conclusion of the second Punic War in 201 BC is a serious misnomer.

Publication of the *History of the World* came in December 1614; printed by William Stansby for Walter Burre for sale in his shop in St Paul's Churchyard at the sign of the Crane. It was priced at 20 shillings and will probably have been printed in a run of up to 500 copies. While this first edition did not carry Walter Ralegh's name, it had an elaborate frontispiece from which the identity of the author might be deduced. This was not a surreptitious imprint. In his invaluable biography, Pierre Lefranc argues that Ralegh will have started writing in January 1609 – following no doubt a lengthy period of planning and research. Guided in part by references in the text to books with known publication dates and to Ralegh's own mention of an eclipse of the sun, Lefranc calculates that by April 15, 1611, when the book was entered into the Stationers' calendar as being Burre's copy, some 650 pages would have been completed. By November 16, 1612, the date of the death of Prince Henry, to whom Ralegh had intended to dedicate his History, the 1,000 page mark should have been reached, leaving the balance in the ensuing two years, with the Introduction being written last in 1614.[39] In Lefranc's opinion, the great bulk of the text was dictated to Ralegh's secretary, John Talbot, who was one of those in his service who were authorised to reside in the Tower.[40]

A book of this length written over several years would also have taken several years to print, starting in 1611. John Racin's detailed study of the History brings out its carefully planned divisional structure – and hence printing complexity : by book, by chapter, by section within a chapter, by subsection within a section and finally by page (Books i and ii having one pagination, Books iii to v having another). This leaves out 42 pages of unpaginated preliminary material and 36 pages of unpaginated tables at the end.

Racin's detailed analysis also uncovers several instances where pages have been cancelled in mid-production so that, while a number of copies carry the corrections, others have escaped such amendments. Most interesting of all is one which in Racin's account points to Ralegh's direct intervention; this relates to the suppression of a comment that was indiscreet and would have given immediate offence to the king.[41] Ralegh's ability to control the production of his work from within the confines of the Tower is telling evidence of the freedoms from which he benefited.

As a self-indulgent digression: Shakespeare's first folio, printed by Isaac Jaggard in 1623, ran to 972 pages – 486 leaves – and was in the press for about 18 months from about February 1622 until October 1623, based on the findings presented by John Buchtel and Peter Blayney.[42] The *History of the World* ran to some 1,570 pages, equivalent to 785 leaves, and on John Racin's calculations would have been in the press for 44 months up to December 1614.[43] This indicates that the *History*, 60 per cent longer than the First Folio, took two and a half times as long to produce. Among the many factors that might explain this contrast, one must be that the speed of the printer (and the number of presses used) of the *History* was largely determined by the pace set by the author – not a constraint on Isaac Jaggard, working on his author's posthumous publication. And when Burre published the third edition in 1621, with Isaac Jaggard as the printer, there is a certain thrill to record that Ralegh was, as it were, a mere two years short of that momentous publishing event in English literature.[44]

Publication in 1617 of the second edition came at a time which saw Ralegh temporarily released (unpardoned), so that he might undertake yet another expedition to Guiana. Fresh editions followed in 1621, 1624, 1628, 1634, and 1652. That of 1677 was the first to include a life of the author. By 1687 some ten editions had been published, as set out in T. N. Brushfield's bibliography.[45] The popularity of the work is further underlined by the publication of abridgements in 1650 and 1698. Most remarkable of all were the two *Continuations of the famous History of Sir Walter Ralegh* that appeared in 1652 and 1708.

Wherein lay the attraction? First of all, Ralegh's *History* was very different from the impersonal annals that were popular in the sixteenth century, having been for the most part a compilation of contemporary notices. His coupling of history with geography had a modern ring to it, while the lacing of the text with his own judgments and experiences added a personal touch. Best of all, he skilfully managed to link his centuries-old accounts to day-to-day developments.[46] For, as Racin writes: "according to Ralegh's view of history, whether the historian's subject matter was ancient or modern made no difference in terms of its moral, political or practical relevance.

Underlying the whole work was an impressive display of scholarship, all the more remarkable in a man of action whose time spent in formal education was limited. There is much of the autodidact about Ralegh. On his sea voyages, he was said to have always travelled with a trunk full of books. His contemporary, Thomas Lodge, a fellow buccaneer and author, found time to write *Rosalynde. Euphues golden legacie*, deservedly celebrated both as a source of *As You Like It* and as an example of narrative art (*Concise Cambridge History of English Literature*), when sailing to the Canaries.[47] Ralegh's own library when in prison, the book list of which is in his own hand and was identified as recently as 1953, contained 515 items. The foreign languages covered were French, Italian, Latin, and Spanish. However, he did not read Greek easily and he relied on outside help when it came to Hebrew. Walter Oakeshott's article in *The Library* makes clear that this was the working library of a historian and of a seafarer, with particular strengths in ancient and modern history, geography, theology, cosmography, but with little space given to belles lettres. Latin titles predominate.[48] He would also certainly have had access to the extensive prison library of his close friend, the Earl of Northumberland; its strengths lay in mathematics, chemistry, the occult and above all the art of war. And there is the (undated but probably c. 1610) letter to Sir Robert Cotton, the celebrated antiquary and collector of manuscripts and books, asking for the loan of 13 titles.[49] What emerges is that the research facilities in the Tower for a writer having Ralegh's interests were indeed extensive.

This leads to the disputed matter of authorship and Ben Jonson's much quoted remark: "the best wits of England were Employed for making of his Historie".[50] Two centuries later, Isaac D'Israeli writes, in his essay "Literary Unions", "we cannot doubt, however, that some specialist studies were prepared for his use". D'Israeli's comment carries much greater conviction than does Ben Jonson's quip. It is also likely that Ralegh would at times have been free with existing texts, most obviously biblical and classical. But, to quote Oakeshott, "The *History* is indeed a highly individual book, and its interpretation of the facts is coloured by the writer's experience".[51] And the painstaking analysis undertaken by Pierre Lefranc serves to demolish the claims for co-authorship of those five or six whose names have at various times been bandied about.[52] At the same time, Lefranc emphasises the assistance Ralegh received from his secretary, John Talbot. (Talbot was destined to die on the outward journey to Guiana in 1617; help for his mother is included in Ralegh's last wishes.)

Perhaps the most enduring appeal of the book to today's reader lies in its English. The tone is set from the start in his Preface: "For myself, if I have in any thing served my Country, and prised it before my private: the generall acceptation can yield me no other profit this time, than doth a faire sunshine day to a Sea-man after shipwrack; and the contrary no other harme than an outrageous tempest after the port attained." The ensuing discursive approach has immediate attraction, accompanied furthermore by the authority of a man who could write: "rarely or never can we consider truly of worldly proceedings unless we have felt the deceits of fortune".[53] The revolt of mercenaries against the Carthaginians leads to a treatise on the use of mercenaries in warfare. Biblical references to Moses are an opportunity to explore legal issues. But he could also be pithy, as witness his account of the battle of Marathon. "So invincible and resistless the Persians esteemed their own numbers to be, and the small troupe of their enemies then in view, rather to be despised than to be fought withall: But in conclusion, the victory being doubtfully balanced for a while, some time the virtue of the Graecians and sometimes the numbers of the Persians prevailed, the Graecians fighting for all that they had, the Persians for that they needed not, these great forces of Darius were disordered and put to rout; the Athenians following their victory even to the Sea Shore; where the Persians, so many of them as lost not their wits with their courage, saved themselves in their ships."[54]

Ralegh's *History* has something of the charm of Montaigne's *Essays*, an extended conversation with the reader; first published in 1580, Ralegh's own copy appears as Number 487 in his catalogue.

On December 22, 1614, a few weeks after publication in early December, Archbishop Abbot, on the king's instruction, ordered the suppression of the

History of the World.[55] The copies with the printer, Stansby, were impounded and further sales by the bookseller forbidden.

A history that included in the Preface a review of English sovereigns, with acerbic comments on many, not omitting Henry VIII, was bound to call for extreme tact on the part of the author. Ralegh's formula on the one hand was to lavish praise on James I in the accepted tone of the day, concluding with "I could say much more of the King's Majesty, without flatterie: did I not feare the imputation of presumption". The hyperbole grates on modern ears, but to James I, who had after all written that "kings are the breathing Images of Gods upon earth", this would not have come amiss – though he might have questioned the sincerity of the author.[56] The second string to Ralegh's bow was to make much of his intention to have dedicated the *History* to James's much loved son, Henry, and to emphasise the prince's close interest in the work: "For it was for the service of that inestimable Prince Henry, the successive hope, and one of the greatest of the Christian World, that I undertook this Worke. It pleased him to peruse some parts thereof, and to pardon what was amiss. It is now left to the world without a Maister." These palliative measures were not sufficient, however, to offset the negative impact on James of the "relentless and repetitive rehearsal of God's judgment on rulers", to cite Anna Beer's happy phrase.[57] While Ralegh never justifies the overthrow of a monarch, he illustrates it again and again. It is, therefore, hugely ironic that the copy in the British Library should have belonged to Princess Elizabeth, daughter of James I and sister of Prince Henry.[58] Following her marriage on February 14, 1613, to Frederick V, Count Palatine of the Rhine – who was later to be elected King of Bavaria – the couple had made their way to Heidelberg , and it was there that she would have taken delivery of and then studied a book condemned by her father.

Prince Henry

From an early age, Prince Henry showed considerable promise – stimulated intellectually by his father's requirement that he and his sister Elizabeth write to him frequently accounts of their activities in Latin, French and Italian.[59] From birth (February 19, 1594) he would have been in the long-distance sights of many looking for some form of patronage. By 1609, aged 15, he started forming his household ahead of his investiture as Prince of Wales in June 1610. The patronage aimed at might be direct remuneration, a pension, a position in the household, political or religious protection, self aggrandisement ... A vehicle for such a request that was frequently chosen lay in the dedication of a book, usually after permission had been granted by the dedicatee.

Prince Henry, as an energetic young man, the heir apparent, wielding considerable power and endowed with a Renaissance-wide range of interests, while firmly committed to the Protestant faith, was a great catch as a patron. At the time of his investiture, his own household already came to 400.[60] By the time of his death in 1612 aged 18 he had received the dedication of 110 printed books, 16 in the year of his death.[61] As John Buchtel notes, the young man had attracted an unrelenting and painstaking instruction whether in printed books, manuscripts, unique presentation copies. Ralegh was by no means alone in dedicating didactic works addressed to the prince, examples being his naval writings. But how literally one should take his statement introducing his pamphlet regarding the proposed marriage of Princess Elizabeth as being written at the behest of the prince may be questionable. Ralegh's assertion that the *History* was a work stimulated by Prince Henry[62] is also matched by John Hayward, who, in 1613, described Prince Henry as both requesting an English History for his own instruction and as urging publication. Both may well be true, but Ralegh's position is clearly not unique.[63] What is certain is that Ralegh made no attempt to secure an alternative patron on the prince's death – as did Francis Bacon, for example, who was quick to re-dedicate a forthcoming edition of his *Essays* to his brother-in-law, Sir John Constable. Many writers were in a quandary at a time when rewards came through patronage and very little from payments made them by publishers (i.e. booksellers). For an imprisoned Ralegh, however, a close association in the public eye with the prince was reward enough, hence a statement that can be mistaken for simple window-dressing .

This brings one to the question of precisely how close Ralegh was to the Prince. One can readily conceive of him as a youngster being drawn to Ralegh, a man of action, highly literate, having an inquiring mind and with all the glamour attached to a participant in Queen Elizabeth's glory years. He is quoted by Roger Coke, citing his father, the great jurist Sir Edward Coke, as having heard him exclaim: "no other king but this Father would keep such

Henry, Prince of Wales,
unknown artist
after Isaac Oliver, c. 1610

a Man as Sir Walter in such a Cage". Prince Henry's vigorous opposition to the bestowal of the Sherborne estate to James's favourite of the day, Sir Robert Carr, is well documented.[64] He carried the day and the property was granted him instead; the prince's avowed intention had been to hold it for Ralegh pending his release. Nonetheless, Roy Strong in his biography of the Prince cautioned that there was no evidence that Ralegh and the Prince had ever met.[65] J. W. Williamson on the other hand takes it for granted that they saw each other in the Tower,[66] as does Pierre Lefranc.[67] And Queen Anne did get Ralegh to supply the prince with a small vial of his Balsam Guiana; this was administered to him on his death bed. Some malicious gossips had it that it was the cordial that finished him off.

It seems reasonable to conclude that, had Prince Henry still been alive in 1618, Ralegh's execution might never have taken place.

Guiana

Throughout his thirteen year imprisonment, the fascination that Guiana exerted on Ralegh remained as an undercurrent. The 1595 expedition had been followed by those of such explorers as Captain Leigh (1604), Robert Harcourt

(1609) and Sir Thomas Roe (1611), testimony to the hold on the imaginations of English risk-takers, but without providing any confirmation of the existence of the city or empire of El Dorado. There remained though in the air the spectre of a gold mine of great richness close to the banks of the Orinoco River. Ralegh seized on this. Playing skilfully on the King's need for money and holding out the possibility of a solution to a massive debt overhang, Ralegh secured his temporary release from the Tower in March 1616 with a view to mounting a full scale expedition. There were two major conditions, one being that the force should not engage in any hostilities with the Spaniards and the other that Ralegh should return to prison whatever the outcome.

Ralegh's release from the Tower had two book related consequences: firstly he was able to leave prison taking with him his library[68] and secondly, following what amounted to the lapse of the ban on the History, the king chose to sell for his own profit the copies that had been confiscated.[69]

One has to marvel at the determination of a man in his sixties, whose health was now indifferent, taking on the physical challenges of a testing voyage of exploration. But there was no lack of energy. He set about raising the money and organising what was to be a fleet of over a dozen vessels, carrying a complement of sailors and soldiers of some one thousand. He spoke the language of a modern promoter: they would be spending three to four months in the Orinoco, equipped with brick ballast and six pairs of great bellows for the conversion of the minerals into ingots. The samples were those brought back from the 1595 expedition, the analysis of which confirmed the presence of gold – no matter that Ralegh had promised £20 to the assayer should he find such traces.[70] All that remained to do was to locate the mineral deposits. The money, amounting to the substantial sum of £30,000, was raised, Bess contributing significantly, as well as close relatives of hers. The fleet set sail from Plymouth on June 12, 1617.

It proved an unqualified disaster: ill health decimated the crews, an ailing Ralegh himself being unable to lead the expedition up the Orinoco. Far from avoiding conflict with the Spaniards, the Spanish fort of San Thomé was overrun with loss of life. Ralegh's son Wat was killed. The force under the command of his loyal aide, Laurence Kermiss, turned back before establishing the existence of a mine; on returning to base and being reproached for his failure, he committed suicide. The homecoming of the bedraggled expedition saw one commitment honoured – Ralegh's re-entry into the Tower, in line with the precedent established in the fourteenth century by the king of France, Jean II, after he had failed to raise the ransom money needed to secure his freedom.

The Royal Proclamation, dated June 9, 1618, will have left few people in doubt as to the fate reserved for Ralegh. The King starts by invoking the strict conditions under which the expedition was authorised, then enumerates the breaches to these instructions and goes on "to make a publique declaration of Our own utter mislike and detestation of the said insolences and excesses". He concludes by calling for further evidence "that wee may thereupon pro-ceede in our Princely Justice to the exemplary punishment and coertion of all such, as shal be convicted and found guilty of so scandalous and enormous outrages". Ralegh was duly executed on October 29, 1618.

From an investor's point of view, Ralegh's one significant success had been in 1592 with the *Madre de Dios*. Otherwise, those who had backed his gambles had experiences that ranged from disappointment to heavy losses. The braggart label that earned him the distrust of many is beautifully il-lustrated in a letter from the Tower of July 1607 to Viscount Haddington: "When God shall permit me to arrive, if I bringe them not to a mountayne nire a navigable river covered with gold and silver oares, let the commanders have commission to cut of my head their".[71] Today's prospector overlooking a depression in Australia and announcing the existence of a diamond bearing deposit has nothing on Ralegh. But Ralegh was also dealing with other peo-ples lives, not simply their money.

Ralegh as a Political Thinker

From having been in the political limelight for more than 20 years up to the death of Queen Elizabeth, the imprisoned Ralegh found himself reduced to a condition of near invisibility. A number of his prison writings can be ex-plained in part as his way of seeking to keep his name in the public eye. Some of these works had so to speak a limited shelf life – advice on royal couplings and on naval construction and tactics. Rules of behaviour to a son by contrast had a relevance that was not limited in time; it was a crowded field, howev-er, and Ralegh's book which enjoyed successive reprints in the 1630's finally lost some of its edge. As a means of keeping the author's name to the fore, the *History of the World* – and the *Dialogue* – were, however, outstanding. This owes much to the fact that Ralegh chose to present historical and political issues in their complexity with the reader having to make his or her judgement – in itself an innovation. But for a man already aged 64 and in the event a mere four years away from death, it was inevitable that personal gratification over the dissemination of his great book was destined to be limited, all the more so that for two of those years following publication the *History* was itself out of bounds. But the wider objective he will have had of a lasting legacy was to be amply fulfilled, as witness the care that he lavished on the text and most importantly the fact that, alone of all his prison writings, he had it printed.

From 1617 the *History* became freely available and remained so throughout the political and religious turbulence of the seventeenth century. Once a text is in the public sphere, as Anna Beer reminds one, it is open to interpretation.[72] And the *History of the World* during the course of its 1,750 pages gave readers of all hues the opportunity to wring significance out of Ralegh's words so as to create their own readings. The posthumous elevation of Ralegh to near-canonical status was also helped by the publication of texts that had previously only circulated as manuscripts: the *Dialogue* in 1628, *Instructions* to his son in 1632 and in 1648 the speech from the scaffold. Carew Ralegh's pamphlet defending his father and pointing to the travails of the Stuarts as a form of divine retribution appeared in 1656. The *History* appealed to Levellers, to regicides, to republicans, to supporters of constitutional monarchs, to parliamentarians, to naval strategists. John Locke recommended it as a cultural experience. Oliver Cromwell gave it to his son, Richard: "Recreate yourself with Sir Walter Ralegh's History: it's a Body of History and will add much more to your understanding than fragments of Story."[73] It also became a vehicle to which spurious works, credited to Ralegh's pen, were attached as a means of promoting special causes. In addition, the *History* provided fertile ground for those careful readers who approached the work for its autobiographical content.

There are some who claim that Ralegh was a notable political thinker. This is not supported in histories of political thought from which his name is typically absent. His real achievement is to have produced writings which then served as a form of scaffolding for political debate lasting well over a century. The more considered judgment that the *History of the World* was one of the most influential works to have been produced from prison seems well founded.

Seventeenth Century – Eighteenth Century

||||||||||||||||||||||||||||||||||||||||||||||||||||||||||||||||||||||||||||||||||||||||||

CHAPTER VI

William Prynne

(1600–1669)

In a long life, remarkable for its turbulence, even by the exacting standards of the seventeenth century, William Prynne was convicted on religious and political grounds on four separate occasions, and this took him to nine different prisons in which he spent a total of some ten years. As an outspoken Puritan, he twice came before the Star Chamber on charges of sedition, which gained him entry into the Tower of London.

He was born at Swainswick near Bath into a family that was comfortably off. From school in Bath he went up to Oriel College, Oxford, and was awarded his BA degree in 1621. A keen developing interest in law led to his admission as a student of Lincoln's Inn, which was destined to have such a formative influence in his life, since it was there that his militant Puritanism was awakened.

In 1628 he was called to the bar. By then he was already the author of several religious tracts, early evidence of what was to occupy so much of his time and earn him the reputation among his contemporaries of being decidedly "wordy". During the course of his life, Prynne's printed output came to an estimated 180 to 200 titles (many of these published anonymously), making him a strong contender for the title of the most prolific pamphleteer of his day.[1] Furthermore, while the term "pamphlet" applied to some publications of little more than a handful of pages, it also included works that ran to hundreds of pages. It has been calculated that from an early age he would need to have written more than one page a day.[2] What is certain is that imprisonment did nothing to stem the flow, thereby confirming Prynne's position as a prominent prison writer.

Prynne is now perhaps best remembered for his courageous endurance when subjected to punishments of great severity for his religious convictions. The first such occasion followed the publication in November 1632 of Prynne's massive work *Histriomastix*. In it, as a good Puritan, he set out the case against the stage, seen as one of the principal sources of immorality, as well as being contrary to the scriptures and indeed against the law. The argument was supported by quotations from all ages, precedents from any number of countries and harsh criticisms of unconcerned clerics, all of which ran to a book of 1,006 pages of text and supporting references.

Unfortunately for Prynne, January 9, 1633, saw the first performance of Walter Montagu's *The Shepherd's Paradise*, written specifically with Queen Henrietta Maria in mind, who, according to a contemporary correspondent, had declared herself "pleased to act a parte for her recreation as for the exercise of her Englishe".[3] Rehearsals had started in September, with the Queen taking the lead role of Belissa and the cast consisting of her six maids of honour and four court ladies, several of whom were called upon to play the male parts. The length of the play weighed heavily on a number of the conscripted players, and this meant that the target date of November 29 – the King's birthday – was not achieved. Another contributor to the missed deadline centred on the erection of an elaborate stage, a temporary structure in the lower court of Somerset House to accommodate Inigo Jones's elegant sets and scenery. After the first performance in January, a second was given a month later on February 2. While the Queen had already appeared in a French masque in 1626 with her French ladies, these were her first stage appearances in English. To this was added the considerable novelty of its being the first play in English known to have been acted by women.[4]

In this context, it was inevitable that some passages embedded in Prynne's book were soon to attract the attention of the Star Chamber, ever on the lookout for royal libels carrying a whiff of treason. At one stage, Prynne roundly declares: "It hath been always reputed dishonourable, shameful, infamous for Emperours, Kings or Princes to come upon a Theatre to dance, to masque, or act a part in any publike or private Enterludes to delight themselves or others."[5] Prynne's plea that his work antedated the staging of the play, that much of the printing had been completed months earlier and that he was innocent of any deliberate insult to the Crown was weakened by the fact that the Queen had participated in the 1626 masque a year into her marriage;[6] moreover, the extended period of rehearsal for the *Shepherd's Paradise* constituted well publicised advance notice.[7] He was consequently committed to the Tower. A year later, sentence was pronounced: the loss of ears on the pillory, the University of Oxford and Lincoln's Inn to degrade and debar him, a fine of £5,000, and life imprisonment. The publisher and bookseller, Michael Sparke, was fined £500, made to stand in the pillory and there hand a copy of the book to the hangman for burning.[8] Prynne duly had one ear cut when in the pillory before Westminster Hall on May 7, 1634, and the other ear when in the pillory in Cheapside on May 10. This harks back to Ben Jonson's *The Alchemist*, published in 1616, where Dol upbraids her companions – her good baboons Subtle and Face – with the promise of the pillory "t'have but a hole, to thrust your hands in, for which you should pay ear-rent".[9]

The clerical Court of High Commission had still to consider his attacks on the clergy. With this in mind, Prynne's personal library was seized and sold on Archbishop Laud's instructions, with the proceeds destined to defray some of the costs of this second trial. In the event, this trial never materialised. Prynne was confirmed, however, in his detestation of Laud, whom he regarded as a closet-papist, corrupting the purity of the Elizabethan church, and the main architect of his own persecution.

He was taken back into the Tower, where one gets a glimpse of the conditions under which a man with his background might experience imprisonment. Financial constraints do not appear to have been at any time a consideration and indeed his father's will – he died in 1620 – did not herald monetary difficulties. References to one or more servants indicate that his day-by-day needs will have been met, though it is not clear if any of them lived in the prison. He will certainly have had ready access to writing materials and books, some no doubt supplied by visitors, perhaps surreptitiously. In the aftermath of his mutilation, this will have been of particular importance given his resumption of pamphleteering in language that was increasingly intemperate, reflecting his deep sense of outrage. On June 11, 1634 he also wrote directly to Archbishop Laud detailing the illegality of his punishment, but also letting fly with personal abuse. By a ruse, he was able to destroy the original letter and thereby escape being hauled before the ecclesiastical court.[10] The continued appearance of militantly puritanical pamphlets,

All fleſh is Graſs, the beſt men vanity;
This, but a ſhadow, here before thine eye,
Of him, whoſe wondrous changes clearly ſhow,
That GOD, not men, ſwayes all things here below.

William Prynne:
engraving after
unknown artist, 1640

which, albeit anonymous, bore his stamp, led, however, to enquiries with a view to confirming their authorship.

News from Ipswich, dated November 1636, was a particularly abusive attack on the church government. The following year saw the appearance of *Brief Instructions for Church Wardens and others to Observe in all Episcopal or Archdiaconal Visitations and Spiritual Courts*, a four-page anonymous pamphlet.[11] This was a defiant publication in which Prynne advised churchwardens how they might use the law to avoid church visitations, and if cited into the ecclesiastical Court of High Commission, how to ignore the church's requirement of statements under oath. The investigation established that the imprisoned Prynne had given to his servant, Nathaniel Wickens, the manuscript and he in turn had taken it to the printer, one Gregory Dexter, who had been commissioned to run off 1,000 copies. The proof was then taken by the printer on an appointed day to the home of Wickens's father, a cheesemonger in Newgate Market. Prynne, having made use of the opportunity given to prisoners to have short leaves of absence from the Tower, if accompanied by a keeper, was already installed at the cheesemonger's, where he was able to read and correct the proof in an inner room. The keeper, for his part, who had been invited to go upstairs and not stay in the shop, had had no contact with Gregory Dexter. The corrected proof was then taken back by Dexter and the pamphlet produced. The one surviving copy in Britain is in the National Library of Scotland, but apparently lacking a title page, which contained a bibliographical curiosity that had caught the attention of E. W. Kirby: this consisted of a capital letter "C" which, when turned on its side, appeared as a pope's head and served as a reflection of Prynne's abhorrence of all things that appeared to him to be papistic.[12]

By March 1637, two other Puritan writers, John Bastwick and Henry Burton, had been imprisoned in the Tower, having given their names to further pamphlets questioning the legality of the ecclesiastical court.[13] These recalcitrant Puritans finally exhausted the opportunities open to them for procrastination as well as episcopal patience. On June 13, 1637, the Star Chamber ordered their trial. The sentence was severe: each was to lose his ears on the pillory at Westminster, to be fined £5,000 and condemned to perpetual imprisonment. (It has to be noted that fines of this scale and imprisonment of this duration must have had symbolic value in quite a few cases.) In addition, Prynne was to be branded on both cheeks with the letters "S" and "L" for "Seditious Libeller". The execution took place on June 30 and was savagely enforced, particularly in respect of Prynne: what may previously have been notches to his ears now involved full excisions, clumsily executed, and the branding was worsened by the hangman having to repeat one letter that he had first applied upside down. With indomitable spirit, Prynne cried out from the pillory "The more I am beat down, the more am I lift up", and on his way back to the Tower recited a punning verse, with a deft reference to his tormentor, that included an alternative to "Seditious Libeller" – "Stigmata Laudis" ("Brandings of Praise").[14]

This was to mark the end of his connections with the Tower of London as a prisoner. Laud wanted him out of the way. After a brief spell in Carnarvon Castle, he was exiled to the Channel Islands, to Mont Orgueil Castle in Jersey, and remained there three and a half years. In November 1640 Charles I, after 12 years of absolute rule, had reluctantly summoned Parliament. The Puritan parliamentarians promptly set about overturning the 1637 convictions. Prynne and his two fellow-sufferers made a triumphant return to London. Prynne was readmitted to Lincoln's Inn and his Oxford degree was restored. Several years later, Prynne was to have the satisfying task of conducting the prosecution for treason in the trial of Archbishop Laud, an impressive recognition of his legal skills. The trial began in 1644 and led to Laud's execution for treason on January 10, 1645.

During his imprisonment in Jersey Prynne's polemical writings were sharply curtailed. He did, however, compose several poems, one collection of which appears in a charming little volume under the title *Mount Orgueil: or Divine and Profitable Meditations* . . . . published in 1641. Claims for the literary merits of Prynne's verse are rare, but what is of interest to this study are the dedications in three of his poems: (a) "To the Right Worshipfull his ever Honoured worthy friend, Sir Philip Carteret, Knight, Lieutenant Governor of the Isle of Jersey"; (b) "A Christian Paradise or a Divine Poesie dedicated to the Worshipfull his ever Honoured Kind Friends, Mrs. Douse and Mrs. Margaret Carteret Daughters of Sir Philip Carteret"; (c) "The Soules Complaint dedicated to Lady Elizabeth Balfoure, Wife of Sir William Balfoure Knight Lieutenant of the Tower of London". This is followed by:

> Madam Your Noble Favour whiles that I
>
> Did in the Tower of London, Prisoner Lye
>
> For Sundry years; may now in Justice call
>
> For some expression of my Thanks, though small
>
> Having no better meanes to testifie
>
> My gratitude, than this small poesie.[15]

On the basis of these dedications written on the publication of these verses in and around 1640 Prynne emerges as a more amenable individual than his other writings would indicate.[16] Secondly, it is clear that in both the Tower of London and Mont Orgueil incarceration did not preclude kindness at the hands of his gaolers, leading to a lessening of constraints and a degree of congenial companionship. At Mont Orgueil, this extended to playing cards with Lady de Carteret and her two daughters, an unlikely pastime, it must be said, for a militant Puritan. Consistent with the status he had acquired as that of a friend of the family, the cell that was fitted out for him was close to the Governor's State Room.[17]

The years 1640 to 1660 saw Prynne very much in the public eye, dispensing a succession of strongly held views, often by no means the received opinion of the day and indeed some of which earned him periods of imprisonment. As his biographer, E. W. Kirby, succinctly comments, "he was to run up and down the gamut of political experiences".[18] This encompassed: sharp criticism of Charles I for his casual observance of the law and contempt of the Commons; condemnation of Archbishop Laud for encouraging the king in these views and simultaneously promoting the clerical encroachment on royal prerogatives; distrust of the Independents infected by Calvinistic enthusiasms; hostility to the army with its republican leanings; strong opposition to the trial and execution of the king; outright opposition to Cromwell in his progress towards dictatorship. Having been elected to Parliament in November 1648, Prynne came just in time to be included in Colonel Pride's Purge of Cromwell's opponents in the Commons, thereby joining the ranks of the "secluded" members – though, true to form, he did not go quietly when barred entry into Parliament. This will have contributed to his strong advocacy of Charles II's restoration since "monarchy is the best of governments whiles it keeps the bounds which Law and Conscience have prescribed".

One direct result of the Restoration was to bring the Tower back into Prynne's life, but this time not as a prisoner but as Keeper of the Records of the Tower of London. This was one of the earliest of Charles II's appointments, made no doubt in recognition of Prynne's contribution to the king's return. It had the additional merit of being a perfect choice for the post.[19]

From an early age, Prynne's enthusiasm for the law had given him a keen interest in what his contemporaries termed his "antiquities". Dating from his imprisonment in 1633, he had been given access to the records in the Tower, no doubt sowing the seeds of his passion for archives and easing somewhat the pains of incarceration.[20] Furthermore, his political pamphleteering did not displace detailed historical studies. *Histriomastix* was an early example; buttressed by a plethora of references, this was to earn him the epithet "Marginal Prynne" given him by John Milton.[21] His imprisonment as a troublesome, seditious writer with royalist sympathies in Dunster Castle in June 1650, which lasted one year, was softened by his being given access to the muniment room by the owner, George Luttrell; he proceeded to make a catalogue of the early deeds and rolls. In 1657 *An exact Abridgment of the Records in the Tower of London From the reign of King Edward the second unto King* *Richard the Third of all the Parliaments holden in each king's reign . . .* was published. This abstract of Cotton's *Records of the Tower* was a large folio running to 716 pages, supplied with a preface, marginal notes . . . by William Prynne Esq a Bencher of Lincoln's Inn. In December 1659 *Histriarchos* appeared, a substantial work on the writs of Parliament, and in September 1660 *A Brief* *Register, Kalendar, and Survey of Several Kinds of Parliamentary Writs, relating* *to the House of Commons.* In the summer of 1661, there is an appealing picture of Prynne, covered in dust in the depths of the White Tower sorting out decaying documents into sundry heaps – 94 parcels of parliamentary writs filed alphabetically.[22] This gave rise to the publication *Brevia Parlamentaria* *Rediviva* of January 1662. As late as 1668 came *Aurum Reginae*; this was a compilation of revenues in the form of dues to which the consorts of monarchs were entitled and which had fallen into abeyance as a result of sundry acts of Parliament, as well as the physical absence of consorts during the reigns of Edward VI, Queen Mary and Queen Elizabeth. Judiciously, it was dedicated to "Katherine, Queen Consort to his Sacred Majesty Charles II, King of England, Scotland, France and Ireland".

Prynne's literary reputation has nothing to do with elegance of style. His contemporaries were at one on this. Nor could he be accused of impartiality: his views, always strongly – but by no means consistently – held, lent themselves to violent language – bishops were "divells", Quakers were "masked papists", the Great Fire was the work of Romish enemies of England. When deploying an argument it was said of him that he has "such accurate skill in the laws that he can find treason in a bulrush, and innocence in a scorpion".[23] His most favoured weapon was a literary battering ram: by sheer volume he aimed to overthrow his opponent, but he would occasionally lose his reader in the process. What is undeniable, however, is that he had huge courage. His physical courage was on display throughout a life full of torments, most memorably on the pillory. His intellectual courage was evident in a lifetime devoted to espousing causes that so often challenged authority and brought down on the author the weight of the law, or as he would define it, the arbitrary action of those contemptuous of the law.

It is perhaps to his antiquarian work that one should look for his most enduring influence. The respect he had for historical evidence based on primary sources sets a standard for objective research that historians of all stripes would do well to follow. It is totally in character that in the preface to his *Abridgment of the Records of the Tower* of 1657 he took to task the great Elizabethan and Jacobean jurist, Sir Edward Coke – and did so without any mincing of words: Prynne castigates those "who commonly take all Printed Statutes and Reverend Sir Edward Coke's oft mistaken Records, for un-doubted Oracles, without comparing them with the original Records them-selves, out of over much laziness or credulity".[24]

CHAPTER VII

Richard Lovelace
(1618–1658)

Incarcerations

Gatehouse Prison at Westminster	*June 1 – 21, 1642*
Peterhouse Prison, Aldersgate	*June 9, 1648 – April 9, 1649*

Two spells in prison, lasting a little over ten months, secured for Richard Lovelace his position in English literature on the back of a dozen or so lyrics. His otherwise extensive output elicits such judgements as "it is to be con-fessed that there is not much true and genuine poetry in Lovelace" (J. A. Longford, *Prison Books*),[1] and more woundingly "His two or three perfect lyrics are buried in a mass of frigid, extravagant and artificial versification which is best forgotten" (*Concise Cambridge History of English Literature*).[2]

The Lovelaces were an old Kentish family with strong ties to the Crown. Lovelace's father was a professional soldier who in 1604 was granted "a li-cence to serve in the wars under any Christian State or Prince in league with His Majesty during pleasure". He saw service principally in the Low Countries. He was knighted by James I in 1609. Richard, the eldest of five children, is said to have been born in Holland. At the age of nine, he lost his father, who was killed in battle at Gryll in Holland. His education took him to Charterhouse and then on to Oxford, matriculating in 1634. By 1639 he was a soldier participating in the inconclusive Scotch Expedition of that year, which had as its objective to teach those Scots who stubbornly opposed the King's ecclesiastical policy a lesson. The Scots fielded a body of troops, many of them experienced in warfare, committed to the Presbyterian cause; by contrast the royalist army was disorganised and lacking in conviction. The two forces confronted each other at Berwick, with the Scots occupying a strong position. What amounted to a stand-off gave birth to a treaty with the unconvincing title "The Pacification of Berwick". Despite the almost total absence of any military engagement, Ensign Lovelace nevertheless found material enough to compose a poem in celebration of his commanding officer, General Goring.

A year later the king set about preparing for a second punitive expedition to Scotland. The religious issues had been further sharpened in May 1640 with the proclamation of a series of Canons summarising reforms promoted by Archbishop Laud. They included the decree that the Doctrine of the Divine Right of Kings be expounded by the clergy to their parishioners at least once a quarter; confirmation of the hierarchy of the Church; compulsory positioning of the Communion table in the East; imposition of an oath on all members of the learned professions that they should never wittingly subvert "the government of the Church by Archbishops, Bishops, deans and archdeacons etc". This predictably became known as the Etcetera Oath, a source of hilarity but also a focus of discontent. The task facing the king of assembling an army was again fraught, with many of the gentry unwilling supporters of a war against the Scots and yet called upon to make what C. V. Wedgwood, grandiosely, describes as "the largest levy of troops within the memory of man".[3] The political decision not to make any significant use of the experienced troops from Ireland and the sensitivity over using officers who were Catholic – albeit favourably disposed towards the king – added to the difficulties. Nonetheless, the king had the devoted support of the body of Cavaliers of which Richard Lovelace was a shining representative. From Ensign he had advanced to Captain.

This second Scotch Expedition, in which Lovelace also took part, had much in common with the first, with the additional characteristics that it involved skirmishes and battles and a nimble foe. On August 20 the Scots crossed the Tweed and advanced without opposition to the Tyne. Having managed the crossing at Newburn, they routed the Royalist forces opposed to them, with the English foot-soldiers, mainly pressed men, taking to their heels, and only the English cavalry giving a good account of themselves. The following day, the Scots entered an abandoned Newcastle. For his part, the king with his forces had only reached York. The next few weeks witnessed a succession of Scottish advances, interrupted by an occasional royalist success. On September 15 the Royalist-held Edinburgh Castle capitulated, and by the end of October an armistice had been signed with the Scots emerging as clear victors in a six-month-long conflict. Aside from the fact that Lovelace was again in General Goring's regiment, little is known of the part he played in the war. Had his tragedy *The Soldier*, written about this time, survived, it could possibly have been mined for autobiographical insights.

Subsequently he returned to his family estate. Only seven months later the political climate had changed dramatically, with the execution on May 12, 1641, of Thomas Wentworth, Earl of Strafford, the king's most effective – and loyal – servant. November 23 then saw the passage in the House of Commons of the "Grand Remonstrance", remarkable evidence of the king's eroding authority, which condemned in detail and at length his policy in Church and State at home and abroad, throughout his reign. Parliament was happily exacting its revenge for the many years when Charles, having dissolved Parliament, ruled as an absolute monarch. But now, cap in hand, his financial needs necessitated a semblance of humility, beneath which the king's long-held ideals remained undisturbed: for his subjects to accept his absolute authority with unquestioned obedience and for them to belong with uniform and regular devotions to the Church established by law.

It was in April 1642 that Lovelace achieved a degree of notoriety at the quarter Session at Maidstone, Kent, where he tore in pieces a "disloyal petition" to Parliament advocating merely "just and regal authority". He followed this up by setting out to deliver to the House of Commons, in conjunction with Sir William Boteler, also of Kent, an alternative petition calling for "the restoring of the King to his rights", the removing of the militia from the county and ensuring the Book of Common Prayer was observed.[4] They were supported by a party of Kentish royalists in their hundreds, some mounted and others on foot, on their way to their chosen assembly spot, Blackheath.

Richard Lovelace:
pen and ink drawing by his
brother, Francis Lovelace,
after Wenceslaus Hollar, 1659

Parliament was alarmed, with Oliver Cromwell calling for a meeting of both Houses, at which the militia were instructed to prevent the mass of Kent men from entering London. Following their hand-delivery of the petition – which was similar to the one that had already been burnt by the hangman – the two leaders were taken into custody, Boteler being sent to Fleet Prison and Lovelace to the Gatehouse, Westminster. Three weeks later they were released on bail.

The Gatehouse, Westminster, was a medieval structure situated within the complex of the Abbey buildings from which the Dean and Chapter derived rental income, the leaseholder being the prison keeper.[5] It is best known, perhaps, for the fact that Sir Walter Ralegh spent his last night there ahead of his execution on the morning of October 29, 1618. In 1776, being much decayed, the prison buildings were demolished.

It was in the Gatehouse that Lovelace composed his song "To Althea, From Prison". She is invoked in the first stanza:

When Love with unconfined wings
Hovers within my Gates;
And my divine Althea brings
To whisper at the Grates . . .

In the third stanza, Lovelace declares his Royalist credo:

When (like committed Linnets) I
With shriller throat shall sing
The sweetness, Mercy, Majesty,
And glories of my KING;
When I shall voice aloud, how Good
He is, how Great should be . . .

And the fourth and final stanza is the prisoner's equivalent to the passage from St Paul's first Epistle to the Corinthians – much used at funerals and memorial services – that comforts the bereaved by depriving death of the faculty to sting:

Stone Walls doe not a Prison make,
Nor I'ron bars a Cage;
Mindes innocent and quiet take
That for an Heritage;
If I have freedome in my Love,
And in my soule am free;
Angels alone that sore above,
Injoy such Liberty.

Lovelace appears to have spent part of the next few years in Holland, returning to England at the height of the Civil War towards the end of 1647 to the beginning of 1648. In May, 1648 he participated in the battle of Maidstone in which Sir Thomas Fairfax's troops were ultimately successful. One participant (John Rushworth) had this to say of the engagement: "The like service, though I have been a member of this army ever since the first going out and have seen desperate service in several stormings, I have not seen before; for every street was got by inches".[6] Nine hundred Royalists were taken prisoner. Richard Lovelace was one of them – as was John Gifford, later to take holy orders and destined to exert a profound influence on John Bunyan as the evangelical minister of St John's Church, Bedford.[7] On June 9 a warrant of commitment was made to send Lovelace to the prison of Peterhouse.[8] Ten months later, on April 9 1649, a little over two months after the execution of Charles I, on January 31, a warrant was issued to the keeper of Peterhouse Prison for the discharge of Lovelace.

Peterhouse

In a bizarre way, Peterhouse, when studied for its role as a prison, can often take on the characteristics of a phantom creation. To researchers in the London Metropolitan Archives it remains stubbornly invisible. It fails to rate mention in histories of London or to feature in scholarly studies covering English penal institutions. Even its precise location is subject to debate. And yet, there were times when it played a significant role as a state prison.

To put some flesh on bare bones, during the course of the sixteenth and seventeenth centuries the strongly Catholic Petre family had substantial land holdings in Essex. At one stage it also occupied a building in London that came to be known as Petre House – which name might well lend itself over time to corruption as Peterhouse.

The 1720 edition of Stow's Survey of London is worth quoting at this point. "Aldersgate street, very spacious and long; and although the Buildings are old, and not uniform, yet many of them are very good and well inhabited; and of the principal of them, two are very large, the one formerly called Dorchester House, as being the Seat of the late Marquess of Dorchester; and Peter House, as belonging to the Lord Peters: Now called London House, being at present the Seat of the Bishop of London" (the then Bishop Humphrey Henchman). In this account of an area that had escaped the Great Fire by reason of its location outside the London wall, there seem to have been two large houses, one belonging to a certain Lord Peters, and this also would have readily given rise to "Peterhouse".[9] But nowhere is there any reference to its being used as a prison. There is, however, one entry in Sir William Dugdale's work, *A Short View of the late Troubles . . .*, published in 1681, where he alludes to somebody having been "committed to that Prison which they made of Lord Peter's House in Aldersgate Street".[10] He dated this event to mid-1642, consequently at around the start of the Civil War

– which some historians place at January 10, 1642, others at August 22, 1642, being the day that the King's standard was raised.

Preserved in the Parliamentary archives, located in the House of Lords, is a petition dated April 1, 1647, which confirms Peterhouse's use as a gaol since 1642 and also illustrates its role in the religious tensions of the day.[11] The summary reads as follows. "Dr Edward Martin, prisoner in the Lord Petre's house in Aldersgate Street. He has been five years in prison, has been plundered to the very clothes on his back and being unmarried can make no plea to a fifth part of his estate; in answer to a petition for relief, the House replied that for maintenance out of his estate it was not in their power to allow it, but they would grant him liberty upon bail on taking the Covenant (i.e. Presbyterian). The petitioner in a long argument shows that, having sworn allegiance to the King and as a member of the Church of England, he cannot conscientiously take the Covenant, and therefore prays that his five years probation may suffice to prove that no means in life or death can move him to enter in to the Covenant ..."

With London largely committed to the Parliamentary cause, its political prison population naturally enough reflected this bias. At times, pressures on resources must have been considerable and this will have stimulated the use of non-traditional prison locations by the state, of which "The Three Tobacco Pipes Tavern" near Charing Cross is a colourful instance; on one occasion, for several weeks it housed Sir Roger Twysden.[12] Other relief gaols included Gresham College and a succession of compters. But it was Peterhouse (The Lord Petre's House) that can be said to have served the Parliamentarians most for a sustained period. How it came into this role is not clear, but the sequestration – at a date that is not now known – of a convenient Catholic-owned property seems a plausible explanation.

From the early 1640s, Peterhouse crops up intermittently in the accounts of royalists and those judged to be royalist sympathisers. Francis Twysden, brother of Sir Roger Twysden, was confined there briefly on charges of engaging in criminal correspondence with France. In April 1645, two servants were released so as to enable them to attend their masters then held in the Tower of London.[13] But it is in the second half of the decade that Peterhouse springs to life, as judged by the frequency of entries in the State Papers, none of which, however, refer to its location in Aldersgate Street.

For the most part, Peterhouse accommodated men guilty of "raising arms against Parliament", sometimes as a group, sometimes individually. The occasional escape from Peterhouse Prison is recorded. October 24, 1648, saw Eleanor Passenger incarcerated "for dispersing and spreading scandalous and unlicensed pamphlets", and a month later, on November 24, she and another woman were released, "having made discovery of the men of whom they had them". In July that year "a report was made to Parliament concerning the great disorder and tumult occasioned by the transport of prisoners to the House of the great disorder and danger of tumult there was in conveying some prisoners hence to Peterhouse.[14] That this committee is of the opinion that it is not safe to bring any more prisoners to London especially persons of quality", Windsor Castle being preferred in such cases. Within this entry lies perhaps a clue to Peterhouse's historical invisibility: having enjoyed a brief period when it was seen to be a state prison of choice for the Parliamentarians, might it not have been then judged no longer suitable for close incarceration? Its days of prison fame could have been comparable to a mere snapshot and readily overlooked by scholars. From June 4, 1648, to the end of that year, Peterhouse Prison featured 46 times in the State Papers and in the following year to December 25, 1649, there were 36 entries. Thereafter nothing. Lovelace's own imprisonment from June 9, 1648, to April 9, 1649, coincided with the period of its most intensive use.

There is little direct information on the prison conditions that confronted Lovelace. He would certainly have been charged rent, with the calculation taking into account the nature of the accommodation and his social position, and have borne costs of food and fuel, some perhaps supplied him from outside the prison. Overall costs could mount up rapidly but could also vary widely from prison to prison, as was the experience of Sir Roger Twysden. When he found himself in what was in effect a relief gaol at the Three Tobacco Pipes Tavern, he paid £1 6s 8d per day, this being the keeper's authorised fee, in addition to the charges for diet and lodging. When transferred in February 1644 to a tried and tested place of confinement such as Lambeth Palace, he was assigned a three-bedroom apartment plus a study that had been occupied by one of the Archbishop's chaplains, for which he paid twelve shillings a week. He was allowed to have food and fuel sent up to him from Kent. He was destined to remain a prisoner for two years. The keeper's fee is not known.[15]

One vignette that throws light on the internal aspects of Peterhouse Prison comes through a letter that Thomas Holder, auditor general to the Duke of York, imprisoned for corresponding with the King, managed to send from prison to the fervent royalist, Peter Barwick.[16] "I was at last betrayed and committed to close Prison; and there this worthy Dean my dear Friend and Confident adventured himself and by my contrivance got to whisper with me through the chinks of a door nailed up ... into the chamber next to mine in Peterhouse, where Major Polwheel was Prisoner on the King's Account, by whose favour we conferred together of which I made this good Use, that by my Directions the Dean found all my Cyphers, Papers etc and burnt them". Holder subsequently escaped and got out of England, demonstrating that there was more than one chink to the Peterhouse Prison.

While Peterhouse's known contribution to prison literature is limited, one polemical author was the controversial Dr Daniel Featley, deprived rector of Lambeth and Acton. Imprisoned as a royalist spy on the strength of intercepted correspondence, he was the author of a number of pamphlets that appeared beneath the title *The Dippers dipt or the Anabaptists Duck'd and Plunged Head and Ears at a Disputation in Southwark*. They were typically signed "Aldersgate London, from prison in Peter-house", one such being dated January 10, 1644 – further confirmation of the prison's location. Little more than a year later, on April 21, 1645, Dr William Leo was called upon to preach at Lambeth his funeral sermon, in the course of which he revealed that Featley "wrote a little tract called 'Sea Gull' against a gross imposture and showed it me in Peter House, what time I came to visit him there with Sir George Sands, Knight, my countryman of Kent, with others".[17] This also illustrates the freedom of communication that could sometimes be enjoyed by the inmates with the outside world.

Lovelace is without question the literary face of Peterhouse. The prison conditions were such that during his incarceration he was able to arrange and revise his poems for publication as well as add to their number. One 14-stanza epode carries the specific label "from prison" and is addressed to Lucasta. Somewhat strangely for a love poem, the opening lines:

Long in thy Shackels, liberty, I ask not from these walls, but thee are interpreted by Lovelace's twentieth-century editor, C. P. Wilkinson, as meaning "I do not ask liberty from my prison but of thee, Lucasta, whose prisoner I have long been , in order that leaving thee for awhile I may be able to turn my fancy to anything else".[18]

The lady's identity has been much debated, the interest being enhanced by the fact that she was the recipient of 22 other poems. While some of these may also have been written from prison, the evidence is lacking. The added complication is that Lovelace's poems circulated in manuscript for many years, giving rise to numerous variants. However, the year 1649 saw the first publication, overseen by the author, and the second came in 1659, one year after his death, a pious act of a surviving younger brother.

Lovelace's literary achievement is summarised by Robert Bell, whose judgment of "To Althea" reads: "there is scarcely any production of the seventeenth century which enjoys such extensive popularity".[19]

|||||||||||||||||||||||||||||||||||||||||||||||||||||||||||||||||||||||||||||||||

CHAPTER VIII

Charles I

(1600–1649)

Principal Places of Detention and Incarceration

Newcastle	*May 13, 1646 – February 3, 1647 (8 months)*
Holmby House (Holdenby) Northants	*February 17 – June 4, 1648 (4 months)*
Hampton Court	*August 24 – November 11, 1647 (3 months)*
Isle of Wight	*November 16, 1647 – December 1, 1648 (12 months)*
Hurst Castle	*December 1 – 19, 1648 (3 weeks)*
Windsor Castle	*December 23, 1648 – January 19, 1649 (1 month)*
St James's Palace & Whitehall	*January 21 – 30, 1649 (10 days)*

The prison writing of Charles I has been buffeted by conflicting claims made by Royalists, on the one hand, and their opponents bearing such titles as Parliamentarians, Covenanters, Independents and Presbyterians. The places of imprisonment varied, and any assessment of the king's literary involvement has to start with some understanding of the conditions that prevailed at different times in the changing locations. But, first of all, the military background leading to Charles's three years of detention needs to be given, as also a key to his complex Scottish origins.

At the battle of Marston Moor, near York, on July 2, 1644, the Royalists suffered a heavy defeat which effectively lost them control of the north of England. In this engagement, Oliver Cromwell as Lieutenant General had the command of a cavalry wing of the Parliamentary forces facing Prince Rupert.[1] Just under a year later, at the battle of Naseby, Northamptonshire, on June 14, 1645, the royalist forces were routed. The New Model Army, formed earlier in the year by the Parliamentarians for service anywhere in the country, whose professional character was epitomised by its leaders being prohibited from taking seats in the House of Lords or the Commons, played a decisive role. At one point, the king was prevented by his officers from making what would have been a suicidal charge at the head of his own troop of horse.[2] Sir Robert Fairfax, the experienced Parliamentary Commander in Chief, was later to describe Naseby as "The greatest victory vouchsafed to the Cause":[3] the king had seen the loss of all his infantry, all his guns, and most of his baggage. Included in the latter was the king's correspondence, revealing tortuous scheming, involving both the king and the queen, in the search for financial and material help whether from Holland, France, Denmark or Ireland. Since 1642 the queen had been intermittently in France for reasons of safety, while at the same time fulfilling an important fund raising role. Rapid publication by Special Order of Parliament in June 1645 of the royal correspondence under the title *The King's Cabinet Opened* served to ensure that scepticism remained an inevitable component in negotiations with the king. As between the king and the queen, the deep affection that had developed is exemplified by the "Dear Heart" and "My dear Heart" that introduced their letters. Of the 39 printed, 19 were from the king to the queen and six from the queen to the king. The queen's touching letter of March 13, 1664 (written four months before Naseby) reveals the strength of this bond:

"There is one other thing in your Letter which troubles me much, where you would have me keep to myself your dispatches, as if you believe that I should shew them to any, only to Lord (Jerman) to uncypher them, my head not suffering me to do it: but if it please you I will doe it, and none in the world shall see them; be kinde to me or you kill me: I have already affliction enough to fear, which without you I could not doe, but your service surmounts all: farewell my dear heart".[4]

One royalist response to *The King's Cabinet Opened* was Edward Symmons's *A Vindication of King Charles or a loyal subject's Duty*. Its delayed publication in 1648 had something to do with the accidental loss of the manuscript: on his taking refuge in France from Cornwall, he was separated from his "Cloak-bag" when it made the crossing in one ship with the author in another, landfall being achieved with a 100-mile gap.[5]

In the aftermath of the crushing defeat at Naseby, the king's moves took him to Oxford, where he had established his headquarters at the outset of the war. The crumbling of support for the royalist cause, however, seriously threatened Oxford's status as a safe haven. Of the two options Charles considered to be open to him, either to trust himself to the generosity of London or to seek refuge with the Scots, he chose the latter. Leaving Oxford in disguise as the servant of his groom, John Ashburnham, he went north to claim the protection of the Scottish army then encamped at Southwell, Nottinghamshire. A letter of May 18, 1646, to the two houses of Parliament and to the Commissioners of the Parliament of Scotland explained this action: having understood that it was not safe for him to come to London and "being certainly informed that the Armies were marching so fast up to Oxford as made that no fit place for Treating (negotiating), did resolve to withdraw Himself hither (to Southwell) only to secure His own Person with no intention to continue this war any longer".[6]

The ambiguities of seventeenth-century political associations are at their most complex when Scotland is involved. Quite apart from the Scottish-English territorial battles extending over many centuries, Charles I had himself not so long ago mounted two punitive Scottish expeditions – in which Richard Lovelace had taken part – in 1639 and 1640. These, however, were aimed at teaching the Scots a religious lesson. Some six years later, he was seeking their protection capitalising on the powerful pull of family and crown. His grandmother, Mary Queen of Scots, daughter of King James V of Scotland, had "mounted" the throne in 1542 when only six days old; a series of regents held power while she was largely brought up in France, marrying at the age of sixteen the Dauphin and becoming queen consort of France on his accession in 1559; François II's sudden death in 1560 brought her back to Scotland as a widow. Marriage to her first cousin Henry Stuart, Lord Darnley, in 1565 was followed a year later by the birth of the future James VI / James I.

Several historical awkwardnesses then intervened: the murder of Lord Darnley in February 1567, swiftly followed by Mary's marriage to Lord Bothwell, the prime suspect, led to her forced abdication in favour of her son, James, who became King James VI, aged a mere 13 months. Mary suffered imprisonment in the island castle of Lochleven, whence she managed to escape 11 months later. In contrast to Charles's progression north in search of security, her path took her south seeking the protection of Queen Elizabeth, her first cousin at one remove, her own grandmother, Margaret Tudor, being Henry VIII's sister. Her presence in England was bound to be highly discomforting in the light of her own claims to the English throne, buttressed by the aura of legitimacy that her Catholicism imparted. Consequently, accommodation for her took the form of confinement in a succession of castles where she became periodically the focus of real or rumoured conspiracies. In 1571, under what was known as the Ridolfi Plot, Elizabeth was to be replaced by Mary, with the help of Spanish troops and the assistance of the Duke of Norfolk, the premier Catholic in the realm. Then came the Throckmorton Plot in 1583 and, most serious of all, the Babington Plot of 1586, in the exposure of which Ralegh played a part. All three called for the assassination of Elizabeth and her replacement by Mary. On this last occasion, incriminating letters confirmed that Mary had sanctioned the attempt. On February 1, 1587, Queen Elizabeth signed her death warrant and on February 7 Mary was executed at Fotheringhay Castle. Had the plot succeeded, Mary would have added to her previous dignities of Queen of Scotland and Queen Consort of France, the Crown of England, a remarkable royal hand. Instead, her execution provided a chilling end – and precedent – to a tumultuous life.

The presence in England at this time of a Scottish army is crisply explained in Winston Churchill's *History of the English-Speaking Peoples* as deriving from a combination of religious fervour and personal cupidity.[7]

As to religious fervour, the Presbyterians were much given to forming bonds or covenants, binding themselves by religious and political oaths to maintaining the causes of their religion and incidentally earning for themselves the label "Covenanters". The most recent covenant was in 1643. Points of continuous concern included rejection of the hierarchical structure of the Church of England and, by Parliamentary Ordinance in January 1645, rejection of the *Book of Common Prayer* which "hath proved an offence, not only to many of the Godly at home, but also to the Reformed Churches abroad".[8] It was replaced by a greatly simplified order of service in *A Directory for the publique worship of God*; this was the work of the Westminster Assembly of Divines, much influenced by Presbyterians (Scottish and English) and by Independents whose extreme distaste for ecclesiastical ladders meant that they looked to local congregations to provide church leadership. The Scots having seen off Charles in 1639 and 1640 when he sought to impose Archbishop Laud's conservative religious practices by force of arms, were now seeking to return the compliment by imposing Presbyterianism on England with the assistance of militant parliamentarians.

In the Civil War, Charles fought strenuous campaigns; of the seventeen or so major engagements, Charles was himself present at about half, but without taking on the role of Commander in Chief in the field. This did nothing to stop him exploring the possibility of diplomatic breakthroughs. As is pointed out in the entry in the *Dictionary of National Biography*, Charles was constantly testing out the possibility of peace, having "greater confidence in my Reason than my Sword". Most recently, efforts had been made in this direction at Uxbridge. But now, what more convenient opportunity could one conceive of than the king voluntarily putting himself into the protective embrace of the Scottish army?

From Southwell, Charles was taken to Newcastle, the Scottish army's headquarters. To his surprise and distress, he came face to face with the proselytizing enthusiasms of Scottish Presbyterians. Over several months he was preached at and argued with and harried. As he lamented in a letter to the queen, "I never knew what it was to be barbarously baited before".[9] There were two familiar stumbling blocks to any wide-ranging agreement. On the one hand, the king held sincerely to his hereditary right of nominating bishops, regarding the Episcopate, based upon the Apostolic Succession, as inseparable from the Christian faith; and for the Established Protestant cause, the dating of its introduction to the time of St Augustine had the additional merit of connecting episcopacy directly to the purity of the Early Church. To the Presbyterians, however, it seemed inextricably linked to the Church of Rome, which was weighed down by a well-rehearsed catalogue of abuses and fanatical beliefs. In short, accepting the right of the king to appoint bishops was agreeing to a decisive step in the re-introduction of the Papacy. And the king was not prepared to enter into any covenant, which was an indispensable condition of Scottish Parliamentary support.

Failure to reach any accord after months of discussions had financial consequences. While the Scottish forces in England had opportunistically seized the chance of promoting their religious objectives, they were in effect in this instance a hired body at the charge of the English Parliament. This was expensive. The Scots were now also eager to disband and go home – though doubtless prepared to return if the terms were right, as demonstrated under the "engagement" that Charles was to conclude, surreptitiously, in December 1647 with the Scottish Commissioners. The English Parliament for its part was ready to commit a lump sum so as to put an end to repetitive payments for the Scottish troops. The outcome was the release of the king to the Parliament for a total of £400,000, 50 per cent on transfer and the balance at a later date – in effect the Churchillian pendant to Scottish religious fervour.[10]

This transaction, which was later to be endued with quasi-religious significance, was struck on January 11, 1647. The king was then escorted by the nine Parliamentary Commissioners whose responsibility he had become to Holmby House in Northamptonshire, one of the 19 royal palaces belonging to the Crown. It had been bought by Charles's mother, Anne of Denmark. The inconveniences of what was house arrest will have been much softened in Holmby since court etiquette prevailed, with the king dining in public, receiving visits from the local gentry, being served by his own pages and grooms and having the opportunity of exercise, including tennis and games of bowls, which he had always enjoyed. His devotions, often several hours a day, were an unchanging element in his prison life. Access to his own chaplains was a source of considerable comfort to him and when, as was to happen occasionally later, this was denied him – or when he was allocated a Presbyterian minister – he was greatly distressed. Another regular feature of his prison life was the time set aside for his correspondence. This was very much conducted behind closed doors and a recurrent comment of those in close attendance on him is that few seem to have observed him writing. Such invisibility was no doubt partly influenced by the king's wish for privacy in a prison environment, thereby facilitating any clandestine communications. In his writings, the use of a cipher served the same purpose.

The picture of a well-regulated, placid existence is, however, deceptive. It obscures a kaleidoscope of intrigues, the pattern of which changed at every shake. Quite apart from anything else, the king was himself game for any number of escapes, mostly stillborn, conjured up by Royalists and often requiring undercover planning. At the same time he was ever seeking to play off one faction of the Rebels against the other. In two letters to the queen written as early as May 1645 he had gleefully pointed to "the Rebels' great distractions as Presbyterians against Independents in Religion and Generals against Generals in point of command" and detected weaknesses on their side with "Fairfax and Browne being at Cudgels, and his men and Cromwell's likewise at blows together".[11] At the same time, Charles might be negotiating with Scottish Royalists and continental powers.

His removal from Holmby in June 1647 arose directly out of just such a rift between the Presbyterians in Parliament and the Army, whose Parliamentary arm made up the Independent faction. The king's person was seized when 500 troopers came to Holmby in defiance of Parliament. They were under the command of Cornet Joyce, whose rough manners the king found offensive. At the time, Cromwell's objective, to quote W. H. Davenport Adams, was a settlement on the basis of religious tolerance and civil freedom – in alliance with the king.[12] This was judged to be more readily attainable with Charles at Hampton Court rather than Holmby. Indeed, during the course of his being moved there, the king, now in the custody of the army, had extensive conversations with all three senior army commanders, Fairfax, Cromwell and Ireton, when the journey was broken at Childerley, near Cambridge. And, once at Hampton Court, contacts between the king and his attendants on the one hand and Cromwell, Ireton and the Army on the other were frequent and seemingly frank and cordial, involving at times discussions during long walks in the park. And at a social level, the presentation to the king of the commanders' wives.[13]

For his part, Charles was also happy enough to return to a court life which came closer to that to which he had been accustomed, with confinement being made deliberately light. The king's routine was similar to that at Holmby, but somewhat more structured. Mondays and Thursdays were the king's set days for writing letters to be sent abroad. He dined in public, received visits from his subjects and took exercise. Nonetheless, after only three months, he addressed a letter to the Governor, Colonel Whalley, in which he pronounced himself "loath to be made a close prisoner under the pretence of securing my life".[14] This served to announce his escape. It also reflected Charles's assessment that he had more to gain from the other negotiations in which he was simultaneously engaged. As a way of souring relations with Cromwell and the Army, it is difficult to see how this might have been bettered.

On November 11, 1647, Charles, in disguise, with two of his Grooms of the Bedchamber, one being the faithful John Ashburnham, slipped out of Hampton Court. Colonel Whalley's account of the escape throws an interesting light on the extent to which royal instructions still remained inviolate. Typically, the king would re-emerge at the end of the day between five and six o'clock from his bedchamber, where the rule was rigidly applied that he should not be disturbed. Colonel Whalley, wishing to see him that afternoon, duly stationed himself in the antechamber at five o'clock; at six the king had not emerged and the grooms on duty did not dare knock.[15] At seven o'clock, still no sign of the king and still no willingness on the part of the grooms to attract the king's attention. By eight o'clock, the Governor had become worried and, accompanied by the "keeper of the privy lodgings", peered through the window to find the room empty and only then did he give instructions to enter. Meanwhile, the fugitives had made good progress on the way, with royalist help; 12 days later, they reached the Isle of Wight, whose governor, Colonel Robert Hammond, was said to be a confirmed supporter of the Crown. This did not, however, mean that he would ignore his accountability to Parliament. A striking instance of conflicting responsibilities in the midst of a civil war within the same family: Robert Hammond's uncle, Dr Henry Hammond, a fervent royalist, was to attend the king as chaplain in November – December 1647, at the same time as his 27-year-old nephew found himself called upon to be the king's gaoler. Another family link of an altogether benign character: in 1648 Robert Hammond's young cousin, William Temple, visited him in the

Isle of Wight, where he met another traveller, Dorothy Osborne, aged 21 . This was to lead to a prolonged courtship and give rise to a correspondence, half of which survived in the form of Dorothy Osborne's enchanting letters, first published in full in 1888. One of the great love stories in English literature.

On 23 November 1647, Charles entered Carisbrooke Castle for what was destined to be his longest spell of imprisonment. Initially, his detention had much in common with his experience at Hampton Court, with the king being allowed a fair degree of liberty; this included enjoyment of the chase in Parkhurst Forest, but inevitably meant an end to the informal walks with Cromwell and Ireton. His daily routine with set times for worship, prayers, exercise and correspondence, interrupted by modest meals, was maintained. As was the formulation of fresh escape plans, and this inevitably led to the curtailment of many liberties. On one occasion, the king found himself wedged in a casement from which he had great difficulty extricating himself.

Throughout this period, evasion attempts notwithstanding, Parliament was working towards a settlement; this eventually took the form of a conference at Newport, Isle of Wight, lasting some three months, between the king and the Parliamentary representatives. One side effect was a considerable relaxation of constraints on the king, the pages of the Bedchamber being able to make arrangements for Charles to correspond regularly through weekly exchanges of despatches between Newport and London.[16] On November 27, 1648, Charles largely agreed the terms of a treaty, containing 11 clauses, which included, among other unprecedented concessions, granting control to Parliament (for a period of 20 years) of the militia, of affairs in Ireland and over the appointment of ministers of state. It was duly submitted to Parliament. By a significant majority vote (129 for, 83 against) the Commons declared itself satisfied that the concessions made by the king were sufficient grounds for Parliament to proceed with a settlement of the king's peace.[17] Three weeks later, for the second time the Army took matters into their hands and seized the king's person, a strong body of horse and foot having been despatched to Carisbrooke.

Charles was transported to Hurst Castle overlooking the Solent, one of the mainland coastal forts built in Henry VIII's reign to guard against French and Spanish invasions. The moated castle stands at the end of a mile-long promontory of shingle surrounded by sea and marshes. The king and his

14 servants were undoubtedly cramped, justifying the comment made by Sir Thomas Herbert, the Parliamentary Commissioner who had attended the king since the move to Holmby, that "His Majesty was very slenderly accommodated in this place".[18] Of all the locations where Charles was confined, Hurst was where he came closest to unvarnished prison conditions.

A feature that Charles and Cromwell seem to have had in common was a readiness to engage in commitments that ceased to be binding at will. Charles's unreliability has already been alluded to; Cromwell's own considered assessment is shorn of nuance: "The king is a man of great parts and great understanding, but so great a dissembler and so false a man that he is not to be trusted".[19] For his part, Cromwell was rated by many as the chief of liars. Thomas Carlyle, who gave room to Cromwell among his Heroes, had nonetheless to concede that "all parties found themselves deceived in him; each party understood him to mean this, heard him say so and behold he turns-out to have been meaning that."[20]

Against such a background it is readily apparent that an accord grounded on mutual mistrust had little chance. To the Army, Charles's stated acceptance of the provisions in the recent treaty was worthless and in Parliament the readiness of the moderate Presbyterian majority to give him the benefit of the doubt delusionary. This conciliatory imbalance was to be corrected quite simply by denying entry to Parliament to the Presbyterians – a process known as Pride's Purge after the name of the Colonel who, on December 5, acted as gatekeeper. It left the Independents, the Parliamentary minority formed by the Cromwellian faction, transformed overnight into a majority and available for the vote on January 2, 1649, that put Charles on trial for high treason in waging war against Parliament.

From Hurst, Charles was taken to Windsor, where royal etiquette once again prevailed and he enjoyed freedom of movement within the castle; his contacts with the outside world were, however, sharply curtailed. It can be presumed that much of his time was taken up with preparations for the forthcoming trial, both in terms of his spiritual state and on the legalistic front.

The trial, held before the High Court of Justice in Westminster Hall, lasted four days, starting Saturday, January 20, 1649. John Bradshaw, President of the Court, acted as prosecuting lawyer, supported by John Cook, Solicitor General. Charles conducted his own defence. The charge against Charles

Stuart, King of England, was that of Treason and High misdemeanours.[21] Further elaborations held him to be a Tyrant, a Traitor, a Murderer and a Public Enemy of the Commonwealth of England. This elicited from Charles the contemptuous assessment:"For the charge I value it not a rush."[22] But far from setting out to discredit such epithets – requiring him to justify his high-handed dealings with Parliament over many years, to cite just one issue – the king's "defence" lay in the much more effective refusal to acknowledge the jurisdiction of the Court. Repeatedly, he was invited to answer the charges but on every occasion he declined to do so until such time as the legality of the whole procedure had been proven. Remarkably, he spoke free of the stammer that affected him from birth.[23] One comes away from a reading of the Official Report of the Trial with heightened admiration for Charles's skill in what was equivalent to a legal ping-pong match with President Bradshaw in which he scored convincingly on points but was fated to lose the match. On the fourth day, Wednesday January 24, sentence of death was given, signed by 59 members of the Court. John Bradshaw headed the list. Oliver Cromwell was the third signatory.

The execution of the king took place on January 30 in Whitehall, a scaffold having been erected to which access was given from the first floor of Inigo Jones's Banqueting House. Two shorthand writers were there to record the scaffold speech, which the king delivered, consulting occasionally notes on a small piece of paper. Among those attending the king was the then Bishop of London, William Juxon.[24]

Prison Writings

Throughout the account of Charles's periods of imprisonment lasting two and a half years, a recurrent feature has been the seemingly automatic provision of facilities for the king's correspondence and other writings. Not for him Thomas More's struggles with charcoal crayons. In part, this reflects the fact that Charles's experience had largely the character of detention rather than rigorous incarceration. It also recognises Charles's continuing, albeit diminishing, responsibilities as sovereign. At the same time, much of his writing activity seems to have been conducted incognito. Since few in his immediate entourage will admit to having seen him pen in hand, this presents difficulties if one wishes to anchor texts to individual prisons. Those that would appear to have given rise to the greatest epistolary and literary output are Holmby, Carisbrooke and Windsor.

Charles's prison writings are as a consequence both varied in character and extensive in volume. They have the additional feature that in the case of the single most influential work, the king's authorship has been questioned. They can be ranged under several headings.

(1) Official documents. It was only after his flight from Hampton Court that the Commons voted that they would make no more addresses to the king and that none might apply to him without leave of the House of Commons upon pain of being guilty of high treason.[25] More generally, however, the Newcastle discussions of 1646 concerning changes of church government, and the Newport treaty negotiations in 1648 will have both given rise to a large number of papers.

(2) Private correspondence, much of it conducted surreptitiously. The impression gained is that successful conduits for limited exchanges of letters were developed in most of the king's "residences".

(3) Devotional writing, which includes *Penitential Meditations and Vows in the king's solitude at Holmby*, *Prayers used by his Majesty in the time of his Sufferings* and *Meditations upon Death*, the latter written at Carisbrooke Castle.

(4) *Suspiria Regalia or the King's Portraiture in his Solitudes and Sufferings*, a work of some length, which most probably dates from his months in Carisbrooke Castle.

(5) His final writings, being the lengthy *Letter to his Son* (the Prince of Wales), other personal letters and the *Speech from the Scaffold*, all composed at Windsor.

(6) The disputed autobiographical work, *Eikon Basilike*.

The King's Book – *Eikon Basilike*

Eikon Basilike, the Greek title chosen for "The King's Portraiture", which replaced at the last moment *Suspiria Regalia* – most probably with the aim of confusing parliamentary censors – was published in 1649 within hours of the execution. It served as a vindication of the king's reign, running to 269 octavo pages, an autobiography written in the third person. Its success was immediate. Within a year, 39 editions had been published in English and 20 in translation on the Continent, appearing in French, German, Dutch and Latin. As Jason McElligott comments, "the *Eikon Basilike* was, quite simply, one of the most powerful weapons that the Royalists possessed".[26]

Its initial appeal undoubtedly owed much to the shocking circumstances of an anointed sovereign being put to death by his subjects – something that was later to lose its unprecedented character with the guillotining of Louis XVI in 1793 and the bayoneting of Czar Nicholas in 1918. The king's contrition at having submitted to Parliamentary pressures in signing the death warrant of his loyal servant, Thomas Wentworth, Earl of Strafford, and his eloquent defence of the queen from her partisan critics make endearing reading. His tone is measured. He denies responsibility for having been the first to take up arms, but confesses to a somewhat chilling royal preoccupation: "It is a hard and disputable choice for a king that loves his people, and desires their love, either to kill his own subjects, or be killed by them." And in the course of 28 chapters, interspersed with extended passages given over to prayers, he reviews, piecemeal, the major events leading up to his trial. To some, this is seen as a self-regarding, self-serving document – a criticism that can be levelled at many autobiographies; to others such as David Hume, writing in his *History of England*, "The *Eikon* . . . must be acknowledged the best prose composition which at the time of its publication was to be found in the English language".[27] A century later, Thomas Carlyle has a different view: "one of the paltriest pieces of shovel-hatted, clear-starched, immaculate falsity and cant I have ever read".[28]

At an early stage, doubts began to be expressed over the authorship. These will have certainly been fanned by the Cromwellians, who had every incentive to denigrate what had become a powerful piece of royalist propaganda. They had also sponsored a point-by-point refutation by their most prominent polemicist, John Milton, which was published towards the end of 1649 under the title *Eikonoklastes (the image breaker) in Answer to a book Intitl'd Eikon Basilike*. It ran to two further editions, one of them in 1650, a far cry from the multiple *Eikon Basilke* reprints.

This marks the start of what became a major pamphleteering contest between believers in Charles's authorship and disbelievers. During much of the Commonwealth it was largely conducted beneath the surface, only bursting into the open on the Restoration with the emergence of an alternative author in the shape of John Gauden, sometime Dean of Bocking, later Bishop of Exeter and briefly before his death on September 20, 1662, Bishop of Worcester. His biographer in the *Dictionary of National Biography* describes Gauden's activities in the 1640s and 1650s as chameleon like, allowing him to be a player for both sides in the Civil War. But as the possibility of the Restoration materialised, so his royalist enthusiasms became more conspicuous and his ambition for ecclesiastical advancement more pronounced.[29] This provides the background to a letter he wrote in 1661 to Edward Hyde, Earl of Clarendon, seeking recognition by way of preferment for the outstanding service rendered by him to the Crown by way of the *Eikon Basilike*: "This booke and figure was wholly and only my invention, making and designe, in order to vindicate the king's wisdom, honor and piety". The figure referred to is the arresting frontispiece print portraying Charles as a Christian martyr. This account was endorsed by his wife as well as by his curate, Anthony Walker. As a widow, she continued to importune the Chancellor.[30]

The John Gauden claims were given a considerable boost when, at a book auction in 1686, the auctioneer selling the library of Arthur Annesley, the first Earl of Anglesea, found a note in the copy of the Eikon Basilike declaring that in 1675 both Charles II and the Duke of York, the future James II, had told Annesley that John Gauden, Bishop of Exeter, not King Charles, had been the author. The high point, so to speak, for the Gauden camp, came in 1692 by which time the Annesley auction discovery was widely known and had been reinforced with the publication of the *True Account of the author of the Book Eikon Basilike* by Anthony Walker, the author being described as a tutor and inmate of Dr Gauden's family.[31] Five years earlier, Robert Chiswell, son-in-law of the royalist publisher, Richard Royston, had published a fresh edition of the *Complete Works of Charles I* in which the *Eikon Basilike* had been relegated to an appendix – tantamount to flying the white flag.

Thereafter, however, doubts brimmed to the surface with respect to the "disinterested" character of Gauden's testimony. There were some also who started to question the significance of the royal sons' evidence quoted by Annesley, given that the elder had been since 1646 as a 16-year-old in exile

Charles I: etching and line engraving by William Marshall, 1649.
The central part of the image is the emblematic frontispiece to the King's
final written testament Eikon Basilike

in France and Holland and the younger had joined him there in 1648. This was seen to degrade what might have been an eye-witness account to the level of hear-say testimony. Against which, from the royalist perspective, the recollections of those courtiers who later claimed to have observed the king on many occasions writing the book founder on the rock represented by the secrecy that accompanied the king's writings throughout his various imprisonments, as amply illustrated above.

The absence of irrefutable evidence on one side or the other gave birth to compromises wherein Charles and Gauden emerged as collaborators. In some cases Gauden was portrayed as the leading spirit with Charles acting as little more than a copy editor and in others the roles were reversed. These rival interpretations were recorded and analysed in detail: Roger Morris, the Puritan minister, left a 1500-page manuscript in 1691 covering the reputation of the *Eikon Basilike* in the 1680s , which incorporated much oral testimony, in what Jason McElligott characterises as "a dispassionate chronicle of public affairs".[32] In 1824 Christopher Wordsworth's *Who Wrote Eikon Basilike?* ran to some 670 pages, including the documentary supplement based on recently discovered letters and papers of Lord Chancellor Hyde and the Gauden family. Throughout the period covered, public interest was sustained by a continuing flow of new editions as recorded in Francis Madan's comprehensive bibliography.

In this 1950 bibliography, Madan was held by a number of scholars to have demonstrated convincingly that Gauden did write the *Eikon Basilike*, but that in doing so he was working from a body of writings produced by Charles I and that Charles had himself revised and edited Gauden's text for the press.[33] In her 1973 biography of Oliver Cromwell, Antonia Fraser roundly states that "the *Eikon* was the work of a royalist sympathiser", an extremist position in the light of the arguments rehearsed since 1649.[34] Fraser herself provides no supporting evidence. By contrast, the work of Andrew Lacey in his scholarly book on the cult of Charles the Martyr, published in 2003, commands considerable attention. He writes that John Gauden "is now credited with editing the *Eikon* from notes and drafts left by the king".[35] This is in line with Jane Roberts's catalogue entry to the Royal Collection 1999 exhibition "The King's Head – Charles I: King and Martyr", which reads "after three centuries of discussion it appears that the king did indeed prepare most of the text: however, it was brought together as a book by Dr. John Gauden . . . The frontispiece too was possibly designed by the King".[36]

In the production of the *Eikon Basilike*, pride of place goes to Richard Royston, the royalist publisher whose production in 1645 of anti-parliamentary tracts had already earned him a short spell in prison.[37] Royston was alerted in November 1648 that the king would be requiring a press for a book; the manuscript was duly delivered to him by Edward Symmons, the king's chaplain, on December 23.[38] Production began promptly in Ivy Lane where he had his business and John Grismond had his press, a proof copy being ready by the second week of January. Ahead of the trial, there was a speculative aspect to the commissioning by the king of the book and a commercial risk to the publisher/printer in undertaking such a politically sensitive "autobiography" that would fill presses over several weeks. Indeed, the authorities, having got wind of the venture, raided Grismond's premises and destroyed the proofs.[39] Reacting quickly, Royston transferred the printing to a press outside London. Notwithstanding this major setback, the first edition, first issue was successfully produced on January 30 and 2,000 copies became available within hours of the king's execution. The second issue of the first edition appeared on February 4. On February 10, William Sancroft, the future archbishop, asked by his father to obtain six copies, took advice and was told they were extremely rare and "if they be Royston's they will be above six shillings".[40] Another source quotes fifteen shillings as the price charged by hawkers. Royston, for his part, had been summoned before John Bradshaw, President of the Council of State, and pressed to deny that Charles had written the book. Royston refused and spent 15 days in custody.

In the ensuing months, publication of the many new editions was in effect shared by an array of bookselling publisher printers, more or less adept at dodging the authorities. William Dugard, Headmaster of Merchant Taylors' School, produced his edition in March; the text was expanded to include four prison prayers of the king – previously published – as well as the letter to the Prince of Wales. Production took place on the four presses Dugard had set up in the school grounds. The premises were duly raided, the stock removed and Dugard briefly arrested. By early April, he was back reprinting the confiscated March edition. One trouble-free source of supply was provided by Samuel Browne, based in The Hague, where his bookshop and printing press accounted for three further editions in English and one in Latin – the latter on Charles II's instructions as a way of reaching the non-English-speaking market.[41] Back in England, throughout the summer of 1649 John Williams produced a succession of readily concealed miniature editions. Parliament, responding to a situation that threatened to get out of hand, passed "An Act against Unlicensed and Scandalous Books" to be implemented by the "Committee for the Suppression of Scandalous Pamphlets" set up by the Council of State.[42] This was to earn Royston, Grismond, Williams and Dugard fresh prison sentences. From a financial point of view, the picture that emerges is one of strong demand for the *Eikon*

Basilike, promising profits to the book trade, providing that the frequency of confiscations and prison sentences was "tolerable". Dugard is an instance of somebody who did his sums and eventually concluded that they did not add up: in April 1650, after a little over a month in Newgate Prison, he submitted to the Council of State, gave substantial sureties and in return was granted the publishing contract for one of Milton's religious titles.[43] This heralded other work of a similar nature.

Royston, nothing daunted, continued to publish royalist material throughout the 1650s, notably the king's collected speeches, letters and messages – *Eikon Basilike* included – which appeared under the title *Reliquiae Sacrae Carolinae*, published under a false Hague imprint. They ran to five separate editions, all dedicated to Charles II, being designated as the king whose reign started in 1649. (In January, 1650, Charles was in fact crowned King of the Scots at Scone, pledged "to maintain the true Kirk of God, Religion, Right Preaching and Administration of the Sacrament").[44] Following the Restoration in 1660, Royston was rewarded by being granted the sole printing and publishing rights on the *Collected Works* as well as on "all or any other works of our Royal Father". In 1666 he received from the king a payment of £300 in recognition of some of the losses he would have suffered as a result of the Great Fire. Royston became Master of the Company of Stationers in 1673.

Sanctification

The feature that distinguishes King Charles's prison writing from all others is the role played by his one book, *Eikon Basilike* (also known as "The King's Book" as well as "The Royal Portrait"), in securing for the author the epithet "Martyr King". In contrast to beatification in Catholic ritual, which is only granted many years after a candidate's death, Charles was declared a blessed martyr from the moment of his execution. On the scaffold, he proclaimed "I was brought hither to undergo Martyrdom for my people".[45] In his own writings from prison, be they prayers or religious musings, he had been preparing the ground. His most fervent supporters equated his passage to the execution block with Christ's path to Calvary, a blasphemous analogy in the eyes of John Milton, who had also argued persuasively that an authentic martyr could not be self-proclaimed.[46]

But Charles was no average candidate for martyrdom. Aside from his blameless moral life, deeply held religious beliefs and assiduous observances, he was credited, as anointed king, with miraculous healing powers over scrofula through the royal touch. In those days the term was often used to encompass most swellings of the neck and face. In virtually all his imprisonments, his healing powers continued to be solicited. And if his biographer, Richard Perrinchief, is to be believed, writing in the 1662 edition of the *Collected Works*, these powers continued to be beneficial beyond the grave. Spectators, eager to secure relics of the king, bought chips off the block and scoops of sand impregnated with his blood to be used as antidotes to scrofula. Perrinchief happily writes: "it was reported that the Reliques failed not of their effect".[47]

For a book that presents itself as a portrait of the king, it is appropriate that the allegorical frontispiece (see page 125) depicting Charles as a Christian martyr should have served as a potent shorthand for the royalist cause. Engraved by William Marshall, partly to the design of the king – or wholly to that of John Gauden if the pushy bishop is to be believed – it shows the king kneeling in prayer, his faith and uprightness symbolised by the storm-beaten rock, his earthly crown beneath his feet, his crown of suffering in his right hand and his upward gaze directed to the heavenly crown. Official recognition of Charles's special status came in 1660, when January 30 was incorporated into the Church of England calendar in the *Book of Common Prayer*. It was only in 1859 that it was dropped.

Such sanctification naturally stirred the displeasure of the Church of Rome. Lambeth Palace Library's copy of the 1662 edition of the Works of Charles I contains remarkable evidence of this hostility through the accident of piracy: the volume was presented to the library on November 1, 1678, by Zacharias Cradock, with an explanatory note as to the provenance. "This book being seized aboard an English ship was delivered by order of the Inquisition of Lisbon to some of the English priests to be perused and corrected according to the Rules of the Index Expurgatoribus. Thus corrected it was given to Barnaby Crafford English merchant there and by him it was given to me the English Preacher resident there Anno Domini 1679 and by me as I then received it to the Library at Lambeth to be there preserved." The corrections throughout the 733 pages are numerous, consisting for the most part of ink strokes against such words as "Sacred", "Majesty", "Popish",

"Priests", "Bishops", "Martyr", "Defender", "Faith", "Deans", "Chapters". Only rarely is the offending word illegible and frequently whole paragraphs and pages are simply crossed off.

The copy has the additional charm of having been consulted on October 7, 1700, by Samuel Pepys , who wished to compare it with his own copy bought, as he records in his diary, on May 12, 1665. Edmund Gibson, Librarian, wrote to Pepys on October 6: "I will order a Fire to be made betimes to morrow morning in a private Room; where the book shall be ready for you at the hour you mention. It is a publick day, but of that you may have what part you please: if you be disposed to goe down to the Dinner, you know, his Grace (Archbishop John Tillotson) will reckon it a Favour: otherwise, to you it shall be as private as you desire."[48]

To have had occasion to invoke Pepys in the course of this work on prison writing is hugely satisfying: first in connection with Paul Lorrain, Pepys's secretary, who became Ordinary at Newgate Prison, and secondly through his association with this astonishing survival in Lambeth Palace Library.

In conclusion, two curiosities which demonstrate again how Charles divided opinion. The Calves Head Club, formed in the 1660s, met every year on January 30 on the anniversary of his death "in order to blaspheme the memory of Charles I" – and also to counter the reunions of Royalists on the same date. Its Republican membership was drawn chiefly from Independents and Anabaptists. The annual club meetings followed a set pattern: a sumptuous feast in one of the taverns in the City, featuring a large dish of calves' heads, a pike with a small one in its mouth and a large cod's head "representing the Person of the King himself" with as decoration an axe hanging on the wall. After the Repast was over, one of the Elders presented an *Eikon Basilike* which was, with great solemnity, burned upon the Table. Another produced Milton's *Pro Populo Anglicano* upon which they laid hands and made a Protestation in the form of an oath, followed by singing of an Anniversary Anthem. From a collection of about ten of these for the years 1690 to 1700, in a book purporting to give the history of the society, as quoted above, the following is a representative couplet:

> Triumphant Laurels too must Crown the Head,
> Whose righteous Hand struck England's Tyrant dead[49]

In a totally different vein, a book produced in 1825 on the Continent bore the title in Greek lettering *Eikon Basilike*. It was addressed to "the King" and consisted of 31 texts in verse and prose honouring him as Henri V. He was the grandson of Louis XVI's brother, Charles X, and hence the survivor of the Bourbon line. In the 1830 Revolution the Crown had passed to the Orléans branch, at whose head stood Louis Philippe, the son of the regicide known as Philippe Égalité, whose vote had been cast for the execution of his cousin. In the copy in my possession, on the guard page, one of the contributors, Alcide du Bois de Beauchesne, has made the symbolic link between Charles I and Louis XVI explicit: "Ce titre de Eikon Basilike fut donné en 1648 [old style] au testament du roi Charles 1er, livre qui fit pâlir Cromwell, comme le testament de Louis XVI fit pâlir ses bourreaux". (This title of *Eikon Basilike* was affixed to the will of King Charles I, a book that made Cromwell change colour, just as the will of Louis XVI made his butchers blanch). An intriguing instance of a mid-seventeenth century English legitimist work doing service some 200 years later to buttress the cause of the French legitimist Bourbons. Powerful evidence also of the extended life of a remarkable prison text.

|||||||||||||||||||||||||||||||||||||||||||||||||||||||||||||||||||||||||||||||||||||

CHAPTER IX

John Bunyan
(1628–1688)

Incarcerations

Bedford Town Gaol	*November 1660 – January 1661*
Bedford County Gaol	*January 1661 – 1666; 1666 – May 1672*
Bedford Town Gaol	*March – September 1675*

Publication in 1678 of Part I of *The Pilgrim's Progress* secures for John Bunyan first place among prison authors in English literature. Having regard to the impact his extraordinary dream had in Britain – sustained through several centuries – as well as the exposure abroad with translations in more than 200

John Bunyan: graphite on vellum drawing by Robert White c. 1679

languages, it has no equal. But John Bunyan's position as a prison author goes well beyond this one title.

Bunyan's imprisonment encompasses spells ranging from six months to two stretches of six years for a total of 13 years, one third of his working life. It is also noteworthy for the fact that at all times his incarceration was grounded on his refusal to conform on religious issues. He was no thief, no adulterer, no murderer – even though he confessed himself to be "the chief of sinners . . . being filled with all unrighteousness . . . more loathsome in mine own eyes then [*sic*] was a toad". His rigid adherence to his principles meant that where he might have avoided the full force of the law, he took no advantage of any such opportunities.[1] Indeed, on occasions he might be said to have even courted imprisonment. As he writes in *A Relation of his Imprisonment* (published posthumously): "I was not altogether without hopes but that my imprisonment might be an awakening of the Saints (i.e. nonconformists) in the country".[2] And in the account of his spiritual development, *Grace Abounding*, he recalls that at moments of deep depression "I was also at this time so really possessed with the thought of death, that oft I was as if I was on the Ladder, with the Rope around my neck; onely this was some encouragement to me. I thought I might now have an opportunity to speak my last words to a multitude which I thought would come to see me die; and, thought I, if it must be so, if God will but convert one Soul by my very last words, I shall not count my life thrown away, nor lost".[3]

As Bunyan discloses, he was born into a very poor family, living in Elstow, a village one mile away from Bedford; his father, a "braseyer" repairing agricultural equipment, will also have been a mender of pots and pans as a tinker;[4] this was how Bunyan started to earn his own living before enlisting in the Parliamentary army at the age of 16. Three years later, he resumed his life as a tinker. Marriage then brought with it children, his first child being blind, and a decisive turn to religion through links with a nonconformist set whose charismatic pastor was John Gifford, a powerful preacher with an unconventional worldly background.[5] By 1655, Bunyan had moved his family to Bedford, was himself acquiring a reputation as a preacher and was taking early steps as an author. And in 1658 he had his first brush with the law, being arrested (but not imprisoned) for preaching without a licence. It would not be until 1660 that he would have his first direct experience of prison life.

At all times, Bunyan was subject to laws and practices derived from the past which were then the subject of adjustments and refinements that also encompassed about turns. Some familiarity with this background may go some way towards an appreciation of the ups and downs that Bunyan experienced throughout his life.

To set the scene, one can usefully go back to the reign of Queen Elizabeth, who, with the objective of protecting the established church, found it necessary to issue numerous proclamations against seditious books, whether of Roman or Puritan persuasions. To this end, she inherited on the one hand the fifteenth-century court of law known as the Star Chamber, made up of Privy Councillors and common law judges. Initially, in the fifteenth century it had served as an adjunct to the established courts, with the time-saving aspect that the sessions were held in secret with no right of appeal. Throughout the 16th century, however, these features meant that the Court of Star Chamber became an increasingly useful political weapon, having a special role to play in curbing verbal and printed dissent.[6] The Star Chamber met the needs of the Crown in somewhat the same way as the *lettre de cachet* in France, when the king of the day chose to exercise it on matters that were of direct concern to him.

The other body that Queen Elizabeth inherited was a trade grouping – able to trace its origins to 1403 – made up principally of printers, bookbinders and booksellers, which received its royal charter in 1557 as The Stationers' Company.[7] As a livery company it was responsible for the smooth running of its trade and the conduct of its members. But, as Marjorie Plant, historian of the English book trade, explains, it came to have as its primary duty helping the Government stamp out sedition.[8] For this and other regulatory purposes it was given right of search and empowered to impose fines and prison sentences and to seize and destroy type and printed sheets. In an early ruling, for a member of the trade to establish that a book was his particular property ("copy") he needed to enter it in the Stationers' Register.[9] This became a valuable statistical resource for both the authorities and the trade, and at the same time served to underline the livery company's dominant position. In carpentry terms, the Court of Star Chamber and The Stationers' Company formed a perfect dovetail.[10]

In June 1586 the Star Chamber strengthened the control of the press, consolidating and extending its powers,[11] while the year 1593 saw the passage of "An Act to reclaim the Queen Majesty's subjects in their due obedience", which made it unlawful to refuse to attend church for a month and to attend "assemblies, conventicles or meetings, under the colour or pretence of any such exercise of religion".

For the book trade, the advent of the Stuarts brought with it further restrictions and persecution, particularly in Charles I's reign, culminating in the Star Chamber Act of 1637.[12] This included a reduction in the number of printers from 25 to 23; a requirement that, in addition to the entry into the Stationers' Register of the names of printers, authors and publishers, each book had to be licensed – law books by the Lord Chief Justice; divinity/philosophy/poetry titles by the Archbishop of Canterbury or the Bishop of London . . . and so forth. All told this amounted to an additional 33 clauses. However, a mere four years later, there was a major about-turn with the abolition in 1641 of the Star Chamber by the Long Parliament, which had little truck with Charles's instruments. The 1637 decree became a dead letter. But only for two years: in 1643 a fresh comprehensive programme of press controls was put in place, which called for the Stationers' Company's master and wardens on the one hand and Parliament's Sergeant of the House of Commons on the other hand to act as censors. Among unintended consequences, this decree gave rise to one of this country's great liberal documents, Milton's *Areopagitica: a Speech for the Liberty of unlicensed Printing*, in the production of which in 1644 he provocatively neglected both to have it licensed and to have its printer named. In the event, the Civil War undermined all such regulations.[13]

It so happened that Bunyan's first books were written in a regulatory environment that was extraordinarily favourable to nonconformists. After a period of some 12 years when Presbyterianism – hierarchical and unclubbable – dominated the religious scene, came the ascendancy of the Independents (Congregationalists). This was a direct result of Oliver Cromwell's assumption of power in April 1653 following his ejection from the Parliament of the Rump. Under Cromwell's "Broad Church", uniformity was replaced by an elastic regime of tolerance, written and spoken (Catholics and Quakers excepted). Since no one form of ecclesiastical organisation had State recognition, it was left to worshippers to decide how they wished to worship and how they should administer themselves. One striking and by no means unusual illustration of this came with the admission of Bunyan's mentor, the nonconformist minister, John Gifford, as pastor of what was a parish church, St John's Church, Bedford.[14] But with his death in 1657, his ministry proved to be short. In September 1658 Cromwell died, and by 1660 the Independents' ascendancy was at an end and St John's Church was once again firmly within the Church of England.

In April 1660 Charles II, on the eve of his return from the Netherlands, had promised liberty to tender consciences and gave assurances that no man should be disquieted or called in question for differences of opinion in matters of religion which did not disturb the peace of the kingdom.[15] This declaration made at Breda was not, however, enshrined in law and was duly ignored when on November 12, 1660, Bunyan was arrested while preaching in Lower Samsell by Hurlington and was imprisoned in Bedford Town Gaol.

At the January 1661 assizes he was sent to Bedford County Gaol, rather than the town gaol – in recognition of his having broken the law outside the city limits. He was indicted for "devilishly and perniciously abstaining from

coming to church to hear divine service, and for being a common uphold-
er of several unlawful meetings and conventicles to the great disturbance
and distraction of the good subjects of this kingdom, contrary to the laws of
our sovereign lord the king".[16] He was gaoled for an initial period of three
months, having refused to give an undertaking not to repeat his offence. His
imprisonment was destined to last a further 12 years.

It should be added that the climate of opinion against dissenters of all
stripes had by then also deteriorated following the Fifth Monarchy Men riot
near St Paul's of January 1661. Under the leadership of the cooper Thomas
Venner, a group of men, inflamed by a literal interpretation of St John's Book
of Revelation, had set out to overthrow the monarchy and set up the reign of
King Jesus.[17] The riot was put down with vigour and accompanied by a proclamation "for restraining all seditious meetings and conventicles under pretence of religious worship and forbidding any meetings for worship, except
in parochial churches and chapels", echoing Queen Elizabeth's Act of 1593,
aimed at reclaiming her subjects to their due obedience.

The coronation of Charles II took place on April 23 1661; on such occasions it was customary for prisoners awaiting trial to be released. Bunyan
missed out: as an already convicted individual, he would have needed to sue
for a pardon, which he was not prepared to do.

And then on May 19, 1662, the Act of Uniformity became law, the fourth of
its kind, under which all ministers were required publicly to assent to the *Book
of Common Prayer*, whose daily exclusive use was ordered – thereby reversing its
abolition by Parliamentary Ordinance 18 years previously in 1644, at which time
it had been replaced by the *New Westminster Directory*.[18] Ministers not episco-
pally ordained were to be deprived. Some 2,000 ministers who refused to conform were ejected from their livings. This is known in dissenting literature as the
"Great Ejectment", whose 350th anniversary fell in 2012, while August 24, 1662
(being the given deadline), is sometimes characterised as the Black Bartholomew
of the English Church. The Act of Uniformity was further strengthened in
October 1665 by the Five Mile Act, which established a no-go area between the
dispossessed ministers and where they previously exercised their ministry.[19]

These religious injunctions were accompanied by additional press controls. The Licensing Act of 1662 had as its major objective the reassertion of
the Royal Prerogative, displacing the authority of the Stationers' Company,

and was accompanied by such measures as the reduction in the number of London printers from a swollen 60 to closer to 20.[20] The creation shortly thereafter of a new office, "Surveyorship of the Imprimery and Printing Presses", led to the appointment of Roger L'Estrange as surveyor, wielding the police powers previously exercised by the Stationers' Company.

The last major section of regulatory scaffolding may be said to have been put in place with the enactment of the Conventicle Act of July, 1664, under which penalties, starting with fines, were imposed on those attending such illegal meetings – a pendant as it were to the penalties in place for those preaching at such meetings.[21] This act expired after three years in March 1667, but its renewal being delayed, it was only in April 1670 that a New Conventicle Act, with even stricter definitions, came into force.[22]

In 1666 Bunyan, having served six years in prison, was briefly released. John Brown, in his magisterial biography of Bunyan, first published in 1885, surmises that the presence of the plague in Bedford around that time may have influenced that decision. Be that as it may, Bunyan was shortly thereafter returned to Bedford County Gaol for a further six years, having been found preaching at a meeting without a licence.

March 1672 was marked by Charles II's Declaration of Religious Indulgence, which suspended the execution of all manner of penal laws in matters ecclesiastical against whatever sort of Nonconformists or Recusants. This decision was explained "by the sad experience of twelve yeares that there is very little fruit of all these forceable Courses".[23] Bunyan's own release was tied to the fact that his was one of several dissenters' names that the Quakers had included in a lengthy list of prisoners to be freed.[24] He was also among those who were granted licences to preach.

Three years later, in March 1675, the Declaration of Religious Indulgence was withdrawn on the grounds that it had been a royal proclamation and was therefore in conflict with the constitutional argument that penal statutes in matters ecclesiastical could only be suspended by Act of Parliament. This led to Bunyan's renewed imprisonment, but this time in the town gaol rather than the county gaol. Six months later, on the strength of a cautionary bond supplied by two parishioners of St Giles Cripplegate, where Bunyan's friend George Cockayne was preacher to an Independent London community, he was released, never thereafter to be imprisoned.

Bunyan's writings

All told, Bunyan's literary output extends to some sixty published titles; these are itemised by John Brown in the appendix to his biography, where he brings up to date the chronological list prepared in 1698 by Bunyan's loyal friend, Charles Doe.[25] Since then, the classification of Bunyan's publications has no doubt been further refined.

Bunyan's first publication, *Some Gospel Truths Opened*, in verse, appeared in 1656 and this was followed by three titles, one per year to 1659. His first prison publication, *Profitable Meditations, Fitted to Man's Different Conditions* was dated 1661. In the first six years of his imprisonment, he had nine works published, the last being *Grace Abounding to the Chief of Sinners* in 1666.

Following his renewed imprisonment lasting six years in Bedford County Gaol, he produced eight titles. And in the six months' incarceration in Bedford Town Gaol he is said to have written the first part of *The Pilgrim's Progress*.

In the period before his imprisonment, the booksellers J. and M. Wright acted as publishers/backers, J. Wright being responsible for his first two titles, M. Wright for the next two. A word of caution is required, since the word "publisher" as it is now understood fits awkwardly with seventeenth-century practices. At that time, it could relate to a stationer, who as a member of the Stationers' Company, whose main business is likely to be that of a bookseller. It could denote a bookseller who is outside The Stationers' Company. In either instance, the bookseller might also have a printing business. A further variant would be an independent printer.

Once imprisoned, Bunyan's main publishing connection was with Francis Smith, whose place of business was at the Elephant & Castle near Temple Bar and the church of St Dunstan in the West.[26] His religious views earned him the name "Anabaptist Smith", alternatively recognized geographically as Elephant Smith, and in the eyes of the Censor, Roger L'Estrange, "a disaffected Person and a Phanatick". This translated into recurrent house searches and periodic seizures of unlicensed books, for the printing and compiling of which he was judged to have been responsible. It also led to convictions, entailing spells in gaol and fines. Some of the hardships affecting dissenters are detailed in an anonymous pamphlet that John Brown believes Smith may have had a hand in writing: *A True and Impartial Narrative of some Illegal and Arbitrary*

Proceedings by certain Justices of the Peace and others, against several innocent and peaceable Nonconformists in and near the Town of Bedford, upon pretence of putting in execution the late Act against Conventicles. Published for general information. Printed in the year 1670. Ten years later, he was the declared author of the *Account of Injurious Proceedings against Francis Smith, 1680.*

Francis Smith was clearly resourceful and determined. As a champion of Bunyan he remained at the heart of his published output for many years. From early in his incarceration, Bunyan was punctilious in underlining his status – as with: "*Christian Behaviour: or the Fruits of true Christianity . . .* By John Bunyan, a Prisoner of Hope. London: Printed for F. Smith at the Elephant & Castle without Temple Bar", the conclusion of which reads "Farewell from my place of confinement in Bedford this 17th of the 4th month, of 1663". Two years later came the publication of his "*Prison Meditations; Dedicated to the Heart of Suffering Saints and Reigning Sinners*: by John Bunyan, a servant of the Lord Christ. London: Printed for Francis Smith". The work, however, that deals most directly with his experience in gaol is *A Relation of his Imprisonment* (cited at the start of this chapter), which remained in manuscript form for about 100 years, being published only in 1765. Its value to historians is considerable since it provides not only a 25-page account of Bunyan's actual imprisonment, but also an insight into his character.

Francis Smith's position suffered what seems to have been a major reverse in 1666 when publication of *Grace Abounding to the Chief of Sinners* was undertaken by George Larkin, another Nonconformist printer. This spiritual journey, composed in prison, harked back to the years of freedom of a 20-year-old pursuing his trade as a tinker within a largely rural setting. It was avidly read, calling for seven further editions. Such later editions also benefited from the inclusion of anecdotes, often homely – such as Bunyan's scruples over the enthusiasm he had for bell-ringing – and had the effect of rounding out the picture of what was also an appealing autobiography.[27] As one of the great books of religious experience, this alone would have secured for Bunyan a prominent position among prison writers.

It has been suggested that the bypassing of Francis Smith may have had something to do with the fact that he was at that time in particularly bad odour with the authorities, whose constant concerns centred on any perceived or imagined threats to a Restoration that was still very young. Be that as it may, Francis Smith resumed his role as Bunyan's prison publisher in the ensuing years up to Bunyan's release in 1672.

The Pilgrim's Progress

The genesis of *The Pilgrim's Progress* is a puzzle facing historians and bibliographers – one that has still to be solved.

Bedford County Gaol is credited by many with having nurtured Part 1. This is true for Richard Greaves (2004) who sees it as having been largely composed there by 1669 and completed by early 1671.[28] Roger Sharrock (1962) envisages a start having been in Bunyan's first six-year spell of imprisonment, while the balance "followed naturally and inevitably on the completion of the spiritual autobiography" (*Grace Abounding*, published in 1666).[29] By contrast, the partisans of Bedford Bridge Town Gaol include the compiler of the *Concise Cambridge History of English Literature* (1941) with an unequivocal "here and then it was that he wrote the first part of *Pilgrim's Progress*".[30] John Brown (1928) also decides "after a careful examination of all the evidence" that it was during his last spell of imprisonment that he wrote his memorable dream.[31] John Alfred Langford for his part is both shaky on urban geography and romantic: "He was a prisoner in Bedford gaol for twelve years, during which time he wrote the first part of *Pilgrim's Progress*, a fact which has made the gloomy cell, which looked upon the waters of the slow moving Ouse, one of the shrines of England" (1861).[32] But then there is Macaulay, who comments that "before he left his prison, he had begun the book which has made his name immortal" (1857).[33] This glimpse of an unfinished prison manuscript awaiting completion may help to explain the two-and-a-half year gap that separates Bunyan's final release from gaol in September 1675 and the *Pilgrim's* publication date of February 1678. What is not open to question is the identity of the publisher.

Nathaniel Ponder, who came from a sturdy Puritan family of Northamptonshire, was apprenticed in 1656 at the age of 16 with Robert Gibbs, a publisher of devotional books and political tracts, at the Golden Ball in Chancery Lane. In 1663 he was made a freeman of the Stationers' Company and the first publication bearing his name appeared in 1668. His first brush with the law came in 1676 when he was imprisoned briefly for having published four years earlier Andrew Marvell's *Rehearsal Transpos'd*, that made light of one of Archbishop Sheldon's chaplains.[34]

On December 22, 1677 Nathaniel Ponder entered *The Pilgrim's Progress* in the Stationers' Register as his copy by virtue of a licence granted by Mr Turner and subscribed by Mr Vere, Warden of the Stationers' Company. And on February 16, 1678, an octavo volume running to 232 pages was published bearing the title:

The Pilgrim's Progress from this world to

That which is to come:

Delivered under the Similitude of a

DREAM

Wherein is Discovered,

The manner of this setting out. His Dangerous Journey; And safe

Arrival at the Desired Countrey.

I have used Similitudes, Hos. 12.10.

By John Bunyan

Licensed and Entered according to Order.

London,

Printed for Nath. Ponder at the Peacock

in the Poultrey near Cornhill, 1678[35]

It was priced at one shilling and sixpence bound.

In a second edition (12mo format) in 1678 and a third early in 1679 Bunyan made a number of significant additions. [Part II of *The Pilgrim's Progress* appeared six years later in 1684]. That Part I should have run to three editions within a year demonstrates its immediate popularity.

The printer of the first edition has not been identified. Frank Mott Harrison, in an extensive article in *The Library* of December 1934 suggests the name of John Darby, whose links with Bunyan were indirect, being the printer of the works of John Owen, a close nonconformist friend of Bunyan's – and incidentally the printer in 1672 of Andrew Marvell's pamphlet that had landed Ponder in gaol.[36] The one printer known to have been involved in the second edition is Thomas Bradyll. Conclusive evidence comes from the fact that he was being pursued in the courts by Ponder within three months of the original licensing of the book. Somewhat simplified, Ponder's accusation is that, having given Thomas Braddill (sic) instructions to print 4,000 copies, the printer had printed an additional 4,000 copies for his own account for selling on unbound to some five selected booksellers.[37] In relation to the economics of piracy, this must count as one of the cleanest methods, with production of the pirated edition escaping all composition charges – barring perhaps an altered title page – and costs being limited to payments for the additional paper and the machine minders' hours of extra work.

Publication of the fourth edition in 1680 was the occasion of renewed accusations by Ponder of illicit printings by Bradyll, but the evidence adduced on this occasion by Ponder of corrupted text indicated that, were there to have been a surreptitious edition, the text would have had to have been composed afresh. Bradyll was also the subject of a law suit brought against him by Ponder as late as 1697. *The Pilgrim's Progress* illustrates the difficulties a publisher could encounter in defending his ownership of a title, albeit exaggerated perhaps in this case by Nathaniel Ponder's litigious character.

The history of the protection of intellectual property is a complex tale. One needs first of all to be reminded of the fact that in Bunyan's day, the rights of the publisher – not those of the author – were the concern of the law. At the same time, F. A. Mumby's succinct account in his authoritative work *Publishing and Bookselling* of the ways into the business illustrates what appears to have been a surprisingly rapid entry available to those who had completed their apprenticeships. "It was certainly easier and less expensive to start simply as a bookseller, without waiting for permission to set up a printing establishment" (apart from the shortest cut of all being to marry a printer's widow). "The young stationer could begin with a bookstall; and he had only to pick up a manuscript – it did not much matter how – have it entered as his 'copy' in the Stationers' register, get someone to print it for him if he had no press of his own, and start publishing at once".[38] Possession of the 'copy' gave him ownership in perpetuity of that book to use or dispose of at will. This obviously leaves unanswered the success or otherwise of such a fledgling enterprise. An ordinance of the Stationers' Company of 1682 strikes a note of caution. Addressed to its members, the by-law reiterated that when a book or copy was entered in their register to any member "such person has always been reputed and taken to be the proprietor of such a book or copy and ought to have the sole printing thereof", a privilege that had been too often violated and abused.[39] Piracy was indeed rife. *The Pilgrim's Progress* was no exception, as already shown with the frequency with which Nathaniel Ponder had recourse to the law.

The Business of Publishing

The financing of much that was published in the seventeenth century centres on the role of booksellers, whose ability to accumulate capital as stationers enabled the more enterprising to take risks and to diversify into publishing. A glimpse into the profitability of a strong selling title is in fact provided by *The Pilgrim's Progress*: in evidence in 1698 two booksellers confirmed their purchase from the printer, Bradyll, of 9,500 copies at three and a half pence a copy. This is in relation to a retail price of one shilling and sixpence, bound. Binding, which would have been the responsibility of the bookseller, might have cost, say one penny, bringing the total cost to the bookseller to four and a half pence. This would indicate that the cost borne by the bookseller represented 25 per cent of his sales price, i.e. a mark-up of four times. Bearing in mind that the bookseller would have been buying firm, carrying the risks of unsolds, as well as facing the threats presented by illegal printings, this multiple does not seem excessive. The obvious caveat is that such calculations are based on unverifiable assumptions. It may, however, go some way towards explaining why Ponder's financial position was often shaky, as demonstrated in a brief spell in King's Bench debtors' prison in 1688, to which his frequent and costly recourse to the law will have also doubtless contributed. He died impoverished in June 1699,[40] notwithstanding the 11 editions of *The Pilgrim's Progress* he published during the author's lifetime and the book's cumulative sales as reported by Frank Mott Harrison of 100,000 copies.[41]

The exceptional role of William Proctor, a wealthy seventeenth-century stationer in Bread Street, as financier to the book trade is explored in David Stoker's article.[42] Surviving ledgers indicate that he loaned money to book sellers at a rate of 6 per cent, on mortgages being sometimes secured on printed copies of the borrower's publications, or on their rights in the copy or on copper plates. Proctor in his role as stationer was characterised by the merchant, John Dunton, as a generous creditor, not chasing arrears, whether

of interest or capital. This amiable quality also benefited the publishing activities of some booksellers, including Nathaniel Ponder. On Ponder's death
significant sums were owed to Proctor. Repayment, whether partial or complete, would have been achieved through the publication of several editions
of both parts of *The Pilgrim's Progress* in Proctor's name, the copyright having
largely or entirely fallen into his hands.

One charge that will not have weighed heavily on Ponder relates to any
payments to John Bunyan. The seventeenth-century view was that an author's work was to be traded like any other commodity and that, were it to
be sold to a publisher – more often than not a bookseller – this represented a
single transaction and one that did not entitle the vendor to any subsequent
additional remuneration. Examples abound. John Stow, author of *The Survey
of London*, received £3 on its publication in 1598. For his *Brief Chronicle* he
received twenty shillings. And in 1604 an appreciative King James I gave him
a beggar's licence, (as it happens one year before his death). Famously, John
Milton's printer, Samuel Symons, paid £5 in April 1667 for *Paradise Lost*, with
a further £5 should the 1,300 copies be sold, thereby justifying a second impression. It is, therefore, hardly surprising that John Brown in his biography
concludes that John Bunyan earned little or nothing from his writings.

This view may, however, need to be tempered by the experience of the
celebrated Puritan divine, Richard Baxter (1615–1691), an exact contemporary of Bunyan's, who also suffered persecution and imprisonment and was a
prolific author. In a letter that is appended to his own biographical narrative,
he comments on the publishing history of his best-known work, *The Saints'
Everlasting Rest*.[43] Published in 1650 by two printers/booksellers, Thomas
Underhill and Francis Tyton, he received £10 for the first printing and similarly £10 for each of the two later editions up to 1665. Thereafter payments
ceased, Underhill having died and Tyton having lost much in the Great Fire
of 1666. Baxter then moved to Nevile Symmons for further writings and was
paid in kind on the basis of one volume for every 15 printed, plus a cash payment of 18 pence per printer's ream of some 500 sheets. The precise sums
cannot now be established, but the interesting feature is that Baxter's letter
was in response to the charge that he, as author, had largely contributed to
the financial distress of his publisher, Symmons – not the other way round.

While Baxter's experience may not have been typical, change was in the air. In March 1699 John Dryden received 250 guineas for 10,000 verses of his *Fables* and in 1709 Queen Anne's Copyright Act took the unprecedented step of including authors and not only publishers in the provision of copyright protection.[44]

Prison Conditions

Little is known of Bunyan's financial position when in prison, aside from his reference to his having earned money from weaving braided laces.[45] Where adequate support came for his wife and children is unclear. And then as a prisoner he would have incurred a variety of costs, the most basic being to supplement the weekly bread allowances and to add to any grants of coals in winter for cells equipped with fire places. The extent to which he may have benefited from gifts from church members is also an unknown but in the circumstances they might well have been at times significant.

John Howard's The State of the Prisons was first published in 1777, some one hundred years after Bunyan's incarceration in Bedford County Gaol – a prison particularly well known to Howard since, as one-time High Sheriff of the County of Bedford, it came under his supervision.[46] His account of the gaol, albeit not contemporary with Bunyan, provides what is probably a reasonably accurate picture of the place where Bunyan spent 12 years of his life. The building was not large: on the first floor a day-room for debtors, which was also used as a chapel, and four lodging rooms. For felons on the ground floor, two day-rooms, one for men and the other for women, without fireplaces, and two cells for the condemned. As of February 12, 1776, the gaol contained eight debtors and five felons. The Gaoler, who received no salary, was most probably the nearby innkeeper, who obtained his remuneration from providing supplies to the prisoners, including drink.

Howard reports that in the 1750s gaol fever (typhus) claimed several lives, including that of the surgeon who attended the prisoners. This led to changes in medication and the installation of a sail ventilator, which was credited with having saved the prison from any serious recurrence of the fever. These, however, were embellishments of which Bunyan had no direct experience. In his day, the discomforts must have been considerable, but not such as to deny him facilities for writing.

The very small Bedford Town Gaol, as seen by Howard on October 16, 1779 had "two new rooms", no apartments for the gaoler, no court, no water. Nor were there any prisoners at the time of his visitation. More to the purpose, the prison had been effectively rebuilt following the flood in 1671 when the Ouse had largely destroyed the bridge house. A point to note is that a prisoner from the newly repaired upper chamber could then go down a staircase to a small island covered in shrubs and greenery. Bunyan's imprisonment lasted six months, from March to September 1675. It is a pleasing thought to imagine him throughout the spring and the early summer months taking advantage of the island garden while engrossed in following his pilgrim on his travels.

Bunyan's prison circumstances are the subject of much debate. They divide conveniently into four periods. The early months to, say, 1661/2 saw him experience a fair degree of freedom, with several absences on parole which on one occasion even extended to a visit to London where he preached. The next four to five years will have seen a sharp tightening of controls which he put to good use, since this period saw the production of several of his most considered prison writings. For the last six years spent at Bedford County Gaol, his involvement with the Baptist church with which he was associated increased significantly, even involving brief forays from prison to admonish erring Baptist church members. In 1671 he was made an Elder of the church, becoming on his release from prison in 1672 its minister. The last imprisonment in the Bedford Town Gaol was the briefest and certainly the least oppressive.

The matter of scale had a powerful and for the most part alleviating influence on his whole prison life. Bedford itself was a town of some 2,000 inhabitants.[47] Bunyan himself was a neighbour: Elstow was only one mile away and he had moved with his family to Bedford in 1655 and had plied his trade as a tinker in and around the town. He would have been known to quite a few as a local but also by reason of his preaching. While his religious views would not have been to everybody's taste, it did not prevent many not numbered as his followers to be sympathetically disposed towards him. In short, he was not the unknown quantity that might have been his experience in a larger town.

In prison, the small scale again applied. This served to enhance the importance of the prison gaoler. Where the gaoler was of a friendly disposition,

Bunyan's privileges increased. Nor does one get an impression of isolation in the gaol itself. He seems to have acted as something of an agony aunt to visiting members of the Bedford Baptist congregation.[48] On one occasion Bunyan found himself with a group of 60 who had been caught at an illegal meeting and were carted off to gaol for their pains.[49] As a prisoner, he was able to preach, attracting some from outside as well as inmates; one of the latter must have surely been the owner of the copy of the first of his prison publications, *Profitable Meditations*, held in the British Library and bearing beneath this fellow prisoner's signature the inscription "now in prison in Bedford 1664".

One is left with a considerable sense of awe at the achievement of a man with very little formal education, with no inherited material advantages of any kind, whose religious beliefs, passionately held and coupled to an indomitable spirit, earned him 13 years of imprisonment. And out of this emerged one of the world's most widely read books, appealing to people of all ages and many cultures.

Bunyan's literary legacy can be assessed at several levels. The Reverend Thomas Scott describes *The Pilgrim's Progress* as "one of the finest and most unexceptionable treaties on the system of Calvinism that can be found in the English language".[50] John Alfred Langford sees it as "the greatest allegory that the world possesses". reflecting Bunyan's ability to give the abstract the interest of the concrete.[51] Hence "Talkative's" all words-no action becomes "his house is as empty of religion as the white of an egg is of savour".[52] Samuel Johnson, for his part, regretted that the book was not longer, describing it as having "great merit, both for invention, imagination, and the conduct of the story; and it has had the best evidence of its merit, the general and continued approbation of mankind. Few books, I believe, have had a more extensive sale."[53] And Lord Macaulay, as quoted by J. A. Langford, writes that while "this wonderful book obtains admiration from the most fastidious critics, it is loved by those who are too simple to admire it".[54] This – to our ears – patronising comment is redeemed by the charming scene where Hopeful and Christian come across a pillar bearing an inscription at its top, but Hopeful "being no scholar, called to Christian (for he was learned) to see if he could pick out the meaning; so he came, and after a little laying of letters together, he found the same to be 'Remember Lot's wife'". A magical image.[55]

||||||||||||||||||||||||||||||||||||||||||||||||||||||||||||||||||||||||||||||||||

CHAPTER X

William Combe
(1741–1823)

Incarcerations

King's Bench Prison, Lambeth   *1785 – 1786*

King's Bench Prison, Lambeth   *1799 – 1823*

The King's Bench Prison that featured so prominently in William Combe's life was not the same building as that whence John Wilkes issued his stirring pledge: "After this tedious and harsh confinement, I hope, Gentlemen, to pass the rest of my life a free man among you, my freeborn countrymen, and give me leave to declare, that on every emergency, whenever the rights of the people are attacked, I shall be ready to stand forwards and to risk all for what is nearest to my heart, the freedom of England." The broadside was dated King's Bench Prison Saturday, June 18, 1768. Ten days previously, his proscription as an outlaw had been lifted. In the British Library, on the verso of a sheet of newspaper clippings from the *St James Chronicle*, Wilkes's much-loved daughter, Polly, had noted "My Papa's Outlawry was reversed the 8 of June 1768" – for a researcher, a touching chance encounter.

Some 12 years later, the building was burnt to the ground in the anti-Catholic Gordon Riots of 1780. The prison was promptly rebuilt so that Combe's initial experience of King's Bench was of a relatively modern construction.

Combe was born in London; his father, a successful wholesale ironmonger, was able to send him to Eton, an experience of which he was hugely proud and one that marked him for life. It seemed to him essential that his aristocratic friends and acquaintances should not be reminded that he came from a tradesman's background. His defensive response was to attach great importance to his personal appearance, to cultivate elegant manners, to acquire a reputation for witty conversation buttressed by an inexhaustible fund of humorous anecdotes. And when any of these supports started to lose some of their force, he was always able to fall back on his own powers of invention. Henry Crabb Robinson, the nineteenth-century diarist, dined with "old Combe" towards the end of his life and recorded that he found him "very amusing & in his manners, gentlemanly. He did not lye so much as usual". Others expressed it more obliquely, using the phrase "Combe's comic infirmity", covering such events as a non-existing spell at Oxford.[1]

In his mid-20s, Combe came into a legacy said to have been worth £2,000. This considerable sum enabled him to live the life of a gentleman: comfortably well off, based in St James's, with his own carriage, and to be seen in fashionable assembly rooms and watering places. Continental travel included Italy and France, where he met Laurence Sterne on his second tour of his *Sentimental Journey*.[2] The picture of a self-indulgent eighteenth-century beau has to be qualified, however: he did not drink, he did not gamble and his amorous adventures appear to have been limited. But his money ran out.

The next few years are shadowy, partly spent on the continent, and much of it in straitened circumstances. Given the need to earn a living, he eventually settled on that of a writer, but as his biographer, Harlan W. Hamilton, notes, with the unusual requirement that his name should never be attached to his compositions: to be seen earning money from his writings would destroy the image of the well-born man of letters, which he was intent on projecting.[3] Occasionally, he would introduce "William Combe Esq." into the list of aristocratic subscribers to a work of which he was the author.[4]

There was nothing amateurish, however, in his approach to his career. Huge industry allied to speed of composition resulted in a mass of material, both prose and verse, often appearing as a series in magazines and later assembled in book form. One aspect of his marriage in May 1777 to the discarded mistress of Lord Hertford's eldest son, Viscount Beauchamp, was financial , with Combe due to receive a donation of £500 plus an annuity of £150. When this failed to materialise, he felt duped and took revenge on his erstwhile friends – notably the Hertfords – with the publication of nine satires in which the claims of candidates for the Throne of Hell are rehearsed. They were eventually published in book form in 1785 under the title *Diaboliad, a Poem Dedicated to the worst man in his Majesty's dominions*. They proved a considerable success.[5] Other productions included two volumes of letters in the style of Sterne and the *R . . . l Register*, purporting to be the king's private notebook, which ran to 19 volumes over a period of seven years.

Financially, however, Combe was on a treadmill. He still had to keep up appearances and he had additional heavy expenses when his wife was admitted to Stephen Carey's madhouse in 1779, where she was to remain until her death in 1814.[6] Matters came to a head in 1784 when one of his creditors caught up with him in Brussels. He signed three promissory notes to John Palmer. On his return to England, being unable to honour these notes, he was taken into custody on October 18, 1785 and, a week later, entered King's Bench Prison for trial in January 1786. Harlan Hamilton notes that he was discharged on May 25, 1786 but, strangely, "released" in August, 1786.

Combe's release, as Hamilton explains, was the result of a three-sided agreement. John Palmer, described as a relatively obscure manager of provincial theatres, had been appointed by the then prime minister, William Pitt, Comptroller General of the Post Office.[7] John Walter, founder of *The Times*, was already using the services of Combe, chiefly in connection with the products of his Logographic Company, and was looking to use his services on *The Times* itself. Palmer, by securing the release from prison of Combe was (a) doing the publisher of *The Times* a favour (hoping perhaps for editorial support in his Post Office work), (b) doing Combe a marked favour and (c) enhancing the prospects of being repaid what he was owed. Some two years later, in 1789, the arrangement was blessed, as it were, by both Palmer and Combe being put on the Treasury payroll to receive £300 and £200 respectively per annum.[8] At the time, Combe's work for the Logographic Company, which had by then become more of a publishing company than a printing company with an innovative typecasting facility, centred on his editing a lavish four-volume *History of Commerce*. Completed in 1789, it proved a loss maker for John Walter.

Combe's second incarceration came in May 1799, a direct result of creditors' claims totalling £352 which included those of his tailor and the suppliers of household furnishings, as well as an unsettled account for one harpsichord.[9] At the same time his income was coming under pressure, with the war with France having a depressing effect generally and leading to the cancellation of some specific publishing projects.

Not long after the Gordon Riots, we get a glimpse of the King's Bench

William Coombe: pencil drawing by George Dance, 1793

Prison from the survey by The Society for the Discharge and Relief of Small Debtors (originally known as The Thatched House Society) undertaken in 1800. At that time, King's Bench held just short of 400 debtors, some 380 on the master's side and a mere 18 on the common side.[10] The author of the survey reports that those on the master's side, "not intending to avail themselves of the benefit of our Institution, desired that their names might not be inserted in the gaol lists kept by the Society". No prizes as to the stand William Combe would have taken had the occasion arisen during his residence. The prison he entered, rebuilt rapidly after the riots, consisted of a large enclosed yard, at one end of which stood the main building containing 176 rooms, each of which was nominally occupied by two prisoners, for which a weekly charge of one shilling was made; for a prisoner to have the room to himself – i.e. not to be "chummed" – the rent was increased and payments needed to be made to the dispossessed room companion.[11] Towards the rear of the main building there were twenty four rooms, forming what

King's Bench Prison, 1808, after T. Rowlandson and A. C. Pugin

was known as "the common side" reserved for those prisoners with little or no means of payment. At the other extreme, in a separate building, known as the State House, there were eight rooms, labelled "commodious", available at a weekly rent of two shillings and sixpence. In the yard itself, there were shops and stalls, some run as private businesses by the prisoners themselves, as well as a coffee house and two public houses. With the prison gates open throughout the day a great variety of pedlars also hawked their wares.

At first glance, there is something anomalous in a debtors' prison being run on commercial lines. But then, a creditor has little incentive in locking up somebody who is destitute, unless of course he is motivated by vindictiveness. Incarceration must have as an objective to enable the debtor to rearrange his finances, shielded from further temptations, and perhaps even to enable him to prosecute his business from within the walls. With a view to his being ultimately repaid, the creditor may also choose to provide the inmate with what is required to pay for the day-to-day necessities of life – for a while. What is beyond doubt, the situation of the impoverished prisoner must have been dire, dependent at its worst on the begging bowl at the gate.

A further very important feature of King's Bench Prison – and one it shared with the other two large debtors' prisons in London, Fleet and Marshalsea – takes one outside the walls into the "Rules". At King's Bench these rules or liberties applied to a large area, carefully defined, extending for about three miles in circumference, within which some 60 to 70 prisoners at any one time could live, provided they satisfied certain conditions. One was to put up security the size of which was determined by the debtor's degree of indebtedness. Combe's security was 25 guineas. He rented quarters from a Mrs Reynes at 12 Lambeth Road.[12] Living within the Rules also entitled residents to a limited number of visits beyond the Rules in the shape of day releases. But should such privileges be abused, punishments ensued: in 1808 Combe was confined again within the prison (Room No. 2 in the State House), only regaining his comparative freedom four years later when he returned to Lambeth Road. As reported in Michael and Edward Walford's *Old and New London* (1892–1893) "these privileges render the King's Bench the most desirable (if such a word may be applied) place of incarceration for debtors in England; hence persons so situated frequently remove themselves to it by 'habeas corpus' from the most distant prisons in the kingdom".[13] This exploited the flexibility introduced into the Act of 1679: the location of the habeas corpus, the requirement that the body of a person be brought before a judge, became to some degree a matter of choice to the debtor.[14]

From the very beginning William Combe was a "working" inmate. He already had his business connections with booksellers and publishers and once he had established himself in what he judged were reasonable quarters, he set to work. His early commissions included the translation of five lengthy volumes covering recent military, diplomatic and antiquarian activities on the continent and in Egypt.[15] They were published in 1799 and 1800 by Debrett and Wright. In 1801 he took on the heavy editorial task of preparing Alexander Mackenzie's account of his explorations in Western Canada for publication in May 1802.[16] At around this time he was again involved in work on *The Times*.

The development that was to play a hugely important part in Combe's life was the public's rising enthusiasm for colour plate books, notably aquatints. An early involvement came through his links with John Boydell, Lord Mayor in 1790, but more to the point a successful dealer in cheap topographical prints. In a decisive move upmarket, he issued a prospectus in 1792 soliciting subscribers for the *Picturesque Views and Scenery of the Thames and Severn, the Forth and the Clyde*. The artist was to be Joseph Farington, an established landscape painter, the engraver the experienced German, Joseph Stadler, and the name of the author responsible for the text left to the reader's imagination – in fact, William Combe.[17] In the event, only the Thames was covered in the work as published in two volumes in 1793–1794. It proved a considerable commercial success and served to confirm the strong demand that existed for tinted topographical illustrations.

While the Boydells were to continue to give Combe useful work, they were to be eclipsed in importance by Rudolph Ackermann.[18] The son of a German coach builder, he came to London, married an English girl, and by 1796 had established a business in the Strand, the "Repository of Arts", which acted as a drawing school, a print shop and a supplier of fancy goods. The print side came to dominate what became a sizeable enterprise employing four aquatint engravers and a team of professional colourists.

One of Ackermann's early experiences with aquatint prints involved Thomas Rowlandson as the artist. But it was nine years later that Rowlandson became an integral part of Ackermann's publishing programme. The year 1808 saw the publication of the first volume of *Ackermann's Microcosm of London*, which set out to present subscribers with views of a great range of buildings within the city; a further two volumes appeared in succeeding years and the total number of plates came to 104.[19] One novel and happy feature to which Rudolph Ackermann drew attention was his use of two artists, the French émigré, Augustus Pugin, for the buildings and Thomas Rowlandson for the figures in each plate. The engraving was largely the work of Joseph Stadler and J. Bluck. The letterpress was supplied by William Henry Pyne for the first two volumes. For Volume 3 it was the work of the anonymous William Combe. Within the plates, London prisons are well represented. King's Bench falls into Volume 2, thereby relieving William Combe of the need to describe his own residence. The *Microcosm* is a considerable achievement which established from the start its position as one of the most desirable holdings in any serious collection of books on London.

Combe's connection with Ackermann was to be shortly formalised in an agreement under which Combe undertook to supply Ackermann with the

Dr Syntax losing his way: *cartoon by T. Rowlandson in William Coombe's*
The Three Tours of Dr Syntax, published 1813, satirising William Gilpin

letterpress for his publications. Combe was given a drawing account.[20] Had
he been paid a lump sum per publication, it was felt that this might have made
him vulnerable to his creditors and their lawyers. Implicit in this argument is
the view that an immured Combe was still capable of generating debts.

The best-known products of this agreement are the three *Tours of Dr.
Syntax*, published in book form in 1812 (*The Tour of Dr. Syntax in Search of the
Picturesque*), in 1820 (*The Second Tour of Doctor Syntax in Search of Consolation*)
and in 1821 (*The Third Tour of Doctor Syntax in Search of a Wife*). These recount the experiences and mishaps which befall an amiable, daydreaming
clergyman/schoolmaster on his travels around England. The encounters are
conjured up by Rowlandson, the text consists of Combe's descriptive verse
in rhyming couplets and the arbiter is Ackermann. Given the pattern of
monthly publication, regular and frequent consultation between the three
principals would normally have taken place. But Combe's special circumstances made this impossible. As Combe explains in the advertisement to
Volume 1 "When the first print was sent to me, I did not know what could
be the subject of the second; and in this manner, in a great measure the Artist
continued designing, and I continued writing, every month for two years, 'till
a work, containing near ten thousand Lines, was produced: the Artist and the

Writer having no personal communication with, or knowledge of each other".[21] Ackermann's role was that of gatekeeper: Rowlandson would submit to
him drawings which, if approved, would then be sent to Combe. Rejections
tended to be on the grounds of propriety. Matthew and James Payne in their
book *Regarding Thomas Rowlandson* quote an acquaintance of Combe who
remembered how Combe used "regularly to pin up the sketch against the
screen of his apartment in the King's Bench and write off his verse as the
printer wanted them" for initial publication in the *Poetical Magazine* under
the title "Schoolmaster's Tour".[22] It was not until 1816 that Rowlandson and
Combe met each other.

Given the considerable success of *The Tour of Dr. Syntax*, Rudolph
Ackermann had every incentive to find further employment beyond Syntax
for his yoked team of Rowlandson and Combe. He settled on another *Dance
of Death*, a theme that was famously developed by Holbein in the sixteenth
century. Ackermann's project called for 72 plates in the series, each with accompanying verse by Combe, to be issued monthly in groups of three. The
first three were published on April 1, 1814 and the last plate on March 1, 1816.

In any consideration of Combe's literary standing, the *Dance of Death* occupies a significant position.[23] Joseph Grego in *Rowlandson the Caricaturist*,
after applauding the contribution of Rowlandson, turns his attention to
Combe: "Combe has worked with a vigour worthy of the occasion; and for
wit, point and felicity we are inclined to believe the versification to the 'Dance
of Death' surpasses all his other contributions to literature in this branch. The
entire series may be accepted as a work of higher character, in all respects,
than its popular predecessors, the better recognised 'Tours of Doctor Syntax';
and it is superior, beyond comparison, to the works which followed it."[24]

Whether or not one accepts this judgement, the point has to be made
that much of his voluminous output was the work of a fluent hack writer.
And in the more considered work where his text was subsequently published
in volume form, his role was always subservient to that of the artist on whose
coat-tails he might be viewed as riding. Nor has his posthumous literary
standing been helped by his passion for anonymity – a major hurdle with
which his biographers have had to contend. Where he can lay claim to special recognition is to have earned his living as a man of letters during twenty-
four years of confinement.[25]

William Combe died on June 19, 1823, aged 82. He was buried in the church of St George the Martyr, close to King's Bench Prison and steps away from Marshalsea debtors' prison. The costs of his funeral were borne by his friends. There was no money for a memorial tablet. At his death, he owed Mrs Reynes £90 in back rent.

(B)
INCARCERATION
IN FRANCE

CHAPTER XI

Clément Marot

(1495–1544)

Incarcerations

Châtelet, Paris	*March 1 – 13, 1526*
L'Enseigne de l'Aigle, Chartres	*March 13 – May 1, 1526*
Conciergerie, Paris	*Mid-October – November 5, 1529*

Clément Marot, often regarded as the first of the Renaissance poets in France, wrote some of his finest poems during brief spells in prison. His widespread literary influence extended to such writers as Ronsard, du Bellay and Rabelais. Marot's life has the considerable additional interest that it offers an insight into the turbulent years of the first half of the sixteenth century viewed from two courts, both remarkable for fostering intellectual curiosity and Renaissance enthusiasms: those of François I, King of France, and of Marguerite d'Angoulême, his sister who, on marriage in 1527 to Henri II d'Albret, King of Navarre, became queen of the small kingdom that straddled the Pyrénées.

Marot was seemingly destined from birth to be attached to a court. His father, Jean Marot, first held a post at the court of Anne de Bretagne and later of François I, fulfilling the role of poet laureate. At the age of 19 Clément Marot became page to the secretary of the king, Nicolas de Neufville,[1] seigneur de Villeroi, and then some four years later in 1518 on the recommendation of François I page to Marguerite d'Angoulême. Jean Marot died in 1526 and a year later Clément himself became *valet de chambre* (in effect secretary) to the king.

Service to Marguerite d'Angoulême brought him into the orbit of a woman of exceptional talent.[2] She had been given a thorough education along with her brother by their formidable mother, Louise de Savoie. Marguerite was to remain greatly attached to him. They both imbibed many of the values of the Italian Renaissance, one aspect of which entailed the promotion of the vernacular. In literature, this meant displacement of Latin by French. In religion it meant the translation of the Scriptures, and this carried potentially dangerous reformist (evangelical) undertones. The Church was deeply suspicious of any divergence from the Latin Vulgate of St Jerome and little was required for the Sorbonne, acting in its historic capacity as arbiter in France of these matters, for a work to be banned. More significantly, enthusiasm for the use of French in church writings was often associated with the wider promotion of church reform, covering abuses such as simony, pluralism and absenteeism among the clergy, and charges against monastic orders often centering on immorality and knavery. Such considerations were widely voiced – Rabelais to the fore with his "hypocritical papal maniacs" (*papimanes*). This line of thought could then lead to Lutheran-held views touching on the purchase of indulgences as a way of diminishing and/or shortening the pains of purgatory and the Calvinistic disbelief that actions on earth, however praiseworthy in themselves, could secure the Christian a position in Heaven.

Marguerite herself was hugely pious and the author of a mass of religious poems, many of them now judged to have limited literary merit. It was only towards the end of her life that she produced the *Heptaméron*, a series of spirited, sometimes racy, tales patterned on those of Boccaccio's *Decameron*. By the time of her death in 1549, she had completed seventy-two out of a planned one hundred;[3] their posthumous publication in 1559 proved extremely popular, with Rabelais even dedicating to her Book III of his great work, inviting her to come down from her celestial residence to follow the further adventures of Pantagruel.

This has presented scholars with the task of finding ways of reconciling two such disparate literary strains in the writings of a polished sixteenth-century princess. The historian of the French sixteenth century, Lucien Febvre, rejects the suggestion that Marguerite should be ranked with "risky"[4] (gaulois) versifiers, arguing that such critics are not in tune with the sixteenth century cast of mind; furthermore, *L'Heptaméron*, on analysis, has a veiled autobiographical content that imbues it with historical value. It is worth noting that Clément Marot at a later stage of his life promoted a poetic competition among a group of courtiers who were to praise certain physical

Marguerite of Navarre (1553–1615)

features of those mistresses to whom they professed eternal devotion. Marot chose to sing the praises of "the beautiful nipple"[5] (*le beau tétin*), others chose the breast, the neck and the winner, the eyebrow. The judge was the cousin of François I, Jeanne de France, duchess of Ferrara, the doughty younger daughter of Louis XII. Nobody took Marot to task for his choice of subject matter. Indeed, he had set a fashion among sixteenth-century poets and rhymers, which only ran out of steam once some 60 other celebrations of the female body had been circulated. More often than not, these were under the counter productions, many earning their rightful place in the Bibliothèque Nationale's collection of works judged a threat to public morality, known by the satanic label "l'Enfer". (In the next century Andrew Marvell was to develop this conceit to perfection in the well-known *To His Coy Mistress* ("Had we but world enough, and time, This coyness, Lady, were no crime").

On an altogether more serious note, scholars have to assess the extent to which Marguerite favoured the reformists at the expense of the orthodox Catholics. What is undeniable is that her court, under her lead, proved a haven of free thought and open discussion. One striking illustration was her commissioning Antoine Papillon, a prominent reformist, to translate Luther's powerful attack against monastic vows (*De Votis Monasticis*).[6] Clément Marot was one of several young men who found such an environment hugely appealing. He, furthermore, was in her employ. But it also meant that he was soon tarred with the reformist brush by outsiders, as was Marot's talented but unscrupulous printer-publisher, Étienne Dolet, who was to take his religious nonconformity to tragic limits some 25 years later.

An historical curiosity is the way that the lives of England's Henry VIII and France's François 1er ran on parallel lines, Henry succeeding to the throne in 1509, aged 18, François 1 succeeding to the throne in 1515, aged 21. Early in their reigns they indulged in competitive grandeur at the meeting in June 1520 in the Pas-de-Calais known as the Field of the Cloth of Gold (*Camp du Drap d'Or*). Henry for his part came with an entourage of more than 5,000, an excursion which proved ruinous to many a noble house called upon to participate. Lasting friendship between these two young bucks was an improbable prospect, and indeed within two years the countries were at war. During the course of their reigns, each was faced with religious turmoil, but they ultimately took up opposite positions. However, the two rulers were destined to be united in death, both dying in 1547.

One event from which Henry VIII had happily distanced himself was the battle of Pavia of February 24, 1525. François 1, who was seeking to confirm his claim to the throne of Milan through his wife, Claude de France, elder daughter of Louis XII, suffered a crushing defeat at the hands of Charles V, King of Spain and Holy Roman Emperor. Most serious of all, he was taken prisoner. His note to his mother, informing her of this disaster and incidentally alerting her to her forthcoming role as Regent, included an assessment of the situation which is a model of brevity: 'Madam, all is lost barring honour' ("*Madame, tout est perdu, hormis l'honneur*").[7] He was incarcerated in the Alcazar in Madrid, fell ill, came close to death but was saved by the attentions of his sister who had managed to make the journey from France and to be given access to him. When there she was also behind a failed attempt at escape and was expelled for her pains.[8] The king was released on March 17, 1526, leaving his eldest son and a younger brother as hostages pending the payment of a massive ransom. Four years later on July 1, 1530 1.2 million gold écus were handed over and the two set free. Marot celebrated the occasion with a poetical "*Chant de Joie*".[9]

For Clément Marot, the Crown's changeable fortunes were of more than academic interest in his capacity as a page at the court of Marguerite d'Angoulême and later as the King's secretary. Indeed, some believe that he was himself at the battle of Pavia. What is certain is that François 1's imprisonment and Marguerite d'Angoulême's consequent preoccupations lost him royal protection at a critical moment in his life. On March 1, 1526, he was imprisoned in the Châtelet prison in Paris on the denunciation of a woman that he had eaten pork in Lent (*"qu'il avait mangé du lard en Carême"*).[10] Such action was typically interpreted as a public statement of reformist religious beliefs. He therefore found himself in prison for suspected heresy, which, if confirmed, could entail torture followed by burning at the stake. Little wonder that by March 7, 1526, he had composed an epistle addressed to a M. Bouchart, doctor of theology, most probably the person assigned to his case.[11] Marot started by denying that he was a Lutheran, a Zwinglian or an Anabaptist, affirming his strong Catholic beliefs. He followed this up with an epistle addressed to his friend Louis Jamet, who had legal connections and held the post of Clerk of Finances. But instead of a passionate plea for release, he made his case by means of an elegant fable. This features a rat caught in a trap, out of which he cannot worm his way thanks to a belly swollen by overindulgence in pork. He is freed by a considerate lion who smashes the trap. The lion in turn finds himself entangled in a net from which he extricates himself with the help of the rat, who gnaws through the twine. The role that Jamet is being asked to play is made explicit in the title of the epistle 'Epistle sent to his friend Lion [rather than Louis] Jamet' (*"Epitre adressée à son ami Lyon Jamet"*).[12] On March 13, less than two weeks after his imprisonment in Paris, he was transferred to Chartres and detained in the inn, 'The Eagle' (*L'Auberge à l'Enseigne de l'Aigle*), answerable to the Bishop of Chartres. The connection between Louis Jamet and the Bishop of Chartres is unclear, but the effectiveness of Marot's fable is unquestionable.

In medieval times Paris had two "Châtelets", small fortified castles protecting the bridges over the north and south arms of the Seine which were the links to the Ile de la Cité. The larger of the two, Le Grand Châtelet, came to serve as the king's administrative centre for the country at large at

La grosse tour du Châtelet du côte de la rue de la Joaillerie;
engraving after a drawing by Dunovy

the head of which was his personal representative known as the Prévôt de Paris. At the same time the municipal administrative centre remained the town hall at the head of which stood the mayor. In Clément Marot's day the Grand Châtelet had been greatly enlarged, having become the focus for decisions encompassing a wide range of judicial, military, jurisdictional and policing matters, and this had led naturally to its being endowed with a prison of its own, known as "*la prison du roi*". From a fifteenth-century description, there were some 15 large chambers – those on the upper floors being the more favoured and attracting the higher rentals – in addition to the familiar accompaniment of insanitary cells, fetid dungeons and jailors skilled in extracting both money and "confessions".[13] (Already in the fourteenth century, however, overflows of prisoners had led to the sporadic use of the prison facilities of the Conciergerie, which were later destined to eclipse those of the two Châtelets). The Petit Châtelet was eventually demolished in 1782 and the Grand Châtelet in 1802).

*

In his own words, confinement at Chartres was in a prison that was bright and clean ("*en la prison claire et nette de Chartres*"). This was a far cry from the horrors he had observed at the Grand Châtelet, the reputation of which for inhumanity even exceeded that of the Bastille and the Conciergerie, with cells that bore such descriptive labels as the Pit, the Chains, the Well. It is in the comfortable security of Chartres that he wrote his lengthy poem of 288 lines on his experiences in the Châtelet, appropriately entitled 'Hell' ("*l'Enfer*").[14] He qualifies the prison as sulphurous, foul-smelling, crowded and cacophonous, where a state prisoner is invited to name his accomplices with promises of leniency. If uncooperative, he is plunged into the building's depths, where measures taken include the stretching of veins and nerves ("*Au fonds l'Enfer ou lui fait alonger Veines & nerfs*").[15] Typically, the guilty have the advantage over the innocent. This applies to all manner of prisoners, who serve as fodder in a legal system that is built around the financial needs of the practitioners. As Marot writes, poverty is no route to justice ("Là sans argent paovreté n'a raison").[16] The judges, lawyers, clerks, officials are said in Marot's poem to occupy Hell's suburbs, effectively encompassing the courts and offices that clustered around the prison itself.

L'Enfer in fact served several purposes for its author. In addition to exposing the horrors of a prison – out of which he had been happily spirited – and the corruption of the judicial system, it also enabled him to reiterate his innocence of the charge brought against him, asserting that the name Clément had nothing to do with Luther ("*Et pour monstrer qu'à grand tort on me triste: Clément n'est point le nom de Luthériste*").[17] More convincingly, he used the poem as a means of demonstrating his close links to and deep affection for the King and his sister. He rejoices in being in the employ of Marguerite, who is foremost among women in literature and eloquence, combining this with great piety and personal elegance. As for François i, in whose service he anticipates finding himself at a later date, he is characterised as the first of that name whose knowledge exceeds his fame. Realistically, however, he accepts that Marguerite's priority is to go to a greater prisoner than him and retrieve her brother from Spain ("*Elle va voir un plus grand prisonnier . . . pour retirer notre Roy hors d'Hespagne*").[18]

In the event, Marot was freed from his Chartres confinement on May 1, 1526. This was little more than six weeks after the king's own return to France;

one is probably entitled to see a close link between the two events. It is likely that he would have taken up again his position at the court of Navarre and it is known that by the spring of 1527 he had achieved his lifelong ambition, being formally appointed *valet de chambre* to the king in succession to his father.[19] The point has to be made that the effectiveness of *L'Enfer* in securing Marot's release did not depend on its publication – this came 13 years later in an unauthorised edition – but rather on its widespread circulation in manuscript form.

It was in October 1527 that Marot next had occasion to demonstrate his talent as a prison writer. This took the form of his epistle "Marot Prisoner, an Address to the King for his Enlargement" (*Marot, Prisonnier, escrit au Roy pour sa déliverance*). The prison this time was the Conciergerie and the occasion was a disorder in the course of which Marot and friends had freed one or more individuals then held by the police.[20] The surrounding circumstances are not known. In typical fashion, his appeal is given in a light-hearted vein. It is only after listing the gifts given to the magistrate – a woodcock, a partridge and a hare – but to no avail, that he importunes the king, his master. In a matter of days he was freed.

In Marot, a solid core of seriousness was overlaid by a thick layer of charm, on which he traded readily, thereby enabling him to survive for a long time in the choppy waters of the French sixteenth century. It also helped that two of those most exposed to his charm should have been the king and his sister. For sheer entertainment, it is hard to better the epistle he addressed to the king on January 1, 1532, recounting the occasion when his servant – "one hailing from Gascony, a glutton, a drunk & certified liar, a cheat, a thief, a blasphemer, with the whiff, a good hundred yards off, of the hangman's noose" (*ung valet de Gascongne, Gourmant, Yvroigne & assuré Menteur, Pipeur, Larron, Jureur, Blasphémateur, sentant la Hart de cent pas à la ronde*) – took advantage of his master's heavy alcohol-induced sleep to ride off with all his money, wearing his finest clothes and choosing the better of his two horses, forgetting only one thing: to bid his master farewell. Marot's assessment "in short, the best of all lads" (*Au demeurant, le meilleur filz du Monde*) quickly achieved proverbial status.[21] Later in the poem, after denying that he had any intention of soliciting a donation, he does saucily say that he would be open to an interest-free loan, repayable once the king ceases to be renowned.[22]

The period 1528 to 1534 was one of poetic fulfilment and increasing recognition. He edited an edition of Villon's poems. He became a published author in 1531 when two unauthorised anthologies appeared in Lyon and Paris respectively. Up to then his verse had circulated in manuscript form, quite often under the counter, and this had the incidental benefit of shielding him from theological investigation. His preparation of an authorised collection (not including "*L'Enfer*") was designed in part to protect him from false attributions crediting him with dangerous views: "*L'Adolescence Clémentine*", published in August 1532, which for once bore the name of the author, proved a considerable success and quickly went into several further editions.

An amusing illustration of publishing pitfalls occurred in 1533 with the condemnation of Marguerite's own anthology, *The Mirror of the Sinful Soul* (*Miroir de l'âme pécheresse*) by the theological faculties of the universities and colleges of Paris, collectively known as the Sorbonne. She had included a number of Marot's early translations of several psalms. This clearly clashed with the Church's opposition to vernacular renditions of the Scriptures and earned Marguerite a very public reprimand.[23] She complained to the king, who demanded an explanation. They backed down promptly, citing an administrative error. Ultimately, Marot's elegant verse translations extended to 50, and were to be much prized by the reformers.

The cause of moderation suffered a damaging setback on the night of October 17, 1534, which was also to have serious consequences for Marot. Posters were fixed on buildings in Paris, as well as several provincial towns, which carried inflammatory messages hostile to the established religion.[24] This came to be known as "The Affair of the Placards" (*L'Affaire des Placards*). The author, a certain Marcourt, a reformist firebrand, together with a group of similarly minded fanatics, set out to challenge the validity of the mass, pointing to the impossibility of the sacrifice made by Jesus being repeated since the Scriptures tell us he is in heaven with God; from this it follows that transubstantiation is a lie and communion no more than a memorial. To achieve maximum impact, posters were fixed onto the church and the château of Amboise, where the king was at the time. From a standpoint nearly five centuries later it is difficult to understand the bill-stickers' motives, unless it were a perverse ambition to reverse any trend towards greater religious tolerance – that initially had the encouragement of the king and consistently that of Marguerite – and instead to bring on a fierce repression. In the immediate aftermath of the affair of the posters, warrants were issued for the arrest of known Lutheran sympathisers, prominent among whom was Marot. He was to feature seventh[25] out of a total of 73[26] in the Paris proclamation of January 25, 1535, listing those who, having fled the city, were banished from France, had their possessions seized and if captured were condemned to be burnt at the stake. (The claims that François I might still have had to the title of a tolerant sovereign were finally to be extinguished in 1545 with the savage persecution of the Quaker-like Vaudois of Provence.)[27]

Marot, who had been at Blois on the night of October 17, will have left immediately for the south. We next hear of him in Bordeaux where he was arrested, pursuant to the orders of the Parlement, Paris's judicial body;[28] having managed to give his captors the slip, he made his way to the safety of Navarre. From December 1534 to March 1535 he remained there under Marguerite's protection. This must have been judged an uncertain long-term refuge for Marot and/or a potential embarrassment for his protector. By April, he was in Italy and had entered the service of Renée de France, duchess of Ferrara, who, in common with Marguerite, had sympathy for the reform movement. He was already known to her having celebrated her marriage on June 21, 1528, to Ercole d'Este in a nuptial poem.[29]

Thereafter Marot was destined to have a peripatetic existence. This had much to do with the heretical cloud that never really left him. From Ferrara, where his presence and that of several other Frenchmen had become a political embarrassment to the Duke, he went to Venice. In November 1536 he took advantage of the king's decree permitting the return of religious refugees, providing they renounced their previous views. By January 1537 he had taken up again his position as secretary to the king and felt sufficiently secure to oversee the following year the publication in Lyon by Étienne Dolet of his collected works (to date), with the prudent exclusion of certain satirical poems. In July 1539 we find him thanking the king for the gift of a house in Paris[30] and later that year saw the publication of the first instalment of his French translation of the Psalms. The impression of a return to the halcyon days of 1528 to 1533 was, however, to prove illusory. With a build-up of reformist sentiment fuelled by suspect publications, the king's predisposition to tolerance was being undermined. Prominent among the publisher-printers involved was Étienne Dolet. Despite having much to thank the king for, getting him out of earlier skirmishes with the authorities, he overplayed his hand and was accused of being at the centre of the production and distribution of a wide range of heretical publications. He was arrested in January 1543, managed to escape abroad, but unwisely returned to France in 1544. Arrested afresh, he was incarcerated in the Conciergerie. Fifteen months later on August 2 1546 he was sentenced to death by hanging, with his corpse and his books being then cast into a bonfire's purifying flames.[31]

It is hardly surprising that Clément Marot should have himself felt insecure. By the end of 1542 he had already left France for good, going initially to Geneva where he proved an uncomfortable presence in Calvin's austere city. His exile eventually took him to Turin, which is where he died in September 1544.

In considering Marot's literary achievement, Claude Mayer, who devoted himself to the study of Marot and his works, describes Marot's translation of the Psalms as his greatest contribution. A more widely held view is that Marot's role in extending to French verse the liberating influences of the Renaissance is where his chief claim to fame lies. For others, his irrepressible humour, his gaiety, his irreverence are what is most captivating.[32]

The Lambeth Palace Library possesses a copy of a 1557 edition of his psalms, published in conjunction with others translated by the Calvinist Théodore de Bèze. An arresting woodcut on the title page features a structure having two stout doors, one narrow and the other wide, overhung by the caption *"entrez par la porte étroite car c'est la porte large & la voie spacieuse qui mène à la perdition"* (enter by the narrow door since the large door, giving on to the easy path, is the route to perdition) – neatly foreshadowing John Bunyan.[33] On the verso of the title page, a certain Estienne du Modilin proposes the following epitaph as a snapshot of Marot's life, covering his origins in the Querci in central France, his career at court, his death in Turin, his world wide renown.

> Querci . . . la Cour . . . le Piémont . . . l'Univers
> Me fit . . . me tint . . . m'enterre . . . me cognut
> Querci mon los . . . Cour . . . tout mon temps . . . eut
> Piémont . . . mes os, . . . et l'Univers . . . mes vers
> [Los – pride]

What may be a suitable note with which to conclude this chapter is provided by an enchanting get-well poem to Marguerite's little girl, Jeanne, ill in bed. The child survived to become the mother of Henri IV.

Ma mignonne,
Je vous donne
Le bon jour.
Le séjour,
C'est prison.
Guérison
Recouvrez,
Puis ouvrez
Vostre porte
Et qu'on sorte
Vistement;
Car Clément
Le vous mande.
Va, friande
De ta bouche,
Qui se couche
En danger
Pour manger
Confitures;
Si tu dures
Trop malade,
Couleur fade
Tu prendras
Et perdras
L'embonpoint
Dieu te doint,
Santé bonne,
Ma mignonne.

Ma mignonne – my pretty one

Le séjour – staying put

Friande de ta bouche – having a sweet tooth

Embonpoint – weight

Dieu te doint – may God give you

|||||||||||||||||||||||||||||||||||||||||||||||||||||||||||||||||||||||||||||||||||||||||||||||||

CHAPTER XII

Lettre de Cachet

In France it was the the *ordre du roi*, later better known as the *lettre de ca-chet* (sealed writ), in England it was incarceration for debt that accounted at times for the bulk of the prison population in those two countries in the seventeenth and eighteenth centuries.

The *lettre de cachet* or sealed writ derives its potency from the concept of the divine right of kings. As the historian Claude Quétel expresses it, an ab-solute monarch's written instructions on an individual basis have the force of law – without the interposition of the courts.[1]

The monarch may exercise this power in matters of state through the in-carceration of those who are seen as a threat to the Crown. This would in-clude traitors, rebels, religious dissidents, fraudsters, scurrilous pamphleteers and their bookselling distributors. It lent itself to ready use where urgency was required and the courts seen to be too slow-moving; where the verdict of the courts was uncertain; when the repression of religious nonconformity was not assured; in cases of political manoeuvring . . .[2] All of this was achiev-able without there being any need to justify such actions nor any facility for appeal against such sentences.

An absolute monarch is also invited to adjudicate on matters that do not touch his own interests. He does this in his paternalistic role of father of the country whose involvement extends down to the level of the family. In this situation, he receives pleas and requests, many of them aimed at shielding family honour – variously defined. The grant of a *lettre de cachet* leading to the detention of the accused has something in common with usage under English debtor laws – but with much wider application. It was coercive in intention, it involved a civil dispute between citizens, it fell ouside the courts. The place and duration were at the whim of the holder. No provision was made for appeal or redress.

Initially the monarch would receive personally the requests from his sub-jects and he would himself assess their worth and pass judgment. In practical terms, this degree of centralisation rapidly became unmanageable. The creation in 1667 of the post of Paris Police Commissioner ("Lieutenant général de police de Paris") and subsequently of bailiffs having similar powers outside Paris served to relieve the additional pressure which had built up – for state reasons – during the years of civil disturbance between 1648 and 1653, known as the Fronde.[3]

The end of the regency in 1661 and Louis XIV's assumption of power were to mark the start of a rapid growth in the issuance of *lettres de cachet* which was to reach its zenith in the second half of the eighteenth century. This was facilitated or fuelled by a degree of standardisation where the personal holograph application could be replaced by a printed form with gaps that needed to be filled in. More importantly, while the pleas were still addressed to the king, only a minority came to his direct attention, the others being processed by ministers and officials – but still in his name.

Among the state prisons, the Paris Bastille occupied a special position since it stood as an appendage within the king's administration, only admitting those confined there under the monarch's orders and functioning outside the judicial system. It also happens to provide a glimpse into the changing pattern of religious intolerance: in the reign of Louis XIV (1643–1715) 372 incarcerations under *lettre de cachet* were recorded, of which 254 were of Protestants and 73 of Jansenists, the quasi-Calvinistic movement within the Catholic church. In the reign of Louis XV (1715–1774) there were 383 incarcerations, a mere 16 of Protestants – more for reasons of scarcity than of tolerance, since many had already fled to the Low Countries and England – and 367 of Jansenists. In the reign of Louis XVI (1774–1792) those who entered the Bastille on the king's bidding did not include any on account of their Protestant or Jansenist beliefs.[4]

Global figures carry weight.[5] One estimate quoted by Quétel suggests that possibly up to 200,000 *lettres de cachet* were issued from the end of the regency in 1661 to the start of the Revolution in 1789 – with Louis XV's minister, Cardinal Fleury, himself issuing no fewer than 50,000 targeting the Jansenists.[6] These are suspiciously round figures. More topically, but still lacking precision, at the time of the Revolution the 500 to 600 places of detention located within the country housed between 7,000 and 8,000 men and women held under *lettres de cachet*.[7]

In the district of Caen in Normandy, for which there are detailed records, a total of 1,723 *lettres de cachet* were issued during the course of the eighteenth century, a mere 2.2 per cent of these on the initiative of the Crown and 97.8 per cent on that of individuals, primarily families.[8] Of those targeted, men outnumbered women three to one. The reasons for confinement varied, with dishonesty (*"délinquence"*) claiming 28 per cent of the men against 12 per cent for women; anti-social behaviour (*"mauvaise conduite"*) 13 per cent for men, 3 per cent for women; insanity 25 per cent for men, 18 per cent for women. Women came into their own, so to speak, in matters of immorality (*"libertinage"*) with 50 per cent compared to 23 per cent for men, and misalliance (*"danger de mésalliance"*) 16 per cent against 3 per cent for men. Some 5 per cent of men were held on the grounds of disobedience, with women enjoying a clean slate by reason no doubt of their not being credited with independence. Finally, dilapidation took care of 3 per cent of the men against 1 per cent of the women.

An application for a *lettre de cachet* had to be backed up by evidence of the alleged misconduct for examination by the appropriate official, or indeed by the king himself in cases in which he might take a direct interest, most probably those involving members of the aristocracy. That this was not a mere formality is indicated by the fact that 20 per cent or so of requests were typically rejected, some to be re-submitted having been buttressed by additional information.[9] This casts a favourable light on the conscientiousness of many civil servants and administrators, which is easily overlooked. The successful applicant(s) would then be required to pay what amounted to a rental charge to the house of detention in which he chose to confine the subject of his plea, and to do so until such time as he chose to release the man or woman in question.

Paradoxically, the best way of protecting the honour of a family might involve imprisonment, providing of course that this was under a *lettre de cachet* to which no opprobrium was attached. It could prove an effective way of dodging the arm of the law in the wake of a criminal act. Similarly, the creditor could be thwarted if the debtor were to disappear within the walls of a secure house of detention. In other circumstances, the *lettre de cachet* was a potentially valuable aid or weapon involving a great range of domestic issues: the stubborn son or daughter intent on an alliance judged unsuitable on financial grounds or considerations of lineage; the improvident father whose actions threaten his wife and children with destitution; the wish to curb sons and daughters who are busy sowing – or close to sowing – their wild oats; its application in defence of one's possessions; as a means of countering anti-social behaviour of all kinds . . . By invoking the highly elastic notion of family honour, no further elaboration was required.

Mirabeau
(1749–1791)

One of the best views of *lettres de cachet* in intensive use is provided by the travails of the revolutionary political figure, Honoré Gabriel Mirabeau. As a young man he was a tearaway, running up debts, forming amorous attachments, ready to pick a quarrel where honour was an issue. During a spell of military service, he compounded his derelictions by going to Paris without leave; this was tantamount to desertion and earned him his first spell of imprisonment in the Île de Ré under a royal order. His father, the marquis de Mirabeau, managed to obtain for him a revocation. The point should be made that his father also had had a wild streak in his youth, and while he subsequently became renowned for his prolific writings on economic subjects, was remarkably unsuccessful in his own financial affairs, chiefly property speculation leading to heavy indebtedness.

Over the next few years Mirabeau lived up to what one commentator described as his "conscienceless prodigality with money". Marriage in 1772 to the 19-year-old heiress Emilie de Marignane, rather than easing his financial position, saw a blossoming of creditors, reflecting the wedding expenses and subsequent outlays on the couple's respective wardrobes and on lavish home improvements.[10] In December 1773 his father obtained a *lettre de cachet*, under which Mirabeau was put under house arrest, and thereby secured him protection from his creditors. This having failed to halt a spending spree, a fresh *lettre de cachet* was secured for detention at Manosque, not far from the family property in Provence. From there he made an unauthorised sortie to Grasse where he encountered the elderly baron de Villeneuve, said to have insulted his sister, and engaged him in physical combat. This earned him a legal action for murderous assault – not, to the embarrassment of the Villeneuve family, a challenge to a duel, the more honourable outcome as between noblemen. His father promptly secured for him in September 1774 a new *lettre de cachet* for confinement in the island fortress near Marseilles, the Château d'If. This time, he was being protected from the arm of the law, rather than his creditors.

In a letter to his father from his new abode, his youthful indignation surfaces at the constraints to which he was subject: "I know that you have heard all sorts of stories involving a serving lass. But really is this not a case of going out of one's way to manufacture a crime to attribute to a young man. At the Château d'If there was only one person who bore the slightest resemblance to a woman. I was 26 years old. What a monstrous action on my part to have fed the suspicion that I found her pretty".[11] ("Je sais qu'on vous a fait mille histoires d'une cantinière. Mais de bonne foi, n'est ce pas forger des crimes à un homme, que de lui en chercher cette espèce? Il n'y avait qu'une femme au château qui ait figure de femme. J'avais vingt-six ans. C'est un furieux délit que d'avoir donné lieu de soupçons qu'elle me paraissait jolie".) But the girl in question had a husband, and this led to Mirabeau being accused of seduction; it was judged prudent to move him yet again: under a fresh *lettre de cachet* taken out in April 1775; he was transferred to Fort de Joux, adjacent to Pontarlier.

Fort de Joux, near the Swiss border, was to be the scene of an altogether more serious attachment. There he met Sophie de Monnier, the 21-year old wife of the marquis de Monnier, 48 years her elder, whose hospitable house at Pontarlier he often frequented. The two fell deeply in love and the comfortable conditions which governed his detention served to abet their romance, the even tenor of which was threatened, however, by measures being taken to transfer him to a prison in Picardy; this was in the wake, yet again, of his abuse of the privileges he had been granted governing absences. Threatened with this prospect, in August 1776 he absconded to Neufchâtel, where Sophie joined him, and the two then sought refuge in the Low Countries, settling in Amsterdam. He had thereby opened himself to the accusation of having subverted and effectively kidnapped Sophie, a capital offence – and another man's wife to boot. Eight months later, the Dutch authorities having agreed to his extradition, he found himself again

Honoré Gabriel comte de Mirabeau,
19th-century lithograph by Frantz Gabriel Fiesinger

under a *lettre de cachet* secured by his father; this time, incarceration was not in one of the more porous places of detention in which he had enjoyed a fair degree of freedom, but in Vincennes, the state prison on the eastern outskirts of Paris. Sophie, for her part, was the subject of a *lettre de cachet* taken out by her family; being three months pregnant, she avoided incarceration in Sainte Pélagie prison, being initially confined in a house of detention designated for prostitutes and the insane, but subsequently in a convent in Gien.

In total, Mirabeau collected at least ten *lettres de cachet*, as calculated by his biographer, Jean-Paul Desprat – the majority on his father's initiative. It should not, however, be assumed that parental wrath was all that motivated the marquis de Mirabeau: during the course of his life, he was granted 67 *lettres de cachet*, his victims including his own wife and a brother – such was his sensitivity when the honour of the family was seen by him to be compromised.[12]

Prison Writings

Mirabeau's letters to Sophie are generally recognised as his prime claim to literary fame, though there are those who dispute this, preferring another prison book, *Erotica –Biblion* – a startling product of the author's fevered prison imagination, and in the judgment of one modern critic, "chef d'oeuvre érudit d'éroticisme philosophique" (an erudite masterpiece of philosophic eroticism).[13] It was first published in 1783 with the humorous attribution "De l'Imprimerie du Vatican".

The letters themselves fill four octavo volumes that cover the 42 months of imprisonment in the Donjon de Vincennes, the first being dated April 1, 1777. Those to Sophie come to 71, with 48 going to prison authorities, one to the King, and four to his father. Nine months into his imprisonment, he put his side of the story of his misadventures in a 150-page Memoir sent to his father. As a means of securing his release from under the parental *lettre de cachet*, it was a clear failure, not least because of the uncompromising tone throughout.

From the start, Mirabeau's hugely affectionate letters to Sophie centre on the forthcoming birth of their child, born January 7, 1778 and baptised Sophie Gabrielle. At an early date, Mirabeau rehearsed the virtues of inoculation against smallpox – a procedure that was contentious at that time and not without risk – insisting that it be "en la manière de Sutton" (i.e. by puncture). Few letters from Sophie are included in this collection, though one charming exception is dated December 1778 "Gabriel (sic) Sophie a quatre dents. Elle est gaie, grasse et se porte à merveille" (Gabriel Sophie has four teeth. She is jolly, plump and in rude good health.)[14]

The letters' frequency varied widely, those to the prison authorities during the first two years exceeding those to Sophie (42 to 28); the pattern was then sharply reversed during the last two years (six to 43). The explanation lies in Mirabeau's anomalous position: his detention under his father's *lettre de cachet* – rather than that of the King – but incarcerated in a gaol reserved for people judged to pose a threat to King and Country. The prisoner total at that time in Vincennes came to around 12; they were known not by name but by cell number and forbidden any contact with other prisoners or the world outside.

Mirabeau had in effect two keepers, firstly the Governor of the dungeon, M. de Rougemont, and secondly M. Le Noir (often Lenoir), Lieutenant

Général de Police, Secrétaire d'Etat, a considerable figure with responsibilities that extended across all state prisons. The former was cast in an inflexible mould. It was to the latter that Mirabeau turned seeking alleviation on subjects that ranged from the hugely important ability to communicate by letter with Sophie, the delivery of his wardrobe and books he had had to abandon in Holland on his arrest, to ways of supplying Sophie with funds following the birth of their child. This led to a stream of letters to Le Noir and fulsome expressions of gratitude to him and to his police clerk (M. Boucher) who acted as the go-between; throughout the correspondence, he was the anonymous "notre bon ange" (our good angel). In the second half of Mirabeau's imprisonment, the virtual drying up letters to the authorities reflects the achievement of a modus vivendi. The flow of letters to Sophie, on the other hand has much to do with the death of their two-year-old daughter in May 1780 when in the care of her wet nurse. This tragedy can be said at the same time to have contributed to a softening of parental and filial intransigence, which led finally to the lifting of the *lettre de cachet*.

Release from detention in October 1780 promptly landed Mirabeau with the legal consequences of the trial of May 10, 1777, in Pontarlier when, in his absence, he had been found guilty of a capital crime of "rapt and seduction". He was sentenced to be beheaded in effigy and to pay fines of 5,000 livres to the King and 40,000 livres to Sophie's husband, the marquis de Monnier. On emerging from prison, rather than seek a royal pardon, Mirabeau chose the risky route of a court trial.[15] Buttressed by three powerful memoranda he had prepared for the purpose, he conducted his own defence and was triumphant: his sentence was quashed and civil rights restored, while Sophie was granted a separation from her husband. For Mirabeau, his revolutionary credentials in combating the oppressive legal institution of the *lettre de cachet* had been greatly enhanced, his oratorical brilliance thoroughly demonstrated and, at a personal level, a love affair that (for him) had long run its course brought to a satisfactory conclusion.

The account of the survival and printing of the letters brings one to P. Manuel, *Citoyen français*, one of the many shadowy figures who have been so vividly brought to life in Robert Darnton's accounts of the revolutionary period. In an extended preface in the first edition of 1792 (published posthumously), Manuel explains that a happy accident led him to the prison archives of the Bastille, which housed the material of other state prisoners, including those from Vincennes, where he found Mirabeau's correspondence to Sophie. Such letters would have either been undelivered and filed away or will have reached their destination, subject to the recipient undertaking to return them to the prison authorities. Mirabeau, as a prolific writer, ever in the sights of the censor, had had many publishing links with Manuel throughout the seventies and eighties.[16] He was then acting as his agent and distributor. But now Manuel re-surfaced with a heavily edited collection of letters as an act of revolutionary piety: "I found them scattered by the revolution, I collected them with great respect" (éparpillées par la révolution, je les ai ramassées, partout d'une main respectueuse).[17] This was to form the fourth title of his series of books created from dossiers held in the Bastille, to which his position as provincial administrator of the police had given him access, and that he had in effect appropriated. Mirabeau's mother, his sole heir, was unconvinced by his explanation and took him to court, on the grounds that Mirabeau's letters, which had survived the sack of the Bastille, were held safe, sealed and stored in a special section of the prison, and that Manuel had no authority to remove them by breaking the seal and using a key from the police headquarters so to do – let alone to have set his sights on publishing them for personal profit.[18] Manuel's defence was that the Bastille and all its contents were now the property of the people. The case was a casualty of the chaos following the overthrow of the monarchy on August 10, 1792, but the arguments seemed heavily weighted in favour of the plaintiff.

Mirabeau's death on April 2, 1791, came at a time when his republican reputation was at its highest: on April 4, 1791, he became the first man to be honoured with burial in the Panthéon. This was the name given to the church of Sainte Geneviève, construction of which had begun in 1757 under the auspices of Louis XV and after many delays was largely completed by 1790. Under a decree of April 1791, the Constituent Assembly gave it a new role as a secular mausoleum reserved for the ashes of Great Figures of a Grateful Nation ("*Aux grands hommes la Patrie reconnaissante*"). This called for deconsecration and the replacement of Christian embellishments with features more in harmony with its position as "Temple de la Patrie" or shrine to liberty. The work was entrusted to the architect with an arresting name, Antoine-Chrysostome Quatremère de Quincy, who set out to eliminate all shameful vestiges of fanaticism (*"de faire disparaître les vestiges honteux du fanatisme"*).[19]

Worrisome doubts, however, began to surface centring on rumours of Mirabeau's clandestine contacts with Louis XVI. To profit from a romantic story having huge potential appeal, Manuel had to mount a robust defence of Mirabeau, which he did in a lengthy presentation that introduced the work. Darnton's account of its marketing has a modern ring to it: the publisher-bookseller, J. B. Garnery, running off 20,000 prospectuses that supported a print run of 50,000 ahead of publication in January 1792.[20] The book will have been usefully profitable. In the course of 1794, however, irrefutable evidence emerged of Mirabeau's dealings with the king. Consequently, on September 21 Mirabeau's ashes were solemnly removed from the Panthéon and replaced the same day by those of Jean-Paul Marat, the revolutionary firebrand assassinated by Charlotte Corday in July 1793.[21] In the wake of the fall of Robespierre on July 27, 1794, Marat's stock had actually risen on the argument that he had been a genuine Jacobin, whereas Robespierre had betrayed the cause through his pursuit of dictatorial powers. Such recognition, however, was to prove short-lived as the backlash against the revolutionary excesses – with which Marat himself was so closely identified – took hold. On February 21, 1795, his ashes in turn suffered expulsion. The Convention then took the wise decision to allow for a cooling off period of ten years before any deceased candidates could be nominated for this honour.

But the prison writing that bears most directly on the subject of this chapter is naturally enough Mirabeau's *Des Lettres de Cachet et des Prisons d'État* (Concerning Sealed Letters and State Prisons): a substantial two volume work written in 1778 and first published "posthumously" in 1782. This is a confusing allusion to the fact that its publication came two years after Mirabeau's release. For censorship reasons it was printed outside France, but not necessarily in Hamburg, as the title page of the first edition indicates, and published anonymously. As Barbara Luttrell points out, a lot of material is taken from "Essai sur le despotisme", another prison writing from his time in the Château d'If.[22] Volume 1 is a broad review of the circumstances of incarceration over the centuries and the injustices to which they gave rise. Volume 2 is more explicitly concerned in considerable detail with Mirabeau's own experience at Vincennes. Bearing in mind the conditions under which the author had to write, with limited access to sources and often in indifferent health, this is a notable scholarly achievement. Such weaknesses as its discursive character, betraying at times a scissors-and-paste application, are understandable. But a work written from a prison cell, extolling liberty and decrying abuses, carries with it a special ring of authority. And who can dispute the author's qualifications to examine the operations of the *lettres de cachet*?

Voltaire
(1694–1778)

Voltaire's connection with *lettres de cachet* is particularly interesting, he being both victim and agent.

Aged 21, he was confined in the Bastille as being the author of a poem that suggested incestuous relations between the Regent, the duc de Bourbon, and his eldest daughter; this earned him 11 months' incarceration. Five years later, the "plebeian" Voltaire quarrelled with the "aristocratic" chevalier de Rohan in the Opera House loge of Mlle Lecouvreur. Voltaire reached for his sword, Rohan his cane and Mlle Lecouvreur her smelling salts.[23] No blows were exchanged but egos had been bruised. Scorning a duel with a man his social inferior – and what's more, a literary upstart – Rohan has Voltaire given a public thrashing. The victim swears vengeance and the Rohan family, fearing the worst (as did the police), requests and secures a *lettre de cachet* from the Regent. Voltaire re-enters the Bastille on April 17, 1728. In this instance, he was being protected from himself, i.e. from what a headstrong young man might do, and the Rohan family was being reassured over the threat to the chevalier de Rohan. At the same time the authorities took note of Voltaire's by then prominent position in literary and social circles, with Voltaire dining at the governor's table and, most importantly, being released 12 days later. This was made subject to his place of exile being at least 50 leagues ouside Paris; he then managed to change the terms to a period of exile in England; it was in 1729 that he was granted permission to return to France, initially to Saint Germain, where he was under house observation, a restriction that was lifted a few months later.

François Marie Arouet de Voltaire known as Voltaire,
after a painting by Maurice-Quentin de la Tour

He took up residence in Paris in a house in the rue Vaugirard, where he had a certain dame Travers as a tenant.[24] On August 16, 1730, he is to be seen drawing up a demand for a *lettre de cachet* from M. Hérault, the then Paris Police Commissioner, against his tenant, claiming that she is the disgrace of the neighbourhood, drunk every day, parading naked, threatening to set fire to neighbours' houses. This request was in Voltaire's own hand – not unexpectedly Voltaire scorned the use of the pre-printed form – and carries his signature and those of several neighbours. M. Hérault calls for an enquiry which reveals that Mme Travers had reasons for complaint, claiming that she had been threatened with Voltaire's servants proposing to blow her brains out.[25] This initial request having gone quiet, Voltaire writes afresh to the Police Commissioner adding to Mme Travers's shortcomings blasphemy (*sic*) and perversion of morals. The *lettre de cachet* is finally granted and on November 25, 1730, she is imprisoned in the women's prison La Salpêtrière. However, a counter-petition made by the woman's sisters against this injustice secures her release within a month.

Voltaire's double role of victim and agent illustrates, on the one hand, the occasional subtleties in the application of what was a heavy-handed extra-legal instrument, and on the other hand its abusive potential – in the grasp, moreover, of that great critic of aristocratic excesses and champion of individual freedoms. The invocation of blasphemy in the catalogue of accusations has special spice.

Voltaire's prison output is much less than is that of Mirabeau, but his period of incarceration was very much briefer, being measured in months rather than years. It was in the Bastille that he completed his tragedy, *Oedipe*, published in 1718. The subject had most recently been treated by Corneille. Voltaire's play was very well received and is often cited by literary critics as marking the start of his literary fame. He also wrote a humorous poem on his arrest and translation to the Bastille. This has several features in common with Clément Marot's own accounts of similar misadventures, dating from the 1530s! But Voltaire was able to enrich the French language by coining the verb "embastiller".[26]

Abolition of the *Lettre de Cachet*

As recently as 1788 Louis XVI declared: "La liberté de mes sujets m'est aussi chère qu'à eux-mêmes; mais je ne souffrirai pas que mon Parlement s'élève contre l'exercice d'un pouvoir auquel les familles ont souvent dû la conservation de leur honneur et l'État sa tranquilité" (I treasure the freedom of my subjects as much as they do themselves, but I shall not tolerate that my Parlement should set itself up in opposition to an authority to which families have so often owed the preservation of their honour and the State of its tranquility).[27]

The Parlement for its part enjoined the king that he could not be indifferent to attacks on the personal liberty of his citizens. And this judicial body assured him that it would not cease to draw to his attention the dangers inherent in these obscure prisons into which people are thrown without any legal process, without examination and lacking any means of redress, such arbitrary decisions being at total variance with the principles of equity.[28]

The case for the *lettre de cachet*, grounded as it was in the divine right of kings and bound in with the inequalities of the old order, was one of the most conspicuous relics of the past and hence one of the most obvious candidates for suppression. Its abolition was decreed on March 12, 1790, by the Constituent Assembly.

The French Revolution

||||||||||||||||||||||||||||||||||||||||||||||||||||||||||||||||||||||||||||||||||||||||

CHAPTER XIII

Madame Roland
(1754–1793)

Incarcerations

La Prison de l'Abbaye	*June 1 – 24 , 1793*
La Prison de Sainte Pélagie	*June 24 – October 31, 1793*
La Conciergerie	*October 31 – November 8, 1793*

During the course of a little over five months of imprisonment, Madame Roland filled five folders, three of historic notes and two of personal memoirs. All told, she covered 700 manuscript pages that give virtually no signs of revision or correction. They are preserved in the Bibliothèque Nationale.

The Conciergerie was well known as a staging post for the guillotine – most famously in the case of Queen Marie Antoinette. Of the other two, l'Abbaye was at the centre of the September 1792 prison massacres. A mob of Parisian patriots devoted five days to assassinating inmates of nine Paris prisons. They were responding to the warning, fanned by Robespierre, Danton and Marat, that the nation was at risk from an uprising from within the prisons of counter-revolutionaries. These were said to be on the point of a breakout at a time when French troops were otherwise occupied protecting the northern frontier from a Prussian-Austrian advance. A total of 1,300 men (among whom were 200 priests), 40 women and 40 young under the age of 18 were killed. Revolutionaries were thereby able to breathe a collective sigh of relief at the successful elimination of what must rank as one of the most implausible threats ever conjured up to justify political murder. Ten months later l'Abbaye opened its gates to Madame Roland.

Marie-Jeanne Phlipon (known as Manon) was born in Paris in 1754, the daughter of an engraver, principally of silver objects. His work shop, where he employed a number of apprentices, was in the Place Dauphine at the west end of the Île de la Cité. He lived with his family above the shop in a comfortable apartment, whence they looked out onto the Pont Neuf and the statue of Henri IV, famous for his religious tolerance and his tragic death in 1610 at the hands of an assassin. The business of Manon's father, Gratien Phlipon, brought him into contact with the more prosperous bourgeois citizens as well as members of the aristocracy and this helped to shed lustre on his own standing. Through his work, he made friends of artists such as the painters Greuze and La Tour. He remained nonetheless firmly rooted in the bourgeois class. The same applied to Manon's mother, though she was a notch or two further up the social scale.

Manon was one of seven children, but the only one to survive, the others dying at birth or shortly thereafter. She was consequently brought up as an only child. From an early age, she gave evidence of great promise, being endowed with an extremely retentive memory, and this fed what can best be described as a hunger for learning. By the age of five she was able to read and write. Thereafter, her father gave her drawing lessons – and also taught her how to use an engraving tool; an uncle took care of Latin (not however destined to be persevered with) and teachers came to instruct her at home in geography, history, music, dance. From the age of seven, much of her time was spent reading and filling notebooks with her précis and commentaries.

Aged eleven, following her first communion, she was placed by her parents in a nearby convent for one year, where she excelled scholastically and made two great friendships. These were to last the rest of her life, being maintained by a sustained correspondence – in effect replacing her childish précis and commentaries.

From an early age her reading was voracious, extending even to a book on heraldry. Thomson's *Seasons*, initially in translation, was one enthusiasm. But there are two authors above all others who had a decisive formative influence on her. The first dates from when she was only nine years old, at which point she was given a copy of Plutarch's *Parallel Lives* of Greeks and Romans. This book by the first century Greek historian, destined to be read and re-read, introduced Manon to the circumstances and potential of republics shorn of monarchical links. The second book, first read much later when she was 20 years old, was Jean-Jacques Rousseau's *Julie ou la Nouvelle Héloïse*. It acted on her as a beacon of feminine liberation. It was also destined to have the same effect on the future Mme de Staël, who added, however, permissiveness to the intellectual freedoms that seduced Manon.

In the course of her teens, she started to question her faith, being offended by the view that a heavenly consummation was reserved for those lucky enough to have been born or brought up Catholic, while her exposure to Descartes, Helvetius and others shattered her acceptance of the concept of infallibility in religion. In history, her enthusiasm for the accounts of republics left her convinced that a republican regime was ideally suited to foster nobility of conduct among both the people and their leaders. An opportunity of viewing at first hand a monarchy in operation came to her as a 20-year-old when she, her mother and a favourite uncle were able to occupy an apartment in Versailles for one week thanks to a relation on her mother's side whose aristocratic genealogy, albeit minor, was much polished and gave her this entry.[1] The visit took place in 1774, shortly after Louis XVI, also aged 20, had come to the throne. By the end of their stay Manon decided that she preferred examining the statues in the gardens to seeing the courtiers in situ. For her the tone of the visit was set from the start when she found that their quarters were in the gods, down a dark passage, smelling powerfully of the nearby privy, an experience moreover shared with the Archbishop of Paris from whose next-door apartment a paper-thin wall separated them – degrading conditions for those dancing attendance at court. That aside, her egalitarian sympathies had been well and truly aroused.

A more pressing issue concerned the quest for a husband that her parents had put in train once she reached the age of 18. This gave rise to much correspondence with her great friend from convent days, Sophie Cannet, with Manon providing entertaining descriptions of the candidates and summaries of the rejection letters she drafted for her father to sign.[2] In June 1775 disaster struck with the death of her much-loved mother. Manon suffered a serious depression, all the deeper since her relations with her father were on the decline. Reduced attention to his own business accompanied by unhappy speculations created additional tensions. The quest for a suitable husband, already fraught since from the start both parents had accepted that to be chosen the

Jeanne Phlipon, Madame Roland, by Johann Ernst Heinsius

aspirant had to be somebody who would share Manon's firmly held views, was made all the more so by the dwindling dowry she might bring to a marriage.

It was in January, 1776, that Jean-Marie Roland de la Platière, a friend of the Cannet family, first came into Manon's life. He was 42 years old (against her 22), of good provincial bourgeois stock, with a successful career as a civil servant acting as an inspector of industries – a job with an important didactic side to it – and with professional recognition coming through membership of a number of scientific societies both in France and abroad. His long spell as a bachelor had given him a prickly disposition and, being very much on his dignity, he deeply resented the affronts that the class structure supplied in spades. But here was a man who was intelligent, honest, hardworking, imbued with a great sense of the public good, and republican in spirit. He was also ready to overlook the absence of a significant dowry. And she was ready to overlook the fact that he was light on humour and that he could not be said to be the obvious answer to a young woman's romantic dreams.

Four years after the first meeting they were married. By then his work had brought him to Paris, where he was also very much involved in writing technical tracts published under the signature of the distinguished philosopher and mathematician, Condorcet, in his capacity as permanent secretary of the Académie des Sciences de Paris.[3] Subjects covered at that time included improvements in the manufacture of woollen fabrics, in that of cotton velvet fabrics and in the exploitation of peat. Manon took on enthusiastically the tasks of secretary, copier and desk editor. This fitted in with her entrenched view that in marriage women should be able to contribute beyond childbearing and household management. At the same time Manon stressed the dutiful and devoted role of wives, and in her marriage she went to great lengths to play down any suspicion of being in competition with Roland. One abiding fear was that she might be taken for a bluestocking and this may have been behind the opinion – surprising for someone who is now clearly associated with the feminist cause – that it was unbecoming in a woman to put herself forward as an author.[4] As young marrieds, they enjoyed an active social life, often centred on academic and professional friends and acquaintances. It comes as little surprise that the Rolands were among those who showed a passing interest in the demonstrations of Mesmer. In Robert Darnton's account of Mesmerism, this was tantamount to being accorded a badge of pre-revolutionary intellectual activity.

Towards the end of 1781 a daughter was born and given the name of Eudora in recognition of the father's enthusiasm for all things Greek. The girl was to prove somewhat of a disappointment, lacking as she did her mother's boundless energy and, most importantly, her thirst for knowledge. These shortcomings are spelled out somewhat brutally in the Memoirs.[5] Manon was to have greater success in promoting the interests of her husband and in furthering his career. There was her editorial help with his important contributions to the Dictionary of Manufactures, Arts and Crafts ("Dictionnaire des manufactures, arts et métiers"). More significantly, finding herself in Paris on family matters – and he at Amiens at the time – she was able to alert him to the vacancy of the important post of inspector of manufactures based at Lyon, and then successfully pleaded his case going the rounds of the relevant government bureaux. The move to Lyon in 1784 represented a major advance for him as to salary and position. It also carried with it acknowledgment that Madame Roland's role was that of collaborator rather than merely assistant.

Revolutionary build-up

At a national level, a continuing source of concern over many years was the state of the country's finances, weighed down as they were by the privileges, some medieval in origin, granted to the clergy, the aristocracy and certain elements within the merchant and professional classes. The repeated failure of Louis XVI to override the interests of the establishment was reflected in a succession of ministerial changes. Reforming finance ministers came and went, never getting the backing of the king, the most remarkable of these being the economist, Turgot. In his resignation letter of May 1776 he even cautioned the young king that it was royal weakness that brought King Charles I to the execution block.[6] In her correspondence, Madame Roland expressed resignation at the turn of events, declaring that little good could be expected under a monarchy unwilling to confront injustices and inequalities. She did not predict its overthrow.

The fuse can be said to have been lit in November 1787 with the king's decision to announce by decree yet another package of onerous measures. This came after he had summoned an Assembly of Notables ("Assemblée de Notables"), made up of 144 prominent nobles whose brief was to advise on a way out of the crisis – with predictable lack of success and, for the king, disturbing evidence of discord among his natural supporters. The decree was deliberately not submitted to the high court of justice, the "Parlement de Paris". Over the centuries, the requirement had arisen that royal edicts be registered in the Paris court – which the court could reject, thereby exercising a rare check on an absolute monarchy. While a strong Crown had ways of overriding such a veto, this was not the case with Louis XVI. The Paris Parlement, itself a body enjoying hereditary privileges, chose a direct confrontation, invoking, rather saucily, what it termed "the fundamental law of the kingdom" whereby taxation was to be the province of the Estates General ("États généraux"), the courts to be the fountain of all laws and, for good measure, the extra-judicial imprisonment by *lettres de cachet* to be abolished.[7] Louis XVI responded by declaring the Paris court to be on holiday, and had the main movers arrested.

Nonetheless, the idea of reconvening the Estates General gained support. It is ironic that an institution that traces its origins to 1302 and came to an end in 1614, should have been resuscitated 175 years later to act as a vehicle for reform. The Estates General, often used in the past as a sounding board by the Crown, was made up of representatives of the clergy (the first estate), the nobility (the second estate) and the largely urban middle class (the third estate) in equal numbers. This guaranteed a conservative slant to its deliberations, so long as the first two estates marched in step. Louis XVI, responding to widespread pressures, agreed to the convocation of a revived Estates General for May 1, 1789. He also met the obvious concerns over bias by allocating to the third estate 600 seats, against 300 to each of the other two estates. Then came the issue of suffrage: was each estate to vote as a separate entity or were all votes to be pooled? In one case the voting pattern might well confirm the traditional bias, in the other case the numerical weight of the commons would come into play. Notwithstanding the king's most strenuous efforts to swing opinion his way, supported by all those of a conservative disposition, he lost the argument.

In the space of a little over seven weeks the revival of a medieval institution set in train the events which led to that of June 20 – one of several dates that punctuate the Revolution and for French historians need little further identification. On June 13 the tripartite Estates General had effectively ceased to exist, being renamed the National Assembly ("Assemblée nationale"). Confirmation of their eclipse came with the vote of June 19, backed by half the clergy and 85 deputies from the nobility, giving the commons a comfortable overall majority. On June 20, 1789, the deputies of the commons having been forbidden access on the king's orders to the hall they had previously occupied, switched to the nearby "Jeu de Paume" (a large indoor tennis court), where they took the solemn vow that they remain together until such time as they had given the country a constitution; David's well-known painting captures this dramatic scene. Once again Louis XVI yielded, and on July 7 a committee was formed for the purpose of drawing up the new constitution, in recognition of which the National Assembly gained the name of the Constituent Assembly ("Assemblée constituante"). This can be said to mark the moment when France ceased to be under the rule of an absolute monarch and instead appeared to have at its head a constitutional king in the making.

The events only a week later of July 14, 1789, put into sharp relief some of the problems of such a transition. That day saw the overthrow of the Bastille, which followed the marshalling of troops on Louis XVI's orders around Paris and the dismissal of the finance minister, Necker, who was occupying that post for the second time. As explained by Pierre Cornut-Gentille, these actions by a king, endlessly reliant on rearguard measures, were feared by some as heralding a counter-revolution on the one hand and national bankruptcy on the other.[8] As a symbol of the old order, the destruction of the Bastille is celebrated every year with the national holiday of "le 14 juillet", trumping June 20 in the republican calendar.

The first phase of the Revolution found the Rolands based in Lyon, well away from the scene of action in Paris, on which they were kept informed by friends, notably the botanist Louis Bosc, a childhood friend and mentor.[9] Roland himself had been seriously ill, only recovering at the end of the year. In her memoirs, his wife recalls that "the Revolution started to unfold and we were carried away" ("La Révolution survint et nous enflamma").[10] It quickly became an all-absorbing event for the couple – and one which had happy side-effects for them in as much as it called for their presence in Paris on two counts. One centred on the precarious financial position of the city of Lyon, where the collapse of the textile (silk) industry had led to massive unemployment, a burden that had led directly to crushing indebtedness for the municipality. Roland, whose vigorous pamphleteering on the subject had drawn attention to his mastery of the problem, was eventually given the task of negotiating for the state to take on the civic debt.[11] The other consideration pointing them in the direction of Paris was of a more personal nature: the job of inspector of manufacturing had the stigma of the old regime and was abolished on September 27, 1791. Roland was therefore facing a significant gap in his income, the filling of which was likely to be easier in Paris, where they both had much stronger ties than in Lyon. He was also hopeful of obtaining a pension.

Reinforcing a move to the geographical centre of the Revolution was their increasing involvement in political debate and the build-up of their contacts with some of the more outspoken revolutionary figures. Jacques-Pierre Brissot, the talented hack writer with strong liberal sympathies, found his voice with the regular publication of *Le Patriote français*. The Rolands had had contact with him in 1787, and Manon had added him to her list of correspondents; starting in mid-1789, he published – anonymously of course

– extracts from her letters in his journal. Roland, for his part, had joined the Société des Amis de la Constitution, but finding it ineffective (40 members) and lethargic, had organised a militant club, La Société populaire, which by the end of 1790 had 3,000 members.[12] The club's role was not simply to explain the actions of the Assembly but also to act as a pressure group influencing their deliberations.

With the king's ratification of the constitution in September 1791, the Constituent Assembly gave way to the Legislative Assembly ("Assemblée legislative"), some two years after the dramatic events in the Jeu de Paume. In a self-denying move, members of the Constituent Assembly declared themselves ineligible to run for the Legislative Assembly. Those elected were largely unknown to the Rolands, barring Brissot and Condorcet, and had a conservative cast. Roland himself failed to be elected as a deputy for Lyon, notwithstanding his earlier success at relieving the city's debt burden.

Once in Paris, a natural magnet for the Rolands was Le Club des Jacobins, named after an erstwhile Dominican house in the rue Saint-Honoré, where their meetings were held. This, the most influential of all the revolutionary clubs, had also established a network of affiliated groups across the country; in its composition it proved protean, accommodating at various times the supporters of the moderate Feuillants, led by Lafayette (famous for his role in the American War of Independence), which favoured a constitutional monarchy, as well as the republican-inclined Brissotins, named after the Rolands' friend; they later became much better known as the Girondins, in recognition of the number that came from the Bordeaux region. The ultra-radical wing, later to be known simply as the Jacobins, eventually rose to prominence under the dominance of Robespierre, who was also to use the authority he came to enjoy within the Club to get the backing of the more radical figures in the 48 Sections into which Paris was then administratively divided.

To begin with, the Club may be said to have served as a warm-up debating facility for its members ahead of their presentations as deputies in the Assembly, helped by the fact that the seating patterns were similar. The meetings gained additional significance with the decision taken in October 1791 to throw them open to the public. Indeed, it became an important chamber for the likes of Brissot and Robespierre, where they might develop their policies and secure their adherents, and can be said to have evolved into a political laboratory attracting many of the most gifted figures of the day.

The Rolands threw themselves enthusiastically into the political arena. Manon took to attending the sessions of the Assembly in the morning and those of the Club des Jacobins in the evening. Thanks to Brissot, they met all the leading revolutionary figures of the day, and throughout the spring and the summer of 1791 the practice arose for a number of the deputies to meet four times a week at the apartment occupied by the Rolands for a frugal meal before going on to the Club. This constituted a mini salon with the distinctive characteristics that discussions were political – not philosophic or literary – and that the attractive woman, imbued with charm, who presided went to great lengths to deny in her memoirs having ever in any way directed the discussion, absorbed as she was sitting at a side table with her letter-writing and her embroidery.[13] In moments of honesty she may have acknowledged to herself that most of the men who were regulars were there in part for being in her thrall and also that the picture of her biting her tongue and staying silent in the midst of political debate was distinctly implausible.[14]

In February 1792, Roland, at Brissot's invitation, entered into the Comité de Correspondance of the Jacobins, the function of which was to keep the allied clubs throughout the land up to date with developments in Paris. This resolved itself into a public relations exercise that Manon took on for her husband. Only a month later, Brissot, who, within the Legislative Assembly had a majority position thanks to the support of the moderates, offered Roland the immensely important portfolio of Minister of the Interior. Three days later, he swore allegiance to a king whose position had been seriously weakened by his botched attempt at fleeing the country with his family in June 1791. This had ended with his interception at Varennes (foreshadowed in a remarkable quatrain of Nostradamus's *Prophecies* of 1555).[15] Forms were preserved, however, with the fiction that the gallant burghers of Varennes had foiled an attempt by persons unknown intent on kidnapping the royal family.

War was one of the most divisive issues that affected the Jacobin Club and the Legislative Assembly. This came to a head with the Declaration of Pillnitz of August 27, 1791, in which the Austrian Emperor Leopold II and the Prussian King Frederick William II, burying hatchets long held, issued "a statement of principled opposition to the Revolution" and demanded that

Louis XVI – at the time under effective house arrest in the Tuileries – be placed, in Christopher Clark's words, "in a position to affirm in the most perfect liberty, the basis of monarchical government".[16] For the revolutionaries this was regarded as particularly provocative, and for the other European powers the Declaration put them on notice that Austria and Prussia saw in the Revolution possibilities of territorial aggrandisement.

The war party in France was led by the Girondins. Their opportunistic argument, as deployed by Jacques-Pierre Brissot, one with which Madame Roland was thoroughly sympathetic, ran as follows. The presence on the northern frontier of a clutch of émigrés led by one of Louis XVI's brothers, forming part, albeit small, of the Austrian and Prussian forces, gave to a pre-emptive strike strong justification. Furthermore, such a move would trigger republican uprisings in Prussia and Austria. Brissot had the support in the Legislative Assembly of the deputies occupying the middle ground, who were relishing the prospect of military success. The King, for his part, was convinced that war against the Prussian-Austrian alliance was bound to lead to the defeat of the revolutionary forces and open the way to a counter-revolutionary uprising in France. It was with this in mind that he did the Girondins' bidding and signed the declaration of war on April 10, 1792, incidentally targeting Marie-Antoinette's homeland.

Within the Club des Jacobins, the anti-war party was led by Robespierre. Displaying, it would seem, statesman-like caution, he was said to be concerned over the costs of such an enterprise at a time when the economy was weak, already depressed by poor harvests. More to the point, he expressed doubts about the steadfastness of a revolutionary army which could still be directed by a king through royalist sympathisers. Madame Roland herself was deputed to try to achieve some kind of reconciliation between the two groups. Over a lengthy dinner with Robespierre in April 1792 she exercised her persuasive powers to no avail. Robespierre's statement, quoted by her in her memoirs: "whoever held different views to his on the war was no sound citizen" ("quiconque pensait autrement que [lui] sur la guerre n'était pas bon citoyen"),[17] marked the start of a fierce struggle in the Legislative Assembly, whose ups and downs for the Girondins and the Jacobins mirrored the military successes/reverses on the ground, with the uncommitted members known mockingly as the Marais (marsh) shifting their support one way and the other.

Acceleration of the Revolution

With Roland plucked, as it were, from obscurity, and now a major figure in a wartime ministry, it was to be expected that Madame Roland's salon should have a fresh lease of life. This took the form of dinners for 12 to 20 in the ministerial apartment every Monday and Thursday, the guests being typically Girondins. Danton, Minister of Justice, a political bruiser with lax financial habits, was not included. This was to earn her a powerful enemy. But in the near term Roland took centre stage: four months of ministerial responsibilities, answerable to a king who excelled in obfuscation and dilatoriness, exposed Roland and the Girondins to heavy criticism from the Robespierre faction. In addition, the war was not going the way they had hoped. On June 10, 1792, the king received a lengthy letter detailing his monarchical shortcomings and outlining the measures that needed taking. It was signed by Roland but written by Manon at one stretch, as she proudly recorded.[18] This act of impertinence led predictably to Roland's dismissal and to the king forming an administration of moderates. The letter was read to the Legislative Assembly and copies were widely distributed throughout the country. If one wishes to single out a specific occasion when Manon influenced the course of the Revolution, this was it: the case for a constitutional monarchy was weakened and that for a republic enhanced.

Thereafter, the pace of change gathered speed:

- JUNE 20: 1792 militants from the Paris Sections invade the Tuileries and compel the king to don the Phrygian cap of liberty;
- JULY 11: the Legislative Assembly declares that the country is endangered and calls for nationwide mobilisation to meet internal counter-revolutionary threats and external military threats;
- AUGUST 9: the Paris Sections which make up the municipal Commune transform themselves into the Revolutionary Commune ("La Commune insurrectionnelle").
- AUGUST 10: the king is deposed and taken from the Tuileries;
- AUGUST 10: section militants, together with bands of patriots from Marseille and Brittany, attack and set fire to the Tuileries and massacre the Swiss guards;

- AUGUST 13: the king and his family are incarcerated in the Temple, the 12th-century building of the Templars, whose central tower served as a state prison;
- The Revolutionary Commune proceeds to dictate its demands to a cowed Legislative Assembly; this includes establishing a Central Supervisory Committee ("Comité central de Surveillance") having over-all control of the supervisory committees at the level of the Sections, all enjoying full powers of search and arrest;
- AUGUST 15: Robespierre, as head of a delegation of the Commune, de-mands the creation of Revolutionary Tribunals ("tribunaux populaires") for exacting vengeance on traitors;
- SEPTEMBER 2 to 7: prison massacres;
- SEPTEMBER 21: The Legislative Assembly is replaced by the National Convention ("Convention nationale") elected on the basis of universal male suffrage (servants excepted);
- SEPTEMBER 22: the Republic is proclaimed.

With the deposition of the king, Roland was once again given the impor-tant Interior portfolio, but instead of being answerable to the king he was answerable to the authority that had taken his place – which was in effect the Commune. As a municipal body, clearly defined geographically, whose writ was to extend to the whole country, this meant an extraordinary concentra-tion of power in a group that could only claim to represent citizens of Paris.

Roland was a member of the six-strong executive committee in the gov-ernment and he and Danton were required to confirm the decrees emanat-ing from the Revolutionary Tribunal made up of one delegate from each of the Paris Sections. The September prison massacres were of direct concern to him as Minister of the Interior. He undoubtedly shared his wife's view ex-pressed in a letter to the fellow Girondin, Henry Bancal: "You know well how enthusiastic I am about the Revolution. I'm ashamed of it. It is being debased by a bunch of scoundrels. It has become hideous" ("Vous connaissez mon enthousiasme pour la Révolution, et bien j'en ai honte! Elle est ternie par des scélérats, elle est devenue hideuse").[19] His own public pronouncements had to be more measured. The speech he promptly made before the Assemblée Nationale on September 3, printed and circulated to the 83 departments throughout the country as well as to the municipality of Paris and the 48 sections, is an energetic response to what was to be the first of six days of massacres: "Yesterday was a day over which it is perhaps best to draw a veil . . . But I know how easy it is for scoundrels, for traitors to misuse [revolutionary] enthusiasms". ("Hier fut un jour sur les développements duquel il faut peut-être laisser un voile . . . Mais je sais qu'il est facile à des scélérats, à des traîtres d'abuser de cette effervescence [révolutionnaire]").[20] He calls on the Commune – the mayor and the section heads – to take immediate action to end all lawlessness. His own powerlessness in the light of the support given to the massacres by his fellow ministers is vividly demonstrated in the lack of response to his urgent call for action. It also surfaces when he concludes with an undertaking to stay at his post, but only so long as he feels – and is seen by others – to be of use. He declares himself ready to resign if another were to be judged more effective. Throughout, Manon's hand is clearly visible.

The next three months were given over to the battle, no holds barred, waged between the Girondins and the Jacobins, each accusing the other of treachery and dictatorial ambitions. The sittings of the Convention provided the platform for the most dramatic confrontations, which in turn supplied copy for a plethora of pamphlets and commentaries for circulation throughout the land – in the production of which Manon will have often had a hand on the Girondin side. The numerical strength in deputies of the Girondins and their allies in the Convention reflected their provincial power base. Ultimately it proved illusory in the face of the Jacobins' dominance in Paris and Robespierre's ability to call on the extremist Section leaders and deploy the armed bands of the scornfully named "sans-culottes" patriots. Some historians point to the debate on November 5, 1792, as marking the start of the eclipse of the Girondins, when an attempt to deliver a lethal blow to Robespierre with a vote of censure backfired. The Jacobins – often known as La Montagne from the elevated position of their seats in the Convention hall – were quick to follow up their success. One month later, on a claim that Roland had links with a royalist group and that his wife had been compromised, she was required to answer the accusation herself before the Convention. This she did very effectively and with a fluency that silenced the accusers. A victory, but one which was to prove shortlived, since the Rolands were increasingly fulfilling the function of a lightning rod for Jacobin attacks on the Girondins. Roland's unbending financial rectitude, which had led him to refuse Marat the use of funds for propaganda purposes, earned him Marat's undying hatred. This in turn led to a sustained scurrilous campaign against the Rolands, much being made of the husband's advanced age and his wife's youthful allure. Danton, already hostile, was incensed by Roland's criticisms of his departmental finances. He led the attack in the Convention, all the more enthusiastically since the Rolands credited him with having encouraged the prison massacres.

The issue of what to do with the king raised questions that went beyond personal rivalries. In the event, Louis XVI was put on trial in December 1792, appearing for questioning before the Convention on December 11 and again on December 26, when his defence lawyer's address lasted three hours.[21] On January 17, 1793, he was condemned to death for conspiring against the state and threatening the freedom of the country. And on January 21 he was guillotined.

This stark recital disguises what was a tortuous process. Throughout, Robespierre was clear in his mind that Louis XVI deserved to die: it was enough that he bore the title of king. The Jacobins were therefore opposed to a trial because that might lead to an acquittal, an impossible outcome in view of his guilt by definition. The Girondins, who were united in the need for a trial, had divided views on capital punishment. Furthermore, many were uncomfortable with a decision that would be made in Paris – in practice by 48 more often than not extremist Sections – and one that ignored the more conservative views held in many of the 83 Departments across the country. Such a call to the people was seen – correctly – as a delaying tactic. But the tide was running strongly against any postponement and the Convention was swimming with the tide.

On January 15, out of 718 deputies, 691 pronounced the king guilty, 27 abstained. On the motion calling for a countrywide vote, 424 were against and only 281 in favour. And then the sentence: out of 721 votes, 366 for the death penalty. This was followed by a recount, which produced 387 for the death penalty, of which 26 carried a reprieve, giving 361 voting for prompt execution against 360. Hence the notorious result: Louis XVI was condemned to death by a majority of one.[22]

The Girondins were left seriously weakened, largely because of their inability to present a common front; this stood in sharp contrast to the unity of the Montagne. On January 22, Roland, deserted by his fellow Girondins and at odds with the other members of the Executive Committee, resigned his portfolio. The draft of his letter, almost entirely in his wife's hand, survives.

Imprisonment

The Rolands had every incentive to leave Paris and return to Roland's family base at Villefranche. For this, Roland needed the Convention to approve his ministerial accounts. His opponents were delighted to prevaricate and keep him on a string, ignoring his repeated requests. The Rolands lived under the growing threat of arrest or assassination. The Girondins' fortunes were clearly on the wane, the latest setback having been their failure to secure a vote of condemnation in the Convention against Marat. It came therefore as no great surprise when on May 31, 1793, six men arrived at Roland's door with a warrant for his arrest; it was signed by the Revolutionary Committee ("Comité révolutionnaire"), which had been constituted the day before by the Jacobin deputies. Roland, having vigorously refused to accept the legality of the warrant, took advantage of an opportunity to take refuge in the house of Louis Bosc. Manon, for her part, rushed to the Convention hall with a view to protesting her husband's innocence, but was not given a hearing. Shortly after returning to their apartment, she received a fresh delegation, this time wielding two warrants, one from the Commune and the other from the newly formed Revolutionary Committee, for the arrest of both Roland and his wife. Seals were affixed throughout the apartment.

She was taken to the Abbaye Prison and given a sordid prison cell – but she was on her own and also had the great privileges of a table, chair, bed and blanket. The prison governor and his wife went out of their way, furthermore, to mitigate discomforts, enabling her, for instance, to see visitors in their own quarters. One early visitor was Grandpré, the Inspector of Prisons, who had been appointed to this post by Roland when Minister of the Interior. For a while, this connection was to help soften the rigours of prison life. Such hope that Manon may have had of a rapid release – she had written immediately in protest against her arbitrary incarceration – were dashed with the news that on June 2 the Convention delegates had been terrorised into ordering the arrest of some 29 prominent Girondins by a 40,000-strong body

of armed sans-culottes patriots fulfilling the role of the national guard; they
were under the orders of the Revolutionary Committee. In effect, this was a
coup d'état, orchestrated by Robespierre and Marat, which left the Jacobins
with the field to themselves. {The period known as "La Terreur" extends from
May 31, 1793, marking the fall of the Girondins, to July 27, 1794, *le 9 Thermidor*
– the fall of Robespierre}.

In the meantime, Roland having managed to avoid arrest in Paris,
worked his way to Rouen where he had lived in his youth and was given
refuge by loyal friends. His sense of loss would have been greatly intensified by Manon's revelation, made to him in the course of 1792, that she had
fallen deeply in love with somebody five years her younger – whose identity
was established some 50 years later, when the letters of Manon Roland and
François Buzot, the prominent Girondist, came into the public domain. As
she was a true follower of Rousseau, an honest admission to her husband was
required of her. At the same time, her virtuous disposition and her respect
for the condition of marriage will have prevented the liaison from taking
on the characteristics of an affair. Then came imprisonment which reduced
any contacts to smuggled letters. To this effect, Marianne Cornevin quotes
a passage from Manon's own writings.[23] "We were both ready to embark on
an ardent love affair, but we both decided to follow the path of virtue. I truly
believe that abiding by the moral code in love gives rise to the most beautiful
of all passions and the most deeply felt. Take morality out of love, what's left
but lust reduced to physical needs. Insist on its inclusion, and it becomes
the most fruitful and purest source of great ideals and noble actions" (Nous
étions donc tous les deux prêts à vivre une grande passion, mais tous les deux
décidés à respecter les barrières de la vertu. Je crois bien que ce respect du
moral de l'amour crée justement les passions les plus belles et les plus écla-
tantes; ôtez ce moral, tout n'est qu'appétit et se réduit aux besoins physiques;
exigez-le, il devient la source la plus féconde et la plus pure des grandes ver-
tus et des belles actions.) Emotionally, this, the first great love of her life,
was somehow fulfilling and liberating. Her letter to François Buzot from the
Abbaye Prison dated June 22 sets the tone: "Don't you also understand that
by finding myself on my own it's with you that I'm living" ("mais ne vois-tu
pas aussi qu'en me trouvant seule c'est avec toi que je demeure").[24]

She still entertained hopes that the Girondins outside Paris might break the stranglehold of the Jacobins in Paris. And, only two days after writing to Buzot, her spirits soared when the authorities released her from the Abbaye Prison. Taking a hackney coach, she arrived at her apartment only to be arrested a second time: the Committee of General Security ("Comité de sûreté générale"), created in April, 1793, was intent on correcting a legal deficiency in the earlier warrants, which had overlooked giving the reasons for her arrest.

Her new prison, Sainte Pélagie, situated near the Jardin des Plantes, had escaped the September massacres, thanks to a courageous act of the prison governor and his wife. On learning that they were next in line for a visit from the rioters, the governor handed over the keys to the prisoners and instructed them to simulate a mass break-out.[25] This included tying the two of them up securely. Their gamble worked and the rioters, deeply disappointed at finding no victims, went on to another target, but first released the governor and his wife. The prison at this time had a population of some 350.[26] It was also noted for its squalor. Manon did, however, secure a cell on her own and gain access to writing materials. As at l'Abbaye, money secured some privileges. She obtained the services of a prisoner who acted as lady's maid. She benefited from the generosity of Madame Bouchard, the governmor's wife, being able to spend much of the day in her quarters – where she received visitors – to enjoy her cuisine and at one stage to have the use of a piano.[27] This removed her from the proximity of her fellow women inmates – often thieves and prostitutes – and the attentions of those men prisoners who made a point of communicating with the women's side. The special privileges that Manon enjoyed were at a later stage curtailed, but by then the quality of the prisoners, men and women, had risen by dint of the fact that the Jacobin purges encompassed many well educated revolutionary opponents, whose wives often shared the same fate as their husbands.

Prison Writing

In this prison environment, Manon once again became an active correspondent and also set to work on her memoirs. At l'Abbaye she had already written the bulk of her *Portraits and Anecdotes*. These involved a detailed account of the period leading up to and including her arrest and her early prison experiences. The narrative is enlivened with spirited sketches of such revolutionary figures as Danton, whom she thoroughly detested; Robespierre, whom she initially admired for his uncompromisingly revolutionary enthusiasms, while overlooking a lack of personal courage and ahead of his espousal of terrorism; and Mirabeau, whose death deprived the Revolution in her view of the balanced leader it needed. In these writings there is a sense of Manon taking advantage of her enforced leisure in order to set the political record straight.

The switch to Sainte Pélagie also brought about a change of emphasis in her writings. It was there that she wrote her *Personal Memoirs*, starting in mid-August following the events of August 10th. The pattern that had evolved was for her to complete a section and surreptitiously hand it to one of her visitors, often Bosc, and if not him Sophie Cannet, and latterly Brissot's close friend, Edmé Mentelle – all packets being for safe keeping by Bosc. The hugely deflating experience of a mere two hours of freedom on June 24 and the absence of any indication that the Jacobin momentum might be reversed had effectively quenched her few remaining hopes. The sense of urgency is conveyed in her entry dated September 5, 1793: "I cut the sheet to enclose what I have written in the little box; for when I see a revolutionary army decreed, new tribunals formed for shedding innocent blood, famine impending and the tyrants at bay, I augur that they must have new victims, and conclude that no one is sure of living another day" (as printed in the English translation published in 1795).

The *Personal Memoirs* are conditioned by the aim of complete honesty that she had given herself. In a letter written not long before her execution, she explained: "Je crois que je suis perdue; sans cette croyance, je ne prendrais pas la peine de me confesser. J'ai fait mon calcul et pris mon parti; je dirai tout, absolument tout, ce n'est que comme cela qu'on peut être utile."[28] (I feel there is no hope for me; without this belief why should I take the trouble to make my 'confession' . . . I have weighed things up and made my decision; I shall say everything, absolutely everything; it's only that way that I can make myself useful). One notable omission: the name of the man she loved. As her editor, Paul Faugère, comments, she also seems to have had the ability to view herself from the standpoint of an outside observer. This extends to quoting the disobliging comment of the Jacobin, Camille Desmoulins, when he expressed surprise that "given her age and her lack of beauty" she should still have managed to have admirers. On her own assessment, she responds to those who interest her – not the case with the Desmoulins of this world – and that gets translated into animation and sparkle.[29]

Those are also the qualities that characterise her *Personal Memoirs*. They form a remarkable document that extends to vignettes that match those of Madame de Sévigné in their vividness and humour; portraiture sometimes fulsome, sometimes gently critical, sometimes acerbic; bursts of indignation at perceived injustices; most of all, recollections taken from all stages of her life whether it be of events, of opinions held at different times, of the ups and downs of an existence that mixed obscurity with prominence – all of this at a rapid pace. As she comments at one point, several years of meditation are being compressed into a few words ("Je trace en peu de mots le résultat de quelques années de méditation"). But perhaps the single feature that distinguishes Madame Roland's memoirs from those of other writers is the stark honesty of somebody counting the hours to her execution.

Her childhood memories take in the onset of puberty – as a flower in bloom – which she recalls as having filled her with a certain joy.[30] Other manifestations – possibly contrary to religious teaching – presented her with a tortuous problem. It was with great difficulty that she evolved a formula for the confessional that would minimise her embarrassment and at the same time satisfy the need for openness vis-à-vis the Lord: "Father, I confess to having experienced emotions that run contrary to Christian chastity" ("Je m'accuse d'avoir eu des mouvements contraires a la chasteté chrétienne"). She felt that Archimedes, finding the solution to the principle of the lever, could not have derived greater satisfaction than she did from this prescription. Elsewhere she gives an explicit account of a narrow escape she had as a young girl as a result of an encounter with an aroused apprentice in her father's engraving shop.[31]

The protracted process of finding her a husband includes six pages of sustained hilarity over the candidature of a doctor, M. Gardanne. He started at a disadvantage since Manon had difficulty being drawn to a man in full medical fig; he also had heavy dark eyebrows that nearly met, and spoke in the sing-song accent of the South. Her father, doing what was expected of a responsible parent, made enquiries in Provence concerning the background and habits of M. Gardanne's family. With what might be viewed as tactless zeal, he even extended his investigations to include the family's servants. That finished off the hapless Gardanne and rejoiced Manon.[32]

A feature of the *Memoirs* is the way Manon as an adult gradually increased in self-confidence, while at the same time resolutely staying in the background. She talks of 12 years working in tandem with Roland, to start with tentatively on his scientific publications, and later, much more significantly, in his political career.[33] By the close, when he was by the standards of the day an elderly man, it can be said that he was lost without her. She notes in her *Memoirs*, in an amused way, how he would derive pleasure from a turn of phrase or a course of argument as being of his creation when in fact they were hers. Once she had renounced the view that women writers should be heard but not seen, the objective of anonymity was jettisoned. How else can one explain the intensely personal recollections, some of them cited earlier, whose modern ring is startling?. And this is what gives the writings of a woman of the eighteenth century such astonishing force today.

The Guillotine

Twenty-one Girondin leaders whose arrest had come on June 2 came up for trial at the Conciergerie on October 24. Manon, still at Sainte Pélagie, had been able to attend. In the optimistic hope of being called upon as a witness – an opportunity she was denied – she had prepared a powerful submission. On October 31 20 were executed, one having committed suicide the night before. That same day, Manon was moved to the Conciergerie.

With her characteristic energy she set about making records of the two interrogations to which she was subjected, preparing her "Projet de Défense", the speech she hoped to deliver in court – and was prevented from so doing – and making arrangements in a long letter for Eudora. But much of her time was spent sustaining the spirits of her fellow prisoners. There are several eye witness accounts of those last eight days of her life, which were marked by an astonishing (outward) serenity that so focused attention on this elegant woman that she captured the wondering admiration of men and women alike.[34] Those who knew her little or not at all were struck by the great purity of her diction and her natural musical delivery. In the women's courtyard at the Conciergerie, where a metal grille separates women from the men, Manon would go over to this barrier and, as it were, hold court, expounding her views on her beloved Revolution and her distress at its de-filement.[35] One fellow prisoner, Comte Beugnot, sums up his experience in his memoirs: "J'éprouvais chaque jour un charme nouveau à l'entendre, moins par ce qu'elle disait, que par la magie de son débit" (Her presence was such that, day by day, I found myself enchanted, not so much by her argument, but rather by the magic of her delivery). And when, on November 8, she was summoned to take her place in the open cart that was to carry her to the Place de la Révolution (today's Place de la Concorde), she gently chided the greatly affected man who was to share the same transport with her when he failed to give her precedence.

But on arrival, it was she who gave up her rights to being executed first so as to shorten the distress of her companion. And then on mounting the scaffold her memorable apostrophe to Frédéric Lemot's huge plaster statue close to the guillotine. "Oh Liberty, how numerous are the crimes we commit in your name" ("O Liberté, que de crimes on commet en ton nom").

Roland, who heard the news of her death on November 10, took his own life that day. Buzot did the same seven months later.

Publication

The two months between April 9, 1795 and June 8, 1795 saw publication in Paris of the four part *Appel a l'impartiale postérité par la citoyenne Roland* ("An appeal to impartial posterity by Madame Roland, wife of the Minister of the Interior or, A collection of tracts written by her during her confinement in the prisons of the Abbey and St Pélagie"). Louis Bosc, the editor, explains his inability to produce the whole work in one run, due to slowness of printing at that date as well as to the views of a number of friends.[36] This disguises prudent considerations when it comes to her political anecdotes and concern over what might be judged as shocking revelations when it comes to her personal memoirs. It was "published for the benefit of her only Daughter deprived of the Fortune of her Parents by Sequestration". Also in 1795, *An Appeal to Impartial Posterity* . . . appeared in an English translation in two octavo volumes printed for J. Johnston, St Paul's Churchyard, again for the benefit of Eudora.

In death, it can be said that Madame Roland was well served when Louis Bosc achieved prompt publication of her historical notes and personal memoirs – to which she had come to attach so much importance – within little more than a year of her execution. Subsequent editions appeared in 1800, 1820, 1823, and 1840. Paul Faugère's two-volume edition of 1864, however, is the first to have been strictly based on the original manuscript, held by Eudora and made available to him for a year. This enabled him to restore Bosc's cautious cuts.[37] It was also in 1864 that he was able to quote from several of Manon's prison letters to Buzot, thereby removing all doubt as to the identity of the man she loved.

It remains to record that the statue to Liberty to which Manon addressed her last words survived until it was taken down on March 20, 1800, on the orders of the consuls, the first consul at that time being Napoleon Bonaparte.[38]

||||||||||||||||||||||||||||||||||||||||||||||||||||||||||||||||||||||||||||||||||||||

CHAPTER XIV

Antoine Lavoisier
(1743–1794)

Incarcerations

Port Libre – ci-devant Port Royal	*November 8 – December 21, 1793*
Hotel des Fermes	*December 21, 1793 – May 5, 1794*
Conciergerie	*May 5 – 8, 1794*

"If clear grasp of its implications be accepted as the test of a discovery, Lavoisier was the discoverer of oxygen" (Charles Singer).[1] "Priestley discovered the gas Lavoisier named oxygen while experimenting with the air given off by the red precipitate of mercury" (Arthur Donavan).[2] "Few, if any, of Lavoisier's experiments in the whole course of his career were entirely original; he followed up the work of others, expanded it, and gave it significance". (J. A. Cochran).[3]

The consequential dethroning of water as one of the four elements identified by Aristotle and its recognition as a compound substance had massive reverberations in the scientific world. It is little wonder that scientists of the day fought each other vigorously in staking their claims to pre-eminence in the evolving researches and experiments. As early as 1772, Lavoisier, then 29, sought to protect his interests by preparing a report on his initial experiments; as a scientist who throughout his career was assiduous in tests and meticulous in analysis, he was still some distance away from reaching any firm conclusions. But, as he engagingly writes, "J'étais jeune, j'étais avide de gloire, et je crus devoir prendre quelques précautions pour m'assurer la propriété de ma découverte"[4] (I was young, hungry for glory, and I thought I should take some steps to secure ownership of my discovery). He goes on to comment that within scientific circles Anglo-French rivalry was sometimes leading to false attributions.

In this 1772 report, however, Lavoisier did praise the insights of one Jean Rey, who in 1630 had deduced the role of a gas, subsequently called oxygen, without the benefit of extended scientific experimentation.[5] But at the same time Lavoisier took care to point out that Rey's insight had only come to his attention after he had composed his own report some 142 years later. In the field of medicine, there is a rough parallel with Michael Servetus divining the circulation of the blood in 1553 and William Harvey's full exposition of the functioning of the heart in 1628. On November 1, 1772, Lavoisier handed his report to the secretary of the Académie des Sciences, with instructions that the seal should be broken only after he, Lavoisier, had published his findings.

The Académie des Sciences, founded in 1666 by Colbert as a counterpart to the Royal Society in London, was already central to Lavoisier's work. His first connection came in 1766 with his winning first prize in a competition for the best method of lighting the streets of a large town. Two years later, as a 25-year-old, he was elected a member of this august body of some 50 members which served as a forum for inventors thereby enabling them to present their findings at its weekly sessions. It also provided the government with the means to assess the worth or otherwise of a host of innovations, projects, phenomena. Over the ensuing 25 years, Lavoisier produced on average eight reports a year (some in collaboration with other members).[6] In 1783, Lavoisier was one of eight members called upon to report on the Montgolfier brothers' "aerostatic machine", a subject on which his own researches made him

Antoine Laurent Lavoisier and his wife Marie Anne Pierette Paulze
by Jacques-Louis David

exceptionally qualified. He later had to pass judgment on the curative powers claimed for Mesmer's "animal magnetism". The first received his strong endorsement, the second his rejection. And it was in 1785 that Lavoisier presented his formal demonstration to the Académie des Sciences that set out to prove that water was a compound of hydrogen and oxygen. It was in this paper that he made what British scientists regarded as slighting references to the work done on gases – some published as early as 1766 – by Henry Cavendish (1731 – 1810) and Joseph Priestley (1733 – 1804).[7]

Not content with his absorbing scientific work, in May 1768 Lavoisier had embarked on a demanding career, becoming in effect a tax gatherer. He bought a junior partnership in the syndicate known as the Fermiers Généraux (The Company of Tax Farmers) – which had nothing to do with agriculture but everything to do with the long-established practice of the French Crown of farming out the collection of taxes: indirect taxes on products such as salt (the gabelle tax) and tobacco, customs duties, sales and excise taxes. These were covered at one stage by over 130 leases, usually renewable every six years, according to which the syndicate members undertook to pay the government a fixed annual sum. Making use of an army of tax collectors, they then secured the dues from which they paid themselves a salary for their administrative role and enjoyed a profit distribution for their risk-taking. The final amount reflected the difference between collection costs and tax receipts, once the payments to the government had been taken care of. While this is a much simplified account of a complex undertaking, it helps to explain the considerable financial benefits that could accrue to the "fermiers" arising out of efficiency and/or abuse of the system.

It does not appear that Lavoisier's name was associated with any of the malpractices. What he was doing was adding to an already comfortable financial position. This greatly increased wealth enabled him to meet heavy costs incurred in the course of his scientific investigations in materials and equipment. An inventory of his laboratory, which was made in 1794, included 250 measuring devices, many of them the work of two craftsmen, Mégnié and Fortin, skilled in the manufacture of the extremely sensitive instruments required for Lavoisier's experiments.[8] The Musée National des Arts et Métiers holds many of them, where they form an attractive and impressive display.

In his role as a "fermier", his effectiveness as an administrator was increasingly recognised. This led to his appointment in 1775 as one of four with responsibility for the production and sale of gunpowder, a government monopoly. The appointment carried with it right of residence in a large apartment at the Arsenal next to which he was able to set up his own laboratory, a huge aid to his research. This also provided his wife, who became a close collaborator in his work, with the opportunity of establishing what amounted to a "salon" for scientists, who were able to meet a convenient two steps away from her husband's workplace. A plaque marking the site of the gunpowder depot honours Pierre Vieille, who a century later was to perfect the powder used in canons. The earlier association with Lavoisier is not mentioned.

A striking instance of Madame Lavoisier's devotion to her husband's interests came in 1787 when she translated *An Essay on Phlogiston* by the English scientist, Richard Kirwan, phlogiston being presented as the combustible force embedded in Aristotle's four elements. Marie-Anne Lavoisier's translation was then published in France with an introduction by Lavoisier and notes by him and professional colleagues, criticising page by page Kirwan's thesis. A point worth noting: the debate was conducted in forceful – at times patronising – terms behind a veil of courtesy. A representative passage from Kirwan's book reads: "Nor have the labours of the antiphlogistians been useless; both Mr.Lavoisier and Berthollet, by carefully distinguishing the component parts, particularly of nitrous air, have thrown great light on the subject, though by neglecting the essential part, namely the phlogiston, they have obliged me to differ from them in some particulars."[9]

In 1785, Lavoisier was assigned the task of recommending the rationalisation of weights and measures. Also in 1785 he was appointed the Director for that year of the Fermiers Généraux. In the leap year 1784, as recorded in the Almanach Royal, the fermiers généraux numbered 45, two being Lavoisier and his father-in-law Jacques Paulze. In the 1780s he had also found time to devote to the management of Fréchines, the estate not far from Blois that he had bought in 1778; he set about converting it into a model farm into which he introduced enlightened employment practices. The year 1789 saw him heavily involved in furthering the diffusion of a totally new chemical nomenclature, developed by the chemist Guyton de Morveau, which Lavoisier adopted in his textbook *Traité Elémentaire de Chimie*.

To quote Arthur Donovan: "Lavoisier was more than a scientist who also took on administrative work or an administrator with an active interest in science. He was, more fundamentally, an unusually competent, ambitious, energetic, and methodical man, whose personal style was marked by a high degree of public spirit and a great respect for detail and rational procedure."[10]

Against this background, it might seem strange that Lavoisier should have incurred the wrath of the revolutionaries. For this there are three principal explanations. In the first instance, he qualified as a member of the nobility – though by recent purchase rather than through long-established inheritance. In 1772, his father, Jean-Antoine, bought the post with the grandiloquent title of "Conseiller-secrétaire du roi, maison, finances, et couronne de France" from the incumbent. This was one of the more sought-after positions out of a total of some 4,000 such posts which were then in existence as virtual sinecures.[11] These had the important attribute of conveying noble status to their possessors and to their descendants. Lavoisier's father's death in 1775 propelled him into that status, though Lavoisier himself seems to have made little overt use of his enhanced social position.[12]

More importantly, as a member of the Fermiers Généraux he was a tax gatherer. From biblical times – and before that no doubt – tax gatherers have been shunned and in this instance the affluence of the "fermiers" gave rise to many claims of embezzlement and of exploitation of the defenceless citizenry. A typical attack on the Fermiers Généraux was J. B. Darigrand's *L'anti-financier*, first published in 1763, in which he charged them with widespread corruption. Circumstantial evidence – on the ground, as it were – was readily to hand in Paris in the rue de Thorigny, where in 1656–58 Pierre Aubert de Fontenay had built what was at the time the largest private Hôtel in the Marais: he had the contract for "*les gabelles*" and this had secured for his magnificent residence the epithet l'Hôtel Salé'.

The third and perhaps most powerful source of antagonism was the indiscriminate hostility of such revolutionary groups as the Jacobins to the past regime and their enthusiasm at rooting out all vestiges of the old order, the Académie des Sciences being one of many. At a personal level, Lavoisier's rejection of a scientific paper submitted by Marat to the Académie des Sciences some years previously had earned him that vindictive man's enduring hatred.

On March 27, 1791, the National Assembly cancelled its contract with the Fermiers Généraux. Cancellation carried with it the requirement that the Ferme's final accounts be submitted according to a deadline of January 1, 1793.[13] The exercise was greatly complicated by the National Assembly's decision to have the accounts backdated to July 1, 1789. The task was given to a Liquidation Committee of six fermiers, not on this occasion including Lavoisier. At the same time, the fermiers were required to continue trading, since their agents were still recovering taxes.

On June 5, 1792, the Liquidating Committee was disbanded.[14] This about-face was prompted by a groundswell of hostility reflecting the popular view, fanned by the ultras among the revolutionaries, that between 300m and 400m livres was owed to the Treasury – money needed urgently, which might slip away in support of the Bourbons given any further "deliberate" delays by the fermiers.

In the light of the increasingly hostile atmosphere, Lavoisier felt it wise to adopt a lower profile and in August 1792 he resigned from the Gunpowder Committee. With this went his lodgings in the Arsenal and the adjoining laboratory which he had occupied since 1776; he moved to a house in the rue de la Madeleine. August 1793 saw the abolition of the Académie des Sciences, in line with the suppression of all learned societies.

Under a decree dated September 27, 1793, of the Convention Nationale (a successor of the Assemblée Legislative and before that of the Assemblée Nationale)) the much set-upon Liquidation Committee was re-activated, Lavoisier being included this time.[15] They were made answerable to a five strong commission set up as a Revising Committee, composed of five former employees of the Ferme, one of whom had been previously convicted of embezzlement and falsification of accounts – not that this debarred him from his new supervisory role. Those on the Committee were given in addition the incentive of rewards whose size would be determined by the scale of the malpractices they uncovered.[16] The Revising Committee reported to two deputies of the Convention, one named Jack, who made a cameo appearance in this role, the other Dupin, who occupied the stage throughout. Dupin, known in his pre-revolutionary guise as André-Simon-Olivier Dupin de Beaumont, had had previous experience of the ferme as "contrôleur général". This new investigative layer was aimed at speeding up the reporting process, with the revolutionaries taking for granted that the fermiers constituted a fraternity of financial leaches soaking up money that belonged to the Republic.[17] A view endorsed by Joseph Cambon, the man behind the creation in 1793 of the "Grand Livre de la Dette Publique", who told the Convention Nationale that he expected to recover 300 million livres from the Fermiers. Dupin was happy to respond to the hue and cry. A revised deadline of April 1, 1794, was given the fermiers.

But on November 8, 1793, patriotic impatience boiled over with the arrest of 32 fermiers on charges of corruption, Lavoisier included.

Imprisonment

Initially, incarceration was in the former Jansenist convent in Paris known as Port Royal. This had been renamed Port Libre to accommodate revolutionary susceptibilities. Its use as a house of detention may be an instance of gallows humour, were it not for the fact that any type of humour is hard to credit to the revolutionaries in power since May 1793 when Robespierre inaugurated the period known as "La Terreur". "Port Libre ci-devant Port

Royal" had more recently served as a maternity hospital. It lent itself to its use as what might now be termed an "open prison", where supervision was light and discomforts tolerable. The inmates, two to a room, were able to communicate freely, while they had access to friends and relations.

The very day following his admission, Lavoisier took up afresh the literary work that had absorbed much of his time in lieu of the scientific experiments which had ceased to be feasible with his loss of the use of the laboratory in the Arsenal.[18] His objective was to assemble the papers presented to the Académie des Sciences over the previous 20 years and to include work from other sources by scientists who were supportive of his own findings. As planned, it was to be an eight-volume work entitled *Mémoires de Chimie*.

Work on the accounts, on the other hand, came swiftly to a halt, with the imprisoned fermiers unable to have access to the archives held in their old headquarters. This obstacle was removed six weeks later when Lavoisier and his fellow prisoners were moved to that very building, l'Hôtel des Fermes, rue de Grenelle-St Honoré, which had also been converted into a house of detention.

There was no interruption to his literary work. In the ensuing four and a half months, Lavoisier, with some help from his wife and Armand Séguin, a colleague of long standing, made preparations for a new edition of an earlier work, *Opuscules physiques et chimiques*. The *Mémoires de Chimie* made rapid progress: by the start of May 1794, the first two volumes and a fragment of the third had already gone to the printers and were available in sheets. At the same time, Lavoisier had become a crucial contributor in the defence of the Ferme. The priorities of prisoners threatened with capital punishment eventually pushed his scientific writing into deep shadow.

During the course of January 1794, all the worldly goods of the fermiers were put under seal.[19] This might have been seen as evidence of how the wind was blowing, but many still felt they had a strong case.[20] Lavoisier was less sanguine: in a letter to his wife dated December 19, 1793, he had already warned against undue optimism.

On January 27, 1794, the Ferme's own Memoir of Justification was delivered to Dupin.[21] Spirits ran high: after all, they had produced their report well ahead of the April 1, 1794, deadline and they knew that the accounts were in very good order. On Dupin's strong advice, however, the report was given no wider distribution, on the grounds that this might prejudice opinion against them.[22] This document was essentially the work of Lavoisier. It was a vigorous rejection of all charges, notably those relating to (a) interest irregularities, (b) "deliberate obfuscation" reflected in the earlier failure to meet deadlines, (c) most important of all –and most eye-catching – falsification of tobacco trading figures by reason of the leaves being wringing wet; the details, which take up six pages of the Rapport des Commissaires, make for some lively reading.

Ever since the appointment of the Revising Committee, the fermiers had received numerous demands for information and clarification, a flow that showed no sign of lessening, rather the reverse. Much of the time, it betrayed the Committee members' ignorance of the inevitably complex accounting practices of the Ferme, giving rise therefore to patient explanatory notes. Other instances were simply vexatious, as when production of material that harked back 19 years – whose very existence moreover was open to doubt – was demanded, for delivery within eight days.[23]

Some two months later, the Revising Committee's own report was submitted by Dupin to the Convention Nationale. It was a hotchpotch: a 60-page report, followed by 44 supporting documents ("pièces justificatives") running to 127 pages, bolstered by numerous tables. Included at certain points were occasional passages taken from the Memoir of the fermiers. The copy before me is said to have belonged to Dupin himself. The startling conclusion reached by the Revising Committee was that, when added up, the Fermiers Généraux owed the State 130m livres.[24] While representing an "improvement" on Cambon's 300m livres, there was little evidence that the defence had been taken seriously.

Notwithstanding numerous assurances given by Dupin to the families of the accused that they had nothing to fear, on May 5, 1794, Dupin presented his final report, which required an initial restitution of 22m livres and called for the fermiers to be brought to judgment before the sinister Revolutionary Tribunal, which held court in the Conciergerie under Fouquier-Tinville.[25] The order for the transfer to the Conciergerie of the prisoners who were destined to stand trial before the Tribunal was given by Fouquier-Tinville two days before Dupin's report had even been released, an "irregularity" that did not go unnoticed.[26] At the trial on May 8, Coffinhal, vice-president of the Revolutionary Tribunal and presiding judge, reportedly guided the jury with the phrase "The Revolution has no need of scientists" – perhaps apocryphal, but too good a comment to dismiss out of hand.[27] Later the same day, Lavoisier, Paulz and 26 colleagues were executed; he was 50 years old, his father-in-law 75. The last piece of prison writing to have survived is a letter to his cousin, Auger de Villers, sent a day or two before his death.

Fifteen weeks later, on July 27, 1794, Robespierre was overthrown, bringing to an end the 14-month-long period of oppression under "La Terreur". "Le 9 thermidor an II" remains one of the pivotal dates of the Revolution.

On May 8, 1795, being the first anniversary of the guillotining of the fermiers, Dupin was to be found on the rostrum of the Convention nationale in what amounted to an expiatory declaration covering the events of a year previously. "Jai le Coeur navré plus que je ne puis vous l'exprimer, en vous disant que le décret que la Convention Nationale a rendu sur mon rapport, au nom des trois comités, a été le tocsin de la mort pour les Fermiers Généraux"[28] (My distress is more than I can express when I tell you that the decree issued by the Convention on the basis of my report and in the name of the three committees sounded the death knell for the Fermiers Généraux). While lamenting the judgment of the jury, he explained his own predicament in that he was being denounced as a creature of the fermiers for the delay in bringing them to justice. In short, his own skin was only to be saved if he orchestrated the executions required of him by Robespierre.

Soon thereafter, on July 11, 1795 the following pamphlet was published: *Dénonciation présentée au Comité de Législation de la Convention Nationale, contre le Représentant du Peuple Dupin, par les Veuves et Enfants des ci-devants Fermiers Généraux*, a 16-page document signed by George-Montclou, fils; Pauline veuve Lavoisier; Pignon, veuve de la Haye; Papillon-Sannois, fils de Papillon-d'Autroche. In addition to pointing out the methods Dupin employed to snuff out all explanations and clarifications given by the fermiers, it was accompanied by a 28-page *Addition à la Denonciation*, largely concerned with Dupin's role in the disposal of the prison possessions of the fermiers. One can safely assume that Madame Lavoisier was the driving force behind this powerful *Dénonciation*.

Dupin was arrested on August 13, 1795, on the grounds that he was both an assassin and a thief.[29] Soon afterwards, however, he regained his freedom under the general amnesty declared in October 1795.[30] He died some 25 years later.

The final accounting for the Ferme, released in 1806, gave effect to vigorous rebuttals to the original charges: far from owing the Republic 130m livres, the fermiers were themselves owed 8m livres.[31]

It now remains to be seen how Lavoisier's scientific writings from prison were to bear posthumous fruit. The new edition of *Opuscules physiques et chimiques* appeared in 1801. The *Mémoires de Chimie* had a longer gestation period. Lavoisier's widow had originally contemplated publication of the two volumes and a fragment of the third, which as noted earlier were already in existence as printed sheets at the author's death, in an edition to which Armand Séguin was to contribute an introduction. But when Séguin's proposed preface failed to include condemnation of Lavoisier's executioners and also presented Lavoisier and Séguin as more or less equal collaborators, she demurred.

It was only in 1805 that Lavoisier's *Mémoires de Chimie* appeared in two volumes, with a two-page introduction supplied by his widow.[32] Her 11-year delay since his death owes much to her impoverishment in the immediate aftermath of Lavoisier's execution, with all her assets sequestered. (She was eventually destined to inherit the fortunes of both her father and her husband.) It can also be explained in part by her hesitation over arranging for the publication of an incomplete work of a scientist well known for his meticulous professional standards. Her scruples were overcome with the inclusion of Lavoisier's 1785 report claiming as his the new chemical theory as to the compound nature of water.[33] As she writes, "C'est donc un devoir envers lui que de fixer l'opinion des savants sur cette vérité" (To establish this scientific truth is an obligation that we owe him). She was also thereby fulfilling the instructions that her husband gave, aged 29, when he handed to the secretary of the Académie des Sciences a sealed envelope that was only to be opened on publication of his findings. In the event, publication was a pious act, with no volumes for sale and all copies sent by Madame Lavoisier to prominent figures of the day. The British Library copy bears an inscription in both volumes, that in volume one being "Donné par la veuve de l'auteur à M. Guillaume van Nieuwerkerke à Paris octobre 1805". On the guard paper, the naturalist, W. C. Trevelyan, has written "This work, the sheets that were collected after the beheading of the author in 1794 and was (sic) done up in two volumes, for presentation to the scientific world – was given to me by Mr. Dr. Nieuwerkerke to whom it had been presented by the widow of Lavoisier".

||||||||||||||||||||||||||||||||||||||||||||||||||||||||||||||||||||||||||||||||

CHAPTER XV

André Chénier

(1762–1794)

Incarcerations

Luxembourg	*March 7 – 8, 1794*
Saint-Lazare Prison	*March 8 – July 24, 1794*
Conciergerie	*July 24 – 25, 1794*

Saint-Lazare

Originally a medieval hospital for lepers, by the time of the Revolution Saint-Lazare had taken on the character of a large monastery run by the monastic order founded in 1632 by St Vincent de Paul. More recently, one function it served was as a lock-up for "les jeunes gens de famille dont les moeurs étaient déréglées" (for those young coming from good families who had slipped into bad habits).[1] On the expulsion of the monks it was designated a prison, receiving its first consignment of inmates on January 18, 1794. Two weeks later, following an intake of 391 prisoners, the prison population amounted to 625.[2]

Chénier was first of all destined for imprisonment in the Palais du Luxembourg, but was turned away for lack of space, a familiar problem that the hard pressed governors of Paris prisons had to confront during the period of the "Terreur". At Saint-Lazare, he found a prison population that was mixed, with a preponderance from the professional and artisan classes and no more than a leavening of those judged to be aristocrats. Women, of whom there were about 100, occupied the first floor, some with young children; men occupied the two other floors.[3] Prisoners were typically two to three to a cell. The regime was initially relaxed, having much in common with that experienced by Lavoisier in Port Royal, notably in respect of ease of contact between prisoners and of access to outside visitors. In a letter dated February 17, 1794,

Recreation at the Saint-Lazare Prison by Hubert Robert

the poet Jean-Antoine Roucher waxed lyrical on the subject of conditions at Saint-Lazare, compared to those he had experienced in Sainte-Pélagie, from which he had just been moved.[4] Another letter described a musical evening given by women prisoners, who had included harps and harpsichords in their cell furniture. Some allowance being made for Roucher's wish to reassure his family, this is nevertheless a comforting picture.

As with so many other prisons, those incarcerated who had the means had the wherewithal to make their daily existence almost agreeable: at its most basic, prison soup would be replaced by dishes brought in from outside, prisoners might furnish their cells with their possessions, incarceration did not extend to the imposition of curfews, random searches, or the locking of cell doors other than from inside. The extensive inventory of household goods and personal possessions drawn up following Chénier's execution contained what must be one of the more startling entries in a prison list: "deux pistolets de poche dans la caisse aux livres" (two pocket pistols in the book chest).[5] Although Roucher's original description had later to be amended as the regime became harsher – partly in response to tightened security – one feature that was of huge importance to Chénier remained intact, namely his ability to study and to write throughout his imprisonment.

André Chénier was born in 1762 in the Galata district of Constantinople (Istanbul); his father, a long time resident since 1741, went there originally as a cloth merchant and later took on the responsibilities of French consul. His mother claimed Greek extraction. Two years after André Chénier's birth, the family moved to France, initially to Marseille. Shortly thereafter, André was taken to Carcassonne to be brought up much of the time by his father's sister, while his younger brother Marie-Joseph and their mother went to Paris. In 1767, their father was appointed French consul in Morocco, a post he occupied until his return to France in 1782. André, aged 11, had by then joined his mother in Paris and entered the Collège de Navarre, where he received a solid grounding in the classics and developed a thirst for learning. From an early age he appears to have been a compulsive versifier and indeed, throughout his life, he is said to have carried with him pen and paper. No stronger evidence of poetic verve can surely be found than the poem he started to compose on a crossing of the Channel on December 6, 1787, when he was suffering the torments of seasickness.[6]

Of the eight children that had made up the Chénier household, three girls had died young, leaving four sons and one daughter: the eldest, Constantin, who became French consul in Alicante, Louis-Sauveur, who achieved the rank of general in the Republican and Imperial armies, Hélène, who may be said to have "married well" as Comtesse de Saint-Ygest, and the two other sons, André and Marie-Joseph, poet and dramatist respectively. Their father was a hard worker, studious, possessed a strong sense of duty and was to make his own literary mark with the massive three-volume *Recherches historiques sur les Maures et l'Histoire de l'Empire du Maroc* (History of the Moors and the Moroccan empire), publication of which in 1787 secured for him professional recognition, but proved a financial drain. The family's social classification was "bourgeois", but with a distinctive cosmopolitan flavour; Louis assumed the aristocratic particle, as did several other members of the family, but not André. The children's mother had ambitions to create a literary-artistic salon in Paris. But throughout their lives they faced the challenges that shortages of money throw up, often linked to the injustices inherent in the "ancien régime". Louis Chénier wasted effort and time in seeking to have

André Chénier by Joseph Benôit Suvée

his years of hard labour as consul adequately recognised, while his applications for positions on behalf of his sons usually fell on stony ground for want of money or social standing. There was one important exception to this catalogue of disappointments: through family contacts involving the Minister of Foreign Affairs, André Chénier secured the position in December 1787 of personal secretary to the recently appointed French Ambassador to the Court of St James, M. de La Luzerne.[7] The work involved was very light, giving him time for studies, Arabic and Spanish being two enthusiasms, and his own writing. He was also very bored. Chénier was to stay abroad close to three years, covering therefore the early stages of the Revolution. It so happened, however, that he was on leave in Paris in August 1789 at the time of the overthrow of the Bastille.[8]

As Gérard Venzac writes, "Louis Chénier parvint à la Révolution avec le sentiment d'être une des victimes de l'ancien régime" (at the onset of the Revolution, Louis Chénier saw himself as one of the victims of the "ancien régime").[9] André Chénier echoed these sentiments. On April 3, 1789, he found himself in Hood's Tavern in Covent Garden, listening to two English Francophobes at the next table. Feeling thoroughly dejected, he lamented "il est dur de se voir négligé, de recevoir, sinon des dédains, au moins des politesses hautaines; il est dur de sentir … Quoi? qu'on est au-dessous de quelqu'un? … Non, mais il y a quelqu'un qui s'imagine que vous êtes au-dessous de lui" (It is hard to find oneself ignored, to suffer, if not contempt, then haughty disdain; it is hard to feel … What? that one is beneath somebody else? Not so, but rather that there is somebody who imagines that you are beneath him).[10] It comes as no surprise to find that the Chénier family greeted the Revolution with enthusiasm.

André and Marie-Joseph both joined the Club Breton in 1789, which became known as the "Société" and then in February 1790 the "Société des Amis de la Constitution". Later, dissension led to one faction becoming known as the Jacobins – named after the monastic Dominican house in the rue Saint-Honoré where they held their meetings – and the other as the Feuillants, so called after the terrace to which its members marched on July 15, 1791, when they split from the Jacobins. The more extremist of the two, the Jacobins, had Robespierre as their leading light, the more moderate, the Feuillants, had Lafayette as their most prominent member. Initially, the Club des Jacobins was open to all, while membership of the Club des Feuillants was restricted, a distinction that was to work greatly to the advantage of the former. By this time, the two Chénier brothers had parted company, Marie-Joseph siding with the Jacobins, André with the Feuillants.

André celebrated in both verse and prose the overthrow of the *ancien régime*. The ode "Le Jeu de Paume à Louis David, Peintre", completed in the first three months of 1791, was penetrated by the notion that "Le genre humain d'espérance et d'orgueil/ Sourit. Les noirs donjons s'écroulèrent d'eux-mêmes" (Mankind is wreathed in smiles of hope and pride. The dismal dungeons have crumbled away). But already he was distancing himself from the blind optimists. In the *Avis au Peuple Français sur ses véritables Ennemis* (The French People put on notice as to who are their real enemies), he strikes a cautious note. This weighty article of some 11,000 words had first appeared as a supplement published on August 28, 1790, to the 13th issue of the *Mémoires de la Société de 1789*. It can be said to have served as a manifesto for the Société – being a model of Revolutionary ambitions couched in moderate terms

linked to a penetrating analysis of what could go wrong – or rather was going wrong.[11] The *Avis* earned Chénier a medal from the King of Poland. He
warned that France finds itself on the edge of a precipice when liberty ceases
to be buttressed by law, given the fact that "la plupart des hommes ont des
passions fortes et un jugement faible dans ce moment tumultueux" (in these
tumultuous times, most men are long on passion and short on judgment).[12]
Tarred by their early association with the Jacobins, he was no lover of the
Girondins, whose enthusiasm for war Chénier also vigorously opposed. It
should be noted that he was well ahead of the Rolands in anticipating the
dangers that lay ahead.

A seemingly minor event, but one that later took on considerable importance, dated back to August 1790, when mercenaries of the Swiss regiment
of Châteauvieux near Nancy rebelled against their officers, stole regimental
funds, and fired on the National Guard. Eventually, they were subdued, but,
in the process, Désilles, a young French officer seeking a peaceful settlement,
was killed. In the aftermath, 23 of the mercenaries were executed, standard
treatment for mutineers, and 41 sent to the galleys. The latter, having benefited under an amnesty in December 1791, were released in February 1792
and sent off as a band of patriots to Paris – well fuelled with alcohol. This is
a curious instance of revolutionary logic, where the extremists in the Jacobin
faction fancied they saw an opportunity for making political capital: it was
decreed that a public celebration should greet these heroic opponents of the
establishment and that this should be capped with an elaborate festival on
April 15, 1792. One of the three signatories giving details of the festivities was
Marie-Joseph Chénier. André Chénier took a different view and on the very
same day, April 15, his poem "Hymne aux Suisses de Châteauvieux" was published in the *Journal de Paris*: a biting satire lauding the action of these foreign mercenaries "qui n'ont égorgé que très peu de nos frères et volé que très
peu d'argent" (who have massacred only a handful of our brothers in arms,
and stolen very little of our money). While sibling rivalry had been building
up for some time, one area of friction being the assessments each made of
the other's literary qualities, this poem was a very public illustration of their
political differences. It also demonstrated the widening gulf that separated
André Chénier from the Jacobins. A later historian called the poem André's
own death warrant.

In June 1791, André Chénier had made himself an elector and hence a potential deputy at the Assemblée Législative. Having become a central figure in the confrontation with the Jacobins, he demonstrated his skills as a powerful political pamphleteer, with many of his writings appearing in the *Journal de Paris* and the *Mercure de France*, and as a gifted orator at the Club des Feuillants. With the publication on 26 February , 1792, in the *Journal de Paris* of Chénier's article "De la cause des désordres qui troublent la France" (The reasons behind the public disorders from which France is now suffering) Chénier mounted a direct attack on the Jacobins. He described the methods used to infiltrate revolutionary societies throughout the country and likened the Jacobins' understanding of liberty to the action of the Harpies, who defecated on all meals prepared by Aeneas's companions. In the build-up to the trial leading to the execution in January 1793 of Louis XVI, he even gave discreet assistance to those preparing his defence. While he was opposed to the king's execution (his brother was to be one of the regicides), he had by no means abandoned his genuine republican principles. However, for the Jacobins that was not enough; he was a wanted man, on the run since August 1792, being the date he had been proscribed in line with the crackdown on all writers critical of the Jacobins. This had led him to take refuge in a small house in Versailles, where he achieved the feat of remaining inconspicuous for more than a year. This may also have coincided with a period of ill health. His literary silence was broken, however, with the appearance in manuscript form of his "Ode à Marie-Anne-Charlotte Corday", Marat's assassin, written on 27 July, 1793, ten days after her execution. Marat is categorised as "le noir serpent" emerging from its foul cave, while Charlotte Corday is saluted as:

> Seule tu fus un homme, et vengea les humains.
> Et nous eunuques vils, troupeau lâche et sans âme,
> Nous savons répéter quelques plaintes de femme
> Mais le fer pèserait à nos débiles mains.

(Alone, you proved yourself a man and avenged mankind, while we, mere eunuchs, a cowardly flock without spirit, all we can do is repeat the womanly laments, since steel would be too much of a weight for our feeble hands).

Two months later, when it was decreed that Marat's bones belonged to those of a national hero requiring preservation, Chénier wrote the powerful iambic "Voûtes du Panthéon" ((Vaults of the Pantheon) in which he castigates by name such Jacobins as Robespierre, Danton and Collot–d'Herbois. Charlotte Corday's courage can be said to have been matched by that of Chénier, "whose writings clearly marked him for the guillotine", to quote Francis Scarfe.

Imprisonment

With these public bursts of outrage, Chénier had ceased to be inaudible. It was only a matter of time before he would also become visible. On March 7, 1794 he was apprehended, having been caught in a round-up under the "Loi des Suspects" passed in September, 1793, the effect of which was to give free reign to denunciations of all kinds.

Once in Saint-Lazare, Chénier appears to have kept very much to himself. A low profile had become habitual during the months of proscription and it still remained the course of wisdom, given the likely presence of spies and informers. It also accorded with his own predisposition, all the more so that it enabled him to concentrate on his writing. As an indication of his success in this respect, there are few known contemporary references to him by fellow inmates, in addition to which the paucity of letters that have survived written from prison suggests that Chénier may again have followed a path of discretion. Gerard Walter concludes: "Tout porte à croire qu'André Chénier se tenait volontairement a l'écart de rencontres oiseuses" (Everything points to the fact that André Chénier chose to avoid tiresome contacts).[13] Other writers, unwilling to credit such unsociable habits, have sought to paint a less monastic picture. Many such efforts have centred on the presence in Saint-Lazare of the gifted and attractive Aimée de Coigny, duchess de Fleury: married in 1784 at the age of 15 to the duc de Coigny, she had then led a colourful life, breaking hearts, making conquests throughout Europe during the ensuing ten years.

Chénier was happily sensitive to feminine beauty. An early poem addressed to his two great friends, the Trudaine brothers, sets the tone:

> Amis, couple chéri, coeurs formés pour le mien,
> Je suis libre. Camille à mes yeux n'est plus rien.
> L'éclat de ses yeux noirs n'éblouit plus ma vue;
> Mais cette liberté sera bientôt perdue.
> Je me connais.[14]

(Much loved friends, whose hearts beat in step with mine, / I am a free man. Camilla is now nothing to me./ I am no longer blinded by her brilliant dark eyes;/ but this freedom will be of short duration./ I know my heart).

This Camilla, the recipient of some ten passionate poems, is believed to have been Madame de Bonneuil, married to the elderly Master of the household of Monsieur, the King's brother.

It is quite possible that André Chénier already knew Aimée de Coigny. It would be unthinkable that he could have failed to notice her in Saint-Lazare, which she entered on March 16, a week after Chénier himself. It takes only a short step to credit her with providing the inspiration for his famous prison poem, "La Jeune Captive", with its intensely romantic lament:

> Je ne suis qu'au printemps. Je veux voir la moisson,
> Et, comme le soleil, de saison en saison,
> Je veux achever mon année.

(I have only just reached my spring. I want to see the harvest, and, as does the sun, move from one season to the next to round off my year.)

Chénier does not name her and indeed teases the readers inviting them to identify her. Some writers were quick to suggest that it must be Aimée de Coigny. This is now accepted as fact, backed up in Monique de Huertas's biography, when she cites the abbé Millin, "Elle ["La Jeune Captive"] a été composée pour Madame de Montrond (Aimée de Coigny), pendant que nous étions ensemble dans la prison de Saint-Lazare, sous le règne de Robespierre.[15] J'ai le manuscrit de sa main" ("La Jeune Captive" was written for Madame de Montrond (Aimée de Montrond by her second marriage) when we were together in the Saint-Lazare Prison during the reign of Robespierre. She handed the manuscript over to me OR I have the manuscript in her own hand.)

Early writers were furthermore swift to suggest that Chénier was also her lover when in prison, thereby embellishing an already romantic tale. This is hard to confirm. In the opinionated memoirs that Aimée de Cogny published in 1817 there is no direct mention of Chénier. A more telling argument is that her inseparable companion of the day – and future husband – the comte de Montrond had been incarcerated with her on March 16 and would have been, at the very least, an inhibiting presence.[16] As a third consideration, the duchesse de Beauvilliers Saint-Aignan is a more plausible candidate for the role.[17] This emerges in Alfred de Vigny's fictionalised revolutionary short story *Stello* of 1832. In a note, Vigny explains that his own mother knew Mme de Saint-Aignan, who spoke frequently about Chénier.[18] She preserved piously a portrait of André Chénier, from which she vowed never to be parted, as well as several prison letters of his. She remembered well the readings of his poems he gave when in prison; these may have formed part of the *bouts-rimés* contests (verse composed to set rhymes) set up by a literary set among the prisoners as a favoured recreation.[19] Providing Madame de Saint-Aignan's recollections are not embroidered, they have the additional value of providing a rare glimpse of Chénier's prison existence.

André Chénier's prison writing extends well beyond "La Jeune Captive". In the first instance, it includes a number of poems written before his incarceration, which were then refined and new copies made. This applies to several of his iambics, poems with alternate lines of twelve and eight feet, and a metric sequence of short/long syllables, inspired by ancient Greek poets, which Chénier fashioned into a powerful satiric tool. One such poem is the "Fête de l'Etre Suprème" (The feast of the Supreme Being). This was the Revolution's way of plugging the hole created by the abolition of Christianity. It was first celebrated on June 8, 1794, with Robespierre as master of ceremonies, resplendent in a sky-blue costume. The same genesis may apply to his searing lines prompted by the "noyades de Nantes" of December 1793 and January 1794, organised by Jean-Baptiste Carrier, when 20 boat-loads of the condemned, chained together, were drowned in the Loire. Towards the end of his incarceration, his poetic output was largely given over to his sustained outrage at the injustices of the revolutionaries, much of which has come down to us unfinished.

Paul Dimoff's edition of the *Oeuvres Complètes* de André Chénier, is largely derived from the collections held in the Bibliothèque Nationale and the Bibliothèque municipale de Carcassonne; the fragmentary nature of many texts may have contributed to the tradition that the constraints to which Chénier was subject meant that much of his prison poetry had to be written in a tiny script on loose leaves and scraps of paper, including laundry tags. This ignores the fact that his methods of poetic composition throughout his life typically entailed neat scribblings in a minute hand on what paper was immediately available. Consequently, his experience has nothing in common for example with the challenges facing Alexander Solzhenitsyn or Irina Ratushinskaya in their gulags. The manuscript preserved in the Bibliothèque Nationale of the poem Chénier wrote on the eve of his transfer to the Conciergerie may provide a key to the origin of this tradition, since it is written on what has been described as paper used for wrapping laundry. "Comme un dernier rayon, comme un dernier zéphyr" (as the last shaft of light, as the last warm breeze) has established itself as one of the most haunting prison poems in the French language, the nearest competitor being perhaps "Le ciel est, par dessus le toit, si bleu, si calme" (The sky beyond the roof, so blue, so calm), but then Paul Verlaine was not facing the guillotine when he wrote it in September 1873.

The actual transmission of his prison texts is rarely spelled out, an exception as already noted being provided by "La Jeune Captive". What is certain is that his father will have been the chief recipient. For much of the time that Chénier spent in Saint-Lazare, regulations were such that prisoners' communications with the outside world were achievable. Visitors could act as couriers, Louis Chénier included. And whenever controls were tightened, guards, once given financial incentives, might fill that role. The situation with respect to Chénier's final poem is unclear, though it might have found its way into the poet's effects, the transfer of which to his father took place after Robespierre's death and the collapse of the Terreur.

The Guillotine

The speed of the journey to the guillotine was to be determined by the "discovery" early in 1794 of a second plot involving mass outbreaks from Paris prisons, with the inmates intent on the Republic's overthrow. This had much in common with the justification for the 1792 September prison massacres.

Military uncertainty was taken by the extremists within the Jacobin faction as an opportunity to concentrate attention once again on lurid external threats, conjured up from within Paris's prison walls. This time there was a new selection of prisons – the Luxembourg, Saint-Lazare, Bicêtre and Les Carmes. Most important of all, Robespierre was facing dissension from within, even after having eliminated a rival such as Danton and survived attempted coups, real or imagined. The need to re-establish his authority was met by the creation of an enquiry to root out all subversive elements within these prisons, the selection of subversives being based on the findings undertaken by Robespierre's close colleague, Martial Herman.[20] With the prisons overflowing with men and women denounced as suspects, it was also important to make room for new entrants. One partial solution came with the legislation of June 10, which was aimed at greatly accelerating the procedures of the Revolutionary Tribunal. Herman, for his part, set to work, starting with the Luxembourg Prison, where he identified 150 conspirators; the chosen were duly sent to the Revolutionary Tribunal for perfunctory trial and thereafter execution.

The next prison Herman investigated was Saint-Lazare; on June 21 Herman reported his findings to the Convention: with the help of an informer, he had come up with a list of 74. Over three days those selected were transferred to the Conciergerie for trial and execution.[21] André Chénier was in the second batch of July 24, the Trudaine brothers, who had been arrested in June, in the third batch. These lists were not cast in stone: occasionally, mistakes of identity were made and were corrected, as when Louis-Sauveur Chénier, already in the Conciergerie, was given as coming from Saint-Lazare.[22] At Saint-Lazare itself, a comic actor named Joly had his name dropped after giving the official a bottle of eau-de-vie (spirits), while Aimée de Coigny and de Montroud achieved the same result with a promised donation in gold of 100 louis. Madame de Saint-Aignan was excused on the grounds of a claimed pregnancy. For André Chénier, any escape was denied him. In the first place, he was a notorious adversary of the Jacobins. And secondly, if this had somehow been overlooked, a desperate initiative of his father would have acted as a vivid reminder: Louis Chénier managed to see Bertrand Barère, president of the Comité de Salut Public to impress on him how staunch a republican his son had been, and he was rewarded with the comforting assurance that André would be out of Saint-Lazare in three days. Louis Chénier followed up the meeting with a letter detailing some of André's patriotic achievements. Three days after the meeting with Barère, André was indeed out of Saint-Lazare and in the Conciergerie, where he was tried and found guilty on three counts: attempted evasion, rebellion against the constituted authorities and plotting against the state.[23]

The Revolution had hoovered up numerous painters and sculptors whose chief "crime" was to have been associated with aristocrats in the routine process of earning a living. In her comprehensive work, *Marking Time: Prison Art in Revolutionary France*, Sophie Matthiesson describes the role played by such artists in "enforced" residence as they strove to meet prisoners' demand for portraits ahead of execution. In the hectic final months of the Terreur, order books expanded and the sense of urgency intensified. At the same time, the minimal gap that typically elapsed between the prison governor's notice of the make-up of the next consignment for trial and the actual transfer to the Conciergerie meant that swiftly executed drawings and watercolours had the edge over oils. An exception was Joseph Benoît Suvée's well known oil of Chénier, completed on July 17, 1794, a full week before he was transferred to the Conciergerie.[24] On July 25, 1794, he was guillotined at the Barrière de Vincennes, now Place de la Nation.

Chénier's Literary Standing

The fact that poetic recognition only came to Chénier well after his death can be explained in part by his own reticence. In 1787 he had started to contemplate converting ten years of verse – often in several states and unfinished – into a format suitable for publication, but this remained no more than a project. Only two poems appeared in print during his life time, the first being the "Jeu de Paume" (the tennis game), the 24-page brochure in verse dedicated in 1789 to Louis David; the second was his "Hymne aux Suisses de Châteauvieux" in 1792. It was not that his verse was unknown, benefiting as it did from circulation in manuscript form. Indeed, as early as 1788 the literary critic Palissot, writing in an article encompassing the Chénier family's literary achievements, characterised André Chénier – on the basis, as he noted, of a scant poetic output – as a man of genius.[25]

It might have been expected that Chénier's premature death, coinciding with Robespierre's overthrow, would have sparked a flurry of interest in his work. That this did not happen can be laid at the door of his brother, Marie-Joseph. The one poem for the printing of which Marie-Joseph was specifically responsible was "La Jeune Tarentine" in 1798, presented as a charming elegy in the old style.[26] This proved to be the sum total from his earlier resolve, announced in his poem "Discours en Vers sur La Calomnie", that he would raise an altar to his brother's memory.[27] This failure may well have been in reaction to the brothers' three years in forceful political discord. An element of literary jealousy may also have weakened his resolve. But perhaps the most important factor was that Marie-Joseph found himself in a false position: as a prominent Jacobin, he was pilloried for not having done more to save his brother, sometimes expressed more forcibly as bearing responsibility for his brother's death, an accusation to which he responded vigorously in "La Calomnie". What the critics failed perhaps to take into account was the wisdom of his recommendation that the adoption of the lowest profile was the best way of avoiding extinction – hence his brother's exile to Versailles. And it is in this context that Louis Chénier's frantic last-minute intervention on behalf of his son had the flavour of a Greek tragedy in its unintended consequences.

With the death of Louis Chénier in 1795, a mere ten months after his son's execution, the family archives went to Constantin, whose career left him little time to act as literary executor, a role for which he probably had little inclination. Marie-Joseph himself died in 1811, by which date he had failed to prepare his own work for a definitive edition, let alone that of his brother.[28]

But already there had been some influential stirrings of interest in André's work within literary circles, marked by Chateaubriand's lament that the Revolution had deprived them of a poet showing particular promise in a pastoral vein.[29] His quotations in the *Génie du Christianisme*, 1802 (The Spirit of Christianity), indicated that he had had sight of a number of Chénier manuscripts; whether these were held in the family or more probably in the hands of a doyenne of a literary salon such as that of Chateaubriand's great friend, Madame de Beaumont, is uncertain.

It was in 1819, 25 years after Chénier's death, that the general public was given access to his verse, with the appearance of Henri de Latouche's first collected edition. To many it proved to be a revelation.[30] This was to be followed by publication of his collected poetry in several ever more comprehensive editions over the ensuing 50 years.

Recognition had come swiftly. A 21-year-old Alexandre Dumas was being recommended Chénier, Lamartine and Hugo among modern poets.[31] In his biography of Alfred de Musset, Henry Sedgwick records how, as an 18-year-old, Musset wrote his first poem, inspired by Chénier, whose slim copy of verse he had just acquired.[32] And the French man of letters Charles Nodier tells in 1830 how delighted he was to find that unpublished poems, said to have been written by Chénier – which he had greatly appreciated – were in fact the work of his daughter.[33] Cumulatively, this helps to demonstrate the anointing of Chénier as a major presence in French literature in the immediate aftermath of the initial publication of his verse. An astonishing feat.

Chénier's position in French literature certainly benefited from the simple impact of what for many was the sudden emergence of a gifted poet. The 25-year posthumous delay also meant that he joined the Romantic poetic wave at a time when it was gathering strength. It is to Sainte-Beuve, the dominant arbiter of literary taste in the first half of the nineteenth century, that much credit should go for having been early in drawing critical attention to the importance of Chénier's influence. Among individual poems, he particularly admired the "Ode à Versailles", written during Chénier's self-imposed exile and under the influence of his attachment to "Fanny" (Madame Laurent Lecoulteux). More generally, Sainte-Beuve saw Chénier as a poet ahead of his time, making him a precursor of the Romantic movement through his sensual, emotive poetry.[34] On this analysis, some critics have seen Chénier as reviving the poetic achievements of the sixteenth century Pléiade – featuring Ronsard and du Bellay – and pointing the way to the coming Romantic verse of Victor Hugo and Alfred de Vigny.

Vigny was to play a particularly influential part in Chénier's posthumous reputation. His own romantic credentials, well established in 1826 with the publication of *Poèmes Antiques et Modernes* and the historical novel *Cinq Mars*, were further enhanced with the appearance in 1832 of the philosophical novel *Stello*, which, as already indicated, gave valuable clues as to Chénier's prison circumstances.[35] What is remarkable is that the portrayal of a poet explaining his struggle to find a meaning to existence in a work of fiction should be adopted by several writers as a substitute for biographical material. This has something to do with the skilful presentation by Vigny of a character he had created in a sympathetic image which did not conflict with what little was known of Chénier or could be deduced from within his own writings and from the occasional anecdotes. It also is a measure of the paucity of authentic historical material.

The popular image that emerged in the early nineteenth century was of a writer driven by his sense of literary destiny, by his sensitivity to beauty in all its manifestations, by his horror of injustice. At the same time, he had contempt for – and a hatred of – the actions of the rabble, directed by individuals who were at best delusionary though more often cynically corrupt. Added to which, there was the appeal of this young man's ardent disposition, and ultimately there was the tragedy of his gruesome death. Ten days earlier, he had sat for the painter Joseph Benoît Suvée. These elements made him an ideal candidate for the role of Romantic hero, on a par with Chatterton and Byron, which position, moreover, made few demands on historical accuracy.

Scarfe mentions four or five bad plays that sustained the romantic tradition.[36] This was carried musically to its most impressive height in Umberto Giordano's well known opera *Andrea Chénier,* first staged in 1898. This late date is itself testimony to the hold that a Romantic tale could have on public imagination. The plot goes roughly as follows. All the action takes place outside the Saint-Lazare prison, barring the final scene. Madeleine (Aimée) first sees Chénier at a ball in the Coigny mansion, where she persuades him to recite a poem, which turns out to be full of republican sentiments, that happen to coincide with hers, and earns him expulsion from the ball. Stricken with love, she follows up this brief meeting with a succession of searing, but anonymous, love letters. Naturally intrigued, Chénier sets about finding who the letter-writer is – a quest that also leads to contact with a rival, a Coigny retainer secretly in love with Aimée from childhood. A meeting is engineered and the two just manage to confess their love before Chénier is taken into custody on Robespierre's orders. The next time they catch sight of each other is at Chénier's trial, when she, Aimée, is one of the spectators. And the final scene is set in the Saint-Lazare prison, where Chénier is shown writing his famous lament, only to be joined by Aimée who has smuggled her way in. They declare their profound love and are last seen walking hand in hand to the guillotine.

Some 50 years later in 1945, Chénier's posthumous fame took a sinister turn, when the imprisoned collaborator, Robert Brasillach, invoked his memory. At a superficial level the two men had much in common: a lifetime of literary achievement, whether in journalism or in verse; deep political commitment in times of huge turbulence, whether of revolution or of war; brief periods of imprisonment put to intensive literary use – earning them the title of prison poets – and finally suffering execution while still in their 30s.

Two tales that gave rise to legends and cults. But those associated with Brasillach bore no resemblance to those linked to Chénier, the one being a fascist, the other having the principles that might have been those of a Solon. As one of the most articulate French exponents from the 1930s onwards of what fitted in with German propaganda, Brasillach then also became an eloquent defender of the Pétain regime, from which he argued France had benefited considerably. Brasillach was much prized by those looking to justify collaboration. His views on the need to rid the country of all Jews tied in neatly with Nazi policy.

It was towards the end of Brasillach's life that his identification with Chénier took shape. When in prison in Frèsnes, in the course of the last 16 days before his execution, he worked on his essay on Chénier, much appreciated by Jacques Benoist-Méchin, a fellow-prisoner: a sympathetic vignette were it not for the fact that he was in search of sanitation by claiming proximity to Chénier.[37] Brasillach saw himself as a victim of society – shades of Lacenaire – and of justice "qui a condamné Socrate et le Christ et André Chénier" (which had condemned Socrates, Christ and Chénier). What Chénier would have made of this distinguished company will never be known, but he would have surely been horrified to read "Comme rien ne paraitra sous mon nom, je choisis comme pseudonym Chénier, sans prénom" (As nothing further will appear under my own name, I take as a pseudonym Chénier).[38]

Fortunately, there is a corrective for which I am indebted to Roger Nichols, writing in the *BBC Music Magazine* of June 2015: "The first orchestral work played in public in Paris at the liberation in 1944 was Albéric Magnard's 'Hymne à la Justice', whose structure follows that of Chénier's poem of the same title."

|||||||||||||||||||||||||||||||||||||||||||||||||||||||||||||||||||||||||||||||||||||||||||||||||||||

CHAPTER XVI

Jean-Antoine Roucher
(1745–1794)

Incarcerations

Sainte Pélagie   *September 14, 1793 – January 12, 1794*

Saint-Lazare   *January 12 – July 24, 1794*

Conciergerie   *July 24 – 25, 1794*

Any quest for an account of a prison existence on a weekly, a daily and occasionally an hourly basis is perhaps best met by Jean-Antoine Roucher's
prison letters to his family and friends. They in turn gave rise to an enchanting, affectionate correspondence with his daughter, Eulalie. She was 17 at the
start of his ten-month imprisonment and 18 when he joined André Chénier
in the cart that took the two poets to the guillotine – within three days of
Robespierre's own overthrow.

Roucher was born into a cultured bourgeois family of Montpellier. He
was educated in the Jesuit seminary and distinguished himself in his classical studies. Helped by a phenomenal memory, he later made himself fluent
in English and Italian. For a while, he seemed destined for the church; indeed, up to the age of 20 he wore *le petit collet*,[1] a preliminary step towards
an ecclesiastical vocation. On coming to Paris in 1768, where he was to pursue his theological studies, the passion for poetry led, however, to a dramatic
change of course, resulting in the eclipse of theology. His first employment
came when he took a position as a tutor in the household of M. Pannetier at
Amel, not far from Compiègne. As evidence of the seriousness with which
he approached his role, he wrote for guidance to Jean-Jacques Rousseau, who
replied at length. This flattering response to a young man will no doubt have
contributed to Roucher's lifelong admiration for Rousseau, bordering on
hero-worship. (This letter did not find its way into the Voltaire Foundation's
Correspondence complète de Jean-Jacques Rousseau.)[2]

Towards the end of 1772, Roucher resigned his post as tutor and returned to Paris. Two years later, he married Marie-Agathe Elizabeth Hachette, a direct descendant of a fifteenth-century heroine who had saved the town of Beauvais from the Burgundian forces of Charles the Bold by axeing his standard bearer. Witnesses at Roucher's wedding included both aristocratic and literary figures. Their daughter, Eulalie, was born in December 1776.

Roucher had by then become a regular contributor of verse to literary periodicals. An earlier composition had been "La France et l'Autriche au Temple de l'Hymen", celebrating the marriage in 1770 of the Dauphin (the future Louis XVI) and Marie Antoinette; through an uncle who was almoner in the household of the Comte de Provence, the king's brother, the poem,[3] circulating as a manuscript, was shown at court and was well received. Some four years later, and with published poems to his credit he was given the sinecure of a "fermier", a tax collector at Montfort-l'Amaury, a location near Rambouillet, close to Paris. As was the experience of Antoine Lavoisier, such a position served to dispel any financial anxieties. The economist, Turgot, a family friend, destined to be the first and – judged by some – the most far-sighted of Louis XVI's finance ministers, appears to have had this appointment in his gift when he spelled out the gentle conditions by which Roucher was expected to abide: "Je veux, mon ami, que vous puissiez travailler pour la gloire elle seule, et que vous soyez tranquille sur les besoins de votre famille. Un commis, qui aura de modiques appointements, pourra toujours vous remplacer et vous éviter un travail aride et étranger à vos goûts et vos talents."[4] (My dear friend, 1 want you to be able to strive wholeheartedly for glory free of any concerns touching the needs of your family. A modestly remunerated employee will always be there to fill in, thereby relieving you of tedious tasks which neither please you nor match your skills.) For a 30-year-old without deep pockets, whether by marriage or in his own right, such help served to underwrite his poetic ambitions.

Roucher's love of the countryside and his passionate interest in botany coloured much of his poetic output, "Hymne à la Nuit" and "Les Jardins" being two instances. These and other poems contain elements that were then incorporated into the great composition, *Les Mois*, on which he can be said to have started work in 1767, with publication coming 12 years later.

As the title indicates, there are 12 chapters or cantos, descriptive of the months of the year, starting with March, in verse that was often admired for its sensitive lyrical qualities. Each month comes with extensive notes, in the course of which Roucher elaborates on rural pursuits, presents earlier versions of the cantos, draws attention to historical associations and invokes parallels from the classics, notably Ovid and Vergil, and, within English literature, from Thomson's *The Seasons*, which he singles out as a major source of inspiration. Roucher does not appear to have known Edmund Spenser's *The Shepheard's Calendar*, which would have come even closer in outline to *Les Mois*. The author also indulges himself in numerous asides covering such matters as the American War of Independence, scientific discoveries and the dismemberment of Poland. In addition, he makes space for three outside contributions, the subjects being free trade in grain, divorce, slavery. Most important of all from a French literary point of view, with the February canto he published for the first time the four letters that Rousseau addressed to Monsieur le Président de Malesherbes, the prominent Genevan political figure he had got to know towards the end of his life. Already circulating in manuscript, they were described by Rousseau as "contenant le vrai tableau de mon caractère et les vrais motifs de ma conduite" (containing a faithful depiction of my character and a true account of my actions).[5] They encapsulated as it were the spirit of the *Confessions* and the *Rêveries d'un Promeneur Solitaire*, and were described by Sainte-Beuve as the most beautiful of his many writings.[6] Their publication also gave rise to a literary vendetta of astonishing virulence.

In February 1780, *Les Mois* appeared in two sumptuous volumes, enriched with numerous full page engravings. it carried a list of 320 subscribers, topped by Monsieur, the king's brother, and ten other members of the royal family. It was dedicated to the memory of Roucher's father, to whom he owed a love of the countryside and a love of poetry. In this final form, the poem extends to 305 folio pages, supported by notes that run to 415 pages.

Its prolonged composition both benefited from and suffered from a facility open to some authors, namely readings at the regular gatherings that certain hostesses organised. To these "salons", which had their greatest vogue in the second half of the eighteenth century and into the nineteenth, each hostess would seek to give a special orientation. We have seen Madame Lavoisier create a salon with a predominantly scientific membership and Madame Roland one that was severely political and largely restricted to the

Girondin faction. One of the best-known literary salons was that of Madame Helvétius in her hotel at Auteuil – the name of which became a conversational shorthand indicating attendance at one of the regular two o'clock to seven o'clock Tuesday lunches. The guest list might include at different times Diderot, d'Alembert, Turgot, Condorcet, Hume, Benjamin Franklin. It was there that Roucher's daughter, Eulalie, acquired the nickname of Minette, given her by Madame Helvétius.[7] The experience of the Trudaine household illustrates the heavy commitment that an active salon called for: throughout the season, each week two lunches, every day an evening supper. Madame du Deffand, blind since the age of 57, continued to give two suppers every week. They spawned as it were another literary supper, when it emerged that Madame du Deffand's helper, Mademoiselle de Lespinasse, had taken to entertaining some of her mistress's guests before they reached their destination.

For a writer such as Roucher, engaged in a lengthy pastoral, such readings could be useful. Moreover, he was an excellent presenter of his own work: a handsome presence, a cultured tone, a modest manner, an outstanding memory and the author of a work which combined sensitivity with solid learning. These were qualities that naturally endeared him to many hostesses. It was also a way for him of testing the market. The monthly division into twelve cantos lent itself to periodic assessments. Indeed, after Rousseau had been shown a draft of the April canto, Roucher took to heart the recommendation that he should recast the chapter.[8] On another occasion, following a salon reading, Rousseau had nothing but warm praise. And even the acerbic critic, Jean-Francois de La Harpe, after attending three early readings, gave – by his standards – a balanced judgment, pointing out in his more general criticisms, the awkwardness of having to differentiate each month from its neighbours, whereas quarterly seasonal contrasts would have been that much more convincing.[9]

Printing was completed by the end of June 1779 and the royal censor gave it a flattering reception on July 9. The author had become a household name with an enthusiastic following and the long-heralded publication in February 1780 guaranteed it maximum publicity and multiple reviews. These, however, turned out to be far from universally favourable. A degree of reader fatigue from over-exposure may by then have taken hold, not helped by a display of learning that smacked of self-indulgence. The frequency of the reverential references to Rousseau will also have grated on some readers. But, without doubt, the most important influence was the lead now taken by La Harpe. His earlier reaction had been converted into a sustained campaign of denigration of the poem and vilification of the author. The problem lay largely with the Académie francaise, the body, established by Cardinal Richelieu in 1635, entrusted with the care of the French language. To La Harpe's huge satisfaction, he had recently become one of the 40 members in 1776, occupying the seat numbered 36.[10] As a relative "new boy", he was outraged that Roucher was preparing to give widespread publicity to Rousseau's contemptuous references to the academicians that appear in the fourth of the letters to M. Malesherbes:[11] "J'estime moi, les paysans de Montmorenci des membres plus utiles de la société que tous ces tas de désoeuvrés payés par la graisse du peuple, pour aller six fois la semaine bavarder dans une Académie; et je suis plus content de pouvoir dans l'occasion faire quelque plaisir à mes pauvres voisins, que d'aider a parvenir à ces foules de petits intrigants, dont Paris est plein, qui tous aspirent à l'honneur d'être des fripons en place & que pour le bien public ainsi que pour le leur, on devrait tous renvoyer labourer la terre dans leurs provinces".[12] (I personally believe that the peasants of Montmorenci [where Jean-Jacques was living] are more useful to society than all those jobless creatures, supported by the sweat of the workers, who go six days a week to chat in the Académie; and I am more than happy to associate with my impoverished neighbours rather than the mass of smallminded schemers, of which Paris is full, all of whom aim to be cock of the walk, and who, in the interests of the country and for their own good, should be sent back to plough their provincial furrows.) La Harpe even led a three-man deputation from the Académie to persuade Roucher to desist, offering as inducements a pension of 12,000 livres and their support for his own election to their august body. Roucher's refusal – and that of his wife, whose help was solicited – secured for him La Harpe's undying hatred. Initially, the vendetta was conducted through the columns of *Le Mercure de France*, sustained over a period of several months.[13] A few years later, as professor of literature at the Lycée, the academy of learning started in 1785 under royal patronage, La Harpe had another platform for his views and judgments. Roucher was even pursued beyond the grave, with La Harpe finding time for a 132-page obsessive critique of *Les Mois*, replete with abuse, published as course material. Little wonder that the contemporary writer, Antoine de Rivarol, best known for his biting wit, characterised *Les Mois* as the greatest poetic shipwreck of the eighteenth century.[14]

The Revolution

The build-up to the Revolution saw Roucher turn his attention increasingly to developments affecting France. As far back as 1778, he had even predicted the advent of the Revolution in an article in the *Journal de Paris*, dated September 28, and placed himself firmly in the ranks of "Les Amis du Peuple". It is in that liberal spirit that he embarked on the translation of Adam Smith's *Wealth of Nations*, being drawn to the study of English political and economic thinking; it was published during the course of 1790, appearing in four volumes under the title *Recherches sur la nature et les causes de la richesse des nations*. His preferred political outcome was a constitutional monarchy. This drew him into a succession of middle-of-the-road groups, notably the Société des 89 in 1790, the Club des Feuillants in July 1791 and three months later the Club de la Sainte Chapelle. It also put him on course for direct conflict with the Jacobins. Indeed, on one occasion he came close to a punch-up with Danton. As for his opinion of Robespierre, this was best summed up in his cryptic comment "Robespierre, surnommé, je ne sais comment, l'incorruptible, par ceux qui ne le sont pas" (Robespierre, labelled goodness knows why, the incorruptible, by those who are not.)[15]

Roucher's direct political involvement came through the Saint Etienne du Mont Paris district, of which he became president, and from being chosen as one of the electors of the Sainte Geneviève section. It was in that capacity that he was called upon to contribute funereal verses (sadly of little distinction) for a hymn honouring J. G. Simoneau, the one-time mayor of Étampes, due to be sung on June 3, 1791, at a solemn gathering in the Champ de la Fédération.[16] Another hymn was called for exactly a year later, for a ceremony that the Assemblée Nationale saw fit to sponsor celebrating the respect for law. Engagingly, the pamphlet carrying the text and music was produced at the Imprimerie des Sourds-Muets (on the presses of the Institution for the Deaf and Dumb). This came a month after Roucher, in common with Chénier, had crossed swords with the Jacobins, intent on organising the massive celebration honouring the achievements of the mutinous Swiss mercenaries at Châteauvieux. Roucher was called upon to represent his section in the grand procession to be held on April 15, 1792, but made it a condition that a bust of Désilles, the courageous French officer, killed while trying to restore order, be carried by the mercenaries so that an astonished Paris might see the murdered man in the midst of his assassins.[17] For their pains, the two poets were then taken to task in incendiary fashion by the Jacobin pamphleteers.

At this point, it is worth noting how the political journeys of Roucher and André Chénier had run together: initial enthusiasm for the Revolution, participation in the moderate Feuillant club, espousal – particularly on the part of Roucher – of a constitutional monarchy, both men chosen to be electors of their respective sections, both equally scornful in print of the Jacobin theatricals of the Châteauvieux variety, and then jointly authors of powerful condemnations of Republican excesses through supplements published by the *Journal de Paris* in the years 1790 to 1792. These insertions, paid for by their authors and sympathisers, revealed at the same time two poets with a marked talent for political debate. Roucher, for his part, contributed eight signed supplements. To quote the biographer, Antoine Guillois, "Roucher et Chénier avaient comme à plaisir attiré sur eux la tempête qui devait les engloutir" (Roucher and Chénier appeared to be deliberately attracting the storm that was to engulf them.).[18]

The differences in age, Roucher an established literary figure of 47, André Chénier, 17 years the younger, a 30-year-old still making his way, probably meant that they were destined to be collaborators sharing similar values rather than close friends. Curiously, for both of them the colourful adventuress, Michelle de Bonneuil, came into their lives at different stages – with Chénier celebrating her under the name "Camille" in his romantic *Elégies*, while Roucher confined himself to dedicating to her his "Stances sur les Fleurs", when they found themselves in prison at Sainte Pélagie.

On August 10, 1793 a mob sacked the offices of the *Journal de Paris* and two days later destroyed the presses. Roucher and Chénier went into hiding. Passage on September 17, 1793 of "La Loi des Suspects" was aimed at catching in its net all miscreants posing – or believed to be posing – a threat to the Revolution. The Paris Commune went one better less than a month later by including "ceux qui n'ayant rien fait contre la liberté, n'ont aussi rien fait pour elle" (those who may not have done anything against liberty but have yet done nothing for liberty). Roucher was duly arrested as a suspect on September 14, 1793, when he chose to return to his Paris house, and was taken to Sainte Pélagie. Chénier, who had found a discreet refuge in Versailles, remained free until denounced by a neighbour and imprisoned on March 7, 1794, in Saint-Lazare.

Prison Conditions

An early judgment: "Ah! Sainte Pélagie! Sainte Pélagie! vous êtes une sale demoiselle" (Ah! Sainte Pélagie! Sainte Pélagie! you're a grubby little number).[19] An assessment four months later when Eulalie had come with her mother to Sainte Pélagie to secure Roucher's possessions on his transfer to Saint-Lazare: "Dieu, quelle odeur, quel air étouffé, quelle atmosphère chargée de tabac, de vin etc ... et que sais-je enore? Cette chaleur puissante d'un poêle dans un corridor privé d'air ... quel antre infecte vous habitiez".[20] (God, what a stench, what a suffocating atmosphere dominated by smoke, by wine etc ... and by who knows what else ... And then the oppressive heat from the stove in an airless corridor, in short what a disgusting den in which to have lived.).

The prison population came to a little over 200 men and women, distributed in cells that typically housed two to three prisoners – very occasionally one – with the women occupying the ground floor.[21] Eight o'clock every evening, the cell doors were bolted and a regular inspection would be made to ensure that the window gratings had not been tampered with. For cells holding two to three beds, a monthly rental of 15 livres was charged. Roucher's experience at Sainte Pélagie involved frequent changes of cells, culminating in the exceptional luxury of one on his own. More typically he had room companions, early instances being a man whose standards of hygiene were distinctly lower than those of Roucher and another who never stopped talking. More happily, his later room companions included his great friend the painter, Hubert Robert, best known for his architectural capriccios that often included classical ruins, and Robert Chabroud, former member of the Constituent Assembly and referred to in the letters as "The Wise Man", whom Roucher encouraged to learn English.

As far as board was concerned, he came to rely on supplies from home. The pattern that became established was for his wife and/or his daughter to come to the prison at around two in the afternoon bringing baskets that contained the home-cooked food – stews, potatoes, beans – and other supplies that might include books from his library, writing materials, elements for his botanical studies. This was a daily event, barring one day in ten, the "décali", which was set aside for the celebration of revolutionary achievements – in lieu of Christian worship. The baskets' hand-over via a turnkey carried with it the much treasured possibility of momentary glimpses between the three. Roucher would often share with others the food hamper. On a more regular basis, two might club together, deciding to "faire table ensemble". On another occasion, he announced in a letter to his daughter that "je dine en ville ce soir", having been invited by a fellow prisoner occupying a cell on the same corridor.[22] At one point, Roucher became known among a small circle of friends for a particularly delicious eau-de-vie, in return for which he received greatly appreciated cups of coffee. One further regular link involved the provision of clean linen. The equipping of his minute cell with his own possessions was undertaken at an early stage, but adjustments were sometimes required following changes of cell.

Political prisoners without means and felons were housed in crowded quarters, making do with straw for bedding and having their meals at the *table commune*, notable for prison fare that was often barely edible. The other more well-off inmates would occasionally be threatened with demotion to the *table commune*.

As soon as the induction into Sainte Pélagie was behind him, Roucher turned to establishing communications with the world outside. From the outset, he learned that family visits were only rarely achievable. One exception came in mid-November, when Eulalie and an uncle managed to see him in his cell, having bribed a turnkey; Roucher forbade any further initiatives of this kind.[23] A contact that was permitted, however, enabled Roucher's four-year-old son, Émile, to spend the occasional day with him. Outside links were therefore effectively limited to the exchange of letters, and this is something of which the family took full advantage. Taking the 168 letters contained in the *Consolations de ma Captivité ou Correspondence de Roucher* and the 315 days of incarceration, this works out at exchanges of letters at a rate of at least one every 48 hours. No allowance is made for letters that were missed or any

Jean-Antoine Roucher by Hubert Robert, ahead of his transfer on 31 January, 1774
(le douze pluviôse an 2) from Sainte Philippine to Saint-Lazare Prison

that might have been deliberately omitted. The book's editor, Marc-Francois Guillois, had married Eulalie shortly after Roucher's death. While we have no way of telling how extensive any editorial work was that he – and also presumably his wife – undertook in preparing the manuscripts for the press, their publication had Roucher's explicit blessing and it was he who had supplied the title for what was to be a posthumous work.[24] In this 1797 edition, there is one clear instance of suppression of material in one of Eulalie's letters (marked by a row of dots) which may well have been home work. The collection is dominated by letters between Roucher and his daughter; those to his wife, while numerous at the start of Roucher's imprisonment, tailed off as it became more prolonged.

The family derived comfort from this frequent epistolary contact. In somewhat the same way, mother and daughter welcomed the daily chores of the hampers. As Eulalie explains to her father after he had passed on to her a rumour that his meals would be at the *table commune*, "c'est dans cette occupation quotidienne de vous, de votre santé, que nous retrouvions je puis dire des consolations" (it is in this daily activity given over to you and your health that we have in a manner of speaking found some solace).[25]

Eulalie's letters to her father are extremely affectionate, typically dutiful in response to her father's instructions and rich in anecdotes, often nicely observed and calculated to lift his spirits. On one occasion, when discussing Madame de Sévigné's famous requiem for the military genius, Turenne, she admires how "avec sa simplicité et son naturel ordinaires ou plus ordinaires plutôt, qu'elle demande des larmes et qu'elle en obtient, après un grand nombre d'années, pour un homme qui en a tant fait répandre" (in her simple and ordinary unadorned way, or rather more than ordinary way, she calls for and obtains tears, many years later, for a man who was himself responsible for the shedding of so many).[26]

Roucher's letters acted in the first instance as a fact sheet, keeping his family informed of his daily prison life. Onto this he grafted a persistently optimistic assessment of his position, influenced in part by his attempt to lift his wife's spirits, whose persistently negative judgments were ultimately to prove to have been the more soundly based. This led to the occasional complaint, with Roucher pointing out that the more normal pattern was for the spirits of the imprisoned to be lifted by the encouragement of the free, and yet he was the person having to do all the encouraging. His daughter would also be called upon to soothe her mother's anxieties. The point has, however, to be made that a few letters to a "Madame L . . ." paint a more realistic picture than do those to his wife.

Roucher's own response to the depression of imprisonment lay in a programme of sustained activity. He went so far as to embark on a fresh translation of Adam Smith's *The Wealth of Nations*; in one of her letters to her father, not that long before his transfer to the Conciergerie, Eulalie passes on to him the message that the publisher, Buisson, was harrying him for the return of page proofs.[27] Most important of all, his regular commitment to letter-writing was made all the more effective as an occupier of his time by the fact that communications with his daughter were those of a teacher as well as those of a parent. In his enlightened view, "J'ai cru bien faire de ne pas te destiner à des occupations manuelles qui donnent aux femmes une si chétive existence"

(I believe I did well by you in not pointing you towards those domestic activities that give a woman such a restricted life).[28] He was determined to
further her education from his prison base.

Writing style is a subject close to Roucher's heart, and there are frequent
exhortations to Eulalie that she should not let a day pass without reading
several letters of Madame de Sévigné and pages of La Bruyère. Interestingly,
he also points her in the direction of Laurence Sterne's *Sentimental Journey*.
Frequently, Roucher wrote late at night or early in the morning, at which
times relative calm descended on the prison. His powers of concentration
could still be taxed as occurred on a day in December following news of a
Republican military success, when the stove opposite his cell door became
the focal point of a thunderous celebration by the imprisoned, keen to express their patriotic fervour.[29]

Perhaps the shining example of Roucher's capacity to concentrate – and
his self discipline – came a few days later.[30] At 7 pm he is to be seen giving
Eulalie an account of William Tell's exploits. Eight hours on, at 3am he in-
terrupts his letter to say that he is being summoned for transfer to Saint-
Lazare. When this move is delayed, he quickly takes up another subject: the
suggestion that the French language is not up to capturing the subtleties of
Latin. He also seizes the opportunity to give her as an assignment the task
of adjudicating between two different French translations of a passage from
Cicero. The letter suffers its final interruption with "le moment du départ ap-
proche" (the departure time is coming close). Today's reader may be forgiven
for feeling that he or she will have shared in the roller-coaster of emotions
that Eulalie experienced when reading her father's prison instructions.

A week later, Roucher sets out to describe in detail the journey from
Sainte Pélagie to Saint-Lazare.[31] Seventy prisoners are lined up in the dimly-
lit prison corridor. Roucher's first act is to entrust to a friendly prison guard
a note that he has prepared for his wife. Then follows the counting out of
the prisoners into the courtyard, where their transport awaits them: a convoy
of ten horse-drawn carts, in which the prisoners can either sit on the side
rails, bending in two in order not to be jolted backwards out of the cart, or
balance themselves as best they can standing upright. The night is cold, the
scene is dimly lit by torches. They set off on what is a four-kilometre journey at around five in the morning, passing close to Roucher's house, not far

from the Jardin des Plantes to which he and Eulalie would go when on their botanical outings. Roucher notes that their cavalcade, under the escort of a handful of soldiers, arouses for the most part only mild curiosity from the occasional passer by. One exception is an elderly woman, at the halfway stage at the rue Saint Martin, who shouts "Qu'on les foute tous à la guillotine, tous à la guillotine" (Let the lot be sent off to the guillotine, the lot to the guillotine).[32] They arrive at Saint-Lazare at seven-thirty, in daylight. Once inside the gate, having been duly counted, they are ordered up to the third floor, where chalk marks on cell doors indicate the number of prisoners allocated per cell, ranging from two to seven. Roucher's cell companion, Chabroud, swiftly installs himself in a cell marked for three; Roucher immediately takes the second slot.

After a week of chaos, Roucher is able to sing the praises of his new prison: "A Saint-Lazare on ne rencontre rien de qui importune les yeux et les poumons" (At Saint-Lazare one comes up against nothing that troubles eyes or lungs)[33] – a miracle of cleanliness compared to Sainte Pélagie, an outlook that is pleasant, a cell which although no longer his alone is shared with two congenial companions, a system of internal controls that leaves doors unlocked, curfews non-existent and internal and epistolary communications unrestricted. But direct contacts with family and friends remain the exception, with one major qualification, namely Roucher's ability to have his four-year-old son, Émile, to stay for weeks at a time; he is made much of in the Prairial Corridor, which houses the women prisoners. To these happy first impressions of Saint-Lazare, there is one important drawback in the considerable distance that now separates him from the family home.

The rhythm of Eulalie's home work is resumed: a lot of Italian, reinforced by some lessons given at home, and English, which would seem to present greater difficulties. She is required to translate some lines of James Thomson, but her father accepts that Laurence Sterne may not be the ideal model for a learner. And yet he decides that she should correspond in English with his cell companion, Chabroud. This excites her wrath, claiming that her father had played her a shabby trick "savez-vous, mon cher papa que vous m'avez joué d'un tour, d'un mauvais tour".[34] On another occasion, on being called upon to have a stab at translating a page of Adam Smith, she has to remind him that she is already fully occupied preparing the daily hampers, delivering them, supplying him with plants for drying and responding to his letters. However demanding he may be, Roucher takes great delight in extolling Eulalie's literary judgments to the point of stunning those fellow prisoners he deems to be worthy listeners ("J'en bats les oreilles de tous ceux que je crois dignes de les entendre").[35] Once she is even asked for her views on a recent composition by André Chénier, a manuscript copy then doing the rounds at Saint Lazare. Roucher follows this up with a detailed critique of the work and a dismissive comment on the output of modern poets. This is the only time that Chénier's name comes up in the published correspondence.[36]

One aspect of imprisonment that puts its stamp, literally and figuratively, on the correspondence centres on the role of the *greffe* (keeper), to whom letters, whether from prisoners or to prisoners, would go. While such scrutiny appears to have been slight at Sainte Pélagie, it became progressively more important at Saint-Lazare, in step with the accelerating march of Robespierre's "Terreur". Roucher advises Eulalie to avoid long passages of English or Italian which can confuse the keeper. The return of books taken from his library provides him with an opportunity to tip in the occasional letter. And for the transfer of a lengthy text – in itself an object of suspicion to the keeper – he gives Eulalie detailed instructions regarding the construction of a shallow, unobtrusive box designed to fit into the bottom of one of their hampers; it came into early use with the account of Roucher's move from Sainte Pélagie to Saint-Lazare.[37]

At a more general level, he goes out of his way to emphasize how careful he is at all times to avoid attracting attention to himself, how much he respects authority, how strong is his support for the Revolution, how confident he is in the wisdom of the Assemblée Nationale and hence in his ultimate freedom. In short, "la loi le veut, je courbe la tête" (such is the law, I submit). Declarations that seem to have the censor in mind just as much as his family.[38]

But in a letter at the end of March, generalisations are suddenly replaced by what reads like a defence lawyer's brief. It revolves around the arrest of three men, allegedly implicated in a counter-revolutionary plot hatched in Sainte Pélagie, who occupied cells in the corridor below his "mais guidé par un sentiment qui est en moi, dans moi, et qui tient pour ainsi dire de l'instinct, je ne m'en étais jamais approché, persuadé qu'eux et moi n'étions pas fait pour respirer le même air" (but guided by a feeling that I have, that is within me and which amounts, as it were, to instinct, I had never got close to them, convinced as I was that they and I were not meant to breathe the same air).[39] Nonetheless, the three had denounced Roucher, thereby confirming him as a "suspect" but not a "conspirator" – which resulted in a 15-day halt to all correspondence.[40] Such was Roucher's professed patriotism that he managed to discern a silver lining to this punishment:

"J'aurais maudit cent fois cette rigueur si je n'eusse pensé à l'utilité générale de la patrie, à la conservation de l'Assemblée Nationale, au salut même des prisons que menaçaient les grands coupables dont on a fait justice" (I would have cursed this harshness a hundred times over had I not considered the country's general needs, the preservation of the Assemblée Nationale and indeed even the welfare of the prisons, when faced by the threats posed by these great scoundrels, who have now had their deserts).[41]

An astonishing passage. One feels entitled to ask how is it that Roucher, a prisoner himself, could have found it possible to praise the firm action (a euphemism for execution) taken by the very Jacobin leaders who, a mere 18 months earlier, were orchestrating the prison massacres that had so repelled Madame Roland.

One answer may lie in a simple moment of panic. Another, that he judged that a show of docility as a prisoner might persuade his gaolers to overlook his well-documented opposition of the past and his aristocratic trappings. Shielding his family from possible persecution was an abiding consideration. Alternatively, he might have simply come to believe in Revolutionary justice. At this point, it can be said that the unity that had characterised Roucher and Chénier in their response to the Revolution as it unfolded was decisively broken: the last few months of Chénier's own captivity – in sharp contrast – saw a poetic outpouring denouncing the injustices of the Jacobin regime.

Roucher's six and a half months in Saint-Lazare mark a period of gradual decline in the hopes entertained by his family – and eventually in his own. Added to which, the deterioration in the family's financial position was accelerating. Already with the cancellation by the Assemblée Nationale of their contract with the "Fermiers" on March 20, 1791, that source of revenue will have ceased. This had been followed by the bankruptcy of the Société des Libraires de Paris, from which Roucher derived income from his writings. The subsequent retrenchment meant that the family had to part company with their servants and that all household chores fell to the lot of Eulalie and her mother, whose time and resources were already stretched meeting the prison needs of Roucher.[42]

Roucher's initial enthusiasm over the living conditions at Saint-Lazare was sustained for a short while. One day in February Eulalie was even able to lunch with him. A seemingly minor improvement was the provision of a screen in his cell. For a man who spent the greater part of the day at the table that served as his desk, this represented a considerable advance. For a writer, any degree of privacy counted as an achievement. As he explains in a letter to his wife, "je fais de l'anglais, et du français et même de l'italien à la journée. Je suis au lit à onze heures et toujours à mon bureau à six heures du matin" (I do my English and my French and even some Italian the day long. I am always in bed by eleven and at my desk at six o'clock every morning).[43]

Roucher dates the hardening of the regime at Saint-Lazare from when the "conspiracy" at Sainte Pélagie was being investigated. The heightened censorship has already been mentioned. This was accompanied by a thoroughly unsettling pattern of shifting rules. Something authorised one day would be forbidden the next, only to be restored a few days later. For Roucher, the presence of his son was an immense comfort to him. Periodically, this would be put in doubt, to his huge personal distress. A moving letter in mid-May tells of a day of acute anxiety that affected the whole prison, when a cell by cell search for treasonable material was conducted: "une grande et vague inquiétude agitant toutes les âmes et troublant tous les visages. Je ne sais quelle sombre terreur sans objet déterminé depuis huit heures du matin jusqu'à huit heures du soir a poursuivi le plus fort comme le plus faible" (a great surge of anxiety affecting all hearts and visible on all faces. I do not know what undefined horror took possession of the strongest and the most vulnerable from eight in the morning to eight in the evening).[44] He reports that Émile was not going to risk the loss of his toys, which he hid beneath his father's bed.

Lessons continued. Madame de Staël's memoirs came up for discussion, as would have Chesterfield's letters to his son, but for the fact that a wodge of English was judged to be too much for the nerves of the guard on duty as a censor. There is also clearly a discernible loss of enthusiasm on the part of the correspondents, with Eulalie admitting that both she and her mother were losing heart and that his letters were capable of leaving them plunged in the deepest gloom. Roucher's own protective shield was visibly wearing thin, with him regretting at one point the "good old days" at Sainte Pélagie.

Perhaps the most remarkable passage comes in a letter that might almost be mistaken for an act of contrition: "Mon malheur est peut-être, d'avoir marché droit dans le chemin tracé par la loi sans regarder ni aux autres ni à moi-même surtout. Aussi quelque soit l'instant de ma mort, me trouvera-t-il aussI pauvre que m'avait fait l'instant de ma naissance" (My misfortune is perhaps to have gone straight down the road indicated by the law without giving thought to others, least of all to my own good. Furthermore, when death comes, it will find me as poor as at the date of my birth).[45] As a confession it fails the test. No admission of any error of judgment. Instead, we have the demolition of a man of straw, since venality never cast a shadow over his reputation.

The end for Roucher came with the spasms that were to mark the death throes of the "Terreur". At Saint-Lazare this took the form of the constant changes of rules that Roucher had already found so unsettling, with the difference that any restoration of privileges became even rarer and the tightening of controls ultimately relentless. This period was characterised by sudden interruptions to correspondence and to the supply from outside of provisions, expulsion of children, restrictions to the freedom of movement within the prison, mandatory attendance at the *table commune*, the banning of candle-light within the cells and as the precursor to total darkness, the banning of the newspaper, *La Convention*, the last chink onto the outside world open to prisoners intent on following the dismal judgments of the Revolutionary Tribunal. The final note he sent to his wife was dated June 29. Then silence.

On July 23 Roucher learned that his name had been added to those proscribed and that he was credited with being the ring leader of the "conspiracy". Émile, the only child remaining in Saint-Lazare, was promptly sent back to his mother. Roucher then entrusted his letters to a fellow prisoner. The last measure he took was to have his portrait drawn by Suvée's pupil Joseph Leroy: a chalk drawing completed in the two hours to spare before his departure from Saint-Lazare.[46]

On July 24, he was in a batch of 30 who were transported to the Conciergerie. At his trial, the charge sheet, signed by Fouquier-Tinville, opened with the phrase "aristocrate puant"(stinking aristocrat) and concluded with "conspirateur à la maison d'arrêt de Saint-Lazare" (conspirator from the Saint-Lazare prison). The same day, he shared the cart that took him,

Jean-Antoine Roucher
by Joseph Leroy from
Pendant la terreur:
Le Poète Roucher
by Antoine Guillois

with André Chénier and thirty others, to the scaffold. Some historians claim that they were overheard quoting Racine's *Andromaque* to each other.[47]

There is no farewell speech from the scaffold, nor is there a concluding statement. What Roucher did leave is a gentle inscription that accompanies the Leroy portrait. It is addressed to his wife, his children, his friends.

> Ne vous étonnez pas, objets sacrés et doux
> Si quelqu'air de tristesse obscurcit mon visage
> Quand un savant crayon dessinait cet image
> J'attendais l'échafaud et je pensais à vous
>
> (Do not be surprised, you who are treasured by me and held dear
> If a certain sadness clouds my face
> When a talented artist drew this portrait
> I was awaiting the scaffold and thinking of you)

Prison Writing

Roucher's writing when in prison was continuous. Some of it served as occupational therapy, notably the translations he made of Italian, English and Latin verse. A second category of writing can be termed income-producing, notably his heavily revised second edition of Adam Smith's *Wealth of Nations*, which achieved publication very soon after his death. The time that Roucher lavished on furthering Eulalie's education meant that much of his writing was pedagogic; while he had access to some books from his own library, he was also heavily reliant on his retentive scholarly memory. Such instruction was then happily intertwined with the personal side of his correspondence.

From the perspective of a book devoted to prison writing, Roucher's letters give the reader a remarkable insight into nine months of a prisoner's life in Revolutionary France on a day to day basis. At times, they have the immediacy of an audio recording.

Roucher's literary reputation, having suffered from the critical battering orchestrated by La Harpe, can be said never to have staged any significant recovery. In an 1856 publication we find the distinguished critic, Sainte-Beuve, complaining "il a manqué par malheur d'invention . . . il n'a que des bons commencements, et ses vers retombent dans le commun" (sadly, he lacks imagination . . . he is only capable of good beginnings before his verses rapidly relapse into the conventional).[48] In 1917, in the *Histoire Illustrée de la Littérature française* he gets a better press from Des Granges, who recognises in Roucher "certains dons du vrai poête, de l'éclat, du pittoresque, de la sensibilité" (certain gifts of a real poet in terms of brilliance, of the picturesque and of sensitivity).[49]

Nonetheless, he rarely gets included in poetic anthologies. Having thus been seemingly forgotten, in 1980 the Société des Amis de Roucher et André Chénier was founded with the objective of holding annual conferences having as the subject poetry of the eighteenth century and into the nineteenth century. The lectures are subsequently published in the *Cahiers Roucher-André Chénier*. The bicentenary of the *Consolations de ma Captivité* was duly celebrated in 1997, followed by a programme of conferences. Publication in 2012 of a fresh edition of *Les Mois*, shorn of its notes, may also be a sign of renewed interest. Intriguingly, an auction held on November 11, 2015, contained 33 items from Roucher archives, relating primarily to *Les Mois* but including some unpublished prison letters.[50] This partial emergence from obscurity helps to remove the stigma of Roucher being best known as the poet who accompanied Chénier to the grave. But for enduring fame, the prison correspondence still provides the soundest foundation.

(C)
INCARCERATION
IN RUSSIA

CHAPTER XVII

Totalitarian Incarceration

Historical Introduction

Prison writing knows no geographic or political boundaries. By way of demonstration, Russia is invaluable with close on a century of (non-czarist) totalitarian rule that has supplied some of the harshest conditions that prison writers have had to confront,

The Soviet labour camps have been the object of extensive scholarly research, notably in the west, and have been enriched by a considerable number of memoirs. The precise conditions under which the imprisoned lived, down to daily grams of black bread to which they were theoretically entitled, are known. Nowhere else in this book is detail on this scale available. But it does not translate into a rich harvest of writings from within the prisons, the most obvious explanation being the severity of conditions prevailing in the camps.

Alexander Solzhenitsyn, Lev Mishchenko and Irina Ratushinskaya managed none the less to earn the title of prison writers in the most hostile environment conceivable.

Anne Applebaum's comprehensive history of the Soviet camps has as its title *Gulag*. From being the term covering the administration of the concentration camps, it came to signify the Soviet system in all its oppressive forms – labour camps, punishment camps, criminal and political camps, women's camps, children's camps, transit camps.[1] Not surprisingly, the statistics for prison numbers are of variable quality and open to multiple interpretations. One figure quoted by Applebaum puts the number of Soviet citizens who passed through the camps and exile colonies between 1926 and 1953 at 18 million.[2]

The opening and closing dates are significant: the first marks the time when Stalin decided to use forced labour as a way of exploiting natural resources in the far north as well as a way of speeding up the pace of industrialisation in the USSR as a whole; the second is that of Stalin's death. Throughout, the

punitive role of the camps as envisaged by Lenin, who in 1918 wanted "unrelia-
ble elements" to be locked up, retained its primary importance.[3]

In Applebaum's account, during the Stalin era the repressive system re-
sembled a vast game of roulette: anyone could be arrested, for any reason,
at any time – peasants, workers and Party bureaucrats alike. For incarceration purposes, the distinction between political and criminal prisoners was
infrequently made, the two categories being jumbled together. In the early
1930s, prisoner numbers were greatly boosted by the agricultural programme
of collectivisation which led to incarcerations and deportations to Siberia
affecting some 2 million.[4] Then came the purges of 1937–38, known as the
Great Terror, "justified" on the argument that the failure of Communism to
fulfil its promise was due to a pervasive fifth column whose eradication was a
patriotic duty. Hence requests by camp leaders to increase the quotas of executions allotted to them. Show trials formed part of the decor.[5]

The semblance of legality was based on a revision in 1926 of the Soviet
Criminal Code. Under Article 58 the definition of "counter-revolutionary
crimes" was expanded from a couple of paragraphs to an elaborate document containing 18 sub-sections, a catch-all ready for implementation
at any time.[6]

The experience of the teacher, Yevgenia Ginzburg, typifies that of many
other professionals in the Stalinist era. A staunch communist, she was accused in 1934 of participating in a Trotskyist group and, as a party member,
of playing a double game. She was deprived of her party card, expelled from
the party and arrested. Over a period of two years in solitary confinement,
interrupted by relentless interrogations, she refused to "confess" her crime. At
her trial in August, 1937, which lasted all of seven minutes, she was sentenced,
with no possibility of appeal, to ten years' imprisonment in a hard labour
camp – subject of course to subsequent extensions.[7] It was, therefore, only in
1949 that she was released from her camp to be sent into exile for five years;
exile was in turn lengthened and it was not until June 1955 that she was allowed to return to Moscow. When in exile she began work on her memoirs,
but having still to exercise great caution. The completed manuscript had to
be smuggled abroad. In 1967 the account of her first three years in the labour
camp under the title *Journey into the Whirlwind* was published successfully in English and then translated into numerous languages. Her death in

1977 came 12 years before her memoirs were officially published in Russia. The Russian text had, however, been circulating since the 1970s in the illegal self-published samizdat form, thereby revealing to those Russians prepared to run the risk of being caught with "a blatantly subversive work" some of the special horrors of imprisonment in camps where criminals and "politicals" were combined and where, at times, the distinctions between the men's wing and the women's wing were ignored.[8] When questioned about the detail in a memoir composed many years after the events described, Ginzburg explained that this did not present any difficulties "since for the whole 18 years remembering everything had been her main object". Her biographer, Olga Cooke, writes that she was motivated by the responsibilities of a survivor to bear witness.[9]

A key feature that distinguishes her prison experience from that of later memorialists lies in her invisibility: the authorities could do what they liked without let or hindrance. At home they had either gulled or cowed the public. Many foreigners seem to have been similarly fooled. In 1933, George Bernard Shaw was referring to Stalin as an interesting gentleman whose personal acquaintance he had had the pleasure of making.[10] And as late as March 1943 he was writing: "The revolution in Russia was saved from utter wreck by Lenin's readiness to recognise and remedy his mistakes, and Stalin's sagacious realism and saving sense of humour."[11]

March 5, 1953, served to rid the world of one despot. It also led to significant changes in the circumstances of political imprisonment in Russia. By mid-September 1953 Nikita Khrushchev had risen to the position of First Secretary of the Central Committee of the Communist Party and by the end of December Stalin's ambitious hatchet man, Lavrenti Beria, had been disposed of. Domestically, Khrushchev's nine-year period of office came to be known as the Great Thaw – but this had no parallels on the foreign front, where suppression of the Hungarian uprising, construction of the Berlin wall and the Cuban missile crisis perpetuated the Cold War. On February 26, 1956, at the Twentieth Party Congress, Khrushchev delivered his "secret speech" in which he – highly selectively – denounced the evils of Stalin. While never published, the speech was circulated to leading party members and the contents became widely known. It is now hard to appreciate the shock that this must have caused to a population that had learnt over many decades uncritical acceptance of authority, whether out of conviction or simply in the interest of survival.

The speech was seen as heralding an end to the further development of the Gulag's camps, so closely associated with Stalin's programme. Within the camps some minor but symbolic clothing regulations governing the political prisoners were eased, women prisoners not being obliged at all times to wear headscarves, and the sewing of convict-style identification tabs on jackets, giving name and number, discontinued. At the time of Stalin's death, the labour camp population had risen to 2,526,402.[12] This astonishingly precise figure had been given by Beria in a memorandum to the Presidium of the Central Committee at the start of his brief spell of power in the Kremlin. Thereafter, the numbers started to decline, reflecting in part amnesties for the criminals and the quashing of convictions for some of the "politicals". And, most significantly, in 1960 the Soviet penal code was revised: night-time interrogations were halted, some of the powers of the KGB were limited and, most important of all, Article 58 abolished, with its all-encompassing definition of counter-revolutionary crimes. More specific clauses took its place.

The advent to power of Leonid Brezhnev in October 1964, with the ousting of Khrushchev, heralded a decisive return to repression, accompanied by the partial rehabilitation of Stalin. Writers came into the spotlight in recognition of the much greater diffusion of information within Russia itself and the danger of its dissemination abroad. The harshness that characterised Brezhnev's 18-year rule was extended – and indeed amplified – for another two years by Yuri Andropov. His experience as head of the secret police and his conviction that dissenters posed a serious threat to the Soviet state earned him a special place in Soviet history. His death in February 1984 was followed by the one-year premiership of Konstantin Chernenko and then by the accession to power of Mikhail Gorbachev – honoured abroad as the dismantler of much of the totalitarian structure and at home often reviled as the dismantler of the Soviet empire.

At this point, a statistical round-up may not be amiss. Anne Applebaum's analysis reaches 28.7 million as representing the cumulative total of forced labour prisoners in the USSR over the period 1929 to 1953.[13] Within this total, using inflow and outflow figures, 18 million passed through the camps and colonies; collectivisation of farms led to the exile of over 2 million kulaks (farmers and labourers); special exiles might have numbered around 7 million made up of Balts, Poles, Tartars, Caucasians, Germans.[14] Excluded from these numbers are the political purges where summary executions of some three-quarters of a million made no call on prison facilities. Also excluded from consideration is the famine of 1953, a delayed consequence of the collectivisation programme, which claimed between 5 and 7 million lives. To quote Alexander Solzhenitsyn, thanks to "ideology" the twentieth century was indeed fated to experience evildoing on a scale calculated in the millions.

Alexander Solzhenitsyn
(1918–2008)

Principal Places of Incarceration and Detention

Brodwitz Prison, Eastern Poland	*February 9, 1945 (3 days)*
Lubyanka Prison, Moscow	*February – June, 1945 (5 months)*
Butyrki Prison, Moscow	*June – July 1945 (1 month)*
Krasnaya Presnya, Moscow transit prison	*August 1945 (2 weeks)*
Novi Jerusalem camp near Moscow	*Mid August – mid September 1945 (1 month)*
Kaluga Gate camp, Moscow	*Mid September, 1945 – July 1946 (7 months)*
Butyrki Prison, Moscow	*July – September 1946 (2 months)*
Moscow Prison Institutes at Rybinsk (*5 months*); Zagorsk (*5 months*); Marfino (*34 months*)	*September 1946 – May 1950 (44 months)*
Butyrki Prison	*May – June 1950 (2 months)*
prison transport	*June – August 1950 (1 month)*

Ekibastuz Kazakhstan Special Camp	*August 1950 – February 1953*
	(29 months)
Kok Terek, Kazakhstan Exile	*March 1953 – April 1956 (36 months)*
TOTAL	*129 months (ten years, nine months)*

On June 22, 1941 war was declared between the Soviet Union and Germany. The 23-year-old Solzhenitsyn promptly tried to join up but was initially refused on medical grounds, only achieving his patriotic ambition in October at a time when the war had taken a dramatic turn for the worse and recruitment barriers had been brushed aside. It was not until July 1943, however, that he was to see action. His subsequent war record was such that by the start of 1945 he had risen to the rank of captain. On February 9, 1945, he was arrested. Letters to his great schoolfriend, Nicolai Vitkevich, had been intercepted which contained some unflattering references to Stalin. In addition to this correspondence, the authorities held a copy of the young man's "Resolution No. 1" with his stated intention to organise a new party.[15] On July 7, 1945, he was sentenced by the Special Board of the NKVD (People's Commissariat for Internal Affairs) to eight years in corrective labour camps and perpetual exile "for anti-Soviet agitation and attempting to found an anti-Soviet organisation".

Nearly 11 years later, his sentence was annulled and his exile lifted. After experiencing in full Stalin-like repression he just managed to benefit from the relaxation introduced by Nikita Khrushchev.

A simple enumeration of Solzhenitsyn's places of imprisonment requires elaboration. During the five months in the Moscow gaol, Lubyanka, Solzhenitsyn was in the hands of the investigator assigned to his case. This could be long drawn out – for Ginzburg it had lasted two years – and relied on psychological pressures of isolation, often interspersed with sleep deprivation, and aimed at unearthing information as well as securing a recantation. The next stop was punitive: Solzhenitsyn's experience of labour camps (Novi Jerusalem and Kaluga Gate) introduced him to the crushing physical demands placed on prisoners classified for general labour. At different times, Solzhenitsyn found himself in the squads unloading timber on the Moscow River and, most memorably, in Novi Jerusalem's clay pits. This involved digging the clay from the

Alexander Solzhenitsyn, 1946

ground with shovels – and in the rain most often with hands – filling up the transport wagons and rolling them to the wet processing plant where the clay was pressed into bricks. All failures to achieve norms being rewarded with re-duced rations. As Michael Scammell succinctly puts it, quoting Solzhenitsyn, the work was so gruelling, the norms set so high, and the food so meagre that the vast majority of prisoners on general duty subsided into scavenging and died of exhaustion and malnutrition.[16] In Kaluga Gate, however, Solzhenitsyn secured briefly some respite by acting as a "trusty", i.e. an informer for the au-thorities, who were ever on the look-out for prisoners' escape plans, thereby enjoying valuable privileges, covering food and accommodation. He had the courage to make this deeply humiliating confession in his history *The Gulag Archipelago 1918 – 1950*, written some 30 years later.[17] Applebaum quotes him as saying that in the event he never reported on anything.[18]

In September 1946 he was unexpectedly reclassified as a "special as-signment prisoner". It may well have saved his life. From an inexperienced,

greenhorn "zek" (slang for prisoner), it converted him into a favoured
research boffin, an existence he was to enjoy for close to four years at the
Rybinsk, Zagorski and Marfino centers. Stalin's prison institutes, known
as "sharashkas", were designed to spur industrial and scientific innovation,
compensating for the arbitrary liquidation of academicians, scientists and
engineers in the purges of the Thirties and the losses incurred during the
war. Solzhenitsyn's qualification as teacher of mathematics, which had been
recorded in his prison induction, secured him positions on several projects,
notably the statistical study of the phonetic properties of the Russsian language, the practical application lying in telephone engineers' scrambling
needs. The atmosphere was in many ways academic: with daily contacts with
fellow prisoners, time for reading and recreation, but overlaid by constant
surveillance and the anxieties that it engenders.

This comparatively comfortable existence came to an end in May 1950. It
had been preceded by a tightening of discipline in the institutes and at the same
time a cooling of Solzhenitsyn's commitment to his own research work. A tactless attack on the head of the institute's own proficiency led to his dismissal and
his transfer to the Butyriki Prison. From there he was transported to the special
labour camp of Ekibastuz in Kazhakstan, some 600 miles short of the Chinese
border, which was to be his "home" for the next two and a half years.

The term "transport" calls for some elaboration. It features prominently in
the accounts of prisoners' relocations across the wildernesses of the USSR.
There were three modes of prison transport: by lorry, by railway cattle-
car, by Stolypin railway car. The open lorry was typically used at night in
the final stages of a journey; the front section was encased in metal cages,
behind which sat armed guards. The prisoners, 25 to a lorry, tightly packed
onto the floor, had to endure hours on end of shaking across roadless terrain.
Prior to that they will have experienced the train. If in the closed cattle cars,
into which the prisoners were crammed, there was minimal ventilation and
for a latrine a hole in the wooden floor. No provision for sleeping. If in the
Stolypin, named after its inventor in the czarist days, but "improved" after
the Revolution, they found themselves in a "normal" passenger coach, mod-
ified to take separate compartments (with bunks to accommodate eight into
which three times that many might be crammed) which gave onto a narrow
corridor that ran the full length of the coach. The compartment doors onto

the corridor were barred. There were no windows whatever, one side of the carriage being blank, the other adorned with deceptive blinds so that from the outside the nature of the cargo was effectively hidden.

During train journeys, the prisoners had to subsist on minimum food and water in all weathers, ranging from extremes of heat and cold. In the Stolypin the calls of nature had to be met by way of a guard escorting a prisoner to the facility at the end of the corridor. The prison numbers were such that this could be a protracted exercise. And a guard could have an attack of deafness or hide behind railway regulations. Irina Ratushinskaya once found herself in a Stolypin, attached to a goods train, that was stopped in a station and giving no sign of movement; prisoners at the end of their tether were met by the rule that use of the railway carriage toilet at stations was forbidden.[19] A cry went up, "start rocking", with some 100 prisoners rushing in unison from one side of their compartments to the other, threatening at any moment to derail the Stolypin – and, most importantly, exposing the guards to the wrath of their superiors: "Game, set and match" to the zeks on this rare occasion. More typically, prisoner transport justified the label "a shortcut to

Butyrka Prison, Moscow

death" from the cold of the winter, the heat of the summer, to be endured on journeys that might run to a week or more.

At Ekibastuz, Solzhenitsyn found himself in a camp that was less than a year old, having grown from a few hundred to close to 4,000 in that period. It formed part of a group of special labour camps in the area of Kazakhstan known as the Dzehezkazgan – an area of semi arid steppe – introduced in 1948 by Stalin with political prisoners much in mind. These presented in the authorities' eyes exceptional risks. Solzhenitsyn had arrived in time to contribute to the construction of the prison. It was also at Ekibastuz that he got the material for the prison "novel" that opened to the world a window on totalitarian Russia and contributed to his being awarded the Nobel Prize for Literature in October, 1970.

Prison Writing

It comes as no surprise that Solzhenitsyn should have turned his mind to writing from early on in his imprisonment. As a schoolboy in love with literature he had also written quantities of verse of his own, as well as short stories, one of which earned him a prize of a bicycle.[20] He had gone on to give himself, as a fervent Marxist, the goal of writing a big novel about the Revolution. Then came the war, his arrest and his first experiences of the hard labour camps Novi Jerusalem and Kaluga Gate. It was when moved to the prison institutes that he read extensively, exploiting the opportunities presented by a well-stocked library – of which at one point he was made librarian. It was there also that he began to write seriously. Reverting to his earlier interests, he embarked on what was to be a lengthy verse composition dealing with Marxism and the Revolution. His fellow prisoner, Lev Kopelev, was also in the throes of literary creation in verse. All of which, strictly forbidden. The sequence of composition began with the verse being written on scraps of paper, then committed to memory, after which the paper was burnt, occasionally swallowed, thereby eluding periodic searches. They could not conceivably be passed off as correspondence, for which there was strictly limited authorisation.

From the time of his departure from the Marfino scientific institute in May, he appears to have been in continuous literary effervescence – whether in the Moscow Butyrki Prison or during the lengthy train journey or in the camp itself. To a considerable extent he had to rely on his memory, which he trained using two ingenious aids. As described by Michael Scammell in his outstanding biography, one of these was based on counting the lines of verse with broken matches; the other had as a prompt a Heath Robinson rosary, made by Catholic Lithuanian prisoners fitted with different-sized "beads" at regular intervals.[21] In the camp itself, where Solzhenitsyn was put on the bricklaying squad, he used scraps of paper (paper and pencil being allowed but anything written had to be handed in) on which he would first write while at work in very small lettering twelve or twenty lines, memorise them, burn the papers in the stove. At the time, the work in question was his revealing autobiographical poem "The Way"; were any of it to have been discovered by the authorities, he would have been in line for severe punishment in the correction cells.

From his job as a bricklayer, Solzhenitsyn had been switched towards the beginning of 1952 to the foundry, a more physically taxing job. But it did not interfere with a final burst of activity: a verse narrative, *Prussian Nights*, a verse play, *Feast of the Conquerors*, and a start on another play, *Decembrists without December*. In recognition of his mental aids, Solzhenitsyn was later to write: "This necklace continued to help me write and remember right up to the end of my sentence – by which time I had accumulated 12,000 lines."[22] On February 9, 1952, he left Ekibastuz to start his exile at Kok Terek.

Of all his books, the most influential and one of the shortest was *A Day in the Life of Ivan Denisovich*. In common with so much of his work, it is grounded on his own prison experience, being based in this instance on his first winter at Ekibastuz.[23] Technically, it cannot be claimed as a piece of Solzhenitsyn's prison camp output, having been written several years after his release. Michael Scammell gives 1952 as the genesis and May 1959 as marking the time when Solzhenitsyn devoted himself without stint to its production. It may, however, be a reasonable assumption that much of its composition – in the author's astonishingly retentive mind – dates back to his imprisonment, thereby justifying its inclusion in this chapter. The autobiographical character is disguised both by its being termed a novel and by ascribing it to Ivan Denisovich Shukov, a labourer. This tallied with Solzhenitsyn's own sympathy with the underprivileged. Consequently, it served greatly to broaden the appeal of his book, giving it a relevance that it would have lacked had the fictional protagonist been, say, an intellectual or a merchant. And crucially, hard labour camps, a subject that stood at the top, or very near to the top, of political sensitivities was handled with extraordinary skill. A key to this success lay in confining the account to the relentless enumeration of the minutiae of 24 hours of struggle in a camp where punitive regulations were imposed in tandem with the harshest climate. Detailed brutalities were avoided, as were contentious judgments. Shukov was therefore able to give his famous summary of "a day without a dark cloud. Almost a happy day". It had started badly, however, with the outside temperature at -30°C: if only it had shown -41°C, then they ought not to be sent out to work.[24] But that aside, "he'd had many strokes of luck that day: they hadn't put him in the cells; they hadn't sent the team to the settlement; he'd pinched a bowl of kasha at dinner; he'd built a wall and enjoyed doing it; he'd smuggled that bit of hacksaw blade through; he'd earned something from Tsezar in the evening; he'd bought that tobacco. And he hadn't fallen ill. He'd got over it". He was then able to sleep fully content.

Nor could the timing be improved upon. Solzhenitsyn's internal exile had been lifted in April 1956.[25] He had subsequently re-established himself in Ryazan, some 300 miles south of Moscow, teaching physics and astronomy in the High School. He remarried his wife Natalia, divorced during the course of his imprisonment. In February 1957, a military tribunal had granted his request for his rehabilitation. All of this reflected the gradual spread of Khrushchev's "thaw". Solzhenitsyn already had to his credit a bulging portfolio of manuscripts and typescripts. This included the writings memorised during his imprisonment and which he had got onto paper once released from Ekibastuz. The political climate now made publication – hitherto an unthinkable proposition for a man with his prison background – theoretically feasible. While some of this material had enjoyed a limited degree of distribution under the counter, what he now needed was a courageous publisher in an established publishing business. He found these in Alexander Tvardovsky, and in the liberal literary magazine publishing house, Novy Mir.

The typescript successfully entered the offices of Novy Mir and onto the desk of the copyeditor, Anna Berzer, with the wife of Solzhenitsyn's friend from the institute days, Lev Kopelev, acting as courier.[26] Berzer, greatly taken by the work's literary qualities but also by its political boldness, then showed it to a colleague, Valeria Ozerova, who endorsed her judgment. To get it to Tvardovsky, one of four section chiefs, who was seen by Kopelev and Solzhenitsyn as likely to prove the most sympathetic, it was essential to bypass the usual hierarchical progress through layers of typically timorous editorial staff capable at any time of killing the project dead. Tvardovsky, who himself was the author of a mock-heroic war poem that Solzhenitsyn had admired in 1943, had one unique attribute: as an observer at the Twentieth Party Congress, he had actually heard Khrushchev's speech, which still had attached to it a "secret" label, notwithstanding its subsequent distribution to party officials. His direct personal experience will have given additional power to his elbow in his enthusiastic campaign for publication of a text that had been craftily handed to him and that he had read through the night of December 12, 1961.[27] The subsequent steps leading to publication included the securing by Tvardovsky of the unanimous agreement of the Novy Mir editorial board – after a number of revisions of a cautious nature – distribution of several typescripts for reviews; these, together with a copy of the revised manuscript, were sent on August 6 to Khrushchev's private secretary, Vladimir Lebedev (already an enthusiastic reader of the story), together with a letter to Khrushchev inviting him to give it his personal attention. Powerful evidence that this request had been taken to heart came on September 23, when Khrushchev ordered that 23 copies be distributed to the members of the Party Presidium, which was to meet in October. There the resolution to publish was proposed by Khrushchev, seconded by Anastas Mikoyan. Five days later, Tvardovsky received a copy of the resolution from Khrushchev during the course of a two-hour long meeting. The official publication day fell on November 17, 1962. A week later, several thousand delegates to the plenary session of the Central Committee were sent off to read "this very important book". *A Day in the Life of Ivan Denisovich* made an ideal fit with Khrushchev's programme of de-Stalinisation.[28] For Solzhenitsyn it was a triumphant achievement: the first book of his to secure publication under a Russian imprint and, furthermore, to have provided him with the delicious satisfaction that this supremely honest document should have seen the light under a totalitarian regime. Without precedent.

It was to prove finely timed. Khrushchev's overthrow in October 1964 brought a swift end to the political internal "thaw" and inaugurated a 21-year resumption of full-scale repression. Solzhenitsyn for his part was deprived of Soviet citizenship on February 13, 1974 and expelled from the country.[29]

Lev Mishchenko
(1917–2008)

Principal Places of Incarceration and Detention

As a German captive:	*October 1941 – June 1945*
Dulag Transit Camp; Fürstenberg-an-der Oder; Oschatz; Leipzig; Buchenwald-Wansleben salt mine; forced march	
As a Russian captive:	*July – November 1945*
Weimar; Frankfurt-an-der Oder	
Transit	*November 1945 – March 1946*
Pechora Corrective Labour Camp	*March 1946 – July 1954*
German Imprisonment:	*3½ years*
Russian imprisonment:	*8¾ years*
TOTAL	*12¼ years*

From the confines of the Pechora Corrective Labour Camp, 2,170 km north-west of Moscow, just short of the Arctic Circle, Lev Mishchenko engaged in an illicit correspondence extending over eight years that gave rise to 647 letters. This archive was supplemented by 599 letters from Svetlana Ivanova, the girl he had first met in 1935 when they were both students in the Physics Faculty of Moscow University. They fell in love, only to have their courtship overtaken by the declaration of war on June 22, 1941.

Lev promptly enrolled in the 8th Volunteer Artillery Division where the rank of junior lieutenant – the fruit of two years of military service –

Sveta and Lev Mishchenko

secured him the command of a small unit moving supplies from Moscow to a battalion at the front.[30] The rapidity of the German advance meant that in the first week of October many thousands of Russian troops, Lev included, found themselves encircled and made prisoners.[31] After a brief spell in a harsh transit camp, conditions improved for Lev in a succession of special prisons where attempts were being made to enrol and train suitable candidates for the role of spies. This Lev resisted; the nearest he came to some sort of cooperation was when he acted as a translator, notably at Oschatz early in 1942 and later at Leipzig, working for a sympathetic Czech functionary.[32] The next challenge that confronted him was when pressure was exerted on prisoners to join the German inspired anti-communist "Russian Liberation Army". Lev, having become a marked man for his lack of enthusiasm for this initiative, judged the time right to escape; he and a colleague enjoyed three weeks of freedom before being recaptured near the Polish border in July, 1943. The next two years were spent in punitive labour camps of increasing severity, ending with seven months in the salt mines at Buchenwald-Wansleben which housed a complex of munitions factories. Shortfalls in prisoner output as well any misdemeanours earned the culprits twenty lashes with a rubber club; from a custodial point of view, this had the considerable merit of being extremely painful, while leaving no mark on the body – thereby dodging the Geneva Convention rules governing the treatment of prisoners of war.

In April 1945 Buchenwald-Wansleben was evacuated with the emaciated prisoners, dragooned into columns, embarking on a forced march, which seemed destined to be a death march. Lev once again decided to take to his heels; together with a fellow-prisoner he managed to escape and on this occasion had the good fortune to encounter American troops shortly thereafter. For the next two months they enjoyed the comforts accorded liberated prisoners of war within the American zone. On June 8 they were taken to the Soviet zone of occupation.

Any Russian soldier who had been a prisoner was automatically an object of deep suspicion to the authorities. And Lev had been a prisoner of the Germans for much of the war. Moreover, during the course of these three and a half years, he had, on his own avowal, acted as a translator. He was promptly arrested as a traitor and transferred to the Weimar prison administered by the NKVD that was home to the special unit known by its acronym SMERSH ("Death to Spies"). His period of interrogation lasted more than a month and featured sleep deprivation and a succession of three- to four-hour night-time sessions. His refusal to sign a confession – he was no spy and he had to his credit two attempts at escape and a spell of seven months hard labour in the salt mines – was however obviated by an admission of guilt. He was tricked into signing what was presented to him as a formulaic preliminary to being found innocent by the military tribunal. The trial, on November 19, 1945, lasted 20 minutes. He was sentenced to death under article 58-1(b) of the Criminal Code reserved for Soviet servicemen – promptly commuted to ten years in a corrective labour camp. At the time, this was a common practice as a means of supplying manpower for extractive industries located in the most hostile environments.

The transfer from Germany to the corrective camp in the Komi Republic was a protracted exercise, lasting more than three months.[33] For Lev, his mode of transport was by railway cattle car, built to accommodate 20 cows and converted to take 60 prisoners.[34] Solzhenitsyn and Ratushinskaya had experienced the Stolypin, a passenger carriage adapted to accommodate some 100 prisoners. Much the same inhumane conditions characterised both: a starvation diet, often limited to 200 grams of bread a day, supplemented by salted fish, and accompanied by minimal provision of water – a diet that frequently proved fatal. One feature that gave Lev's experience an added level of horror was the mixing of criminals and politicals, where the former terrorised the others and did so with the connivance of the guards, who shared in any extortion and satisfied any sadistic urges.

The Pechora Correction Camp had been established in 1937 as a Gulag settlement. By 1946 it had become the industrial hub of the region with a prison population of 10,000; this included the Wood Combine, a vast wood processing centre, employing 1,600 prisoners.[35] The sub-arctic climate gave Pechora an average January temperature of -22.5°C; a low of -49°C was recorded by Lev in one of his letters, described in translation as "biting frosts".[36] On Lev's arrival that March, close to one-third of the consignment of prisoners was directed to the infirmary. Lev, toughened by his experience in German camps, was despatched to one of the 12 barracks serving the division known as the Second Colony, one of two situated in the Industrial Zone; the third was located at some distance outside. Lev's quarters were light on amenities – no running water, nothing but outside privies – but there was warmth and, critically, his companions were overwhelmingly political prisoners, from among whom Liubka Terletsky who was to become his closest friend.[37]

Assigned to the hauling team at the wood combine, his task was to drag tree trunks up from the river to the processing plant; in a 12-hour shift the quota was 60 cubic metres (equivalent to the contents of a small garage); if this was met the prisoner stood to be rewarded with a bread ration for the day of 600 grams, if he fell short of that figure, his ration was cut to 400 grams, and if he exceeded it he received 800 grams.[38] With prisoners standing, day in, day out, in icy waters, having to summon up the strength to shift heavy weights, more often than not in poor health, little wonder that mortality rates were high. Indeed, the route to survival for prisoners classified for general labour often depended on a reclassification. This was Solzhenitsyn's experience when he became a "special assignment prisoner". Somewhat the same transformation came to Lev when the head of the research laboratory, Georgii Strelhov, an old Bolshevik serving a 25-year sentence, came across him trying to enjoy a little warmth in the timber-drying plant and discovered Lev's engineering background. He was recruited at a time when Strelhov was under pressure to accelerate drying times and Lev, three months into this back-breaking work, was questioning his own powers of endurance.[39]

For the purposes of this book, the change of job was of capital importance since it was only then that Lev felt able to consider communicating with anybody outside the camp. Physically, he had escaped the debilitating condition experienced when clothes are always wet, the cold often intense and the workload hugely oppressive. Indeed, his new tasks in the wood drying unit exposed him at times to extremes of heat. Psychologically, to be part of Strelhov's research team came to have some characteristics of club membership. It was presided over by a man who was fair but strict, who had managed "to play the system" capitalising on his key role in the functioning of the wood processing unit. He had been able to create for himself what amounted to a civilised capsule in a thoroughly unpromising environment, where his friends might enjoy lively conversation, play cards or chess; he had built himself a radio, made home-brewed vodka, cultivated flowers in window boxes, weather permitting, and shared some of these amenities with a cat.[40] When in the autumn of 1946 Lev was transferred from the drying unit to the electric power station of the wood combine, the quality of life improved further: his working day was reduced to eight hours, to get to the generator room in the morning took him eight minutes, and when work consisted in keeping an eye on the machinery this was not in itself taxing; furthermore, he had secured valuable free time at the end of the working day.

In effect, Lev had become a non-person since his capture in October, 1941: he had disappeared from view, and as the months passed the chances of his having survived at all must have seemed to friends and relations more and more remote. And from Lev's point of view, he needed first to establish if the news of his survival after a gap of five years was going to be disruptive or welcome. A letter dated June 2, 1946, to Olga, a much-loved aunt who had helped bring him up (his parents had both been executed by the Bolsheviks for alleged complicity with the White Russians when he was four) was designed to sound out the situation, tactfully implying that it need not be shown to Sveta. Aunt Olga having happily ignored instructions, the situation was made crystal clear to him in a letter sent on July 12, 1946: "How many times have I wanted to nestle in your arms but could only turn to the empty wall in front of me? I felt I couldn't breathe. Yet time would pass, and I would pull myself together. We will get through this, Lev."[41] Much the same message was to be given thirty-six years later to Irina Ratushinskaya when her husband cried out at the end of her trial, "Hold on, darling, I love you". In both cases mutual support was being given at what was to become an endurance test lasting years.

Lev's reply was a shout of joy: "Sveta, Sveta, you are so close to me – it feels as if the last five years never happened, although it's also distance that separates us now, 2,170 kilometers. And to me you look practically the same – an imperceptible something, hardly noticeable in the photograph, says that your heart has aged a little, that is all . . . . Sveta, as you said, we'll get through this."[42]

This marked the start of a correspondence that was to last eight years from July, 1946 to July, 1954, 647 letters from Lev, 599 from Sveta, for a total of 1,246. This means that, between them, there was a weekly output of some three letters. As Orlando Figes points out, each letter being dated and numbered, there are no indications of any gaps. This meticulous book-keeping had the double merit of confirming to the recipient safe delivery and untangling any jumble arising from the fact that prison postal deliveries typically came two to three times a month. Sveta put the situation concisely: "When I was writing my first letter you were writing your second, but I sent my second when you were receiving my first, and I was writing my third when I received your first – and *La Traviata* was playing on the radio."[43]

The extent of official censorship is harder to establish. Figes judges it to have been relatively light, often undertaken by the wives of guards, who would merely block out the odd phrase as evidence of their presence. The real censorship was self applied, with Lev describing the advent of Spring rather than random killings by drunken guards, and generally trying to put a neutral slant on happenings in the camp – with a view to allaying Sveta's concerns, as well as avoiding the attention of censors. They also used code words, with officials of the MVD (Ministry of Internal Affairs) becoming "uncles" or "relatives", the prison system portrayed as being "the umbrella" and money for bribes "Vitamin D".[44]

Potential pitfalls throughout Stalin's dictatorship abounded. Just communicating with a prisoner was dangerous, and when the prisoner was dubbed a traitor all it took was for a correspondent to be denounced by a malicious neighbour and then to be accused of anti-Soviet agitation, for which the corrective was imprisonment.

That this prison correspondence should have taken place at the height of Stalin's dictatorship is altogether astonishing. At one level, it illustrates the complexity of the Gulag system, with camps differing widely one from the other. Within camps, there was the need to respond to what Yevgenia Ginzburg calls "the complicated hierarchy of Article 58" and the consequent segmentation of prisoners by group, according to the "crimes" imputed to them.[45] There is also the haphazard factor whereby centrally decreed procedures were often applied erratically or not at all. In short, incarceration in Pechora of political prisoners within the Second Colony differed much from Solzhenitsyn's and Ratushinskaya's experiences in Novi Jerusalem, Kaluga Gate, Ekibastuz or Barashevo.

The distinctiveness of Pechora is perhaps at its most stark in the freedom of movement allowed political prisoners within the camp. Once Lev's shift had been reduced to eight hours from 12, he had time after work to drop in to his unofficial "club", Strelhov's laboratory, or the Wood Combine clubhouse, where he might meet friends and make others. There was no question of roll calls during the day; prisoners were free to come and go from the barracks, only having to record their return at the close of day; no question of searches, whether regular or spot; the barracks left unlocked at night. And when at work in the Electric Power Station, he would be very much his own master, often having time to write letters, a much more convenient place than when in the barracks.

In searching out the reasons for these freedoms, the single most important influence will have come from the ubiquitous presence of free workers; in 1946 they numbered 445.[46] Many were themselves ex-prisoners, who, having served lengthy sentences, chose to stay put on a modest salary. Having doubtless lost the contacts they had before their imprisonment, many may well have lacked the self-confidence or drive to try to make a new life from scratch. Others may have been simply denied their exit papers, the MVD not wishing to lose their skills. They mingled freely with the prisoners, and while their living quarters were in the part of the Wood Combine known as the Settlement, which was distinct from the prisoners' Industrial Zone, it was only in 1949 that a barbed-wire barrier was set up. This proved pretty in-effective. There were cases of cohabitation between free workers' families and prisoners, to the distress of the authorities. One consequence of this pop-ulation mix that was of considerable importance to Lev and Sveta was the existence of a pool of men, who enjoyed full exit and entry privileges, some of whom might be prepared to smuggle letters in and out of the camp, whether out of sympathy or with the stimulus of a bit of "Vitamin D". They would of course be exposing themselves to punishment if caught.

Over time, Lev made firm friends with three or four free workers who became central to his clandestine correspondence, thereby enabling him and Sveta to bypass the normal prison mail room, whenever important matters had to be discussed. The procedure was that Sveta would send her letters to Lev's chief go-between, an academic journalist and author of popular sci-entific books, Lev Izrailevich, who had settled with his wife and family in a near-by town.[47] As a railroad despatcher he had frequent occasion to do contract work in the camp and consequently had a pass which gave him free entry at any time. He would hand on her letters and take Lev's for post-ing. In their correspondence, he was always known as Lev's namesake. When Sveta wished to get money to Lev, his address saved it from being pinched by the censors. The namesake was a keen photographer, which became a small source of income to him, and Sveta was able to send him supplies of photographic paper. Another important friendship was with Alexandr Aleksandrovsky, a Russian Civil War veteran.[48] Imprisoned for speaking up, out of turn, for a military hero, he later married a girl who had been evacuat-ed to Pechora from Moscow in the war. They were friends of Strelhov. Maria worked in the telephone exchange. For communications that lacked urgency, Lev had a wider circle of acquaintances who would help out with trips to the post office, thereby sidestepping whatever the prevailing Gulag rules cover-ing letters might be. All such helpers ran risks.

The bulk of the correspondence had the character of a conversation. Sveta would write about her work in Moscow at the Scientific Research Institute for the Tyre Industry, where she was employed in the physical and mechanical testing laboratory. This involved journeys of inspection to other centres, publi-cation of articles in the technical press and countless internal reports. She also took charge of the laboratory when her boss, Mikhail Tsydzik, was on holiday or unwell. He was only one of two non-family members to know at this time of her links to Pechora. An old friend of her father, he was an avuncular figure and very supportive. Lev also wrote about certain aspects of his work, notably when at the power station. Professional pride seems to have been sometimes felt by prisoners once they found themselves in jobs that relied on specific skills. Irina Ratushinskaya, who had no quarrel with the work as such, reported with some pleasure when able to achieve her daily quota of seventy industrial gloves. Solzhenitsyn, seen through the eyes of Ivan Denisovich, was chuffed to have met a demanding deadline in the construction of a wall. And Lev wrote about his satisfaction at having improved the working of the power plant, thereby raising productivity at the Wood Combine.[49]

For Lev, there was the additional incentive that whatever was seen as demonstrating his value in his work might strengthen his position. One rumbling worry was that he might be transferred back to the haulage team. But his abiding fear was to wake up one morning to learn that he was being relocated, say to a fresh Colony of the Pechora complex or to another camp altogether. At its worst, such a development would sever all the links that he had carefully built connecting him to Sveta and perhaps consign him, as far as she was concerned, back to the status of a nonperson. For both, such anxieties surface in the recurrent bursts of anguish when letters fail to arrive and wild thoughts are given free reign.

Orlando Figes is perhaps correct when he suggests that, psychologically, the strains on Sveta were particularly severe. From her adolescence, she was subject to moods which she called her darknesses and may have been an aspect of depression. At various stages in her letters she refers to bouts of tearfulness and then blames herself for inflicting her darknesses on Lev. The passage of time is likely to have weighed more heavily than on Lev. She was aged 29 when Lev was given his ten-year sentence, which meant that she would be 39 on Lev's release – providing all went according to plan – not the best time for having children. And if the five years that preceded his trial are taken into account, she will have been "Lev's girl" for over 15 years. Little wonder that a sense of hopelessness occasionally took hold of her. Her response was to shake herself and plan for the future, but one that had a much closer horizon: a visit to Pechora. As she wrote "I must live, not simply wait. Otherwise, when the waiting is over I may well find myself incapable of building our life together. I have always had this fear that love is not enough."[50]

Such a project was beset by challenges. In the first place, while visits to prisoners were not formally banned, few were granted, and those that were might be for 20 minutes, overseen by a guard, or as long as two days; this depended on the whim of the official concerned – perhaps influenced by some Vitamin D, but certainly unrelated to the length of the journey that had been undertaken. For Sveta, however, the real stumbling-block was that such visits were restricted to members of the prisoner's family, and she did not qualify. Her trip would therefore have to be illegal.[51]

To begin with, as an employee in an Institute that did work for the military, to be seen to be in contact with a convicted traitor was in itself highly hazardous. More than that, she would be travelling without papers. And, if she escaped detection on the journey, the task that confronted her on arrival was to gain entry into a closely guarded labour camp without having secured police (MVD) approval, and on entry to make contact with Lev, unobserved. The account of this venture, as seen through the letters selected by Orlando Figes and his accompanying commentary, keeps the reader on the edge of his seat as would a first-class spy thriller. It also illustrates what could be achieved through planning, guile, the courage of all those who helped as well as that of Sveta and of Lev – lubricated by good fortune.

As she would be entering illegally into the Gulag zone, she travelled on a ticket bought by her father from a military officer, and posed as his personal assistant. She wore a dress run up by a friend out of the khaki wool from an old army uniform; this proved an invaluable camouflage that served to deflect the attention of the inspector when faced with her invalid ticket.[52] Features special to incarceration in Pechora played a critical part in the visit's ultimate success, one of them being the ability to circulate relatively freely once inside the camp and the other the support of Lev's close free worker friends. On arrival, Sveta stayed in Lev Izrailevich's house. The following day he escorted her to the camp as being the wife of a free worker. The guard manning the entrance demanded that the "husband" should be summoned to claim his wife; the candidate, previously selected by Lev Izrailevich, was finally produced, wringing wet, having had to be revived from a drunken stupor with a bucket of cold water.[53] The place for the assignation – with

Lev already there – proved unsatisfactory, with the real wife taking a dim view of Sveta and also being fearful of becoming compromised. Eventually, a solution was found when they were taken in by the Aleksandrovskys, whose house was in the Settlement. They spent two nights there. One evening, they went to Stelkov's laboratory, where Sveta's pluck was much admired.

While Sveta's return journey had its moments of tension – at any time she might be stopped to have her documents checked – it was accomplished without any major disaster. But what had been achieved by this astonishing visit was confirmation that six years without seeing each other had left them feeling as committed as ever. It also gave them the encouragement to plan further annual visits. Four more were to be made. A degree of familiarity made them less fraught. Furthermore, some of the rules were relaxed, visitors for example no longer needing to be family members, so that Sveta found herself on the right side of the law. And following the construction of a new amenity, known as the "house of meetings", it proved possible in 1950 for Lev and Sveta to spend three whole days together.[54]

The next few years were affected by the ill health of Sveta's parents plus the demands on her at work, while Lev still had to cope with the insecurity of a prison existence, where a new boss at the power station proved to be a bully and a threat. But with Stalin's death on March 5, 1953, the old order was turned upside down, starting with amnesties for criminals, later extended to politicals and eventually to those with a traitor's stigma. Lev had to wait until July 17, 1954, to be released, thereby bringing to an end eight years and four months of imprisonment.[55] This did not mean, however, reunion with Sveta since, under the terms of his exit papers, Moscow was out of bounds to him – barring the occasional visit lasting no more than 24 hours. He was registered to work and live in the Kalinin area, some 100 kilometres to the north. It was only in September 1955 that, under an amnesty granted to Soviet citizens who had collaborated with the Germans, he was allowed to return to Moscow as a legal resident.

On September 27, 1955, Lev and Sveta registered their marriage, both aged 38.[56] This was one year less than the figure Sveta had come up with when calculating the age she would need to have reached before being able to contemplate having a family. December, 1955 saw the birth of their daughter, Anastasia, and January 1957 that of their son, Nikita.[57]

All that now remains is to describe how this love story came to be preserved as an extraordinary instance of prison writing. While letters to those
imprisoned in the camps have often survived, letters from the camps are
much scarcer. To find both sides of a correspondence, in autograph, is unprecedented. In the first instance, this owes much to the effectiveness of Lev's
furtive skills: Sveta's own letters, some that came through the normal postal
system (and were therefore overseen by censors) some smuggled in, were first
hidden in a cache beneath the floorboards of his barracks, to be periodically made into a parcel for surreptitious despatch to Sveta. For her part, she
had no trouble preserving his letters, whatever the route taken. This built up
into a pious archive. Another feature by which the modern reader is struck
is the apparent effectiveness of the normal postal service. This enabled Sveta,
for instance, to keep in close touch with Lev by letter via Lev Izrailevich,
from the different railway stops on her journey to Pechora and back to
Moscow. The modern method of "texting" would seem to be only marginally
more efficient.

In 2007, Lev and Sveta presented to the Memorial headquarters in
Moscow a vast accumulation of family papers comprising thousands of
letters, diaries, notebooks . . . packed into three trunks.[58] Both clearly had
well-developed magpie characteristics, perhaps a reflection of their scientific
training. The smallest of these trunks contained the love letters. Memorial,
the inspiration of a group of young historians in the 1970s, took its present form in the late 1980s and now has a structure made up of more than
50 member groups spread across the country. In Anne Applebaum's words,
writing in 2003, it is "the most important centre for the subject of Soviet
history, as well as for the defence of human rights".[59] Lev had already been in
touch with them when beginning work in 2000 on a short memoir, covering
mainly his war time experiences.

Orlando Figes tells the story of how Irina Ostrovskaya, Senior Researcher
at Memorial, introduced him to the letters in 2007 and his excitement as
the first bundles were untied.[60] What followed was their transcription, a
challenging task since they were written in a minute hand, this being especially the case with Sveta's letters, and liberally sprinkled with code words.
Transcription took two years, financed by The Leverhulme Trust.[61] Figes
records the help he received from many at Memorial, the involvement of

members of its academic council, and the assistance he received from various sources with his translation. Most of all, Figes benefited from the extensive interviews he was able to conduct with Lev and Svetlana (Lev was to die in August 2008, with Svetlana surviving him a further year and a half). To quote Figes, "Lev had a photographic memory and a remarkable ability to reflect on his recollections of the past."[62] Among the archives deposited with Memorial, a brief account by Svetlana of her visits to the labour camp proved of particular value. Were the present efforts by Russia's Justice Ministry aimed at the liquidation of Memorial to bear fruit – by blocking funding from abroad and hindering domestic sources of finance – access to Memorial's huge archive would no doubt be compromised and any additions would cease. And tomorrow's scholar would be denied the thrill of coming across the concluding paragraph to one letter: "The point of all this is that I want to tell you just three words – two of them are pronouns and the third is a verb (to be read in all tenses simultaneously: past, present and future)".

Irina Ratushinskaya
(1954–2017)

Principal Places of Incarceration and Detention

Butyrki Prison, Moscow	*December 10 – 20, 1981 (10 days)*
KGB Investigative Prison, Kiev	*September 1982 – March 1983 (7 months)*
Barashevo Camp, Mordovia	*April 1983 – August 1985 (29 months)*
PKT Prison, Yavas	*August 1985 – January 1986 (6 months)*
Barashevo Camp, Mordovia	*January – July 1986 (7 months)*
KGB Investigative Prison, Kiev	*July – October 9, 1986 (4 months)*
TOTAL	*53 months (4½ years)*

Irina Ratushinskaya, born in Odessa, was of part Polish extraction. Her upbringing was conventional, but her developing attachment to Catholicism put her at odds with her parents, who did not waver in their faith in

Communism.[63] From university in Kiev, the Odessa Pedagogical Institute, she graduated with a degree in physics in 1976. It was also at around that time that she was introduced to Russian poets of the Silver Age, Pasternak being an early enthusiasm, and took her own first poetic steps. In 1979 she married the human rights activist Igor Gerashchenko.[64] Her husband records that it was some two years earlier that she had realised that poetry was to be her vocation, a career that launched her into what was defined as the "dissemination of slanderous documentation in poetic form". Her works were by no means overtly political, but gently nostalgic. Official recognition came, as it were, to her in August 1981, when the KGB demanded that she stopped writing poetry. She and her husband were also promised arrest if they continued with their human rights activities. Both lost their jobs. Their several applications to emigrate – which were refused – naturally also caught the attention of the authorities, as did their attendance on December 10, 1981, at the annual demonstration in defence of human rights in Moscow's Pushkin Square, which earned them ten-day gaol sentences.[65]

On September 17, 1982 Irina Ratushinskaya was arrested under Article 70[66] in her capacity as a writer of poetry.[67] Prolonged searches of the flat she and her husband occupied in Kiev and of the premises of known sympathisers had been duly made, supplemented by close questioning of the occupants. She was taken to the Investigative Prison at Kiev and held there for the next seven months in "solitary". In her account of the incarceration, the KGB did not try "any physical methods" by way of extracting a confession or information, relying instead on psychological pressure.[68] This was to be achieved in the first instance by qualifying her "solitary" status by giving her as cell companion a common criminal, one of their most seasoned and aggressive plants. Later, Irina was assigned to a cell on her own, the only interruptions being the extended sessions with her dedicated investigator, Lukyanenko. After deploying the full panoply of investigative weapons, comprising threats of psychiatric treatment (outward signs of distress could be seized on to justify consignment to a lunatic asylum), heightened prison punishments, increased KGB interest in the careers of family members and acquaintances, mixed with rewards on any signs of cooperation, Irina managed to make clear that she would take no part in the investigation and that she would

Irina Ratushinskaya

talk of nothing that might be connected with the case being put together against her.

The trial, when it came, extended over three days, an improvement over Ginzburg's, which had been measured in minutes, but otherwise the two had much in common. Having refused the services of the KGB-appointed lawyer, she was not allowed to select one herself. She was also refused permission to conduct her own defence. And, because she had been arrested under the politically sensitive Article 70, this had the merit from a KGB perspective of the trial being closed to anybody other than KGB "extras" and prosecution witnesses, drummed up for the occasion. Bizarrely, her husband Igor was one of them. This had the perverse consequence of confirming to Irina that he was alive and free and of enabling him, not having seen her for more than six months, to shout out before being hustled out of the court – and after having given the judge a crisp insight into his views – "Hold on, darling, I love you".[69] On March 5, the day after her 29th birthday, she received the maximum sentence applicable to her "crime" of seven years of strict regime camps, to be followed by five years of internal exile.

The Small Zone

The camp to which she was assigned was one of a network of 14 built in Stalin's time in Mordovia, some 300 miles south-east of Moscow. They bore the name Dubrovlag (Oak Leaf Camps), were centrally administered from the town of Yavas and had the distinction of containing, in Zone 4 of Corrective Labour Colony Number 3 at Barashevo, the only known labour camp for women dissidents in the USSR at that time.

In the 1980s there were four types of regime regulating conditions of imprisonment in labour camps: Ordinary; Intensified; Strict; Special, each entailing a progressive reduction in prisoners' rights. Prisoners under the Special regime were held in cells. Irina, being under the Strict regime, was housed in what was known as the Small Zone, a unit reserved for women political prisoners, separate from, but adjoining the quarters occupied by the criminals, whether men or women. Within the Small Zone, there was a wooden building, which at various times during her incarceration was to hold from five to a high of 11 prisoners. At her induction, she found herself with four fellow prisoners, Tanya Osipova, Raya Rudenko and Tatyana Velikonava, all three human rights activists, and Natasha Lazareva, producer of an illegal journal dealing with day-to-day feminist issues.[70]

As a strict regime "political", Irina learned her "entitlements": (a) on completion of half her sentence, one parcel weighing five kilos once a year; (b) to receive three meetings a year with relatives, one a "long" meeting lasting from one to three days at the discretion of the camp authorities, and two others, at least six months apart, of two hours, across a table with an administration official present; (c) to make purchases at the prison kiosk of up to five roubles a month, potentially to supplement the near-starvation fare of the prison, but often absorbed in the purchase of soap – which the authorities favoured, since it served to reduce the incidence of scabies; by law, prisoners had to be able to wash once a week; (d) prison food made up of a porridge (kasha) for breakfast and lunch, often doused in salt (a direct cause of swollen legs through fluid retention), a daily ration of bread and an evening meal of "skilly", the standard prison dish, also experienced by Solzhenitsyn, being a thin broth often enriched by maggots; (e) the right to receive and send letters, subject to censor scrutiny and normally involving delays of three months; (f) work six days a week, from 7am to 4pm at sewing machines producing industrial gloves – in itself recognised by the prisoners as an acceptable task albeit in very unhealthy conditions – tied to daily quotas per prisoner of 70 pairs. All of these "entitlements" were subject to adjustment, without notice, the cancellation of visitor permissions being much favoured: Igor was to make the long journey from Kiev to Barashevo eight times, but only twice did he manage to see his wife. The punitive docking of food allocations had to compete with the impact of shrinkage at the different stages of cooking and distribution. The richest punishment harvest came from infringements to the plethora of prison regulations. Clothing was contentious: the convict-style labels on jackets were once again mandatory, as was the wearing at all times of headscarves; the addition of an extra layer of underwear in the depths of winter was a gross breach of rules. The upkeep of the house that housed them gave rise to meticulous instructions, extending to how beds should be made up. And woe betide a summer initiative of supplementing the diet by growing herbs in their yard, referred to as the Street: promptly condemned as illegal and dug up.[71]

While the Small Zone was not occupied by warders, it was subject to spot checks and regular visits, with one particular warder having sadistic inclinations. The hut being bugged, any conversations of significance had to be in the open. The prison authorities took every opportunity to come down hard on lapses – whether real or invented – and to search out the slightest signs of illicit contacts with the outside world. Helping them in their task was the SHIZO, the name given to punishment cells located in Camp Number 2, some distance from their own Camp Number 3, and reached by a dedicated small train, known affectionately as the "cuckoo".[72] In the SHIZO each cell held up to four people, was six yards long, not quite four across, with a wooden floor rotted by damp, for sleeping wooden benches, light bedding removed during the day, no changes of clothes, and with every other day a "hungry" one indicating the bread ration but no skilly. "Housekeeping" chores centred on dealing with the night soil: the iron cell bucket, 12 kilos empty, 44 kilos if full, had to be moved in all weathers to the cesspit by the thoroughly weakened inmate(s). By law, the cell temperature might not fall below 16 degrees centigrade; the warders' thermometers showed at all times 15.5°C, independent (illegal) prisoner thermometers 9°C to 11°C.[73] Thirteen days worth of SHIZO, which left the prisoner dizzy from hunger, were guaranteed to heighten existing infirmities and were the harbinger of new ones, pneumonia being a strong contender and kidney failings a frequent feature. In summer, whenever the camp was struck by a wave of dysentery, the situation of those sent to SHIZO was particularly deplorable. More generally, low-level fever was a debilitating commonplace in the Small Zone.

Irina Ratushenskaya's statement of engagement so to speak is set out in her book, *Grey is the Colour of Hope*.[74] "We may be crammed into a small house, we may be dressed in rags, they can carry out searches and lightning raids in our quarters, but we retain our human dignity. We will not get down on all fours to them. We will not carry out demeaning or senseless commands because we have not surrendered our freedom ... we remain free. For this reason, we study every camp rule carefully." This led to incessant battles with the camp administration over subjects ranging from the need for urgent medical attention to the most trivial rights. This was one of the main features of daily life. It also gave rise to a flow of letters addressed to the Procurator, backed up by references to the Penal Code and the camps' "Rules of Internal Order". For the most part, they elicited no response.

What I have called Irina's "statement of engagement" stands in striking contrast to the experience of "politicals" in Solzhenitsyn's day: then, she would have been laughed out of court – something that she was swift to recognise. As she writes in her memoir *In the Beginning*: "We are better off than the earlier ones. We're a new generation of dissidents, following a trail blazed by others."

Underlying Irina's improved circumstances was the major shift in Russia's exposure to the outside world. Some of the steps leading to the heightened visibility of Russia's domestic affairs can be readily itemised. In the 30 years that separated Irina from Solzhenitsyn, the USSR, having already signed the 1948 United Nations Declaration of Human Rights, became a signatory of the Helsinki Treaty of 1976, which incorporated agreements on human rights that recognised "freedom of thought, conscience and belief".[75] This spawned monitoring groups that sought to check on the Soviet Union's observance of the Treaty, Tanya Osipova being just such a monitor. Russia's comfortable legal invisibility had already been breached in the notorious 1964 trial of the poet Joseph Brodsky, when notes taken by a journalist were smuggled out to the United States, thereby exposing Russian court practices in all their corruption.[76] Significantly, the four-year sentence was later reduced to two years, an early instance perhaps of Russian sensitivity to foreign opinion.

Amnesty International, founded in 1961, took an early interest in Russia. In 1963, a campaign backed by some seven thousand cards from Amnesty members secured the release from prison in Siberia of the Ukrainian Archbishop. In 1971, Slava Aidov, imprisoned five years earlier for attempting to buy a printing press, was freed on the back of another letter writing campaign.[77] The role played by PEN International (founded in 1921) should not be overlooked. Russia was by no means neglected by its worldwide community of writers in their tireless promotion of freedom of expression. Striking evidence of this had already come on August 25, 1968, when a demonstration mounted by no more than seven people was held in Red Square in protest against the invasion of Czechoslovakia. The dissidents, who chose the corner of the square favoured by tourists, unfolded their banners carrying the slogan "Hands off the CSSR"; they were promptly pounced upon and thrown into police wagons.[78] That evening Western radio channels were reporting the event.

Earlier in the year, the first issue of a new samizdat (a self-published journal) appeared on April 30, 1968, bearing the title *Chronicle of Current Events*[79]; this was the document, compiled in Moscow, of the human rights "Democratic Movement", itself founded in 1963. Samizdat, the term used for underground literature, could take any number of forms: at its most primitive a manuscript poem, that was first typed, circulated, retyped, circulated, retyped and so on in the manner of a round-robin letter, achieving thereby a modest circulation; handwritten newsletters, bulletins, transcripts of foreign broadcasts might follow suit, benefiting perhaps from mimeographing; another medium consisted of cassette tapes; and at the top end of the range, the professional production of journals and books, dependant on underground typesetting and printing often located in Communist Poland. Anne Applebaum amusingly writes that, in delayed response perhaps to the détente under Khrushchev, the samizdat formula grew into a national pastime.[80] They were of course illegal.

The *Chronicle* was more illegal than most. One of its founders, Pavel Litvinov, was to be one of the seven Red Square demonstrators.

The *Chronicle* had the activities of dissidents as its subject matter. The objective was that it should be factual and descriptive, a neutral recording of otherwise unpublished news events. In its fifth issue, it gave as its patriotic aim "seeing that the Soviet public is informed about what goes on in the country".[81] The United Nations having designated 1968 as the International Human Rights Year, the Chronicle took as its masthead the right to freedom of expression as proclaimed in the UN's Universal Declaration of Human Rights. Over the 15 years of its existence, from 1968 to 1983, making up a total of 64 issues, its liberal values encompassed those persecuted for their religious convictions, for their ethnic origins (Crimean Tartars), for their national loyalties (Lithuanians) as well as for their political convictions. It is under this last heading that the *Chronicle*'s relevance to prison writers is most evident. Regular features included "Inside the Prisons" and "Inside the Punishment Cell". The entries might record how on September 13 Zhukanska found a white worm in his soup, how on October 10 Balkharov was taken by force to attend a meeting of the camp's Education Committee, as well as providing a tabulated record covering the first eleven issues: 37 arrests, 85 trials, extrajudicial persecution affecting 250, the fate of 102 forced labour camp inmates and of 27 mental hospital inmates.[82]

Peter Reddaway suggests that the Democratic Movement may have had 2,000 mainstream, acknowledged members.[83] While the Chronicle portrayed itself as legal, the KGB typically waged a war against it, anybody implicated in its editorial production being a candidate for incarceration – as was the experience of Tatyana Velikonava; the dedicated correspondents, as well as those caught with copies, were also at serious risk. The KGB's chief concerns, however, did not lie in the domestic circulation, amounting to only a few thousand copies, but rather in its leakage abroad. A public relations triumph was to come in November, 1984, when the Small Zone managed to send a congratulatory telegram to President Reagan on his re-election, which reached him with a two-day delay and promptly became front-page news.[84] The achievement was all the more remarkable for the fact that the two who masterminded this coup, Irina Ratushinskaya and Tanya Osipova, were at the time serving sentence in SHIZO.

It is in the context of a country where communications had to a limited extent broken free of the totalitarian grip – and critically had achieved an international dimension – that the activities of the Small Zone dissidents can be considered. This conjunction gave the prisoners a new "weapon" in their struggles against a totalitarian regime trampling on human rights: a hunger strike. In Solzhenitsyn's day, it would have been a matter of supreme indifference if a zek were to choose to go down that self-destructive path. The one exception was the coordinated strike, putting a camp's economy at risk. In Irina's time, a hunger strike could exert influence at two levels. Firstly, with hunger strikes having to be reported to central authorities, the camp officials had the worry that such strikes might be held against them. Secondly, hunger strikes by political prisoners were newsworthy events, and were they to prove fatal they would be certain to attract foreign attention.

A case study concerns Natasha Lazareva, in bad health, who after some six months of Small Zone campaigning gets to see a doctor; he has her admitted to the camp hospital, only for her to be discharged for socialising with the maintenance staff.[85] She is then accused of malingering over the sewing of industrial gloves and earns spells in SHIZO. At that point, in Irina's words, the Small Zone unit convenes and decides on a collective hunger strike aimed at securing medical attention for Natasha. The first few days without solid food are accompanied by severe hunger pangs; these then subside, to be followed by spells of dizziness and nausea. By the seventh day the pangs come back and the ability to swallow any water is affected. And it is also at that stage that the authorities might switch to force feeding. Irina, en route to where this procedure takes place, well away from Number 3 Camp, but within the hearing of other criminals' quarters, manages repeatedly to shout out her Kiev telephone number and the reasons for their strike – in the hope that the news will reach her husband in Kiev so that he can secure maximum publicity.[86] And when she arrives where the tube is to be forced down her throat or into her nostril she finds the strength to struggle so much that she is thrown head first onto the wooden trestle and knocked senseless.[87] She is then force fed.

From the outset of her imprisonment, she decided to take careful note of all that happened to her, as did Yevgenia Ginzburg. On her calculations, she spent when in Barashevo 120 days and nights in SHIZO.[88] She was also given six months' "solitary" in the internal camp prison, PKT, at Yavas "for her repeated protests against camp practices".[89] The one advantage at Yavas was slightly fuller rations.

Prison Writing

At all times during her imprisonment, Irina Ratushinskaya managed to write. Typically, composition started with her committing the verse to memory . This might be for want of pencil and paper when in SHIZO or PKT; in the court room, where an accused was not expected or allowed to while away the time in literary composition; whenever she was transported away from the Zone, be it to and from SHIZO, the PKT, or the hospital, often by the "cuckoo". Occasionally, as a memory prompt, the initial text was on a bar of soap, onto which several lines of verse were written, a match stick serving as a graver. Once memorised, what bibliographers might justifiably term "the very first state of utmost rarity" would be washed away. The poems would then be transcribed, a laborious process requiring minute lettering on cigarette paper four centimetres wide, that invaluable medium for clandestine communication.[90] Irina, taking a page as it were out of Solzhenitsyn's experience, found a way of combining her creative writing with her daily manual work: when at her sewing machine, she would compose poems, jotting lines down on small slips of paper which would be concealed under a pile of unsewn gloves. When the poem was complete, she would commit it to memory, burn the preliminary bits of paper and later transcribe the poem onto cigarette paper.[91] In her own words, "the poems would be tightly rolled into a small tube, the thickness of a little finger and made moisture-proof by a method of our own devising". They were destined for transmission to Igor in Kiev, ever ready to convert them into a typed samizdat for distribution not only within Russia, but also abroad.

In addition to verse, the Small Zone was an extremely important source of copy for the Chronicle of Current Events by reason of its newsworthiness, being the only place of detention for women political activists, and for the presence in its midst of Tatyana Velikonava, described as acting as the "backbone" to the *Chronicle* after its founder, Natalya Gorbanevskaya, was arrested.[92] It is impossible to establish how much of the day-to-day reporting was

Irina's work. Early in 1985, a 23-page "Diary of the Small Zone", covering the months of August 1983 to April 1984, started circulating through unofficial channels. This remarkable, very detailed document had been smuggled out of the camp by Irina's husband on one of the two visits when he had been able to see his wife; at the same time, he had taken back with him Irina's first collection of prison poems. The Diary will have been a joint effort, with Irina one of a group of seven at that time. In any assessment of Irina's prison writing, an unquantifiable, but surely significant, part of the Diary can be put to her credit.

"By one means or another, everything became known "outside" sooner or later".[93] This bold statement points to the complex information network that had been built up, supplementing such direct contacts as were achieved with visiting relatives. The precise details are still hard to establish. Irina was circumspect on the subject, anxious to leave open channels of communication for those still remaining in Russian prison camps or subject to prison-camp-style imprisonment. It is indeed a sobering consideration that as of today her experiences are a mere 35 years old.

A feature of the camps that deserves attention is that they had populations that were by no means static. The turnover on the criminal side (with the majority of prisoners down for theft) was typically extremely high. This made for continuous streams of prisoners moving into the camps and out of them. Those departing did so because they had completed their prison term or were beneficiaries under an amnesty. All this oscillation gave rise to opportunities of contact for the normally isolated politicals. Soldiers on escort duty – here today, gone tomorrow – were potentially among the most promising; departing zeks, demob-happy on the eve of freedom, but bearing with them their well-practised skills in concealment, came a close second. From among the resident population of guards and prison personnel, some might be open to bribery and others could be influenced by humanitarian considerations. But enlisting their help in the transfer of material to the outside world depended on timing and judgment. A minor refinement mentioned by Anne Applebaum: the Mordovian camps, having been organised towards the end of Stalin's era, had the reputation of being manned by guards who were not as hardened as the veterans from the longer-established labour camps.

The wherewithal for bribes available to the Small Zone prisoners was undoubtedly limited. They did, however, have access to modest sums of money from "home"; furthermore, bribes often did not need to be large and might indeed be in kind, as for instance a cigarette lighter from Moscow, or perhaps something saved from one of those rare parcels to which prisoners were entitled. And for those leaving the camp, the reward might come, on delivery, at the address of the contact that had been surreptitiously given them.

This leaves open the question of how in practice the transfer of the illicit writings was made from the Small Zone. The key seems to lie in the frequency with which the prisoners themselves were required to leave the Zone en route for SHIZO, PKT, re-education sessions, the hospital … Irina gives us occasional glimpses of how it worked: "I managed to send this poem off ('I sit on the floor, leaning against the radiator') during the transportation back to the Zone from SHIZO. First it went to 'unnamed people', and then to Igor. This poem reached him before I was to go into SHIZO again."[94]

Her mode of travel was the red zek carriage of the rattling "cuckoo" train, where she would find herself in a noisy throng of prisoners.[95] Revealingly, her conclusion was that these periods of transportation were the most valuable feature of going to SHIZO. And in one rather charming boast of a young woman, "if there had been at least one transport on which I had not managed to pass poetry and information to those who 'fronted' for Igor, I would never have said that zeks were not zeks, and guards are not guards. Or I must be out of my mind". Covert help was indeed something she was able to secure.

Reference to those who "fronted" for Igor serves to highlight Igor's own contribution from outside the camp. He was helped by "ordinary Kiev workers (in typing and duplicating), by former zeks, by Moscow professors, and even by some of my gaolers".[96]

Publications

Irina's publishing achievements while still imprisoned are considerable. Two collections of prison poems were spirited out of the Barashevo Camp, the first, which included poems from the Kiev Investigatory Prison, and the second some two years later, confined to poems written in the Small Zone and the PKT in Yavas. These collections entered the samizdat distribution system. The collaborative prose "Diary of the Small Zone" appeared in the Number 17 issue of the unofficial journal *Materiali samizdata* of May 20, 1985.

Circulation of Irina's verse abroad culminated in 1984 with *Poems by Irina Ratushinskaya*, published by Ann Arbor, in association with PEN, the original Russian being accompanied by translations in English and French.[97] Aside from the powerful literary endorsement that this represented, it was a considerable achievement in the cause of human rights. Irina, for her part, saw publication in the West "as a safe deposit for the preservation of our persecuted culture". She first learned of the Ann Arbor edition when the KGB came to interrogate her on the subject, pointing out helpfully that foreign publication might well earn her a hefty addition to her prison sentence.

The last work of hers to appear at a time when she was still imprisoned was her collection *No, I'm Not Afraid*, published in June 1986 by Bloodaxe Books in the English translation of David McDuff. In a neat public relations move, copies were sent to Mikhail Gorbachev and Ronald Reagan.

On the eve of the Russia/USA summit meeting at Reykjavik of June 9, 1986, Irina Ratushinskaya and Tanya Osipova were among those prisoners of conscience freed, marking the start of Gorbachev's policy of releasing such dissidents. Having served four and a half years of her prison sentence, she was excused the remaining two and a half years and the whole of her five years of internal exile. She and her husband were allowed to leave Russia in December 1986. Several years later, they returned to Russia. She died in January 2017.

Conclusion

One is left with an abiding admiration for the disinterested courage of the inmates of the Small Zone in their fight against intolerance and their espousal of human rights, defined to encompass all and sundry. And to choose to fight a totalitarian regime by courting death through hunger strikes takes one's breath away. The wonder grows on finding in Irina Ratushinskaya a poet wielding a pen full of the gentlest irony – as when she turns to the natural world for enlightenment.[98]

The spider-mathematician (hard to imagine a sorrier creature)

Keeps trying to count his thin little legs.

But sensibly he doesn't believe the tiny number he ends up with

And angrily mutters "The damned thing won't work out again!"

He has woven diagrams, assiduously measured the angles,

He solves the problem of which is the wolf and which the goat

With a cabbage leaf, but doesn't believe the result and once again

Rustles hopelessly and sighs: "I know the answer, but how to prove it?"

O potty genius, crucified on coordinates,

Eccentric Pythagoras, half-witted prison prophet!

Wait before you creep away: I believe your results!

Spread out your diagram, and count the days of my sentence, please.

KGB Investigative Prison, Kiev, January, 1983

(D)
CONVICTED
MURDERERS

CHAPTER XVIII

Pierre-François Lacenaire

(1803–1836)

Incarcerations

La Force; Bicêtre; Poissy; Beaune; Dijon	*1829 – 1835*
Conciergerie	*October 28, 1835 – January 8, 1836*
Bicêtre	*January 9, 1836*

Lacenaire is unusual on many counts: a self-confessed murderer, with a strong poetic vein, who achieved cult status – in his lifetime and beyond – and devoted the last two months of imprisonment ahead of his execution to burnishing his literary legacy.

Lacenaire was born in Lyon, the fourth in line in a family of eight, having two older sisters and one elder brother. At the time, his father, Jean-Baptiste, was a prosperous merchant. Lacenaire's education took him to a succession of schools from several of which he was dismissed, once for outspoken reformist religious views and on another occasion for having entered into a fight with a teacher. Throughout, he appears to have distinguished himself scholastically, notably in the literature classes. On completion of his studies in September 1819, he was taken first of all into a solicitor's practice for one year, then for six months into a notary's practice and spent two years as a junior in a bank. This was followed by a spell in Paris, staying with an aunt; it was there that he first tried to embark on a literary career, writing poems, composing songs for a vaudeville, doubtless for one of the theatres in the Boulevard du Temple, and contributing articles to newspapers. Failure to be remunerated adequately led him to join, using a false name, a Swiss regiment serving under the French flag, where he was placed in the quartermaster's office. Before long he deserted, returned to Lyon, whence he worked as a travelling salesman dealing in spirits, and this took him to England and Scotland. At about this time he started passing forged bills of exchange.

Pierre François Lacenaire
by Théophile Junca,
lithographer

Early in 1828 saw him in Geneva where he engaged in a duel – the first of eight on his own count – which pitted him against a man who had denounced him as a swindler.[1] Lacenaire took the precaution of supplying his opponent with an unloaded pistol, with predictable consequences.[2] Back in France, he signed up with an infantry regiment for eight years, again on the quartermaster's side, was punished for accounting irregularities, went with his regiment to Spain and in March 1829 deserted once more. On his return to France, he learned that his father had become a bankrupt and had left for Belgium with his mother and the other members of the family, thereby leaving him without any potential financial backstop and, more to the point, reducing to zero his "expectations". His response turned him to theft, including that of a one-horse chaise in Paris in June 1829. His second lethal duel also took place at this time, the victim being the nephew of the early-nineteenth-century politician and author, Benjamin Constant. The theft of the chaise, not the duel, led to his first term in prison, amounting to one year, initially in La Force, later at Bicêtre and Poissy, where he was put to work assembling boxes.

On his release from Poissy in September 1830 and after an additional month's detention in recognition of his record as a deserter, a series of burglaries put his finances into better order – only to have the benefits squandered at a gaming house. He took to earning some money as a scrivener, being employed as a copyist, for which he showed ability, and later working on his own account. The July Revolution of 1830, which saw the departure of Charles X, Louis XVI's surviving brother, and his replacement by Louis-Philippe (the Orleanist Bourbon) as a constitutional monarch, created buoyant market conditions for scriveners struggling to meet the demand for countless applications for jobs, petitions for grants, claims for compensation. His income from these sources was supplemented by his participation in a homosexual blackmail ring. The theft of silver from a restaurant in July 1833 earned him, however, a second imprisonment; this time it was for 13 months, initially in La Force and later at Poissy. On his release in August, 1834, he and fellow ex-convicts suffered several disappointments, failing to relieve on two occasions company messengers of their satchels and one of missing out on the winnings of a gambler returning home from the card tables. This was not for want of the use of force on their part. His own attempt at killing Javette, a stallholder in the Saint Jacques market, who presented a danger to him as a witness of one of his acts of aggression, was also thwarted.[3] A reliable source of income came from burglaries using skeleton keys. And on December 14, 1834, Lacenaire with two accomplices, his friend Victor Avril and another jail-bird called François Martin, went to the apartment of their prison acquaintance Jean-François Chardon, a 38-year-old with depraved tastes and a long criminal record, who lived with his mother in a lodging in the Passage du Cheval Rouge, off the rue Montorgueil near the Halles. One attraction had been a treasure trove, rumoured to amount to 10,000 francs.[4] Another, for Lacenaire, had been the opportunity to cap his rebellion against society with a murder. In the event, the "hoard" amounted to no more than 500 francs, but the double murder of Chardon and his mother left Lacenaire well satisfied.

With the murders unsolved, Lacenaire and his colleagues were able to pursue their criminal course for a few more weeks in Paris. Indeed, a mere 14 days later, he devised an elaborate financial trap, which had required, after recruiting an assistant, the rental of an apartment to which the targeted bank was to deliver cash from the exercise of a fraudulent bill of exchange. The messenger escaped with his life, though wounded, and Lacenaire was left empty-handed. Lacenaire quickly picked himself up, and early that January left Paris for Geneva with another big forgery in his sights. This also involved visits to Lyon, Dijon and Beaune, and it was in Beaune that the law caught up with him and he was arrested for the Geneva swindle. His false names – Gaillard, Jacob Lévi, Mahussier – were stripped off him and it was as Lacenaire that he was transferred back to Paris to La Force on April 18, 1835, where he was housed in the felons' wing. One month later he chose to reveal to M. Allard, the chief detective in the Parisian force, his responsibility for the double murder; this later led to his being roughed up by prisoners who took a dim view of his having implicated his partners in the murders, his justification being that he felt they had already betrayed him.[5]

The frequency with which La Force features in this curriculum vitae calls for some comment. This prison, situated halfway between the Hôtel de Ville and the Bastille, originally consisted of two separate establishments in adjoining buildings: la Petite Force, which housed prostitutes who had not kept up the regular monthly charges set by the police or were there on the score of disorderly behaviour; and la Grande Force, whose intake was of men remanded in custody pending their trial, which would either lead to their release or, on conviction, to their transfer to prisons for the condemned.[6] By the 1830s debtors had taken the place of the prostitutes and the prison became known simply as La Force. The building, parts of which dated back to medieval times, had been acquired in 1764 by the École Militaire and came to be used as a place of incarceration. The central section, which featured two courtyards planted with trees, accommodated the better-off – the English equivalent being the state side. One wing included special apartments, as well as the infirmary. The other wing, built at the start of the Revolution, was known as the Bâtiment-Neuf: a massive four-storey building with huge vaulted rooms containing row upon row of pallets, together with a complement of cells and dungeons. This was given over to the destitute and to those judged to be the more dangerous felons. The English equivalent was the common side.

As a remand centre, where the innocent rubbed shoulders with the yet-to-be-proved guilty, conditions had by then become less harsh than in many other prisons.[7] Its population was extremely mixed, with all kinds and sorts from all walks of life being jumbled together. The freedoms they were granted enabled some of the more affluent to put their wealth to good effect, thereby enjoying a comfortable lifestyle and incidentally boosting the takings of prison authorities and prison guards. The prisoner turnover was normally relatively rapid, the length of stay being determined by the speed of the legal processes – but this still could extend to several months or even years; incarceration on remand would sometimes provide the authorities with a convenient way of silencing awkward elements in society. Another prominent feature of imprisonment in La Force was the extent to which it assumed the character of a school of crime. Lacenaire himself claimed that up to three-quarters were recidivists.[8] Wisely, he put his first spell in La Force to good use by rapidly mastering the vocabulary of criminal slang. He also honed his thieving techniques.

Financially Lacenaire's position, while never comfortable, was never desperate, thereby enabling him to avoid the consequences when in prison of extreme poverty. In this, he was greatly helped by an aunt who, unbidden, sent him money throughout his spells in prison; this had two additional benefits, since it enabled him to escape manual labour, to which he would otherwise have been reduced in Bicêtre and Poissy and, most importantly, freed him to pursue his literary labours.

Throughout his life – whether in or out of prison – he was devoted to poetry, an enthusiasm he owed, in one of his few acknowledgements, to his schoolteacher, Reffay de Lusignan, who had introduced him to the works of Horace. In his memoirs he calculates that his lifetime output of odes, epigrams and songs extended to 30,000 lines and, with commendable modesty, declares that perhaps no other person ever enjoyed this same facility for versification.[9] For a time, he was reticent about publication of any of his prison works, perhaps a defensive response to his earlier failure to earn a living as a writer. By 1834, however, when imprisoned in Poissy he had supplied Vigouroux, editor of the journal *Bon Sens*, with some 17 poems. During his second imprisonment in La Force, his poem "A Thief's Petition to the King" (Pétition d'un Voleur au Roy) found its way into the columns of the November 7, 1835, issue of the *Gazette des Tribunaux*. But it was in the Conciergerie, to which he was moved on October 28, that he was to secure his position as a voluminous prison writer and demonstrate his skills in self-promotion.

The Trial

His trial and that of his two accomplices lasted three days from November 12 to November 14. It had been preceded by numerous newspaper articles drawing the public's attention to certain unusual features: a handsome, smartly turned out, intelligent, well-educated young man, 33 years old, with a passion for literature, who had acquired over little more than seven years an intimate acquaintance of the insides of Parisian and provincial gaols and was now to be tried as a self-confessed murderer. All of this made for a compelling tale, to which Lacenaire was anxious to contribute further. One of the concerns that he was to voice in his memoirs was that he might be lost sight of in a provincial setting. His end, whatever it might be, needed to be in the limelight and hence Paris.

The trial was held in the Assize Court of the Seine, sitting in the Palais de Justice which adjoined the Conciergerie. Not surprisingly it received considerable press coverage, was attended by numerous members of the public, many of them women, and had the bizarre feature that the accused would frequently be seen acting for the prosecution, correcting points of detail. Avril and François for their part pleaded not guilty and sought to conjure up alibis. Lacenaire was remarkable for his calm throughout the three days, had a smile on his face much of the time, was consistently courteous and at no time gave any indication of remorse. His own lawyer in his summing up was reduced to describing Lacenaire as having "un caractère effrayant de sincérité" (frightening candour) and invited the jury to find Lacenaire insane and thereby to deny him the accolade of public execution.[10] Lacenaire was duly found guilty. Both he and Avril were condemned to death on the guillotine and François to imprisonment for life with hard labour.

Over the ensuing eight weeks ahead of his execution on January 9, 1836, Lacenaire had to find time for: writing his memoirs, which in published form were to run to some 375 pages; sitting for a number of artists, many of whose sketches and portraits are preserved in the Bibliothèque Municipale de Lyon, one having even been commissioned by M. Allard, the Police Chief;[11] initiating and responding to a flurry of correspondence concerning genuine and spurious texts attributed to him and dispositions for future publications; submitting to a plaster cast being made of his head by a phrenologist; receiving a steady stream of visitors. All of this activity was centred on a small ground-floor cell in the Conciergerie, which contained two pallets, the second being for his guard, four chairs, one table and a stove.

Furthermore, in the wake of the part he chose to play during the course of the trial, he was then given an unprecedented editorial role in the preparation for publication of the official account by the Bureau de l'Observateur des Tribunaux (Office of the Court Recorder).[12] Eugene Roch, as publisher, marvelled at the sight of Lacenaire, only a few days away from his execution, labouring over details of punctuation as well as issues of substance.

Reference to the shaping of a plaster cast of his head testifies to a developing interest, during the 1830s and extending into the 1850s, in the potential applications that phrenology might have in criminology, giving rise to a rich harvest of books on the subject. As Benjamin Appert points out, the Chief Prosecutor of the day at the Assize Court of the Seine, Maître Dupin, was by way of being a convert.[13] In his detailed work on prisons published in 1836, Appert ties numerous case studies of criminals to their phrenological reports. In that of Lacenaire, the phrenologist, a M. Dumoutiers, oversaw the waxing, and Dr Fossati, a disciple of the movement's founder, François-Joseph Gall, was able to report that "L'examen de la tête de Lacenaire vient complètement confirmer la vérité des principes phrénologiques" (the cranial study of Lacenaire is wholly consistent with the principles governing phrenology). It was said to have revealed both positive and negative tendencies.[14] This would have pleased Lacenaire, who had no time for phrenology.

The Memoirs

The bookseller-publisher Olivier had announced as publication date for the *Memoirs* January 10th, the day after Lacenaire's execution. In the event, the *Memoirs* were released some four months later on May 28, available from "les marchands de nouveautés", indicating a book fresh off the press.[15] The publisher was not identified. The original timetable, if taken at face value, clearly indicated that the *Memoirs* were being fed to the printer section by section as the work advanced. One other possibility was that Lacenaire, who revealed that he had started on an earlier autobiographical text when in prison in La Force – and had abandoned the task for reasons he declined to give – may have been able to revive it, making thereby near-instantaneous posthumous publication a more plausible proposition.[16]

The *Memoirs*, as printed in 1836, have led some scholars to argue that the final somewhat breathless pages written within hours of Lacenaire's death may have been supplied by another, possibly the editor. An exception is made of the very last entry, dated January 8, 1836, and timed at 10 o'clock in the evening from the Conciergerie. It opens with two crisp sentences: "On vient me chercher pour Bicêtre. Demain sans doute ma tête tombera" ("They have come to take me to Bicêtre. Doubtless, tomorrow is the day I lose my head").[17] The salient feature of this edition, however, relates to suppression rather than addition: there are numerous marks of censorship indicated by lines of dots. On the evidence of a few surviving manuscript leaves that escaped the censor's red pencil, it would seem that passages will have qualified for deletion on religious or moral considerations, but most importantly on political grounds.[18]

Louis-Philippe's assumption of power in 1830, having been notably smooth and untroubled, was gradually punctuated by death threats and conspiracies, the most serious occurring five years into his reign, when the king was the target of an assassin. The occasion was a military review held on July 28, 1835, when Louis-Philippe was accompanied by his family as well as the governmental and military establishments.[19] The central figure was a 46-year-old Corsican, Giuseppe Fieschi. He had served in the army, participated in the retreat from Moscow, but retained an unshakeable admiration for Napoleon.[20] Later on, while working in a wallpaper merchant's business in Paris, he had made his services available to two republican militants. Their attention had been caught by an ingenious invention of his – one worthy of Heath Robinson: a vehicle of destruction which combined 25 guns, each stuffed with up to 12 bullets, linked for simultaneous discharge by a single trail of gunpowder and operated by one man wielding one firebrand. Installed in a first-floor apartment overlooking the boulevard du Temple, it was put to use on July 28. In the ensuing carnage from what was to be dubbed by French historians "La machine infernale", 18 were killed, including Mortier, duc de Trévise and Maréchal de France, 22 were wounded, but the king and his family escaped unharmed.[21] Today's visitor to the Archives Nationales in the rue des Francs Bourgeois will find intact the "machine infernale", complete with

Giuseppe Fieschi (1790–1836), portrait drawn at his trial in 1835. A disaffected Corsican, who had made available a lethal device of his own creation to a couple of militant republicans, put it to use on July 18, 1835 on the occasion of a military review overseen by King Louis Philippe. The resulting carnage – 18 killed, including the Maréchal de France, 22 injured – earned it the epithet "La Machine Infernale".

Fieschi.

As a prime exhibit in the subsequent trial that led to Fieschi's conviction and execution, the device is preserved in the Archives Nationales. Until recently, it was to be seen near the museum's entrance: a wooden cradle holding 25 pipes. On the day, each pipe had been

stuffed with up to 12 bullets, all 25 linked by a trail of gunpowder and operated by one man, Fieschi, wielding one firebrand for simultaneous discharge.

its 25 pipes serving as barrels laid on their wooden frame. It owes its survival to its having been a critical exhibit, a "pièce de conviction au dossier du procès", in the prosecution's case against Fieschi.

In the aftermath, security procedures were greatly tightened, and that autumn laws were passed limiting press freedoms and broadening the definition of traitorous activities to include the diffusion of anti-royalist and republican sentiments. Théophile Gautier's novel *Mademoiselle de Maupin*, which was said to promote moral disobedience and political indifference, was the kind of target the new legislation had in its sights.[22] The *Memoirs* of a man whose own life was an enactment in extreme form of rebellion on many fronts fell inevitably into the censor's lap. This also serves to explain the postponed publication date and perhaps the change of publisher. Coincidentally, Fieschi and Lacenaire were guillotined within a few weeks of each other, on February 16 and January 9 respectively, and the two men's profile busts shared the same litho plate in Appert's phrenological analysis.[23]

After what has been a prolonged exercise setting out the background to the *Memoirs*, it is now possible to start to consider where Lacenaire stands in any list of prison authors. While he was extremely proud of his poetic talents and affected to disdain expressing himself in prose on the grounds of boredom, there is no doubt that the *Memoirs* were the work to which he attached the greatest importance. In the last two months in the Conciergerie he was to be seen working on them late into the night, intent on leaving to posterity the thoughts of a man whose great promise had been done down by the system.

He writes with considerable fluency and his narrative skills are regularly in evidence in accounts of his criminal exploits. Very occasionally, there is a touch of humour, as when he describes the way he and his brother used to deflect cash from the hidden household reserves, his brother claiming from their mother 'x' number of kisses, the number mentioned then acting as a marching order for Lacenaire to extract the same amount in francs.[24] But the reader is not allowed for long to escape the repetitive character of Lacenaire's explanations of how he came to embrace crime, Lacenaire's analysis of human nature, Lacenaire's judgment on society. It takes a strong stomach to work through some of the passages.

Favouritism by both father and mother for the elder brother is said to be at the root of his sense of injustice, dating from early childhood. The fact that at one stage he was sent to boarding school and his brother had tutors at home grated considerably, as did the junior status to which the accident of birth consigned him. With this initiation into inequalities, he withdrew into himself seeing injustice everywhere, whether at school or beyond, and as he explains, this led him to view others with contempt but without at this stage wishing them ill. It was when he was making his way in the world, whether it were getting work experience as a solicitor or employment in a bank, trying his hand as a journalist or as a soldier, or working as a travelling salesman and then as a copyist, that he came to appreciate what he saw as persecution. An underlying complication centred on his lifelong horror of finding himself with little or nothing in his wallet when allied to the enthusiasms of a spendthrift.[25] His numerous failures to earn a living at a level that satisfied his aspirations – plus, it should be said, his father's bankruptcy – conspired to convince him of the injustice of the world and converted the earlier indifference to society into hatred requiring "revenge". The self-serving arguments are at their richest in the following passage:[26] "Lorsque je me vis sans ressource, et sans qu'il y eut de ma faute; lorsque la meilleure envie d'en gagner par mon talent, d'une manière honnête et de quelque manière que ce fût, de la manière la plus modeste; lorsque je me vis repoussé, dédaigné partout; lorsque j'y vis arriver la misère et avec elle la faim; la haine succéda au mépris, haine profonde et rongeuse dans laquelle je finis par envelopper tout le genre humain. Dès lors, je ne combattis plus pour mon intérêt personnel mais pour la vengeance ... Non, c'était l'édifice social que je voulais attaquer" ("It was when I found myself without means – and without this being in any way of my own doing; when my greatest wish was to earn a living on the basis of my skills, and to do so in the most straight forward way and by whatever route chosen having the most modest of goals; when I found myself rejected and spurned; when I faced destitution and with that hunger; hatred replaced contempt, a deep and gnawing hatred which came to encompass the whole of mankind. From then on I no longer fought to further my own interests but to exact vengeance ... No, it was the whole social structure that was in my sights").

His jaundiced opinion of mankind was coloured by his view that man was governed by selfishness. Even friendship was egotistical since it was based on the expectation of obtaining thereby some personal benefit.[27] For his part he felt able to report that among the greatest virtues stood "sincérité" and "sensibilité", the one covering candour and the other sensitiveness.[28] He himself attached a high value to being open – and in this respect his *Memoirs* were to be the crowning evidence – and as far as sensitiveness was concerned, he had no hesitation in declaring that all his life he had been very charitable and done what he could to help the unfortunate. There were times, however, when he was reduced to stealing from the poor and he admits that this did weigh on his conscience.[29] But such considerations could not be allowed to stand in the way of his declared objective of justifying his life in a bloody protest against the society that had rejected him. Following the death sentence, he was able to write: "Il ne restait en moi qu'un sentiment d'amour propre . . . par le fait que j'éprouve plaisir à me voir arriver aux résultats que je me suis proposé" ("All that remained was the feeling of pride . . . . from the pleasure I derive that accompanies the achievement of objectives I set myself"). All the more satisfying for a man who gloried in the knowledge that he was unique in his field.

It comes, therefore, as no surprise to read in his letter from the Conciergerie dated October 31, 1835, addressed to his old school master, Reffay de Lusignan, "Je suis coupable de tout ce dont je suis accusé. Je l'avoue, je l'avouerais toujours; cependant ma conscience ne me reproche rien, je suis sans remords, sans regrets, sans craintes" ("I am guilty of all of which I am accused. I admit this and shall always do so; however, my conscience is clear, I have no feeling of guilt, I regret nothing, I am free of fear").[30]

Lacenaire's Reputation

From all that has gone before, Lacenaire might appear an unlikely candidate for the cult status that he subsequently acquired. To start with, however, his life story had the ingredients of a detective thriller with the added advantage that it was an historical account. Furthermore, it was in the tradition of the celebrated poacher turned game-keeper, Eugène François Vidocq, whose own memoirs had appeared in four volumes in 1828–1830. It will be recalled that Vidocq embarked as a teenager on a life of crime, featuring multiple incarcerations, primarily for thefts broadly defined, and numerous prison escapes, many incorporating clever disguises. In 1809, aged 34, he had had a change of heart and switched to the role of police informant; this then led to the creation of a plain-clothes unit which in turn was transformed by Napoleon into the Sûreté Nationale (equivalent to the British CID – Criminal Investigation Department) with Vidocq at its head. Vidocq's memoirs, which cover both aspects of his life, proved highly popular. Lacenaire credits Vidocq with having given him an understanding of the underworld and enabling him to take his first steps towards mastering prison slang. They may also have served as a useful model for his own work.

Another consideration guaranteeing that his trial and execution would be no two-minute sensational wonder was his membership of the writing fraternity. He had his newspaper contacts. He knew and corresponded with the prominent literary figure Eugène Scribe, prolific novelist and dramatist. He ends a fulsome letter from prison dated December 24 with sententious praise: "Quant à vous, Monsieur, vous pouvez vous rendre cette justice que si j'avais rencontré plusieurs hommes comme vous, ils m'auraient réconcilié avec l'espèce humaine et fait tomber le poignard des mains." ("You, Sir, may take credit for the fact that had I met several men of your stamp, this would have reconciled me to the human race and made me drop my dagger.")[31] One of his last acts was to entrust the manuscript of his play *L'aigle de la Selléide* to his old teacher, to do with it what he judged best.[32] Stendhal, for his part, worried what would become of his writings; several years later he was to create in his (unfinished) novel, *Lamiel*, a character (Valbayre) directly inspired by Lacenaire.[33]

Théophile Gautier, in a jocular letter to his publisher two days after the execution asking for 200 francs, concludes by likening booksellers/publishers to a string of tight fists, with Lacenaire as a certified thief being a last minute addition to the list.[34] As a rebel himself, Gautier, was drawn to Lacenaire, seeing in him a strongly anti-clerical, anti-royalist figure. Irreligious he was, but Lacenaire's political opinions, while critical, were relatively mild. This illustrates an aspect of Lacenaire's influence whereby people took from his writings what they wanted, enabling them to sidestep all that was an uncomfortable fit. At times they even settled on what they wanted to see, rather than what was there on view.

Jacques Simonelli, in the introduction to his thoroughly researched edition of Lacenaire's *Memoirs* credits him with having made individual acts of violence one of the preferred methods open to rebels intent on denouncing the establishment of the day, the twisted reasoning behind this being that since crimes are committed every day in the name of society, the private individual is entitled to follow suit.[35] The long hold this had on popular thinking was illustrated 45 years later in the case of Lucien Morisset, a young clerk in a solicitor's office. Having lost his job after a string of thefts, he went for a stroll in Tours on July 17, 1881, shot and wounded three people whose conversation irritated him, and then wounded fatally a man sitting on a bench. He announced he was taking revenge on society, and at his trial went out of his way to heap praise on Lacenaire, a copy of whose book he owned.

Lacenaire's literary influence was spread widely. Stendhal has already been mentioned. Dostoevsky, who was on familiar ground from having written about him in a series of articles on the lives of famous French criminals, can certainly be said to have been in Lacenaire's debt when he was later to develop the character of the cultured murderer Raskolnikov in *Crime and Punishment*.[36] Other names include Balzac and Victor Hugo, who, explicitly or implicitly, made use of Lacenaire's experiences in their work. Baudelaire, for his part, will have included him as "un des héros de la vie moderne" ("One of the heroes of our times"). He interested the Goncourt brothers and caught the attention of de Tocqueville. But it is in the film that the influence of Lacenaire has been the most conspicuous.

Les Enfants du Paradis (the "Children of Paradise" or alternatively "Children of the Gods" in the English title), directed by Marcel Carné, with as scriptwriter the poet Jacques Prévert, was released in France on March 9, 1945, and in the United States on November 15, 1946. Its release in France came a matter of months after the liberation of the bulk of the country in the autumn of 1944 and a mere two months before the German surrender of May 6, 1945. It shows Lacenaire at two periods of his life, first of all during the late 1820s, coinciding with the vaudeville days of the Boulevard du Temple, renamed in the film the Boulevard du Crime, and then several years later in his role as assassin. Lacenaire is one of four men courting a beautiful courtesan, Garance, the others being Baptiste Debureau, a famous mime of the time, Frédéric Lemaître, a well-known actor of the day, and the Duc de Mornay, presented in the film as Comte Édouard de Montray. Lacenaire is portrayed as "le dandy du crime" and in the film is also credited with being discreetly homosexual. Some historians regard this as unproven.

Film poster: Les Enfants du Paradis, *1945*

The ambiguities associated with the film's creation in occupied France, the timing of its release and the subsequent debate centring on its "political" message guaranteed the film intense attention.[37] Its cast lacks nothing in impressiveness: Jean-Louis Barrault as the mime, Pierre Brasseur playing Frédéric Lemaitre, Marcel Herrand as Lacenaire and Arletty playing Garance. Arletty's arrest as a collaborator took place in the autumn of 1944, ahead therefore of the film's release. In court, she had famously explained "mon coeur est français, mon cul est international" (my heart is French, my arse is international). Such complications aside, *Les Enfants du Paradis* rapidly took its place as an outstanding entry into what was recognised as the Golden Age of French Cinema.

An assessment of Lacenaire's position as a prison author has two sides to it, the first being his own contributions. These relate almost entirely to his imprisonment in the Conciergerie, where he clearly benefited from a regime that placed no obstacles in his path as a writer. The *Memoirs* stand out as remarkable, being composed within just a few weeks. When it comes to verse, the published results are much less visible; they are admittedly more widely dispersed, given Lacenaire's contributions over a period of time to journals made from a number of prisons. For more lasting recognition as a poet, a trawl through the London Library's holdings of French anthologies produced only one result: a ten-line song written from the Conciergerie which features in Jacques Collard's *Anthologie de la Littérature Argotique*; this came equipped with Lacenaire's own translation for those unfamiliar with prison slang.[38] A more impressive, albeit fugitive, endorsement was to come in 1853. Victor Hugo's novel, *Le Dernier Jour d'un Condamné* ("A condemned man's last day"), a vivid first-person account of a young murderer's last six weeks in the Conciergerie – which foreshadowed in some respects Lacenaire's own experiences – had been published in 1829 and quickly ran to several editions. It had been deliberately left unfinished, and some 24 years later Adèle Hugo recorded in her diary entry for December 20 that her husband had become fascinated by the thought that it should be completed either by André Chénier or by Lacenaire – a surprising coupling. Victor Hugo envisaged that the putative collaborators would need to be reached at a spiritualistic séance with "table tournante" (Ouija board) for which he had developed an enthusiasm during his exile in Guernsey.[39]

It is when one turns to Lacenaire's position as an author – at one remove as it were – that his impact becomes hugely impressive. That a man who had so much about him that was repellent should be associated with major works of literature and that he should give rise to a film, described by many as beyond compare, invites simple disbelief. From his place in Hades, Lacenaire will be preening himself.

||||||||||||||||||||||||||||||||||||||||||||||||||||||||||||||||||||||||||||||||||||||

CHAPTER XIX

William Chester Minor
(1834–1920)

Hospitalisation & Incarceration

St Elizabeth's Hospital, Washingon D.C.	*September 1868 – February 1871*
Horsemonger Lane Prison	*February – April 1872*
Broadmoor Criminal Lunatic Asylum	*April 1872 – April 1910*
St Elizabeth's Hospital, Washington D.C.	*April 1910 – October 1919*
The Retreat, Hartford Connecticut	*October 1919 – March 1920*

"For the next twenty years, he would do almost nothing at Broadmoor except enfold himself and his tortured brain in the world of books, of their writings, and of their words". A quotation from Simon Winchester's *The Surgeon of Crowthorne*.[1]

William Chester Minor, the son of missionaries, was born in Ceylon, where he lived till the age of 13; his father and stepmother, his mother having died when he was only three and his father having remarried two years later, sent him to an uncle in the United States where the family had a substantial retail china business in New Haven, Connecticut. The Minors could trace their American origins to within ten years of the arrival of the Pilgrim Fathers, when their forebears settled in New England. William Minor grew up with many cultural interests – he played the flute and was a watercolourist and above all a bibliophile, in what were fairly affluent circumstances. He also developed a powerful libido, which later on was said to have amounted to a state of insatiable lust. Having embarked on lengthy medical studies at Yale University, he graduated in February 1863. Four months later, on June 29, he joined the Union Army as an army surgeon, three days before the Battle of Gettysburg. It was, however, not until May 4, 1864, at the Battle of Wilderness at the Rapidan River crossing that he first saw action.

The event that separates this shortened curriculum vitae from the

William Chester Minor

quotation cited earlier took place on February 17, 1872, when George Merrett, a stoker at the Red Lion Brewery, Lambeth, was shot dead by W. C. Minor in the early hours of the morning.

In the build-up to this event, the role of the hugely bloody American Civil War was judged to have been central in the unhingeing of Minor's mind. The sheer scale of the conflict was horrifying: the Union Army, which reached 2.9 million, suffered casualties of 360,000 and deserters of 287,000. The Confederate Army, whose strength attained 1.3 million, suffered proportionately heavier losses at 258,000, but a somewhat lower rate of deserters at 103,000.[2] In terms of Minor's own experience, the Battle of Wilderness supplied the horrors of hand-to-hand fighting on terrain that gave no scope for any other form of engagement. And to this were added bush fires. Private Warren Goss, attached to the Unionist 2nd Massachusetts Artillery regiment, describes how "the wind drove the blinding smoke and suffocating heat into our faces. This, added to the oppressive heat of the weather, was almost unendurable. The fire was the most terrible enemy of our men that day, and few survivors will forget this attack of the flames on their lines."[3]

To a surgeon's role on the field of battle was added the part he was called upon to play in its aftermath in the punishment that was meted out to some deserters, who would be branded with the letter "D" on the buttock, the hip or the cheek. The army surgeon would often be called upon to play the role of executioner. Branding as a form of punishment has a long history. We have already seen William Prynne as a victim in the seventeenth century, while suffering at the same time the loss of his ears. By the mid-nineteenth century the barbaric character may well have appeared more pronounced, and this is emphasized in Winchester's emotive narrative account. For Minor, there was the special feature that the deserters in question might often be from among the 150,000 Irishmen who had volunteered to join Unionist forces, encouraged in the thought that they were indirectly fighting the English, known to favour the Confederates. The possibility of a Fenian retaliation against the man who had wielded the branding iron lodged in his brain.

Minor's Civil War experience subsequently found him moving around the Union hospital system, his work being much appreciated. By 1866, he had achieved the full rank of a commissioned captain, based at Fort Jay Hospital on Governor's Island, New York City. It was around then that he started to show signs of being under increasing stress, carrying a gun at all times when off duty and finding relaxation in brothels and louche bars. This led to his demotion and assignment to the quieter environment of Florida. The move did nothing to halt a deteriorating mental condition, leading to his being diagnosed as suffering from "monomania" and admission to the Hospital for the Insane (later called the St Elizabeth Hospital) in Washington, DC. He retired from the army, but retained his pension entitlements. Two and a half years later, in February 1871, he was discharged and the following October set sail for England to recuperate, intending to stay in Europe for a year or two. He came with an introduction to John Ruskin given him by a Yale University professor.

Once in London, he first chose as his base a small hotel in a smart West End district, whence he travelled widely on the Continent. Back in England, Minor took rooms in Lambeth, an insalubrious area, one of whose chief attractions to him being proximity to brothels. He had his watercolour equipment with him, a continuing source of pleasure, but not powerful enough to offset his increasing paranoia: as his landlady testified, he was convinced that he was under attack, chiefly at night, from malevolent forces composed for the most part of vengeful Irishmen. On the night of February 17, 1872, Minor "saw" a man standing at the foot of his bed, reached for his gun beneath his pillow, and gave chase down the stairs into the street, shouting at him to halt. By this time, the mythical intruder had been replaced by George Merrett, heading to work at 2.30 that morning. Thoroughly alarmed at encountering a gun-toting stranger who seemed to have it in for him, Merrett took to his heels. Minor fired three shots, one of which proved fatal.

Broadmoor Criminal Lunatic Asylum

Minor became a patient in Broadmoor Criminal Lunatic Asylum in Crowthorne, Berkshire, on April 17, 1872 after a period in London's Horsemonger Lane Prison ahead of his trial at the Surrey assizes, when he was sentenced to be confined "Until Her Majesty's pleasure be known". He was entering a new building completed nine years earlier; it was made up of eight blocks, six for men, two for women, and built to accommodate up to 200 inmates. Minor's prison circumstances were unusual: a thirty-seven year-old American, distinguished in appearance, whose incarceration drew the solicitous attention of the American Consulate, naturally concerned over the arrangements being made for a US citizen, an alumnus of Yale University, and furthermore a retired military surgeon on a US army pension. What also differentiated him from most of the other inmates were his cultural background and intellectual and artistic attainments. In addition, he was judged to be a low suicide risk and was not subject to epileptic fits.

Many of these considerations worked powerfully in his favour from the time of his admission. Most conspicuously, he was assigned two connecting cells on the top floor of Block 2, known as "the swell block" (that had reminded one visitor of the Athenaeum Club), from which he had views of gardens and the countryside.[4] At the end of the corridor, the guard (known as the attendant) kept watch over the 20 men on his floor. During the day the cells were unlocked, permitting prisoners to go to the bathroom unescorted, and also enabling them to light up their cigarettes and pipes on the small gas jet next to where the guard had his seat. The tobacco was supplied free from the contraband confiscated at the ports and distributed to prisons. At night, the cells were bolted from the outside.

It is perhaps in the furnishing of the two cells that Minor's privileged position becomes most evident. In response to an enquiry from the US Consulate, the asylum superintendent, William Orange, had declared that Dr Minor could have anything he liked so long as it did not prejudice his safety or the disciplined running of the asylum. He had a full wardrobe, he was reunited with his drawing materials and paintbox, and he took up the flute again, occasionally giving lessons to other inmates. Most important of all, he set about converting one cell into a library, equipped with a writing desk, two chairs and floor–to-ceiling teak bookshelves (for which he paid himself).[5]

The number of prisoners able to improve their lot at their own expense has been a familiar feature in this survey of prison writers. William Minor was himself in that happy position. The furnishing of his cell library began with the transfer from New Haven of the books he had already collected in America. These were then supplemented over the years by books bought in large quantities in England, including antiquarian titles. A pleasing detail has it that he was allowed to employ another inmate to help him with a number of domestic chores, included in these being the help he gave towards tidying the books. Access to books time and again has been one of the facilities most sought after by prisoners and its denial one of the most hurtful. But rarely has provision extended to the possession of a private library. There were two occasions, however, when the Tower of London proved an exception, accommodating Sir Walter Ralegh's personal working library and the Earl of Northumberland's scientific library with its strong position in the occult – the run of which he gave Ralegh. It is greatly to the credit of Broadmoor's administration of the day that Minor should have had the enjoyment of his books, thereby satisfying the bibliophilic needs of a collector.

This picture of bookish bliss has, however to be qualified. Firstly, there was the matter of confinement, albeit softened by the uncensored regime he enjoyed in respect of outgoing and incoming correspondence, plus visitor privileges. Secondly, there was the unchanging reality of his mental condition, which generated piercing anxieties emanating from delusions of persecution as represented by the malevolent creatures that inhabit the interstices between floors and ceilings out to do him harm, some of whom being responsible for the "continuing defacement of my books".[6] The role played by the Governor of the prison was as ever important in establishing the environment within which Minor coped with his nightmares and pursued his literary and artistic interests. The long-serving Governor, Dr Nicholson, proved to be a sympathetic figure with a fund of patience as the recipient of countless letters from Minor detailing his accounts of nightly visitations and his need for protective action by the prison authorities. One is reminded in a totally different context of the rapport that John Bunyan managed to establish with the Governor of Bedford County Gaol. Once Nicholson retired in 1895, making way to a governor fashioned in the mould of a martinet, many of Minor's privileges were gradually withdrawn.

In Simon Winchester's painstaking analysis of hospital records, Minor's condition from the date of his admission to Broadmoor in April 1872 through to the early 1880s had shown, if anything, a gradual deterioration. The cut-off date is important because of the fortuitous insertion in a book delivered to Minor from a London bookseller of a pamphlet calling for volunteers to help in the production of the most comprehensive English dictionary ever devised – to which Minor had responded.

The *Dictionary*

At a meeting in the London Library of the Statistical Society and the Philological Society on November 5, 1857, the need for a dictionary to encompass the language in its entirety was recognised, having as a guiding principle rigorous dependence on quotations that would illustrate the sense of every single word in the language.[7] The speaker was Richard Chenevix-Trench, Dean of Westminster. This marks the start of an undertaking that came to fruition 70 years later with the publication on December 31, 1927, of the complete *Oxford English Dictionary* in 12 volumes, with definitions for 414,825 main words and illustrative quotations numbering 1,827,306.[8] For comparative purposes, Samuel Johnson's dictionary of 1755 contained definitions for 43,500 words.

An early decision of considerable importance was to solicit the help of volunteer readers of designated books who would make word lists needed in the supply of descriptive slips to the *Dictionary* team. The first editor of what was then known as *The New English Dictionary*, appointed in 1859, was the erudite Herbert Coleridge, grandson of the poet. One of his first measures was to construct shelving having 54 pigeon-holes that would hold 100,000 slips. This proved to be the earliest and by far the smallest of the lexicographic dovecotes that were to mark the progress of the *Dictionary*. Coleridge's death within two years – a considerable setback to the venture – earned him posthumous fame for his last, or near-last, words, "I must begin Sanskrit tomorrow".[9] His successor as editor was the ever enthusiastic Frederick Furnivall, not renowned, however, for administrative skills and totally lacking in tact, a condition generously expressed as "known to have an itching for annoying people".

The volunteers were invited to distinguish between three periods in the preparation of their slips, whether from designated books or ephemera:

(a) 1250 to 1526 (being the proximate date of publication of William
    Tyndale's translation of the *New Testament*);
(b) 1526 to 1674 (being the year John Milton died);
(c) 1674 to "the present day".

The slips for despatch to the *Dictionary* team had to comply with a strict format: the top left-hand side to bear the target word, beneath which came the details of the work cited – date, author, title, volume, page number. At the foot of the slip came the complete sentence that illustrated the use of the word in question. Throughout, neatness and accuracy were essential.

The brochure that Furnivall devised for the recruitment of volunteers was displayed in magazines, and newspapers and distributed widely in bookshops, where it would also often be inserted in the books themselves, in libraries and newsstands and kiosks. In the first few years, the build-up of slips received was rapid, requiring the enlargement of the facilities for housing them in shelving equipped with suitable pigeonholes. But sustaining the level of enthusiasm year in, year out, was proving difficult, and coping with the volume of incoming material was taxing the existing resources, whether of equipment or manpower. Two developments came to the rescue. In 1878 James Murray, then assistant headmaster at Mill Hill School in North London, obtained agreement for the halving of his school duties, and this enabled him to take on the editorship.[10] In March 1879 the vexed question of who was to be the publisher was settled, with Oxford University Press filling that role. These two developments were to prove critical to the ultimate success of the project. In Murray it had an editor, skilled in philology and marvellously disciplined – he was to give as his daily objective the definition of 33 words, while accepting that the absolute rule never to relax editorial standards meant that some words would inevitably leave that target in tatters. OUP was the publisher of international standing that was needed.

The appointment of OUP also enabled the *Dictionary* team to plan the progressive publication of sections, known as fascicles, thereby generating revenues for the publisher that would go against the costs of succeeding sections. From the start, financial arrangements had been complicated by the fact that the *Dictionary* was to be the Philological Society's *Dictionary*; it was only in 1902 that the Society relinquished its rights, in return for what was a modest sum spread over ten years. Well before then, financial responsibility had in practice been borne by the OUP, thereby abandoning some tortuous attempts at making the editor pay for support staff and sundry costs out of his own salary, for which he stood to be compensated were the team to meet set production targets.

A disciplined relaunch of the whole project now became feasible, starting with a fresh call for volunteers through "An Appeal to the English speaking and English reading Public in Great Britain, America and the British Colonies".[11] Two thousand leaflets were printed. The urgency of this appeal was further underlined by the evidence that much of the work done over the previous 20 years had been slipshod, with moreover some archives lost, some destroyed, a consequence of little or no central management. Only about 10 per cent of the quotations submitted turned out to be usable.[12]

At all times, the drumbeat of Noah Webster's *American Dictionary* was audible: first published in 1825, containing 70,000 words, and thereafter issued in ever-expanded editions, that of 1884 containing 118,000 words. Developments on the Continent will also have acted as a competitive spur. Emile Littré's *Dictionnaire de la Langue française*, the work of one man, begun in 1843, had already appeared in four volumes in 1873. Littré took as his starting point the classical language as used in the seventeenth century and also set out to present an authoritative account of the use of each word based on the various meanings the word had held in the past.[13] In Germany, Jacob and Wilhelm Grimm had begun work on the *Deutsches Wörterbuch* in 1838 and in the process had pioneered the use of volunteers. The Grimms took the analysis back to the High German of the mid-fifteenth century; their historical linguistic approach was in line with that chosen by Littré and the *New English Dictionary/Oxford English Dictionary* – the starting-point for which was 1150. While all three traced their beginnings to the middle years of the nineteenth century, they differed widely on final publication date: 30 years for Littré, 70 for the *OED* and 122 for the *Deutsches Wörterbuch* – in 1960. Multiple reasons can be adduced for this wide spread.

It is not known exactly when Minor responded to the recruitment brochure, sending his application to "Dr. James Murray, Mill Hill, Middlesex N.W." and giving as his own address "Dr. William Minor, Broadmoor, Berkshire" or "Dr. William Minor, Crowthorne, Berkshire" depending on whether one relies on Simon Winchester's biography or his entry in the *Dictionary of National Biography*. For a likely date, Simon Winchester suggests some time around 1880. The precise moment that Minor's interest was aroused is of little importance. The crucial point is that he found himself dealing with a going concern following the relaunch, rather than a shambles, enabling it thereby to become the consuming passion that was to occupy him over the ensuing 20 years.

Minor's listing of his academic achievements and literary interests will have made him in Murray's eyes a perfect fit for the role of volunteer; the confirmation letter will have included an information pack spelling out the procedures to be followed and enclosing an example of a slip. But instead of responding immediately, firing off a clutch of slips on the off-chance that some might match the current needs of the editors, Minor set about creating an inventory of his own, book by book. This was a laborious exercise, since for any one title it might take three months to build a full word list. By the autumn of 1884 he felt sufficiently confident to enquire which were the letters on which the editors were currently working. Armed with that information, he would look up his word lists, extract the appropriate references, complete the slips with the supporting quotations and send them off to the editors, confident of their immediate relevance – unless of course some other volunteer had already noted the same words in the same book with the same quotations. For James Murray and his team, it represented a huge time-saver.

For Minor he had the satisfaction of a frequently repeated virtual byline, albeit anonymous. Regular publication of the dictionary sections also had a morale boosting benefit for volunteers who could scan each text and see which of their submissions had made it into print. Additional glory would come whenever a quotation established the first known instance of that particular word's use.

By the time Minor got into his stride, the first fascicle, "A–Ant", had already been published. He was therefore able to contribute to "Anta–Battening", the second fascicle published in autumn 1885, followed by "Battentlie–Bozzom" in 1887, "Bra – Byzen" in 1888 and thereafter. Murray, having left his position as teacher at Mill Hill School in 1884 to become full time lexicographer, Minor's slips now had to be sent to Dr James Murray. 78 Banbury Road, Oxford. The tin shed, officially known as The Scriptorium and more colloquially as the Scrippy which contained the massive collection of slips in hundreds of pigeon holes in the school grounds had been replaced by an even larger tin shed in the garden at Oxford, while retaining its Scriptorium and Scrippy names. The pigeon hole count had risen to 1,029, sheltering over five million slips. The volume of incoming mail was such that the only address needed was "Dr Murray, Oxford", somewhat in the vein of Victor Hugo's experience once he had sought refuge in Guernsey from Napoleon III's regime, who would receive correspondence addressed to "M. Victor Hugo, l'Océan".

At the same time, outgoing mail was voluminous. As Murray rather charmingly explained at a meeting of the Philological Society , the letters he "absolutely must do in my own handwriting take always one, more normally two, sometimes three hours of the freshest part of my working day". In recognition of his needs, the Post Office set up a pillar-box outside his house. It still exists, but when last seen was in the process of being decommissioned.

Murray welcomed receiving any number of quotations, illustrating shades of meaning, from which to choose the most apposite. Some special problems of definition occasionally arose, as in the case of "altar" over which "his theological helpers had disputed greatly, and its meaning had been reduced to inoffensiveness". The more general difficulty lay in tracing the history of the development of the meaning of a word and getting the changes into a logical order. One can but sympathise when he writes: "you sort your quotations into bundles on your big table and think you are getting the word's pedigree right, when a new sense, or three or four new senses start up, and you are obliged to begin afresh, often three or four times."

The flow of submissions from Broadmoor started as a trickle in the spring of 1885. By the autumn of that year, they had become a monthly packet. Later the frequency became weekly, at a rate of 100 slips. A degree of public recognition came in 1888 with the publication of Volume I of the *Dictionary*, covering the A–B entries, which contained a reference to Dr W. C. Minor of Crowthorne, Berks.[14] His industry had earned him a place as a productive volunteer in the 5,000 to 8,000 quotations band. Nine years later, the flow of submissions had assumed a torrential character. In the annual statement for 1897, Murray was able to report to the Philological Society that during the past year 15,000 to 16,000 additional slips had been received, half of them by W. C. Minor, the product of his reading 50 to 60 books of the sixteenth and seventeenth centuries, some of them bought from antiquarian booksellers.[15] Two years later, Murray announced that Minor occupied the supreme position among the hundreds of volunteer readers "who during the past two years has sent in no less than 12,000 quots.[16] These have nearly all been for the words with which Mr. Bradley (Murray's eventual successor as editor) and I were actually occupied for Dr. Minor likes to know each month just what words we are likely to be working on during the month, and to devote his whole strength to supplying quotations for those words". Minor had ceased to be a shadowy figure.

From an early stage, Minor's productivity had been a cause for celebration to the editorial team all the more so for the condition of his slips, noted for their neatness, legibility and accuracy, evidently the work of a highly disciplined mind.

The numbers of volunteers – at one stage 800 in England and between 400 and 500 in the United States – meant that links with the editorial team were necessarily epistolary. But James Murray's regular reports to the Philological Society highlighted some individual achievements. Following publication of Volume 3 of the *Dictionary* and with Queen Victoria having accepted the dedication of the whole work, the time was judged ripe for a celebration. This took the form of a grand dinner in the hall of Queen's College on October 12, 1897. It also entailed the creation of a guest list made up of all those most involved in the production of the *Dictionary*. The absence of Dr Fitzgerald Hall, a champion supporter over 40 years – and incidentally another American – was readily explained by his being a recognised recluse, now living in East Anglia. But what about Dr Minor, living not far away in Crowthorne, within easy train distance to Oxford, why did he find himself unable to accept?

James Murray had long ago noted that Minor was based in Crowthorne and when Broadmoor cropped up occasionally in the address he assumed that Minor might have been a medical officer associated with the hospital and now enjoying the ample free time that came with retirement. It was only when the Harvard Librarian, Justin Winsor, passing through Oxford some time between 1887 and 1890, visited the Scriptorium and referred to the benefits that "poor" Dr Minor was securing from his association with the *Dictionary* that Murray learned with astonishment the circumstances of this "poverty".[17] A revelation of this kind in the academic setting of Oxford was to prove invaluable raw material for journalistic improvement. In the gripping account given in the September 1915 issue of the *Strand Magazine*, Hayden Church, an American journalist based in London, had Murray visit Minor in his truly imposing residence and, on being ushered into the presence of the Governor of the asylum, had him express great satisfaction at finally making the acquaintance of one of his most prolific volunteer readers. Sad to report, the then editor, Henry Bradley, took great exception to the article.

It was in January 1891 that the two men first met, permission having been granted to Murray to visit Broadmoor, after he had established that this would be welcome to Minor.[18] He found him courteous and cultivated, but reserved. This was to be the start of a succession of trips to Crowthorne over the next ten years and the development of warm friendship founded on their shared passion for philology. They exchanged letters, often daily, while Minor's submission rates of slips were sustained at around 20 a day. Occasionally, Murray would be accompanied by his wife. One physical peculiarity was that the two men, both equipped with generous beards, bore a striking resemblance to each other. These were civilised, professional contacts, with Minor's insanity apparently contained. As the decade wore on, however, Minor's prison behaviour would occasionally turn belligerent and his introspection extending to self-loathing more and more intense. In December 1902 this led to an extreme redemptive act when he sliced off his penis.

Already Minor's dictionary work had been slowing down and Murray's train journeys to Crowthorne, now often with his wife, took on increasingly the character of the sympathetic visit to a friend in hospital. The Murrays were among those who pressed the authorities to enable him to be released from a British asylum for transfer to the US authorities. This was achieved in 1910. Minor was to live a further ten years, dying in 1920, having spent 51 years of an 86-six-year life confined in asylums or prisons.

Conclusion

"I always thought it possible that a man might find such a Libertie within a Prison, as to the Prisoner might seem an Enlargement beyond the extent of Ayres." Thus wrote Thomas Haynes Bayley in the introduction to his curious book *Herba Parietis or the Wall Flower as it Grew out of the Stone Chamber belonging to the Metropolitan Prison of London called New Gate.* The year was 1650. Some two and a half centuries later, Minor escaped the confines of Broadmoor by immersing himself in the production of a dictionary.

For Minor, much of the "liberty" within Broadmoor came through relief from such mundane daily concerns as room and board: being commodiously lodged, regularly fed and benefiting from medical attention whenever needed. This converted into a wealth of free time, a commodity which in the hands of a dedicated lexicographer is priceless. To his immense credit, Minor managed to put to one side for long the depressing aspects of his condition so as to engage in meticulous, disciplined research. There is no doubt that the *Dictionary* gave him an objective that sustained him for many years and also secured him the friendship of James Murray. By the early 1900s, his condition had worsened markedly, leading to his self-inflicted injury, thereby bringing to an end his work on the *Dictionary*.

One rewarding aspect of Minor's prison life should not be neglected – his enduring love of books. This dates from his adolescence when he started building up a collection in New Haven. And once incarcerated in Broadmoor, the conversion of one cell into a library followed swiftly – into which he fed his American holdings. In the period of eight years before his involvement with the *Dictionary*, his prison library met the needs of a bibliophile. In the 12 years that followed, it also became a working library. Many of the books that the volunteers were invited to study will have already been on Minor's shelves – obviating the need for the *Dictionary* team to supply copies to him. And of those that he did not already own he is likely to have purchased many himself. The 50 to 60 books of the sixteenth and seventeenth centuries to which Murray referred when discussing the contribution to the *Dictionary* made one year by Minor conjures up a vision of brown paper parcels from the Maggs and Quaritches of this world being delivered to the top floor of Block 2 to an excited collector. His attachment to his books was seen in his distress at the damage he imagined that they were suffering at the hands of his tormentors. And most conspicuously, when he wrote from Elizabeth's Hospital to Lady Murray (James had been knighted in 1908) offering her the books that had been sent to the Scriptorium from Broadmoor on his departure for the United States in 1910, and which were still in the Scriptorium at the time of James Murray's death in 1915. He also expressed the hope that they might eventually go to the Bodleian.

The dispersal of his prison books must have been a protracted affair, keeping step perhaps with the erosion of the special privileges granted him by Nicholson, the previous governor, and culminating in his transfer to the prison sanatorium just ahead of his departure for America. This would help to explain how limited the number is of Minor's known holdings, making up as it were a sad little detachment of prison refugees. The Bodleian records reveal that a total of 16 titles formed Minor's gift, but that six were returned since they constituted duplicates. Of the ten titles now in the Bodleian, three are from the sixteenth century, four the seventeenth century, two the eighteenth century and one lacks a date. These books are registered as having been donated to the Bodleian by Dr Minor through Lady Murray. Of the five volumes I consulted, three had pasted in the note "This volume was given by Dr. Minor", followed by the date, 8 . 1 . 23, being the registration date of the donation. Two of the books appear to have been supplied by the antiquarian bookseller, Walter T. Spencer, 17 New Oxford Street (better known for his Dickensian stock), in one of which his label appears. Somewhat to my surprise, I was unable to identify any markings or annotations, happy evidence perhaps of the care that Minor lavished on his holdings.

To conclude, it is worth noting that Minor's lexicographic influence went beyond his own contributions to the first edition. Two other Broadmoor patients were to follow in his footsteps: Arthur Graham Bell started sending in quotations from the beginning of October 1958, and J. B. T. Norris did so from a date in the 1960s until his release in August 1986. Peter Gilliver reports that neither came close to matching Minor's output whether in terms of volume or of quality, and indeed the editor of the Supplement, R. W. Burchfield, was moved to write of Bell that he was "not one of our favourite correspondents".[19]

This chapter brings to an end what has been a brief journey through the rich literature of prison writing. It is pleasing to be able to mark its completion with an account recording Minor's unique achievement as a prison-bound lexicographer, whose experience of confinement was furthermore softened by the civilising influence of bibliophily.

Snapshots of Prison Writing

CHAPTER I

Theodore von Neuhoff 18th-century champion of Corsican independence from the Genoese, was duly elected King. But when dethroned in a counter coup, continued to pursue his cause from debtors' prisons by way of a sustained epistolary campaign lasting several years. He bequeathed his kingdom to his creditors.

CHAPTER II

Newgate has given its name to literary endeavours as has no other prison (Newgate Calendar, Newgate Novel). The Prison Ordinary (chaplain), **John Villette**, occupies prime position as author and publisher of the accounts of executions, one covering that of **William Dodd**, befriended by Samuel Johnson. It is at the end of the 18th century and into the 19th century that the prison takes its place as a literary hub for dissenters of many stripes, the editorial seat of a number of periodicals and the source of numerous polemical pamphlets.

CHAPTER III

The Tower of London outclasses Newgate on the score of literary excellence, having harboured Sir Thomas More and the Earl of Surrey in the 16th century and Sir Walter Ralegh in the 17th. Both the Tower and Newgate were called upon by Henry VIII to punish at the stake the poet, **Anne Askew**, for her (then) errant religious views. She was tortured, compiled records of her two lengthy Privy Council examinations, composed and reputedly sang her well-known prison "Balade" from Newgate. Thirty-five years later, in Queen Elizabeth's reign, seven Catholic priests were hanged, drawn and quartered. The eighth, **John Martin**, having abjured, escaped execution at the last moment and wrote the account of their imprisonment.

It was in the 12th-century Bell Tower that **Sir Thomas More** managed to write – and spirit away out of his cell – his great spiritual testament *A Dialogue of Comfort against Tribulation*, judged by many to be his finest work in English.

CHAPTER IV

The Earl of Surrey earned an incarceration in the Tower that lasted five weeks by posing a threat to the succession of of Henry VIII. The evidence came in the heraldic decoration he was incorporating into his Mount Surrey property in Norwich. From childhood, verse was in his veins. Surrey's poetic development took him well beyond the conventions of the day. Metrical experiments led to the introduction of blank verse into English poetry, as well as influencing the form taken by the sonnet. When In the Tower Surrey found comfort in verse having a marked biblical flavour. His execution as a traitor came three days before the death of the king.

CHAPTER V

During the course of his thirteen years in the Tower, **Sir Walter Ralegh**'s literary output was remarkable, covering naval matters, royal betrothals, filial admonitions and classical history. It is in the last category that the *History of the World* (1570 pages long and going no further than the Second Punic War) takes him well beyond the roles of buccaneer, courtier, explorer to that of influential political historian. His execution as a traitor, following temporary release from the Tower, says much for the rules of conduct he recognised.

CHAPTER VI

William Prynne spent ten years in a succession of prisons. Dissent governed much of his life, arising initially from strongly held Puritan views. Twice he courageously endured severe punishment at the pillory. At all times, in and out of gaol, the printing press was put to intensive use, with up to 200 pamphlets to his name, some running to hundreds of pages. "Wordy" was the label he secured – but with no claims to literary elegance. His final years were spent in the Tower, no longer as a prisoner, but as the Keeper of the Records.

CHAPTER VII

The royalist, **Richard Lovelace**, owes his position in a book dealing with prison writing to a single poem "to Althea, from Prison", written in the Gatehouse, Westminster, containing the ringing lines "Stone Walls do not a Prison make Nor Iron Bars a Cage". Later in the Civil War, he was captured in the Battle of Maidstone and held in Peterhouse, used briefly by the Parliamentarians as a London detention centre. Lovelace's ten-month stay in Peterhouse enabled him to prepare for publication a collected edition of his verse.

CHAPTER VIII

Charles I's detention, lasting a little more than three years, was spread over seven locations. At all times, his daily routine included a period for correspondence and other writings. Following his flight from Hampton Court on November 11, 1647, however, all official correspondence ceased. Private correspondence was maintained, often surreptitiously. Other writings included numerous devotional tracts, the lengthy letter to his son and more personal accounts such as "The King's Portraiture in his Solitudes and his Sufferings". Most important of all, there was the *Eikon Basilike*, published clandestinely on the day of his execution. Presented in the third person as a vindication of the King's reign, it was an immediate success, running to thirty-nine editions in the first year alone. As a powerful piece of royalist propaganda, its authenticity was immediately called into question by the Parliamentarians, heralding an historical debate that lingers to this day.

CHAPTER IX

At one level, **John Bunyan** is perhaps best remembered as the impoverished tinker who courted an imprisonment that was to last 13 years in harsh Bedford gaols, for having preached the Gospel without securing the mandatory licences. At another level, he is remembered for some sixty published titles, largely written while in prison, that included "Grace Abounding", the marvellously homely account of his spiritual development. And at a third level, he is remembered for giving the world "the wicket gate", Christian, Faithful and Hopeful by way of the astonishing publishing phenomenon of *Pilgrim's Progress*. Publication of Part 1 came in 1678 and thereafter was sustained over several centuries by countless English editions and over 200 translations. Where *Pilgrim's Progress* first saw the light of day is much debated, depending on whether Bedford County Gaol or Bedford Bridge Town Gaol is given the credit. One calculation not open to dispute is that despite eleven editions in England, published during Bunyan's lifetime with cumulative volume sales estimated at 100,000, Bunyan received no royalties.

CHAPTER X

William Combe was in a precarious financial position once he had gone through what was at the time a significant legacy. This landed him in the King's Bench prison, which was to be his home until his death twenty-four years later. But the urge to spend did not leave him. And there was the need to raise funds to meet daily expenses - and perhaps even to pay back some of the money owing to his creditors. His first solution was to attract orders for French translation. More significantly, as a fluent versifier, he managed to profit from the popularity of aquatint prints that needed some textual support. This was achieved when he became a client of the printer/entrepreneur, Rudolph Ackermann, notably with the monthly publication of episodes in *Dr. Syntax's Tours*, for which Thomas Rowlandson provided the illustrations, with Combe the accompanying text, anonymously. For a long time, illustrator and writer never met since a condition established by Combe was that nobody should know from where he conducted his business.

At his death, aged 82, he was buried in the nearby Church of St George the Martyr. The costs of the funeral were borne by his friends. His landlady (he had been living in the "rules" outside the prison building) was owed the tidy sum of £90.

CHAPTER XI

The sixteenth century French poet, **Clément Marot**, was attached to two glittering courts, those of François I and his sister, Marguerite d'Angoulème – later to become Reine de Navarre. Both brother and sister stimulated intellectual curiosity and at the outset espoused Renaissance values. This led their courts into the dangerous waters of religious reform. Marot, their devoted follower, was credited with Lutheran views and briefly imprisoned as a heretic, making him a candidate for the stake. His successful pleas for enlargement, some addressed to the king, took the form of humorous fables. A lively sense of fun protected him for a while when other prison spells materialised. Typically, they gave rise to verse that contributed to his position as the first Renaissance poet in France.

CHAPTER XII

Honoré Gabriel comte de Mirabeau is well known for his role in the earlier stages of the Revolution. For the purposes of this book, he also serves as a prime instance of the operation of the "lettre de cachet" (the sealed writ), under which private requests addressed to the king or his representative for the incarceration of those threatening family honour or disturbing public order were granted as an extra legal instrument. At the behest of his father, Mirabeau was the recipient of ten such writs. At the national level, in the second half of the eighteenth century those detained under a "lettre de cachet" in France were as numerous as those imprisoned for debt in England.

The spell of three and a half years of imprisonment in the Donjon de Vincennes was in recognition of his abduction of Sophie, the married woman with whom he had fallen in love, the two being extradited from their refuge in the Netherlands. Mirabeau's prison writings once in Vincennes were extensive. Best known are his very affectionate love letters to Sophie in her convent. The title that touches his situation most directly, however, is a two-volume study entitled "Des Lettres de Cachet et des Prisons d'Etat" – an astonishing work coming from a serving prisoner.

Voltaire completed his tragedy, *Oedipe*, when in the Bastille. He was later to demonstrate how a life supporting much of the time individual freedoms, is no bar to the wielding of a medieval instrument, the *lettre de cachet*, for personal advantage.

CHAPTER XIII

Next to Charlotte Corday, the assassin of Marat, **Madame Roland** is the best known of the women revolutionaries, a leading figure within the Girondin faction. Together with her husband who twice occupied the post of Minister of the Interior, they fell foul of Robespierre and the Jacobins. Her husband managed to slip away to the country, she was imprisoned for five months before being guillotined. Writing occupied much of her time, first of all with a series of lively political portraits and anecdotes. Later, once the hope of freedom had evaporated, she turned to her personal memoirs, which she hoped would be a model of complete honesty. The memoirs of this elegant, cultured woman have a freshness that is captivating.

CHAPTER XIV

Lavoisier, co-discoverer of oxygen and thereby dethroner of water as one of the four elements, is a surprising presence in this book. He owed his six-months imprisonment ahead of the guillotine to his links with several "ancient regime" institutions, including that of the tax gathering "fermiers". From the moment he entered the Port Libre ci-devant Port Royal prison, he took up the chemical history on which he had been working. This then had to be set aside when he was called upon to justify the accounts of the tax gatherers – then accused of embezzlement on a grandiose scale – with Lavoisier producing a massive report. The mood of the day was illustrated in the declaration by the vice-president of the Revolutionary Tribunal that the Revolution had no need of scientists. It was only with the final accounting in 1806 that it was established that the tax gatherers were owed money, rather than the reverse.

CHAPTER XV

In common with many from intellectual and artistic bourgeois backgrounds, **André Chénier**, having been at the onset of the Revolution an enthusiastic supporter, switched to a vocal critic over Jacobin excesses - without abandoning his republican ideals. He had become a marked man and in due course was arrested and incarcerated. In prison, his lyrical verse was sustained, as with the memorable "La Jeune Captive". And at the same time he extended his metrical innovations. The bulk of his prison texts was, however, given over to bursts of outrage at revolutionary injustices.

The cult status that Chénier was to acquire owes much to the romantic tragedy of a gifted young man being denied life at the age of thirty-two. But much more is owed to the posthumous publication in 1819 of the first collection of his lyric verse, just in time to be taken up by the swelling romantic wave of the day. His emergence from literary obscurity was a revelation.

CHAPTER XVI

The response to the Revolution of the poet, **Jean-Antoine Roucher**, traced a familiar pattern of initial enthusiasm, changing into fierce criticism of Jacobin tactics, followed swiftly by incarceration. From prison, he continued to fulfil his role as teacher of Eulalie, his seventeen-year-old daughter. This was achieved through an exchange of letters, largely involving his daughter, that ran to one hundred and sixty-eight. Aside from the pedagogic aspect, the correspondence carried news about the circumstances in prison and what was happening at home. Eulalie's affectionate letters have great charm and those of Roucher keep the reader at times informed on an hour to hour basis of prison developments. This comes as close to an audio recording as one can get.

CHAPTER XVII

With Russia having supplied the world with a wealth of material covering the harshest of prison conditions, the specific experience of prison writers within the camps throws a startling light on the special challenges they faced in the actual creation of their texts and in their transmission.

Throughout his life, **Alexander Solzhenitsyn** can be said to have been in constant literary effervescence. Once in prison, writing was either rendered impossible or attracted a range of severe punishments. When posted to the Special Eastern Siberian Camp of Ekibastuz, then in course of construction, he was assigned to the brick laying team; He was destined to remain in Ekibastuz for two and a half years. His work presented a special challenge to an aspiring author. Having brought pencil and paper on shift, he would first write on scraps of paper ten to twenty lines of verse in a minute hand; once committed to memory, he destroyed the paper. The training of his memory, aided by an ingenious rosary used by Catholic Lithuanian missionaries, meant that by the end of his sentence he had memorised some 12,000 lines. In so doing, he had neatly side stepped problems of transmission.

In the case of **Lev Mishchenko**, once he had managed to escape the lethal physical work of the log hauling team at the Pechora camp, the challenges he confronted were those of transmission rather than composition. Having effectively disappeared from sight during the war first as a German captive then as a Russian traitor, he had to establish how his re-appearance might be viewed – if at all – by Sveta, the girl with whom he had fallen in love when they were at university together in the thirties. Her enthusiastic response was to mark the start of a correspondence that would last eight years and build up to more than twelve hundred letters.

With incoming and outgoing postal mail subject to inspection, Lev had to devise routes that escaped such surveillance whenever he and Sveta judged this to be necessary. One hugely important feature of the Pechora gulag was its position within a major industrial complex that received daily movements of workers and suppliers. This in turn led to political prisoners enjoying a high degree of freedom of movement within the camp. These two features made it possible for Lev to build up gradually a clutch of contacts, some of them having entrance and exit passes, who were prepared to take on the hazardous role of a go between. Much of the anxiety that surfaces in the letters concerns the fragility of laboriously constructed arrangements that could at any moment be shattered – thereby plunging Lev again into invisibility.

As a writer of poetry (married to a human rights activist), **Irina Ratushinskaya** received the maximum sentence for her "crime" of seven years strict regime and four years internal exile. Twenty-five years on from Solzhenitsyn's Ekibastuz and Mishchenko's Pechora, the Barashevo camp presented many differences. What remained unchanged were challenges of composition, plus those of transmission in an even heightened form.

Irina found herself in a unit known as the Small Zone, adjoining the regular prison, which housed around ten women political dissidents. They were put to work operating sewing machines in the production of industrial gloves. Irina, taking a leaf out of Solzhenitsyn's techniques, would manage to scribble a few lines onto scraps of paper to be hidden under a pile of half finished gloves. Once committed to memory, the paper would be destroyed. The next stage was to transcribe, unobserved by the guard on duty, the memorised verse onto thin strips of cigarette paper for eventual delivery to her husband two thousand kilometres away in Kiev, where they would join the self-publishing samizdat flow and occasionally achieve overseas publication. As with Mishchenko, such a procedure was only possible by reason of the ever-changing composition of Barashevo's population. The major additional hurdle was the Small Zone's physical isolation – with outside contacts only occurring intermittently on outings to the prison surgery, on the rare authorised visits from family members, on occasional transfers between Barashevo detention centres and, most productively, through the movement in and out of those punitive cells outside the Small Zone that Irina and the other politicals were sent to so often.

CHAPTER XVIII

As a self-publicist, **Pierre-François Lacenaire**, self-confessed murderer, cannot have improved on the final seventy days of his existence: holding court in the Conciergerie after a spectacular trial and writing at breakneck speed his *Memoirs*. When eventually published they ran to 377 pages. Two thirds of the way through, he paused "une halte, j'ai besoin de me reposer" (a break, I need a rest).

What would have pleased him even more would have been for him to have learned that he had subsequently attained cult status as a rebel against society and had caught the attention of such literary figures as Dostoevsky, Stendhal, Balzac, Victor Hugo, Baudelaire and had been the source of inspiration for the outstanding post-war film *Les Enfants du Paradis*.

CHAPTER XIX

William Chester Minor's 38-year-long incarceration in Broadmoor Criminal Lunatic Asylum included a period of eighteen years when, as a volunteer lexicographer, he became a greatly-valued contributor in the creation of the Oxford English Dictionary. For much of the time, he managed to avoid revealing his place of work, shunning, in common with William Combe, a prison address.

Within Broadmoor, he encountered a sympathetic governor, who was intent on welcoming an inmate with an un usual background – a Yale educated retired American army surgeon in whose welfare the U.S. Consulate took an interest. On a practical level, this translated into his being allocated two cells; in recognition of his literary enthusiasms, one was converted into a library (with shelving paid for by Minor) to house initially his books from Yale. With room and board supplied by the Crown, plus having access to the prison infirmary and to medical attention, it can be said that Broadmoor provided the ideal setting for a single-minded, highly disciplined lexicographer to pursue his overwhelming interest. It remains to be said that the prison will also have done much to allay for a while the searing anxieties of a deranged mind.

Acknowledgements

For a work such as *Guarded Words* that has been many years in gestation, the author's obligations are innumerable. In the Preface, reference has already been made to my reliance on the British Library, the archives at Kew, the London Metropolitan Archives, the House of Lords Records Office and the Parliamentary Archives. At a more intimate level, my warmest thanks go to Lambeth Palace Library and the London Library, whose remarkable holdings I have been able to plunder, as it were, with the connivance of the ever-helpful members of staff.

Editorially, encouragement has come from many publishing friends. One, at an early stage, said that I should broaden the geographic scope beyond England and France to include Russia. China had been considered, but discarded for linguistic reasons and for the limited supply of prison-bound writing – a telling commentary on the effectiveness of a repressive regime. To another friend, I owe the enigmatic title *Guarded Words*. Travel at home and abroad occasionally introduced me to lapidary texts on buildings. Having the historian, Linda Kelly, as a great friend naturally led to delightful discussions, one of her books having been *Women of the French Revolution*.

At the practical level, I have received considerable help from my sister-in-law, Sheila de Bellaigue, who, among other things, taught me how to introduce accents into the typescript. Malcolm Welchman has repeatedly resolved Microsoft Word crises. Cai Parry-Jones has brought professional standards of referencing into the creation of the notes.

To Christine Shuttleworth I am greatly indebted on two counts. First of all, the provision of an index. In the second place, it is to Christine that I owe my introduction to Unicorn Press and hence to my publisher, Hugh Tempest-Radford.

Under Hugh's auspices, my earlier exposure to high standards of precision at the hands of Cai and Christine has stood me in good stead. He and his team, Andrew Barker, designer, Susannah Stone, picture researcher, with Lauren Tanner, publicity manager, have created a book of great typographic elegance, equipped with arresting images. This is held together by a publisher, who also sets a high score on communication – a precious attribute.

But for constant support and companionship during the book's extended genesis, I turn to John Sharpe, retired Civil Servant, book binder and collector. Every chapter was scrutinised by him, giving rise to extended correspondence that drew attention to inconsistencies, inaccuracies and suggestions for further analysis, the seventeenth century being a particular enthusiasm of his.

Notes and Bibliography

CHAPTER I

Principal Published Sources

Anon, *The piercing cryes of the poor and miserable prisoners for debt: In all Parts of England. Shewing The Unreasonableness and Folly of Imprisoning the Body for Debt, from the Laws of God and Reason, Custom of Nations, Human Policy and Interest* (1714).

Roger Lee Brown, *A History of the Fleet Prison, London: The Anatomy of the Fleet* (Lampeter: Edwin Mellon Press, 1996).

Richard Byrne, *Prisons and Punishment of London* (London: Harrap, 1989).

W. B. Carnochan, 'The Literature of Confinement' in Norval Morris and David J. Rothman (eds.), *The Oxford History of the Prison: The Practice of Punishment in Western Society* (New York: Oxford University Press, 1995).

Edward Farley, *Imprisonment for debt unconstitutional and oppressive, proved from the fundamental principles of the British Constitution, and the rights of nature* (London, 1788).

John Howard, *The State of the Prisons in England and Wales* (Warrington, 1777).

Geoffrey Howse, *A History of London Prisons* (Barnsley: Wharncliffe Books, 2012).

James Neild, *Account of Persons Confined for Debt, in the Various Prisons of England and Wales: Together with their Provisionary Allowance during Confinement: as Reported to the Society for the Discharge and Relief of Small Debtors* (London, 1800).

Aylmer Vallance, *The Summer King: Variations by an Adventurer on Eighteenth-Century Air* (London: Thames and Hudson, 1956).

Antoine Laurent Serpentini, *Théodore de Neuhoff, roi de Corse: Un aventurier européen du XVIIIe siècle* (Corsica: Albiana, 2012).

Christopher Harding, Bill Hines, Richard Ireland and Philip Rawlings, *Imprisonment in England and Wales: A Concise History* (London: Croom Helm, 1985).

Sean D. M. McConville, *A History of English Prison Administration, Vol. 1 1750–1877* (London: Routledge & Kegan Paul, 1981).

Ralph B. Pugh, Imprisonment in Medieval Britain (Cambridge: Cambridge University Press, 1968).

Jerry White, *Mansions of Misery: A Biography of the Marshalsea Debtors' Prison* (London: The Bodley Head, 2016).

Nigel Stirk, 'Arresting Ambiguity: The Shifting Geographies of a London Debtors' Sanctuary in the Eighteenth Century', *Social History*, 25, 3 (2000).

Robert Twigger, *Inflation: the Value of the Pound 1750–1998* (London: House of Commons Library, 1999).

A Report from the Committee Appointed to Enquire Into the State of the Goals [sic] of this Kingdom: Relating to the Marshalsea Prison; and Farther Relating to the Fleet Prison. With the Resolution of the House of Commons Thereupon (London, 1729).

Ian W. Archer "The Charity of Early Modern Londoners" Transactions of the Royal Historical Society 2002.

Notes (CH. 1)

1 Norval Morris and David J. Rothman (eds), *The Oxford History of the Prison: The Practice of Punishment in Western Society* (New York: Oxford University Press, 1995), p.34.

2 Pat Rogers, 'Contributors and Reviewers', *The Book Collector*, 63/2 (2014), 249.

3 Common-place Book (*c.*1760), MS 4912, Lambeth Palace Library.

4 Ralph B. Pugh, *Imprisonment in Medieval Britain* (Cambridge: Cambridge University Press, 1968), p.46.

5 Roger Lee Brown, *A History of the Fleet Prison, London: The Anatomy of the Fleet* (Lampeter: Edwin Mellon Press, 1996), p.4.

6 Christopher Harding, Bill Hines, Richard Ireland and Philip Rawlings, *Imprisonment in England and Wales: A Concise History* (London: Croom Helm, 1985), p.76.

7 Richard Byrne, *Prisons and Punishment of London* (London: Harrap, 1989), p.110.

8 John Howard, *The State of the Prisons in England and Wales, with Preliminary Observations, and an Account of Some Foreign Prisons and Hospitals* (Warrington, 1784).

9 Sean D. M. McConville, *A History of English Prison Administration, Vol. 1 1750–1877* (London: Routledge & Kegan Paul, 1981), p.51.

10 Allen Reddick, *The Making of Johnson's Dictionary, 1746–1773* (Cambridge: Cambridge University Press), p.93.

11 Pat Rogers, 'Samuel Johnson (1709–1784)', *Oxford Dictionary of National Biography* (online ed.). Oxford University Press (2004).

12 Nigel Stirk, 'Arresting Ambiguity: The Shifting Geographies of a London Debtors' Sanctuary in the Eighteenth Century', *Social History*, 25, 3 (2000), 318.

13 Jerry White, *Mansions of Misery: A Biography of the Marshalsea Debtors' Prison* (London: The Bodley Head, 2016), p.2.

14 Howard, *State of Prisons*, p.281.

15 Byrne, *Prisons and Punishment*, p.44.

16 James Neild, *Account of Persons Confined for Debt, in the various prisons of England and Wales; together with their provisionary allowance during confinement, as reported to the society for the discharge and relief of small debtors* (London, 1800), p.37.

17 Neild, *Account of Persons Confined for Debt*, p.42.

18 White, *Mansions of Misery*, pp.7–10.

19 Neild, *Account of Persons Confined for Debt*, p.32.

20 Pugh, *Imprisonment in Medieval Britain*, p.213.

21 Legacy book, i.e., notes of bequests to Society and progress in obtaining payment of them, Vols. I–III (1773–1865), Society for the Relief of Persons Confined for Small Debts, A/RSD/05/001-003, London Metropolitan Archives.

22 Edward Farley, *Imprisonment for Debt Unconstitutional and Oppressive* (London, 1788), p.139.

23 William Fennor, *A true Description of the Lawes, Justice and Equity of a Compter, the Manner of sitting in Counsell of the twelve eldest Prisoners; &c. &c.* (London, 1629).

24 *A Report from the Committee Appointed to Enquire Into the State of the Goals [sic] of this Kingdom: Relating to the Marshalsea Prison; and Farther Relating to the Fleet Prison. With the Resolution of the House of Commons Thereupon* (London, 1729).

25 White, *Mansions of Misery*, p.98.

26 *A Report from the Committee Appointed to Enquire Into the State of the Goals [sic]*.

27 Aylmer Vallance, *The Summer King: Variations by an Adventurer on Eighteenth-Century Air* (London: Thames and Hudson, 1956), pp.168–170.

28 Vallance, *The Summer King*, p.170.

29 Vallance, *The Summer King*, p.172.

30 Antoine Laurent Serpentini, *Théodore de Neuhoff, roi de Corse: Un aventurier européen du XVIIIe siècle* (Corsica: Albiana, 2012), p.428.

31 Geoffrey Howse, *A History of London's Prisons* (Barnsley: Wharncliffe Books, 2012), p.82.

32 Byrne, *Prisons and Punishment*, p.51.

CHAPTER II

Principal Published Sources

Arthur Bryant, *Samuel Pepys – The Years of Peril* (Cambridge, 1935).

Commonplace book compiled by Andrew Coltée Ducarel (1713–85), Lambeth Librarian and antiquary (c.1760), MS 4912, Lambeth Palace Library.

Michael T. Davis, Ian McCalman and Christina Parolin (eds), *Newgate in Revolution: An Anthology of Radical Prison Literature in the Age of Revolution* (London: Continuum, 2005).

William Dodd, *Thoughts in Prison; in Five Parts, viz. The Imprisonment, the Retrospect, Public Punishment, the Trial, Futurity. By the Rev. William Dodd, LLD. To which are added . . . Other Miscellaneous Pieces* (London, 1777).

Stephen Halliday, *Newgate: London's Prototype of Hell* (Stroud: Sutton, 2006).

William Hodgson, *The Commonwealth of Reason* (London, 1795).

William Eden Hooper, *The History of Newgate and the Old Bailey, and a survey of the Fleet prison and Fleet marriages, the Marshalsea and other old London jails, etc.* (London: Underwood Press, 1935).

John Keane, *Tom Paine: A Political Life* (London: Bloomsbury, 1995).

J. C. Lettsom, *Hints respecting the Prison of Newgate, Extracted from the Fourth Volume of Memoirs of the Medical Society of London* (London, 1794).

Sean D. M. McConville, *A History of English Prison Administration, Vol. 1 1750–1877* (London: Routledge & Kegan Paul, 1981).

Jennifer Mori, *William Pitt and the French Revolution, 1785–1795* (Edinburgh: Keele University Press, 1997).

James Neild, *Account of Persons confined for Debt, in the various prisons of England and Wales: together with their provisionary allowance during confinement: as reported to the Society for the discharge and relief of small Debtors* (London, 1800).

The complete Newgate calendar; being Captain Charles Johnson's general history of the lives and adventures of the most famous highwaymen, murderers, street-robbers and account of the voyages and plunders of the most notorious pyrates, 1734; Captain Alexander Smith's compleat history of the lives and robberies of the most notorious highwaymen, foot-pads, shop-lifts and cheats (London: Navarre Society, 1925–1926).

The Malefactor's register, or, The Newgate and Tyburn calendar: containing the authentic lives, trials, accounts of executions, and dying speeches, of the most notorious violators of the laws of their country (London, 1779).

John Villette, *A Genuine Account of the Behaviour and Dying Words of William Dodd, LLD, who was Executed at Tyburn for Forgery, on Friday the 27th of June, 1777* (London, 1777).

Tim Wales, 'Paul Lorrain (d.1719)', *Oxford Dictionary of National Biography* (online ed.). Oxford University Press (2004).

Marcus Wood, *Radical Satire and Print Culture, 1790–1822* (Oxford: Oxford University Press, 1994).

Notes (CH. II)

1 G. D. H. Cole and Raymond Postgate, *The Common People, 1746–1938* (London, 1938), p.60.

2 John Stow, *A Survey of the Cities of London and Westminster, and the Borough of Southwark, Vol. 2 Appendix* (London, 1720), p.59.

3 William Eden Hooper, *The History of Newgate and the Old Bailey, and a survey of the Fleet prison and Fleet marriages, the Marshalsea and other old London jails, etc.* (London: Underwood Press, 1935), p.111.

4 McConville, *A History of English prison administration. Volume I 1750–1877*, p.75.

5 Tim Wales, 'Paul Lorrain (d.1719)', *Oxford Dictionary of National Biography* (online ed.). Oxford University Press (2004).

6 Diary and correspondence of Samuel Pepys F.R.S.: vol 6. (London, 1879), p.229.

7 Vivienne Aldous, 'The archives of the freedom of the City of London, 1681–1915', *Genealogists' Magazine*, 23/4 (1989), 128–133.

8 Commonplace book compiled by Andrew Coltée Ducarel (1713–85), Lambeth Librarian and antiquary (*c*.1760), MS 4912, Lambeth Palace Library.

9 Paul Lorrain, *A Narrative; or, the Ordinary of Newgate (P. Lorrain)'s account of what passed between him and James Sheppard; who was try'd . . . for high treason . . . and executed . . . on Monday last, being the 17th inst.* (London: J. Morphew, *c*.1717).

10 Simon Heighes, 'J.S. Bach: A Life in 10 Masterpieces', *BBC Music Magazine* (Dec, 2016), 33.

11 Keith Hollingworth, *The Newgate Novel, 1830–1847: Bulwer, Ainsworth, Dickens & Thackeray* (Detroit: Wayne State University Press, 1963), p.43.

12 McConville, *A History of English Prison Administration*, p.75.

13 John Villette, *A Genuine Account of the Behaviour and Dying Words of William Dodd, LLD, who was Executed at Tyburn for Forgery, on Friday the 27th of June, 1777* (London, 1777).

14 William Jackson, *The New and Complete Newgate Calendar, or, Malefactors' Universal Register, Vol.1* (London, [1800–1812]), p.5.

15 Michael T. Davis, Ian McCalman and Christina Parolin (eds), *Newgate in Revolution: An Anthology of Radical Prison Literature in the Age of Revolution* (London: Continuum, 2005), p.xviii.

16 Hooper, *The History of Newgate and the Old Bailey*, p.119.

17 John Stow, *A Survey of the Cities of London and Westminster, and the Borough of Southwark, Vol. 1, Book III* (London, 1720), p.194.

18 William Dodd, *Thoughts in Prison; in Five Parts, viz. The Imprisonment, the Retrospect, Public Punishment, the Trial, Futurity. By the Rev. William Dodd, LLD. To which are added...Other Miscellaneous Pieces* (London, 1777).

19 Davis, McCalman and Parolin, *Newgate in Revolution*, p.70.

20 Davis, McCalman and Parolin, *Newgate in Revolution*, p.75.

21 J. C. Lettsom, *Hints respecting the Prison of Newgate, Extracted from the Fourth Volume of Memoirs of the Medical Society of London* (London, 1794).

22 Dodd, *Thoughts in Prison*, p.73.

23 Jennifer Mori, *William Pitt and the French Revolution, 1785–1795* (Edinburgh: Keele University Press, 1997), p.108.

24 William Hodgson, *The Commonwealth of Reason* (London, 1795).

25 Davis, McCalman and Parolin, *Newgate in Revolution*, p.129.

26 Marcus Wood, *Radical Satire and Print Culture, 1790–1822* (Oxford: Clarendon Press, 1994), p.90.

27 John Keane, *Tom Paine: A Political Life* (London: Bloomsbury, 1995), pp.304–306.

28 Keane, *Tom Paine*, p.331.

29 Davis, McCalman and Parolin, *Newgate in Revolution*, p.118.

30 Wood, *Radical satire*, pp.xi–xii.

31 Winston Churchill, *A History of the English-speaking Peoples. Vol. 3: The Age of Revolution* (London: Cassell, 1957), p.233.

CHAPTER III

Principal Published Sources

Peter Ackroyd, *The Life of Thomas More* (London: Chatto & Windus, 1998).

William Allen, *An apologie and true declaration of the institution and endevours of the two English colleges, the one in Rome, the other now resident in Rhemes : against certaine sinister informations given up against the same* (Rheims, 1581).

H. J. Byrom 'Richard Tottell – His Life and Work', *The Library* 4, 8 (1927), 199–232.

R. W. Chambers, *Thomas More* (London, 1935).

Eamon Duffy, 'William Allen (1532–1594)', *Oxford Dictionary of National Biography* (online ed.). Oxford University Press (2004).

Laurence Echard, *The History of England from the First Entrance of Julius Caesar & the Romans, to the End of the Reign of King James I*, 3rd ed. (London, 1718).

M. A. E. Green, *Elizabeth, Electress Palatine and Queen of Bohemia, revised by her niece S. C. Lomas* (London: Methuen & Co., 1909).

John Guy, *A Daughter's Love: Thomas & Margaret More* (London: Fourth Estate, 2008).

Brian Harrison, *A Tudor Journal: the diary of a priest in the Tower, 1580–1585* (London: St Pauls, 2000).

Nigel Jones, *Tower: an Epic History of the Tower of London* (London: Hutchinson, 2011).

Thomas M. C. Lawler, Germain Marc'hadour and Richard C. Marius (eds.), *The Complete Works of St Thomas More, Vol. 6* (New Haven: Yale University Press, 1981).

Diarmaid MacCulloch, *Thomas Cranmer: A Life* (New Haven: Yale University Press, 1996).

Louis L. Martz and Frank Manley (eds.) *The Complete Works of St Thomas More, Vol. 12 part 1* (New Haven: Yale University Press, 1976).

Clarence H. Miller (ed. and transl.), *The Complete Works of St Thomas More, Vol. 14 De Tristitia Christi* (New Haven: Yale University Press, 1976).

Ministry of Works, *The Tower of London* (London: HMSO, 1961).

Thomas More, *The Workes of Sir Thomas More Knyght, Sometyme Lorde Chauncellour of England, Wrytten by Him in the Englysh Tonge* (London, 1557).

Clare Murphy and David Souden (eds.), *Prisoners of the Tower: The Tower of London as a State Prison, 1100–1941* (Hampton Court Palace: Historic Royal Palaces, 2004).

Geoffrey de C. Parmiter, 'The Indictment of St Thomas More', *The Downside Review* 75 (1957), 149–66.

Geoffrey Parnell, *The Tower of London: Past & Present* (B. T. Batsford, 1993).

John Hungerford Pollen, *Acts of English martyrs hitherto unpublished* (London: Burns and Oates, 1891).

Arthur W. Reed, 'The Editor of Sir Thomas More's English Works: William Rastell', *The Library*, 4/4 (1923).

E. E. Reynolds, *Lives of Saint Thomas More [by William Roper and Nicholas Harpsfield]* (London: Dent, 1963).

Louis A. Schuster, Richard C. Marius, James P. Lusardi and Richard J. Schoeck (eds), *The Complete Works of St Thomas More, Vol. 8* (New Haven: Yale University Press, 1973).

Alvaro de Silva, *The Last Letters of Thomas More* (Cambridge: William B. Eerdmans, 2000).

Notes (CH. III)

1 Clare Murphy and David Souden (eds), *Prisoners of the Tower: the Tower of London as a State Prison, 1100–1941* (Hampton Court Palace: Historic Royal Palaces, 2004), p.20.

2 Nigel Jones, *Tower: an Epic History of the Tower of London* (London: Hutchinson, 2011), p.18.

3 Jones, *Tower*, p.139.

4 Laurence Echard, *The History of England from the First Entrance of Julius Caesar & the Romans, to the End of the Reign of King James I* (London, 1718), p.734.

5 Murphy and Souden, *Prisoners of the Tower*, pp.29–32.

6 Murphy and David Souden (eds), *Prisoners of the Tower*, p.37.

7 Brian Harrison, *A Tudor Journal: the diary of a priest in the Tower, 1580–1585* (London: St Pauls, 2000), p.24.

8 John Hungerford Pollen, *Acts of English martyrs hitherto unpublished* (London: Burns and Oates, 1891), p.208.

9 Harrison, *A Tudor Journal*, p.13.

10 Eamon Duffy, 'William Allen (1532–1594)', *Oxford Dictionary of National Biography* (online ed.). Oxford University Press (2004).

11 E. E. Reynolds, *Lives of Saint Thomas More [by William Roper and Nicholas Harpsfield]* (London: Dent, 1963), p.vii.

12 Harrison, *A Tudor Journal*, p.24.

13 William Allen, *An apologie and true declaration of the institution and endevours of the two English colleges, the one in Rome, the other now resident in Rhemes: against certaine sinister informations given up against the same* (Rheims, 1581), p.71.

14 Allen, *An apologie*, p.111.

15 Allen, *An apologie*, p.113.

16 Allen, *An apologie*, p.24.

17 Harrison, *A Tudor Journal*, p.50.

18 Harrison, *A Tudor Journal*, p.35.

19 Harrison, *A Tudor Journal*, p.87.

20 Harrison, *A Tudor Journal*, p.92.

21 Harrison, *A Tudor Journal*, p.180.

22 Harrison, *A Tudor Journal*, p.105.

23 Harrison, *A Tudor Journal*, p.218.

24 Harrison, *A Tudor Journal*, p.50.

25 Harrison, *A Tudor Journal*, p.93.

26 Harrison, *A Tudor Journal*, p.42.

27 Harrison, *A Tudor Journal*, p.73.

28 Harrison, *A Tudor Journal*, p.26.

29 Harrison, *A Tudor Journal*, p.26.

30 Eamon Duffy, 'William Allen (1532–1594)', *Oxford Dictionary of National Biography* (online ed.). Oxford University Press (2004).

31 Harrison, *A Tudor Journal*, p.61.

32 Harrison, *A Tudor Journal*, p.42.

33 Harrison, *A Tudor Journal*, p.221.

24 Alvaro de Silva, *The Last Letters of Thomas More* (Cambridge: William B. Eerdmans, 2000), pp.58–59.

35 Letter 22, 3 June 1535, in de Silva, *The Last Letters*, p.118.

36 Letter 16 in de Silva, *The Last Letters*, p.101.

37 de Silva, *The Last Letters*, p.192.

38 Jones, *Tower*, p.26.

39 Thomas M. C. Lawler, Germain Marc'hadour and Richard C. Marius (eds.), *The Complete Works of St. Thomas More, Vol. 6* (New Haven: Yale University Press, 1981), p.ii.

40 John Guy, *A Daughter's Love: Thomas &*

Margaret More (London: Fourth Estate, 2008), p.195.

41 R. W. Chambers, *Thomas More* (London, 1935), pp.32–33.

42 Lawler, Marc'hadour and Marius, *The Complete Works of St. Thomas More, Vol. 6*.

43 Louis A. Schuster, Richard C. Marius, James P. Lusardi and Richard J. Schoeck (eds), *The Complete Works of St. Thomas More, Vol. 8* (New Haven: Yale University Press, 1973), p.1345.

44 Schuster, Marius, Lusardi and Schoeck, *The Complete Works of St. Thomas More, Vol. 8*, pp.1247–1251.

45 Lawler, Marc'hadour and Marius, *The Complete Works of St. Thomas More, Vol. 6*, p.603.

46 Lawler, Marc'hadour and Marius, *The Complete Works of St. Thomas More, Vol. 6*, p.675.

47 Lawler, Marc'hadour and Marius, *The Complete Works of St. Thomas More, Vol. 6*, p.491.

48 Lawler, Marc'hadour and Marius, *The Complete Works of St. Thomas More, Vol. 6*, p.603.

49 Guy, *A Daughter's Love*, pp.197–198.

50 Letter 8 in de Silva, *The Last Letters*, p.64.

51 Thomas More, *The Workes of Sir Thomas More Knyght, Sometyme Lorde Chauncellour of England, Wrytten by Him in the Englysh Tonge* (London, 1557), p.1431.

52 Clarence H. Miller (ed. and transl.), *The Complete Works of St. Thomas More, Vol. 14 De Tristitia Christi* (New Haven: Yale University Press, 1976), p.695.

53 Miller, *The Complete Works of St. Thomas More, Vol.14*, p.1077.

54 Chambers, *Thomas More*, p.315.

55 Louis L. Martz and Frank Manley (eds.) *The Complete Works of St. Thomas More, Vol. 12 part 1* (New Haven: Yale University Press, 1976), pp.lxv–lxvi.

56 Louis L. Martz and Frank Manley (eds.) *The Complete Works of St. Thomas More, Vol. 12 part 2* (New Haven: Yale University Press, 1976), p.lxix.

57 Miller, *The Complete Works of St. Thomas More, Vol.14*, p.696.

58 Arthur W. Reed, 'The Editor of Sir Thomas More's English Works: William Rastell', *The Library*, 4/4 (1923), p.42.

59 More, *The Workes of Sir Thomas More Knyght*.

60 H. J. Byrom, 'Richard Tottell: His Life and Work', *The Library*, 4/8 (1927–28), p.202.

61 Byrom, 'Richard Tottell', 205.

62 Byrom, 'Richard Tottell', 205.

63 Byrom, 'Richard Tottell', 202.

64 Byrom, 'Richard Tottell', 207.

65 Chambers, *Thomas More*, p.309.

66 Letter 20 in de Silva, *The Last Letters*, p.114.

67 Guy, *A Daughter's Love*, p.247.

68 Letter 21 in de Silva, *The Last Letters*, p.189.

69 Letter 18 in de Silva, *The Last Letters*, p.186.

70 Letter 23 in de Silva, *The Last Letters*, p.120.

71 Letter 16 in de Silva, *The Last Letters*, p.100.

72 Miller, *The Complete Works of St. Thomas More, Vol.14*, pp.695–697.

73 Martz and Manley, *The Complete Works of St. Thomas More, Vol. 12 part 2*, p.18.

74 Jones, *Tower*, p.26.

75 M. A. E. Green, *Elizabeth, Electress Palatine and Queen of Bohemia, revised by her niece S. C. Lomas* (London: Methuen & Co., 1909), p.19.

76 Robert Lacey, *Sir Walter Raleigh* (London: Phoenix Press, 1973), p.316.

77 Green, *Elizabeth*, p.19.

78 Geoffrey Parnell, *The Tower of London* (London: Batsford, 1993).

79 Jones, *Tower*, p.29.

80 Jones, *Tower*, pp.34–36.

CHAPTER IV

Principal Published Sources

Elaine V. Beilin, *The Examinations of Anne Askew* (New York: Oxford University Press, 1996).

Susan Brigden, 'Howard, Henry, earl of Surrey (1516/17–1547)', *Oxford Dictionary of National Biography* (online ed.). Oxford University Press (2004).

Gerald Bullett (ed.), *Silver Poets of the Sixteenth Century: Sir Thomas Wyatt, Henry Howard Earl of Surrey, Sir Philip Sidney, Sir Walter Ralegh* (London: Dent, 1947).

Guy Cadogan Rothery, *ABC of Heraldry* (London, 1915).

Edwin Casady, *Henry Howard, Earl of Surrey* (New York: Modern Language Association of America, 1938).

Jessie Childs, *Henry VIII's Last Victim: The Life and Times of Henry Howard, Earl of Surrey* (London: Jonathan Cape, 2006).

David M. Head, *The Ebbs and Flows of Fortune: The Life of Thomas Howard, Third Duke of Norfolk* (Athens: University of Georgia Press, 2009).

Elizabeth Heale, 'Women and the Courtly Love Lyric: The Devonshire MS (BL Additional 17492)', *Modern Language Review* 90 (1995), 296–313.

Paul Marquis, 'Tottell's Songs and Sonettes', *The Book Collector*, 56 (2007)

Frederick Morgan Padelford (ed.), *The Poems of Henry Howard, Earl of Surrey* (Seattle, 1920).

William A. Sessions, *Henry Howard, The Poet Earl of Surrey: A Life* (Oxford: Oxford University Press, 1999).

Felix E. Schelling, *English Literature during the Lifetime of Shakespeare* (New York: Russell & Russell, 1973).

Neville Williams, *Thomas Howard, Fourth Duke of Norfolk* (London: Barrie and Rockliff, 1964).

The Poems of Henry Howard Earl of Surrey (London, 1866).

Notes (CH. IV)

1 Susan Brigden, 'Henry Howard, Earl of Surrey (1516/17–1547)', *Oxford Dictionary of National Biography* (online ed.). Oxford University Press (2004).

2 Jessie Childs, *Henry VIII's Last Victim: The Life and Times of Henry Howard, Earl of Surrey* (London: Jonathan Cape, 2006), p.160.

3 David M. Head, *The Ebbs and Flows of*

Fortune: The Life of Thomas Howard, Third Duke of Norfolk (Athens: University of Georgia Press, 2009), p.220.

4 Head, *The Ebbs and Flows of Fortune*, p.118.

5 Neville Williams, *Thomas Howard, Fourth Duke of Norfolk* (London: Barrie and Rockliff, 1964), p.3.

6 Childs, *Henry VIII's Last Victim*, p.183.

7 Childs, *Henry VIII's Last Victim*, p.186.

8 William A. Sessions, *Henry Howard, The Poet Earl of Surrey: A Life* (Oxford: Oxford University Press, 1999), p.231.

9 Sessions, *Henry Howard*, pp.115–116.

10 Childs, *Henry VIII's Last Victim*, p.315.

11 Guy Cadogan Rothery, *ABC of Heraldry* (London, 1915), p.144.

12 Childs, *Henry VIII's Last Victim*, p.223.

13 Head, *The Ebbs and Flows of Fortune*, p.222.

14 Sessions, *Henry Howard*, p.380.

15 Childs, *Henry VIII's Last Victim*, p.270.

16 Williams, *Thomas Howard*, p.14.

17 Susan Doran (ed.), *Henry VIII: Man and Monarch* (London: British Library, 2009), p.261.

18 Sessions, *Henry Howard*, p.416.

19 Childs, *Henry VIII's Last Victim*, p.301.

20 Brigden, 'Henry Howard, Earl of Surrey (1516/17–1547)'.

21 Childs, *Henry VIII's Last Victim*, p.311.

22 Head, *The Ebbs and Flows of Fortune*, p.226.

23 Frederick Morgan Padelford (ed.), *The Poems of Henry Howard, Earl of Surrey* (Seattle, 1920), p.36.

24 Head, *The Ebbs and Flows of Fortune*, p.221.

25 Williams, *Thomas Howard*, p.21.

26 Gerald Bullett (ed.), *Silver Poets of the Sixteenth Century: Sir Thomas Wyatt, Henry Howard Earl of Surrey, Sir Philip Sidney, Sir Walter Ralegh* (London: Dent, 1947), p.iii.

27 Felix E. Schelling, *English Literature during the Lifetime of Shakespeare* (New York: Russell & Russell, 1973), p.274.

28 The Devonshire manuscript, Add. MS 17492, The British Library.

29 E. Heale, 'Women and the Courtly Love Lyric: The Devonshire MS (BL Additional 17492)', *The Modern Language Review*, 90/2 (April, 1995), 300.

30 C. Shirley, 'The Devonshire Manuscript: Reading Gender in the Henrician Court', *English Literary Renaissance*, 45/1 (2015), 36.

31 Childs, *Henry VIII's Last Victim*, p.270.

32 Paul A. Marquis, 'Editing and Unediting Richard Tottell's "Songes and Sonnettes"', *The Book Collector*, 56/3 (2007), 353–376.

33 Sessions, *Henry Howard*, p.355.

34 Elaine V. Beilin, *The Examinations of Anne Askew* (New York: Oxford University Press, 1996), p.xx.

35 Beilin, *The Examinations*, p.xxxiii.

36 Sessions, *Henry Howard*, p.226.

CHAPTER V

Principal Published Sources

A. F. Allison, *Thomas Lodge, 1558–1625: A Bibliographical Catalogue* (Folkestone: Dawsons, 1973).

G. R. Batho, 'The library of the "Wizard" Earl of Northumberland, 1564–1632', *The Library*, 5/15 (1960).

Anna R. Beer, *Sir Walter Ralegh and His Readers in the Seventeenth Century: Speaking to the People* (London: Macmillan, 1997).

T. N. Brushfield, *The Bibliography of the 'History of the World' and of the 'Remains' of Sir Walter Raleigh* (London: Dryden Press, 1886).

John Buchtel, 'Dedicating Books to Henry, Prince of Wales', in Timothy Wilkes (ed.), *Prince Henry Revived: Image and Exemplarity in Early Modern England* (London: Southampton Solent University in association with Paul Holberton, 2007).

By the King, A Proclamation declaring His Maiesties pleasure concerning Sir Walter Rawleigh, and those who adventured with him (London, 1618).

David Cecil, *The Cecils of Hatfield House* (London: Constable, 1973).

Charles Derrick, *Memoirs of the Rise and Progress of the Royal Navy* (London, 1806).

Michael Franks, *The Court, the Atlantic and*

the City: Sir Walter Raleigh v. William Sanderson (Mapledurwell: South and West Books, 2009).

M. A. E. Green, Elizabeth, Electress Palatine and Queen of Bohemia, revised by her niece S. C. Lomas (London: Methuen & Co., 1909).

Robert Lacey, Sir Walter Raleigh (London: Phoenix Press, 1973).

Agnes Latham and Joyce Youings (eds.), The Letters of Sir Walter Ralegh (Exeter: Exeter University Press, 1999).

Pierre Lefranc, Sir Walter Raleigh: écrivain, l'œuvre et les idées (Paris: A. Colin, 1968).

Joyce Lorimer, Untruth and consequences: Ralegh's Discoverie of Guiana and the 'salting' of the gold mine (London: Hakluyt Society, 2007).

Walter Oakeshott, 'Sir Walter Ralegh's Library', The Library 23, 4 (December, 1968).

John Racin, 'The Early Editions of Sir Walter Ralegh's "The History of the World"', Studies in Bibliography, 17 (1964).

John Racin, Sir Walter Ralegh as Historian: An Analysis of the History of the World (Salzburg: Institut für Englische Sprache und Literatur, Universität Salzburg, 1974).

Sir Walter Ralegh, [Remains of Sir Walter Raleigh; viz. Maxims of State. Advice to his Son, etc.] (London, 1702).

A. L. Rowse, Ralegh and the Throckmortons (London: Macmillan, 1962).

A. L. Rowse, The Elizabethan Renaissance: The Cultural Achievement (London: Macmillan, 1972).

Roy Strong, Henry, Prince of Wales and England's Lost Renaissance (London: Thames & Hudson, 1986).

J. W. Williamson, The Myth of the Conqueror: Prince Henry Stuart, a Study of 17th Century Personation (New York: AMS Press, 1978).

Notes (CH. V)

1 Robert Lacey, Sir Walter Raleigh (London: Phoenix Press, 1973), p.16.

2 Lacey, Sir Walter Raleigh, p.21.

3 Charles Derrick, Memoirs of the Rise and Progress of the Royal Navy (London, 1806), p.25.

4 Lacey, Sir Walter Raleigh, p.39.

5 Lacey, Sir Walter Raleigh, p.88.

6 Lacey, Sir Walter Raleigh, p.102.

7 Alfred L. Rowse, Ralegh and the Throckmortons (London: Macmillan, 1962), pp.166–168.

8 Michael Franks, The Court, the Atlantic and the City: Sir Walter Raleigh v. William Sanderson (Mapledurwell: South and West Books, 2009), p.55.

9 Lacey, Sir Walter Raleigh, p.162.

10 Winston Churchill, A History of the English-Speaking Peoples. Vol 2: The New World (London: Cassell, 1956), p.108.

11 Franks, The Court, p.31.

12 Lacey, Sir Walter Raleigh, p.207.

13 Lacey, Sir Walter Raleigh, p.201.

14 Lacey, Sir Walter Raleigh, p.231.

15 Rowse, Ralegh and the Throckmortons, p.202.

16 Lacey, Sir Walter Raleigh, p.263.

17 Lacey, Sir Walter Raleigh, p.286.

18 Lacey, Sir Walter Raleigh, p.274.

19 Lacey, Sir Walter Raleigh, p.296.

20 Letter 170 in Agnes Latham and Joyce Youings (eds.), The Letters of Sir Walter Ralegh (Exeter: Exeter University Press, 1999), p.259.

21 Letter 178 in Latham and Youing, The Letters, p.277.

22 Letter 176 in Latham and Youing, The Letters, p.272.

23 Letter 177 in Latham and Youing, The Letters, pp.273–276.

24 Letter 178 in Latham and Youing, The Letters, p.277.

25 Walter Oakeshott, 'Sir Walter Ralegh's Library', The Library, 23/4 (December, 1968), 285–327.

26 G. R. Batho, 'The library of the "Wizard" Earl of Northumberland, 1564–1632', The Library, 5/15 (1960), 246–61.

27 Lacey, Sir Walter Raleigh, p.320.

28 Batho, 'The library of the "Wizard"', 248.

29 Letter 165 in Latham and Youing, *The Letters*, pp.247–49.

30 Letter 172 in Latham and Youing, *The Letters*, pp.263–65.

31 Letter 165 in Latham and Youing, *The Letters*, p.249.

32 Latham and Youing, *The Letters*, p.xxvi.

33 Anna R. Beer, *Sir Walter Ralegh and His Readers in the Seventeenth Century: Speaking to the People* (London: Macmillan, 1997), p.92.

34 Beer, *Sir Walter Ralegh*, p.89.

35 Beer, *Sir Walter Ralegh*, pp.184–185.

36 *Sir Walter Rauleigh, his Lamentation, who was Beheaded in the Old Pallace of Westminster, the 29th of October, 1618* (1618), Pepys Ballads 1.110–111, Pepys Library, Magdalen College, Cambridge.

37 Latham and Youing, *The Letters*, p.lvii.

38 Beer, *Sir Walter Ralegh*, p.123.

39 Pierre Lefranc, *Sir Walter Raleigh: écrivain, l'œuvre et les idées* (Paris: A. Colin, 1968), pp.639–642.

40 Lefranc, *Sir Walter Raleigh*, pp.268–270.

41 John Racin, *Sir Walter Ralegh as Historian: An Analysis of the History of the World* (Salzburg: Institut für Englische Sprache und Literatur, Universität Salzburg, 1974), p.15.

42 John Buchtel, 'Dedicating Books to Henry, Prince of Wales', in Timothy Wilkes (ed.), *Prince Henry Revived: Image and Exemplarity in Early Modern England* (London: Southampton Solent University in association with Paul Holberton, 2007), p.129, fn.65.

43 Buchtel, 'Dedicating Books to Henry' in Wilkes, *Prince Henry Revived*, p.129, fn.60.

44 John Racin, 'The Early Editions of Sir Walter Ralegh's "The History of the World"', *Studies in Bibliography*, 17 (1964), p.209.

45 T. N. Brushfield, *The Bibliography of the 'History of the World' and of the 'Remains' of Sir Walter Raleigh* (London: Dryden Press, 1886), pp.2–4.

46 Racin, 'The Early Editions of Sir Walter', 203–204.

47 A. F. Allison, *Thomas Lodge, 1558–1625: A Bibliographical Catalogue* (Folkestone: Dawsons, 1973), p.7.

48 Oakeshott, 'Sir Walter Ralegh's Library', 288.

49 Letter 203 in Latham and Youing, *The Letters*, p.319.

50 Lefranc, *Sir Walter Raleigh*, p.260.

51 Oakeshott, 'Sir Walter Ralegh's Library', p.290.

52 Lefranc, *Sir Walter Raleigh*, pp.262–268.

53 A. L. Rowse, *The Elizabethan Renaissance: The Cultural Achievement* (London: Macmillan, 1972), p.303.

54 Sir Walter Ralegh, *The Works of Sir Walter Ralegh, Vol. 2* (1829), ch. 21, sec. vi. p.21.

55 Beer, *Sir Walter Ralegh*, p.60.

56 Racin, *Sir Walter Ralegh as Historian*, p.9.

57 Beer, *Sir Walter Ralegh*, p.46.

58 Sir Walter Raleigh, *The History of the World* (London, 1614).

59 Green, *Elizabeth*, pp.24–25.

60 Buchtel, 'Dedicating Books to Henry' in Wilkes, *Prince Henry Revived*, p.114.

61 Buchtel, 'Dedicating Books to Henry' in Wilkes, *Prince Henry Revived*, p.104.

62 Raleigh, *The History of the World*, p.62.

63 Beer, *Sir Walter Ralegh*, p.31.

64 Racin, *Sir Walter Ralegh as Historian*, p.5.

65 Roy Strong, *Henry, Prince of Wales and England's Lost Renaissance* (London: Thames & Hudson, 1986), p.51.

66 J. W. Williamson, *The Myth of the Conqueror: Prince Henry Stuart, a Study of 17th Century Personation* (New York: AMS Press, 1978), p.3.

67 Lefranc, *Sir Walter Raleigh*, p.680.

68 Oakeshott, 'Sir Walter Ralegh's Library', 293.

69 Beer, *Sir Walter Ralegh*, p.102.

70 Letter 192 in Latham and Youing, *The Letters*, p.297.

71 Letter 193 in Latham and Youing, *The Letters*, p.300.

72 Beer, *Sir Walter Ralegh*, p.14.

73 Beer, *Sir Walter Ralegh*, p.173, fn.12.

CHAPTER VI

Principal Published Sources

An Exact Abridgement of the Records in the Tower of London, from the Reign of King Edward the Second, unto King Richard the Third. Collected by Sir Robert Cotton, revised, rectified, and supplemented by William Prynne (London: William Leake, 1657).

J. E. Harris, *Mont Orgueil, Jersey* ([St. Helier]: Public Works Committee, States of Jersey, 1973).

Ben Jonson, *The Alchemist* (London, 1732).

Ethyn W. Kirby, *William Prynne: A Study in Puritanism* (Cambridge, Mass., 1931).

C. H. Firth, 'William Prynne' in *The Dictionary of National Biography* (London: Oxford University Press, 1975).

William Lamont, 'William Prynne (1600–1669)', *Oxford Dictionary of National Biography* (online ed.). Oxford University Press (2004).

Walter Montagu, *Shepherds' Paradise*, Malone Society Reprints, 159 (Oxford: Malone Society, 1997).

Sarah Poynting, '"The Rare and Excellent Partes of Mr. Walter Montagu": Henrietta Maria and her Playwright' in Erin Griffey (ed.), *Henrietta Maria: Piety, Politics and Patronage* (Aldershot: Ashgate, 2008).

William Prynne, *Histrio-Mastix: The Players Scourge or Actors Tragædie* (London, 1633).

William Prynne, *Mount-Orgueil: or, Divine and Profitable Meditations [in verse]. A Poem of The Soules Complaint Against the Body &c. are Annexed* (London, 1641).

William Prynne, *Aurum reginae: or A compendious tractate, and chronological collection of records in the Tower, and Court of Exchequer concerning queen-gold: evidencing the quidity, quantity, quality, antiquity, legality of this golden prerogative, duty and revenue of the queen-consorts of England . . .* (1668).

Notes (CH. VI)

1 William Lamont, 'William Prynne (1600–1669)', Oxford Dictionary of National Biography (online ed.). Oxford University Press (2004).

2 Ethyn W. Kirby, *William Prynne: A Study in Puritanism* (Cambridge, Mass., 1931), p.172.

3 Walter Montagu, *Shepherds' Paradise*, Malone Society Reprints, 159 (Oxford: Malone Society, 1997), p.viii.

4 Sarah Poynting, '"The Rare and Excellent Partes of Mr. Walter Montague": Henrietta Maria and her Playwright' in Erin Griffey (ed.), *Henrietta Maria: Piety, Politics and Patronage* (Aldershot: Ashgate, 2008), p.9.

5 William Prynne, *Histrio-Mastix: The Players Scourge or Actors Tragædie* (London, 1633), p.848.

6 Karen Britland, 'Queen Henrietta Maria's Theatrical Patronage' in Griffey, *Henrietta Maria*, p.56.

7 William Lamont, *Marginal Prynne, 1600–1669* (London: Routledge & Kegan Paul, 1963), p.29.

8 Kirby, *William Prynne*, p.28.

9 Ben Jonson, *The Alchemist* (London, 1732), Act I, Scene 1, Line 148.

10 C. H. Firth, 'William Prynne' in *The Dictionary of National Biography* (London: Oxford University Press, 1975).

11 Kirby, *William Prynne*, p.38.

12 Kirby, *William Prynne*, p.40.

13 Lamont, *Marginal Prynne*, p.38.

14 Kirby, *William Prynne*, p.45.

15 William Prynne, *Mount-Orgueil: or, Divine and Profitable Meditations [in verse]. A Poem of The Soules Complaint Against the Body &c. are Annexed* (London, 1641), p.175.

16 J. E. Harris, *Mont Orgueil, Jersey* ([St. Helier]: Public Works Committee, States of Jersey, 1973), p.8.

17 Harris, *Mont Orgueil*, p.12.

18 Kirby, *William Prynne*, p.75.

19 Lamont, *Marginal Prynne*, p.205.

20 Kirby, *William Prynne*, p.33.

21 Kirby, *William Prynne*, p.172.

22 Kirby, *William Prynne*, p.160.

23 Kirby, *William Prynne*, p.170.

24 *An Exact Abridgement of the Records in the Tower of London, from the Reign of King Edward the Second, unto King Richard the Third.* Collected by Sir Robert Cotton, revised, rectified, and supplemented by William Prynne (London: William Leake, 1657), p.4.

CHAPTER VII

Principal Published Sources

Peter Barwick, *The Life of the Reverend Dr. John Barwick* (London, 1724).

Robert Bell, *Lives of the Most Eminent Literary and Scientific Men of Great Britain: English Poets* (London: Longman, Orme, Brown, Green & Longmans, 1839).

Daniel Featley, *Katabaptistai Kataptustoi. The Dippers Dipt. Or, the Anabaptists Duck'd and Plung'd over Head and Eares, at a disputation in Southwark* (London, 1646).

C. H. Hartman, *The Cavalier Spirit and its Influence on the Life and Work of Richard Lovelace* (London: Routledge, 1925).

Frank W. Jessup, *Sir Roger Twysden, 1597–1672* (London: Cresset Press, 1965).

Keith Lindley, *Popular Politics and Religion in Civil War London* (Aldershot: Scolar Press, 1997)

H. C. B. Rogers, *Battles and Generals of the Civil Wars, 1642–1651* (London: Seeley Service, 1968).

Walter Thornbury and Edward Walford, *Old and New London: The Southern Suburbs, Vol. 6* (London: Cassell, 1893).

C. H. Wilkinson, *The Poems of Richard Lovelace* (Oxford: Oxford University Press, 1930).

C. V. Wedgwood, *The King's Peace, 1637–1641* (London: Collins, 1945).

C. V. Wedgwood, *The Great Rebellion, Vol. 2, The King's War 1641–1647* (London: Collins, 1958).

Notes (CH. VII)

1 J. A. Longford, *Prison Books and their Authors* (London: W. Tegg, 1861), p.202.

2 George Sampson, *The Concise Cambridge History of English Literature* (Cambridge: Cambridge University Press, 1970).

3 C. V. Wedgwood, *The King's Peace, 1637–1641* (London: Collins, 1945), p.336.

4 Frank W. Jessup, *Sir Roger Twysden, 1597–1672* (London: Cresset Press, 1965), pp.50–51.

5 Edward Walford, *Old and New London: A Narrative of Its History, Its People, and Its Places, Vol. III* (London: Cassell & Co., 1881), p.489.

6 H. C. B. Rogers, *Battles and Generals of the Civil Wars, 1642–1651* (London: Seeley Service, 1968), p.274.

7 John Brown, *John Bunyan: His Life, Times, and Work* (London: The Hulbert Publishing Company Ltd., 1928), p.78.

8 C. H. Hartman, *The Cavalier Spirit and its Influence on the Life and Work of Richard Lovelace* (London: Routledge, 1925), p.294.

9 John Stow, *A Survey of the Cities of London and Westminster*, Book III (London, 1720), p.121.

10 William Dugdale, *A Short View of the Late Troubles in England* (Oxford, 1681), p.568.

11 Petition of Dr. Edward Martin and Dr. Richard Sterne, prisoners in the Lord Petre's house in Aldersgate Street (1 April 1647), House of Lords: Journal Office: Main Papers 1509–1700, HL/PO/JO/10/1/229, Parliamentary Archives.

12 Jessup, *Sir Roger Twysden*, p.60.

13 Calendar of State Papers, Domestic Series, of the Reign of Charles I, 15 April 1645.

14 Calendar of State Papers, Domestic Series, of the Reign of Charles I, 12 July 1648.

15 Jessup, *Sir Roger Twysden*, p.60.

16 Peter Barwick, *The Life of the Reverend Dr. John Barwick* (London, 1724), p.94.

17 Daniel Featley, *Katabaptistai Kataptustoi. The Dippers Dipt. Or, the Anabaptists Duck'd and Plung'd over Head and Eares, at a disputation in Southwark* (London, 1646).

18 C. H. Wilkinson, *The Poems of Richard Lovelace* (Oxford: Oxford University Press, 1930).

19 Robert Bell, *Lives of the Most Eminent Literary and Scientific Men of Great Britain: English Poets* (London: Longman, Orme, Brown, Green & Longmans, 1839), p.273.

CHAPTER VIII
Principal Published Sources
The Kings Cabinet Opened; or, Certain Packets of Secret Letters & Papers, Written with the Kings Own Hand, and Taken in His Cabinet at Nasby-Field . . . Together, with Some Annotations Thereupon (London, 1645).

Richard Baker, *A Chronicle of the Kings of England: From the Time of the Romans Government unto the Death of King James . . . Digested into a New Method* (London, 1660).

Thomas Carlyle, *Sartor Resartus: On Heroes and Hero-Worship* (1908).

James Jude, *Hurst Castle: An Illustrated History* (Wimborne: Dovecote Press, 1986).

Jim Daems and Holly Faith Nelson (eds.) *Eikon Basilike: The Portraiture of His Sacred Majesty in His Solitudes and Sufferings* (Peterborough, Ont.: Broadview Editions, 2006).

W. H. Davenport Adams, *The White King: Or, Charles the First, and the Men and Women, Life and Manners, Literature and Art of England in the First Half of the 17th Century, Volume 1* (London, 1889).

George Hillier, *A narrative of the attempted escapes of Charles the first from Carisbrook castle . . . including the letters of the king to colonel Titus* (London, 1852).

Antonia Fraser, *Cromwell: Our Chief of Men* (London: Weidenfeld and Nicolson, 1973).

Mark A. Kishlansky and John Morrill, 'Charles I (1600–1649)', *Oxford Dictionary of National Biography* (online ed.). Oxford University Press (2004).

Andrew Lacey, *The Cult of King Charles the Martyr* (Woodbridge: Boydell Press, 2003).

F. F. Madan, *A New Bibliography of the Eikon Basilike of King Charles the First: With a Note on the Authorship* (London: B. Quaritch, 1950).

Jason McElligott, 'Roger Morrice and the Reputation of Eikon Basilike in the 1680s', *The Library 7*, 6:2 (2005).

Jason McElligott, *Royalism, Print and Censorship in Revolutionary England* (Woodbridge: Boydell Press, 2007).

Richard Ollard, *The Image of the King: Charles I and Charles II* (London: Phoenix Press, 1979).

Richard Perrinchief, 'Life of Charles I' in *The Workes of King Charles the Martyr* (London, 1662).

Catherine M. Phillimore (ed.), *Eikon Basilike, the Portraiture of His Majesty King Charles I* (Oxford and London, 1879).

Jane Roberts, *The King's Head: Charles I – King and Martyr* (London: Royal Collection Enterprises, 1999).

H. C. B. Rogers, *Battles and Generals of the Civil Wars, 1642–1651* (London: Seeley Service, 1968).

Brian D. Spinks, 'John Gauden (1599/1600?–1662)', *Oxford Dictionary of National Biography* (online ed.). Oxford University Press (2004).

G. S. Stevenson, *Charles I in Captivity: From Contemporary Sources* (London: Arrowsmith, 1927).

Edward Symmons, *A Vindication of King Charles: or a Loyal Subjects Duty, Manifested in Vindicating his Soveraigne from Those Aspersions Cast Upon him by Certaine Persons, in a Scandalous Libel, Entituled, The Kings Cabinet Opened* (London, 1648).

Edward Ward, *The Secret History of the Calves-Head Club: or, the Republican unmask'd . . . by them Called Anthems, with Reflections Thereupon* (London, 1709).

C. V. Wedgwood, *The Great Rebellion, Vol.2, The King's War 1641–1647* (London: Collins, 1958).

Christopher Wordsworth, *Who wrote Eikon Basilike?* (1824).

Notes (CH. VIII)

1 H. C. B. Rogers, *Battles and Generals of the Civil Wars 1642–1651* (London: Seeley, 1968), p.146.

2 Rogers, *Battles and Generals*, p.239.

3 C. V. Wedgwood, *The Great Rebellion, Vol.2, The King's War 1641–1647* (London: Collins, 1958), p.456.

4 *The Kings Cabinet Opened; or, Certain Packets of Secret Letters & Papers, Written with the Kings Own Hand, and Taken in His Cabinet at Nasby-Field . . . Together, with Some Annotations Thereupon* (London, 1645), p.32.

5 Edward Symmons, *A Vindication of King Charles: or a Loyal Subjects Duty, Manifested in Vindicating his Soveraigne from Those Aspersions Cast Upon him by Certaine Persons, in a Scandalous Libel, Entituled, The Kings Cabinet Opened* (London, 1648), p.32.

6 Richard Perrinchief, 'Life of Charles I' in *The Workes of King Charles the Martyr* (London, 1662), p.235.

7 Winston Churchill, *A History of the English-speaking Peoples. Vol. 1 The Birth of Britain* (London: Cassell, 1956) p.217.

8 *Lambeth Palace Library Annual Review* (2013), p.10.

9 Wedgwood, *The Great Rebellion*, p.561.

10 W. H. Davenport Adams, *The White King: Or, Charles the First, and the Men and Women, Life and Manners, Literature and Art of England in the First Half of the 17th Century, Volume 1* (London, 1889), p.54.

11 *The Kings Cabinet Opened*, p.11.

12 Davenport Adams, *The White King*, p.54.

13 Davenport Adams, *The White King*, p.54.

14 Davenport Adams, *The White King*, p.57.

15 Davenport Adams, *The White King*, p.57.

16 G. S. Stevenson, *Charles I in Captivity: From Contemporary Sources* (London: Arrowsmith, 1927), p.4.

17 Stevenson, *Charles I in Captivity*, p.123.

18 James Jude, *Hurst Castle: An Illustrated History* (Wimborne: Dovecote Press, 1986), p.32.

19 Davenport Adams, *The White King*, p.59.

20 Thomas Carlyle, *Sartor Resartus: On Heroes and Hero-Worship* (1908), p.444.

21 Stevenson, *Charles I in Captivity*, p.196.

22 Stevenson, *Charles I in Captivity*, p.212.

23 Stevenson, *Charles I in Captivity*, p.13.

24 Jim Daems and Holly Faith Nelson (eds.) *Eikon Basilike: The Portraiture of His Sacred Majesty in His Solitudes and Sufferings* (Peterborough, Ont.: Broadview Editions, 2006), p.320.

25 Davenport Adams, *The White King*, pp.59–60.

26 Jason McElligott, 'Roger Morrice and the Reputation of Eikon Basilike in the 1680s', *The Library*, 7, 6:2 (2005), p.121.

27 Richard Ollard, *The Image of the King: Charles I and Charles II* (London: Phoenix Press, 1979), p.25.

28 Ollard, *The Image of the King*, p.194.

29 Daems and Nelson (eds.) *Eikon Basilike*, p.120.

30 Daems and Nelson (eds.) *Eikon Basilike*, p.xiv.

31 McElligott, 'Roger Morrice', p.128.

32 McElligott, 'Roger Morrice', p.117.

33 McElligott, 'Roger Morrice', p.123.

34 Antonia Fraser, *Cromwell: Our Chief of Men* (London: Weidenfeld and Nicolson, 1973), p.295.

35 Andrew Lacey, *The Cult of King Charles the Martyr* (Woodbridge: Boydell Press, 2003), p.78.

36 Jane Roberts, *The King's Head: Charles I – King and Martyr* (London: Royal Collection Enterprises, 1999).

37 F. F. Madan, *A New Bibliography of the Eikon Basilike of King Charles the First: With a Note on the Authorship* (London: B. Quaritch, 1950), p.164.

38 Jason McElligott, *Royalism, Print and Censorship in Revolutionary England* (Woodbridge: Boydell Press, 2007), p.145.

39 Madan, *A New Bibliography*, p.165.

40 Lacey, *The Cult of King Charles the Martyr*, p.85.

41 Lacey, *The Cult of King Charles the Martyr*, p.59.

42 McElligott, *Royalism, Print*, p.151.

43 McElligott, *Royalism, Print*, p.135.

44 Richard Baker, *A Chronicle of the Kings of England: From the Time of the Romans Government unto the Death of King James . . . Digested into a New Method* (London, 1660).

45 Stevenson, *Charles I in Captivity*, p.265.

46 Lacey, *The Cult of King Charles the Martyr*, p.10.

47 Perrinchief, 'Life of Charles I', p.92.

48 Miscellaneous Letters and Papers, Bound in One Volume, No.2, MS 4239, Lambeth Palace Library.

49 Edward Ward, *The Secret History of the Calves-Head Club: or, the Republican unmask'd . . . by them Called Anthems, with Reflections Thereupon* (London, 1709).

CHAPTER IX

Principal Published Sources

Johnson Ball, *William Caslon, 1693–1766: The Ancestry, Life and Connections of England's Foremost Letter-Engraver and Type-Founder* (Kineton: Roundwood Press, 1973).

Richard Baxter, *Reliquiae Baxterianae: or, Mr. Richard Baxter's narrative of the most memorable passages of his life and times. Faithfully publish'd from his own original manuscript, by Matthew Sylvester* (1696).

John Brown, *John Bunyan (1625–1688): His Life, Times, and Work* (London: The Hulbert Publishing Company, 1928).

John Bunyan, *A Relation of the Imprisonment of Mr. John Bunyan* (1765).

John Bunyan, *The Pilgrim's Progress* (1863).

Henry W. Clark, *History of English Nonconformity, from Wiclif to the close of the nineteenth century* (London: Chapman, 1911).

Frank Mott Harrison, 'Nathaniel Ponder: The Publisher of the Pilgrim's Progress', *The Library*, 4/15 (1923).

Joyce Godber, 'The Imprisonments of John Bunyan', *Transactions of the Congregational Historical Society*, 16 (1949–51), 23–32.

John Howard, *The State of the Prisons in England and Wales: With Preliminary Observations, and an Account of Some Foreign Prisons* (1777).

Ivor Bertram John (ed.), *Macaulay's Lives of Bunyan and Goldsmith* (London, 1914).

J. A. Langford, *Prison Books and their Authors* (1861).

Anne Laurence, W. R. Owens and Stuart Sim (eds.), *John Bunyan and his England, 1628–1688* (London: Hambledon Press, 1990).

Roger Sharrock (ed.), *Grace Abounding to the Chief of Sinners* (Oxford: Clarendon Press, 1962).

Robert Southey, *Select Lives of Cromwell and Bunyan* (London: Murray, 1849).

David Stoker, 'William Proctor, Nathaniel Ponder and the Financing of Pilgrim's Progress', *The Library*, 7/4 (March, 2003).

Notes (CH. IX)

1 John Bunyan, *A Relation of the Imprisonment of Mr. John Bunyan* (1765), p.109.

2 Bunyan, *A Relation*, p.117.

3 John Bunyan, *Grace Abounding to the Chief of Sinners* (1685), p.102.

4 John Brown, *John Bunyan (1625–1688): His Life, Times, and Work* (London: The Hulbert Publishing Company, 1928), p.37.

5 Brown, *John Bunyan*, pp.78–81.

6 https://en.wikipedia.org/wiki/Star_Chamber.

7 Marjorie Plant, *The English Book Trade: An Economic History of the Making and Sale of Books* (London: George Allen & Unwin Ltd., 1965), p.61.

8 Plant, *The English Book Trade*, p.144.

9 F. A. Mumby, *Publishing and Bookselling: A History from the Earliest Times to the Present Day* (London: Cape, 1954), p.61.

10 Mumby, *Publishing and Bookselling*, p.10.

11 Mumby, *Publishing and Bookselling*, p.72.

12 Mumby, *Publishing and Bookselling*, p.103.

13 Mumby, *Publishing and Bookselling*, p.107.

14 Eric Stockdale, 'A Study of Bedford Prison'

in John Bunyan, *The Pilgrim's Progress*
(London: Charles Griffen and Co., 1863),
p.1.

15 Brown, *John Bunyan*, pp.127–128.

16 Brown, *John Bunyan*, p.143.

17 Brown, *John Bunyan*, p.182.

18 Brown, *John Bunyan*, p.184.

19 Brown, *John Bunyan*, p.190.

20 Plant, *The English Book Trade*, pp.144–145.

21 Brown, *John Bunyan*, p.190.

22 Brown, *John Bunyan*, p.204.

23 Brown, *John Bunyan*, p.214.

24 Robert Southey, *Select Lives of Cromwell
and Bunyan* (London: Murray, 1849), p.247.

25 Brown, *John Bunyan*, pp.468–475.

26 Mumby, *Publishing and Bookselling*, p.127.

27 Brown, *John Bunyan*, p.170.

28 Richard L. Greaves, 'John Bunyan (bap.
1628, d.1688)', Oxford Dictionary of
National Biography (online ed.). Oxford
University Press (2004).

29 Roger Sharrock (ed.), *Grace Abounding to
the Chief of Sinners* (Oxford: Clarendon
Press, 1962), p.30.

30 G. Sampson, *The Concise Cambridge
History of English Literature* (Cambridge:
Cambridge University Press, 1941), p.374.

31 Brown, *John Bunyan*, p.239.

32 J. A. Langford, *Prison Books and their
Authors* (1861), p.228.

33 Ivor Bertram John (ed.), *Macaulay's Lives of
Bunyan and Goldsmith* (London, 1914), p.15.

34 David Stoker, 'William Proctor, Nathaniel
Ponder and the Financing of Pilgrim's
Progress', The Library, 7/4 (March, 2003),
262.

35 Stoker, 'William Proctor', 267.

36 Frank Mott Harrison, 'Nathaniel Ponder:
The Publisher of the Pilgrim's Progress',
The Library, 4/15 (1934), 262.

37 Harrison, 'Nathaniel Ponder', 268.

38 Mumby, *Publishing and Bookselling*, p.92.

39 Harrison, 'Nathaniel Ponder', 270.

40 Mumby, *Publishing and Bookselling*, p.128.

41 Harrison, 'Nathaniel Ponder', 266.

42 Stoker 'William Proctor', 65.

43 Richard Baxter, *Reliquiae Baxterianae: or,*

*Mr. Richard Baxter's narrative of the most
memorable passages of his life and times.
Faithfully publish'd from his own original
manuscript, by Matthew Sylvester* (1696),
p.117.

44 Johnson Ball, *William Caslon, 1693–1766:
The Ancestry, Life and Connections of
England's Foremost Letter-Engraver and
Type-Founder* (Kineton: Roundwood Press,
1973), p.226.

45 Rev. Thomas Scott, 'The Life of Bunyan', in
Bunyan, *The Pilgrim's Progress*, p.13

46 John Howard, *The State of the Prisons in
England and Wales: With Preliminary
Observations, and an Account of Some
Foreign Prisons* (1777).

47 Brown, *John Bunyan*, p.92.

48 Brown, *John Bunyan*, p.160.

49 Brown, *John Bunyan*, p.152.

50 Thomas Scott, 'The Life of Bunyan', in
Bunyan, *The Pilgrim's Progress*, Charles
Griffin and Company 1863 p.18.

51 Langford, *Prison Books and their Authors*,
p.225.

52 Bunyan, *The Pilgrim's Progress*, p.110.

53 James Boswell, *The Life of Samuel Johnson,
Vol.5* (London, 1876), pp.281–282.

54 Langford, *Prison Books and their Authors*,
p.292.

55 Bunyan, *The Pilgrim's Progress*, p.142.

CHAPTER X

Principal Sources

Bernard Adams, *London Illustrated, 1604–1851:
A Survey and Index of Topographical
Books and Their Plates* (London: Library
Association, 1983).

Roger Lee Brown, *A History of the Fleet
Prison, London: The Anatomy of the Fleet*
(Lampeter: Edwin Mellon Press, 1996).

Joseph Grego, *Rowlandson the Caricaturist,
Vol. 2* (London: Chatto & Windus, 1880)

Harlan W. Hamilton, *Doctor Syntax: a
silhouette of William Combe, Esq. : (1742–
1823)* (London: Chatto & Windus, 1969) .

James Neild, *Account of Persons Confined for*

*Debt, in the various prisons of England
and Wales; together with their provisionary
allowance during confinement, as reported to
the society for the discharge and relief of small
debtors* (London, 1800).

Matthew Payne and James Payne, *Regarding
Thomas Rowlandson, 1757–1827: His Life,
Art & Acquaintance* (London: Hogarth
Arts: Distribution by Paul Holberton
Publishing, 2010).

Walter Thornbury and Edward Walford, *Old
and New London: The Southern Suburbs,
Vol.6* (London: Cassell, 1893).

*The History of The Times. [Vol. 1], "The
Thunderer" in the making, 1785–1841*
(London: The Times, 1935).

Notes (CH. X)

1   Harlan W. Hamilton, *Doctor Syntax: a
    silhouette of William Combe, Esq.: (1742–
    1823)* (London: Chatto & Windus, 1969),
    pp.266–267.
2   Hamilton, *Doctor Syntax*, p.48.
3   Hamilton, *Doctor Syntax*, p.x.
4   Bernard Adams, *London Illustrated, 1604–
    1851: A Survey and Index of Topographical
    Books and Their Plates* (London: Library
    Association, 1983), p.250.
5   Hamilton, *Doctor Syntax*, p.65.
6   Hamilton, *Doctor Syntax*, p.137.
7   Hamilton, *Doctor Syntax*, p.141.
8   Hamilton, *Doctor Syntax*, p.181.
9   Hamilton, *Doctor Syntax*, p.197.
10 James Neild, *Account of Persons Confined
    for Debt, in the Various Prisons of England
    and Wales: Together with their Provisionary
    Allowance during Confinement: as Reported
    to the Society for the Discharge and Relief of
    Small Debtors* (London, 1800), pp.21–22.
11 Hamilton, *Doctor Syntax*, pp.204–209.
12 Hamilton, *Doctor Syntax*, p.239.
13 Walter Thornbury and Edward Walford,
    *Old and New London: The Southern Suburbs,
    Vol.6* (London: Cassell, 1893), pp.66–69.
14 Roger Lee Brown, *A History of the Fleet
    Prison, London: the Anatomy of the Fleet*

(Lewiston: Edwin Mellen Press, 1996),
    fn.110, p.172.
15 Hamilton, *Doctor Syntax*, p.208.
16 Hamilton, *Doctor Syntax*, p.209.
17 Adams, *London Illustrated*, p.177.
18 Adams, *London Illustrated*, pp.223–225.
19 Matthew Payne and James Payne,
    *Regarding Thomas Rowlandson, 1757–1827:
    His Life, Art & Acquaintance* (London:
    Hogarth Arts: Distribution by Paul
    Holberton Publishing, 2010), pp.296–301.
20 Hamilton, *Doctor Syntax*, p.245.
21 Hamilton, *Doctor Syntax*, p.246.
22 Payne and Payne, *Regarding Thomas
    Rowlandson*, p.283.
23 Payne and Payne, *Regarding Thomas
    Rowlandson*, p.321.
24 Joseph Grego, *Rowlandson the Caricaturist,
    Vol. 2* (London: Chatto & Windus, 1880),
    p.317.
25 Hamilton, *Doctor Syntax*, p.272.

CHAPTER XI
Principal Published Sources

Marc Chassaigne, *Etienne Dolet: portraits et
documents inédits* (Paris, 1930).

Lucien Febvre, *Autour de l'Heptaméron: Amour
Sacré Amour Profane* (Paris: Gallimard,
1944).

Alfred Fierro, *Histoire et Dictionnaire de Paris*
(Paris: Robert Laffont, 1996).

C. J. F. Hénault, J. Lacombe, and P. Macquer,
*Abrégé chronologique de l'histoire d'Espagne
et de Portugal, Vol 2* (1765).

Clément Marot, *Oeuvres Poétiques Complètes,
Tome 1* (Paris: Bordas, 1993).

Claude Albert Mayer (ed.), *Clément Marot's
Œuvres satiriques* (London: Athlone Press,
1962).

Claude Albert Mayer, *Clément Marot* (Paris:
A.-G. Nizet, 1972).

Ernest Lavisse, *Histoire de France: depuis les
origines jusqu'à la Révolution, Tome 5.1*
(Paris: Hachette, 1903).

Henri Pigaillem, *Claude de France* (Paris:
Pygmalion, 2006).

Jean Plattard, *Marot: sa carrière poétique, son oeuvre* (Paris: Boivin & cie, 1938).

Augustin Renaudet, *Humanisme et Renaissance* (Genève, 1958).

Alison Saunders, 'Sixteenth Century Collected Editions of Blasons Anatomiques', *The Library* (Dec, 1976).

Barbara Stephenson, *Power and Patronage of Marguerite de Navarre* (1988).

J. de la Tynna, *Dictionnaire topographique, étymologique et historique des Rues de Paris* (Paris, 1812).

Notes (CH. XI)

1 Jean Plattard, *Marot: sa carrière poétique, son oeuvre* (Paris: Boivin & cie, 1938), p.17.

2 Plattard, *Marot*, p.26.

3 Lucien Febvre, *Autour de l'Heptaméron: Amour Sacré Amour Profane* (Paris: Gallimard, 1944), p.161.

4 Febvre, *Autour de l'Heptaméron*, p.162.

5 Alison Saunders, 'Sixteenth Century Collected Editions of Blasons Anatomiques', *The Library* (Dec, 1976), 358–360.

6 Febvre, *Autour de l'Heptaméron*, p.118.

7 C. J. F. Hénault, J. Lacombe, and P. Macquer, *Abrégé chronologique de l'histoire d'Espagne et de Portugal, Vol 2* (1765), p.166.

8 Febvre, *Autour de l'Heptaméron*, p.35.

9 Plattard, *Marot*, p.48.

10 Plattard, *Marot*, p.33.

11 Plattard, *Marot*, p.34.

12 Clément Marot, *Oeuvres Poétiques Complètes, Tome 1* (Paris: Bordas, 1993), pp.92–94.

13 Alfred Fierro, *Histoire et Dictionnaire de Paris* (Paris: Robert Laffont, 1996), p.1109.

14 Clément Marot, *Oeuvres Poétiques Complètes, Tome 2* (Paris: Bordas, 1993), pp.19–33.

15 Lines 208–281 in Marot, *Oeuvres Poétiques Complètes, Tome 2*, p.27.

16 Line 55 in Marot, *Oeuvres Poétiques Complètes, Tome 2*, p.21.

17 Lines 348–350 in Marot, *Oeuvres Poétiques Complètes, Tome 2*, p.29.

18 Lines 436–438 in Marot, *Oeuvres Poétiques Complètes, Tome 2*, pp.31–32.

19 Plattard, *Marot*, p.42.

20 Claude Albert Mayer, *Clément Marot* (Paris: A.-G. Nizet, 1972), p.143.

21 Mayer, *Clément Marot*, p.179.

22 Mayer, *Clément Marot*, p.183.

23 Barbara Stephenson, *The Power and Patronage of Marguerite de Navarre* (1988), p.7.

24 Ernest Lavisse, *Histoire de France: depuis les origines jusqu'à la Révolution, Tome 5.1* (Paris: Hachette, 1903), p.371.

25 Marot, *Oeuvres Poétiques Complètes, Tome 1*, p.xii.

26 Mayer, *Clément Marot*, p.269.

27 Ernest Lavisse, *Histoire de France: depuis les origines jusqu'à la Révolution, Tome 5.2* (Paris: Hachette, 1903), p.121.

28 Mayer, *Clément Marot*, p.267.

29 Mayer, *Clément Marot*, pp.168–169.

30 Marot, *Oeuvres Poétiques Complètes*, Tome 1, p.xiv.

31 Marc Chassaigne, *Etienne Dolet: portraits et documents inédits* (Paris, 1930), p.344.

32 Plattard, *Marot*, p.196.

33 *Pseaumes de David, mis en rime Françoise, par Clement Marot, et Theodore de Besze: avec le Cantique de Simeon, et les Dix Commandemens* (Geneva: De l'imprimerie de P. Jaques Poullain, et Antoine Rebul, 1557).

CHAPTER XII
Principal Published Sources

Guy Chaussinand-Nogaret, *Mirabeau* (Paris: Éditions du Seuil, 1982).

Robert Darnton, *The Devil in the Holy Water or the Art of Slander from Louis XIV to Napoleon* (Philadelphia: University of Pennsylvania Press, 2010).

Jean-Paul Desprat, *Mirabeau: l'excès et le retrait* (Paris: Perrin, 2008).

François Furet et al., *La Gironde et les Girondins* (Paris: Payot, 1991).

Ian Germani, *Jean-Paul Marat: Hero and*

Anti-Hero of the French Revolution
(Lewiston: E. Mellen Press, 1992).

Alexia Lebeurre, *Le Panthéon: Temple de la
Nation* (Paris: Editions du Patrimoine,
2000).

Barbara Luttrell, *Mirabeau* (London:
Harvester Wheatsheaf, 1990).

Claude Quétel, *De par le Roy* (1981).

Claude Quétel, *La Bastille: Histoire Vraie d'une
Prison Légendaire* (Paris: Robert Laffont,
1989).

René Augustin Constantin de Renneville,
*L'inquisition françoise ou l'histoire de la
Bastille* (1724).

[H. G. Riquetti, Comte de Mirabeau], *Des
Lettres de Cachet et des Prisons d'État*
(Hambourg, 1782).

Honoré Gabriel de Riquetti, Comte de
Mirabeau, *Lettres Originales de Mirabeau,
Vols.1–4* (1792).

Oliver J. G. Welch, *Mirabeau. A Study of a
Democratic Monarchist* (London, 1951).

Notes (CH. XII)

1 Claude Quétel, *La Bastille: Histoire Vraie
d'une Prison Légendaire* (Paris: Robert
Laffont, 1989), p.40.

2 René Augustin Constantin de Renneville,
*L'inquisition françoise ou l'histoire de la
Bastille* (1724), p.105.

3 Claude Quétel, *De par le Roy* (1981), p.123.

4 Quétel, *De par le Roy*, pp.69–78.

5 Quétel, *De par le Roy*, p.205.

6 Quétel, *La Bastille*, p.345.

7 Quétel, *De par le Roy*, p.117.

8 Quétel, *De par le Roy*, p.123.

9 Quétel, *De par le Roy*, p.128.

10 Oliver J.G. Welch, *Mirabeau. A Study of a
Democratic Monarchist* (London, 1951), p.38.

11 Honoré Gabriel de Riquetti, Comte de
Mirabeau, *Lettres Originales de Mirabeau,
Vol.1* (1792), pp.343–344.

12 Jean-Paul Desprat, *Mirabeau: l'excès et le
retrait* (Paris: Perrin, 2008), p.232.

13 Desprat, *Mirabeau*, p.192.

14 Honoré Gabriel de Riquetti, Comte de

Mirabeau, *Lettres Originales de Mirabeau,
Vol.4* (1792), p.327.

15 Barbara Luttrell, *Mirabeau* (London:
Harvester Wheatsheaf, 1990), pp.52–53.

16 Robert Darnton, *The Devil in the Holy
Water or the Art of Slander from Louis XIV
to Napoleon* (Philadelphia: University of
Pennsylvania Press, 2010), p.213.

17 de Riquetti, Comte de Mirabeau, *Lettres
Originales de Mirabeau, Vol.1*, p.29.

18 Darnton, *The Devil in the Holy Water*, p.239.

19 Alexia Lebeurre, *Le Panthéon: Temple de
la Nation* (Paris: Editions du Patrimoine,
2000), p.18.

20 Darnton, *The Devil in the Holy Water*, p.238.

21 Lebeurre, *Le Panthéon*, p.17.

22 Ian Germani, *Jean-Paul Marat: Hero
and Anti-Hero of the French Revolution*
(Lewiston: E. Mellen Press, 1992), p.186.

23 Quétel, *La Bastille*, p.184.

24 Quétel, *La Bastille*, p.185.

25 Quétel, *La Bastille*, p.186.

26 Quétel, *La Bastille*, pp.446–447.

27 Quétel, *La Bastille*, p.346.

28 Quétel, *La Bastille*, p.345.

CHAPTER XIII

Principal Published Sources

*An Appeal to impartial posterity, by Madame
Roland, wife of the Minister of the Interior;
or, a collection of tracts written by her during
her confinement in the prisons of the Abbey,
and St. Pélagie, in Paris* (1795).

*Lettre de M. Roland, Ministre de l'Intérieur, à
l'Assemblée nationale, en lui envoyant la lettre
qu'il a adressée au Roi, etc.* (Paris, 1792).

[F. W. Blagdon], *Paris – its Historic Buildings*
(1849).

Christopher Clark, *Iron Kingdom: The Rise and
Downfall of Prussia, 1600–1947* (London:
Penguin Books, 2006).

Charles-Aimé Dauban, *Étude sur madame
Roland et son temps, suivie des lettres
de madame Roland à Buzot et d›autres
documents inédits* (Paris, 1864).

Charles-Aimé Dauban, *Les Prisons de Paris*

sous la Révolution, d'après les relations
des contemporains, avec des notes et une
introduction, par C. A. Dauban. Ouvrage
enrichi de onze gravures, etc. (Paris, 1870).

Monique Delon, La Conciergerie: Palais de la
Cité (Paris: Patrimoine, 2000).

M. P. Faugère, Mémoires de Madame Roland
etc., Tome 2 (Paris, 1864).

François Furet et Mona Ozouf, La Gironde et
les Girondins (Paris: Payot, 1991).

Pierre Cornut-Gentille, Madame Roland: une
femme en politique sous la Révolution (Paris:
Perrin, 2004).

P. F. F. J. Giraud, Histoire Générale des Prisons
sous le Règne de Buonaparte (Paris, 1814).

Nouveau petit Larousse illustré (Larousse, 1948).

Ernest Lavisse, Histoire de France: depuis les
origines jusqu'à la Révolution, Tome 9 (Paris:
Hachette, 1910).

Jean-Jacques Lévêque, Victor R. Belot,
Guide de la Révolution française: les lieux,
les monuments, les musées, les homes (Paris:
Horay, 1986).

Claude Perroud, Lettres de Madame Roland,
Tome 2 (Paris, 1903).

Marie-Jeanne Roland, Appel à L'Impartiale
Posterite', Par La Citoyenne Roland, Femme
du Ministre de Intérieur, ed., Louis-
Augustin-Guillaume Bosc (Paris: Louvet,
1795).

Marianne Cornevin, La véritable Madame
Roland (Paris: Pygmailion, 1989).

Michael J. Sydenham, The Girondins (London:
Athlone Press, 1961).

Notes (CH. XIII)

1   M. P. Faugère, Mémoires de Madame Roland
    etc., Tome 2 (Paris, 1864), pp.99–100.

2   Faugère, Mémoires de Madame Roland,
    Tome 2, pp.156–161.

3   Faugère, Mémoires de Madame Roland,
    Tome 2, p.97.

4   Faugère, Mémoires de Madame Roland,
    Tome 2, p.217.

5   Faugère, Mémoires de Madame Roland,
    Tome 1, p.18.

6   Ernest Lavisse, Histoire de France: depuis les

origines jusqu'à la Révolution, Tome 9 (Paris:
    Hachette, 1910), p.50.

7   Lavisse, Histoire de France: depuis les origines
    jusqu'à la Révolution, Tome 9, p.343.

8   Pierre Cornut-Gentille, Madame Roland:
    une femme en politique sous la Révolution
    (Paris: Perrin, 2004), p.145.

9   Cornut-Gentille, Madame Roland, p.143.

10 Faugère, Mémoires de Madame Roland,
    Tome 2, p.250.

11 Cornut-Gentille, Madame Roland, p.172.

12 Cornut-Gentille, Madame Roland, p.170.

13 Faugère, Mémoires de Madame Roland,
    Tome 1, p.57.

14 Michael J. Sydenham, The Girondins
    (London: Athlone Press, 1961), p.98.

15 Les vraies Centuries et Prophéties de Maître
    Michel Nostradamus (Paris, 1669), p.20.

16 Christopher Clark, Iron Kingdom: The
    Rise and Downfall of Prussia, 1600–1947
    (London: Penguin Books, 2006), p.286.

17 Cornut-Gentille, Madame Roland, p.211.

18 Faugère, Mémoires de Madame Roland,
    Tome 1, pp.253–255.

19 Claude Perroud, Lettres de Madame Roland,
    Tome 2 (Paris, 1903), p.436.

20 Lettre de M. Roland, Ministre de l'Intérieur,
    à l'Assemblée nationale, en lui envoyant la
    lettre qu'il a adressée au Roi, etc. (Paris, 1792),
    p.5.

21 Cornut-Gentille, Madame Roland, p.281.

22 Cornut-Gentille, Madame Roland,
    pp.287–289.

23 Marianne Cornevin, La véritable Madame
    Roland (Paris: Pygmalion/Gérard Watelet,
    1989), p.282.

24 Faugère, Mémoires de Madame Roland,
    Tome 2, p.316.

25 Pierre F. F. J. H. Giraud, Histoire générale
    des prisons sous le règne de Buonaparte (Paris,
    1814), pp.72–73.

26 Charles-Aimé Dauban, Les Prisons de
    Paris sous la Révolution, d'après les relations
    des contemporains, avec des notes et une
    introduction, par C. A. Dauban. Ouvrage
    enrichi de onze gravures, etc. (Paris, 1870),
    p.377.

27 Faugère, *Mémoires de Madame Roland,*
   Tome 1, p.210.

28 Faugère, *Mémoires de Madame Roland,*
   Tome 1, p.ix.

29 Faugère, *Mémoires de Madame Roland,*
   Tome 2, p.95.

30 Faugère, *Mémoires de Madame Roland,*
   Tome 2, p.91.

31 Faugère, *Mémoires de Madame Roland,*
   Tome 2, p.32.

32 Faugère, *Mémoires de Madame Roland,*
   Tome 2, pp.155–158.

33 Faugère, *Mémoires de Madame Roland,*
   Tome 2, p.180.

34 Faugère, *Mémoires de Madame Roland,*
   Tome 2, pp.335–337.

35 Faugère, *Mémoires de Madame Roland,*
   Tome 2, pp.285–286.

36 Faugère, *Mémoires de Madame Roland,*
   Tome 2, p.327.

37 Faugère, *Mémoires de Madame Roland,*
   Tome 1, p.viii.

38 [F. W. Blagdon], *Paris—its Historic*
   Buildings (1849), p.279.

CHAPTER XIV
Principal Published Sources

Rapport des Commissaires réviseurs des trois
   compagnies de Finances aux Représentants
   du Peuple chargés de surveiller leurs travaux
   , et lu aux Comités des Finances et de la
   Comptabilité (Paris, 1794).

Bernadette Bensaude-Vincent, *Dans le*
   laboratoire de Lavoisier, livre illustré (1993).

J. A. Cochran, *Lavoisier* (London, 1931).

Arthur Donovan, *Antoine Lavoisier: Science,*
   Administration and Revolution (Oxford:
   Blackwell, 1993).

Sydney J. French, *Torch & Crucible. The Life*
   and Death of Antoine Lavoisier (Princeton:
   Princeton University Press, 1941)

Édouard Grimaux, *Lavoisier, 1743–1794.*
   D'après sa correspondance, ses manuscrits,
   ses papiers de famille, et d'autres documents
   inédits, etc. (Paris, 1888).

Richard Kirwan, *An Essay on Phlogiston, and*
   the Constitution of Acids (London, 1787).

Antoine Laurent Lavoisier, *Mémoires de*
   Chimie, Tome 2 (1805).

Georges Montcloux, *Dénonciation présentée*
   au Comité de législation de la Convention
   nationale contre le représentant du peuple
   Dupin par les veuves et enfans des ci–devant
   Fermiers généraux (Paris: Du Pont, an 3,
   1795).

Georges Ponchet, *Les Sciences pendant la*
   Terreur d'après les documents du temps et les
   pièces des Archives nationales (Paris, 1896).

Charles Singer, *A Short History of Science to*
   the Nineteenth Century (Oxford: Oxford
   University Press, 1941).

Notes (CH. XIV)

1 Charles Singer, *A Short History of Science*
   to the Nineteenth Century (Oxford: Oxford
   University Press, 1941), p.289.

2 Arthur Donovan, *Antoine Lavoisier: Science,*
   Administration and Revolution (Oxford:
   Blackwell, 1993), p.142.

3 J. A. Cochran, *Lavoisier* (London, 1931),
   p.58.

4 Antoine Laurent Lavoisier, *Mémoires de*
   Chimie, Tome 2 (1805), p.78.

5 Lavoisier, *Mémoires de Chimie, Tome 2,*
   pp.83–84.

6 Cochran, *Lavoisier*, p.115.

7 Bernadette Bensaude-Vincent, *Dans le*
   laboratoire de Lavoisier, livre illustré (1993),
   p.40.

8 Bensaude-Vincent, *Dans le laboratoire*, p.33.

9 Richard Kirwan, *An Essay on Phlogiston,*
   and the Constitution of Acids (London, 1787),
   p.35.

10 Donovan, *Antoine Lavoisier*, p.126.

11 Cochran, *Lavoisier*, p.128.

12 Donovan, *Antoine Lavoisier*, p.113.

13 Édouard Grimaux, *Lavoisier, 1743–1794.*
   D'après sa correspondance, ses manuscrits,
   ses papiers de famille, et d'autres documents
   inédits, etc. (Paris, 1888), p.258.

14 Grimaux, *Lavoisier, 1743–1794*, p.259.

15 Grimaux, *Lavoisier, 1743–1794*, p.263.

16 Grimaux, *Lavoisier, 1743–1794*, p.264.

17 Georges Moncloux, *Dénonciation présentée au Comité de Législation de la Convention Nationale contre le Représentant du Peuple Dupin par les Veuves et Enfans des ci-devant Fermiers Généraux* (Paris: Du Pont, 1795), p.6.

18 Cochran, *Lavoisier*, p.226.

19 Cochran, *Lavoisier*, p.249.

20 Grimaux, *Lavoisier, 1743–1794*, p.74.

21 Grimaux, *Lavoisier, 1743–1794*, p.279.

22 Moncloux, *Dénonciation présentée au Comité*, p.9.

23 *Rapport des Commissaires réviseurs des trois compagnies de Finances aux Représentants du Peuple chargés de surveiller leurs travaux, et lu aux Comités des Finances et de la Comptabilité* (Paris, 1794), p.180.

24 Grimaux, *Lavoisier, 1743–1794*, pp.280–282.

25 Cochran, *Lavoisier*, p.251.

26 Moncloux, *Dénonciation présentée au Comité*, Pièce Justificative no. 1, p.42.

27 Bensaude-Vincent, *Dans le laboratoire*, p.73.

28 Moncloux, *Dénonciation présentée au Comité*, Pièce Justificative no. 1, p.41.

29 Grimaux, *Lavoisier, 1743–1794*, p.318.

30 Grimaux, *Lavoisier, 1743–1794*, p.320.

31 Grimaux, *Lavoisier, 1743–1794*, p.321.

32 Antoine Laurent Lavoisier, *Mémoires de Chimie, Tome 1* (1805), introduction.

33 Antoine Laurent Lavoisier, *Mémoires de Chimie, Tome 2*, p.245.

CHAPTER XV

Principal Published Sources

Anne Brassie, *Robert Brasillach ou encore un instant de bonheur* (Paris: Editions Robert Laffont, 1987).

André Chénier, *Oeuvres Complètes* (Paris: Gallimard Pléiade, 1958).

Marie-Joseph Chénier, *Poésies Diverses de Marie-Joseph Chénier* (Paris, 1818).

Jean Fabre, *André Chénier, l'Homme et l'Oeuvre* (Paris: Hatier-Boivin, 1955).

L. Becq de Fouquières (ed.), *Oeuvres en Prose de André Chénier* (Paris, 1872).

L. Becq de Fouquières (ed.) *Documents Nouveaux sur André Chénier* (Paris, 1875).

André Marc Grange, *Journal d'Aimée de Coigny* (Paris: Librairie académique Perrin, 1981).

Monique de Huertas, *Aimée de Coigny* (Paris: Pygmalion, 2001).

Alice Yaeger Kaplan, *The collaborator: the trial & execution of Robert Brasillach* (Chicago: University of Chicago Press, 2000).

André Lagarde, *XVIIIe siecle, Les grands auteurs Franais du programme, 4* ([S.l.] : Bordas Collection Textes et Litterature, 1965).

Hervé Leuwers, *Robespierre* (Paris: Fayard, 2014).

Sophie Matthiesson, 'Marking Time: Prison Art in Revolutionary France' (unpublished, 2017).

Francis Harold Scarfe, *André Chénier: His Life and Work, 1762–1794* (Oxford: Clarendon Press, 1965).

Léon Séché, Études d'histoire romantique: Alfred de Musset (Paris: Société du Mercure de France 1907).

G. Venzac, *Jeux d'Ombre et de Lumiere sur la Jeunesse d'André Chénier* (1957).

Oscar de *Vallée, André Chénier et les Jacobins* (Paris: Michel Lévy frères, 1881).

Alfred de Vigny, *Oeuvres Complètes, Tome 2* (Paris: Gallimard, 1993).

Gérard Walter, *André Chénier: Son Milieu et Son Temps* (Paris, 1947).

Henry D. Sedgwick, *Alfred de Musset, 1810–1857* (Indianapolis: Bobbs-Merrill Co., 1931).

Notes (CH. XV)

1 Monique de Huertas, *Aimée de Coigny* (Paris: Pygmalion, 2001), p.98.

2 Gérard Walter, *André Chénier: son milieu et son temps* (Paris, 1947), p.287.

3 Walter, *André Chénier*, p.268.

4 Jean-Antoine Roucher, *Consolations de ma Captivité ou Correspondance de Roucher Mort Victime de la Tyrannie Décemvirale, le 7 Thermidor, an 2 de la République Française, Tome 1* (1797), Lettre 84, p.273.

5 Francis Harold Scarfe, *André Chénier:*

His Life and Work, 1762–1794 (Oxford: Clarenden Press, 1965), p.351.

6 Paul Dimoff (ed.), *Oeuvres Complètes d'Andre Chenier, Tome 2* (1910), pp.157–158.

7 Walter, *André Chénier*, p.90.

8 Walter, *André Chénier*, p.127.

9 G. Venzac, *Jeux d'Ombre et de Lumiere sur le Jeunesse d'Andre Chenier* (1957), p.188.

10 Scarfe, *André Chénier*, p.371.

11 L. Becq de Fouquières (ed.), *Oeuvres en Prose de André Chénier* (Paris, 1872), p.1.

12 Fouquières, *Oeuvres en Prose*, p.12.

13 Walter, *André Chénier*, p.291.

14 André Chénier, *Oeuvres Complètes* (Paris: Gallimard Pléiade, 1958), p.148.

15 Huertas, *Aimée de Coigny*, p.112.

16 L. Becq de Fouquières (ed.) *Documents Nouveaux sur André Chénier* (Paris, 1875), p.122.

17 Scarfe, *André Chénier*, p.330.

18 Alfred de Vigny, *Oeuvres Complètes, Tome 2* (Paris: Gallimard, 1993), p.79.

19 Huertas, *Aimée de Coigny*, p.102.

20 Walter, *André Chénier*, p.305.

21 Fouquières (ed.), *Oeuvres en Prose*, p.163.

22 Fouquières (ed.), *Oeuvres en Prose*, p.79.

23 Fouquières (ed.), *Oeuvres en Prose*, p.74.

24 Sophie Matthiesson, 'Marking Time: Prison Art in Revolutionary France' (unpublished work, 2017), p.166.

25 Fouquières (ed.), *Oeuvres en Prose*, p.110.

26 Scarfe, *André Chénier*, p.198.

27 Marie-Joseph Chénier, *Poésies Diverses de Marie-Joseph Chénier* (Paris, 1818), pp.95–96.

28 Jean Fabre, *André Chénier, l'Homme et l'Oeuvre* (Paris: Hatier-Boivin, 1955), p.114.

29 Walter, *André Chénier*, p.348.

30 Walter, *André Chénier*, p.354.

31 David Zimmermann, *Alexandre Dumas le Grand: Biographie* (Paris: Julliard, 1993), p.99.

32 Henry D. Sedgwick, *Alfred de Musset, 1810–1857* (Indianapolis: Bobbs-Merrill Co., 1931), p.32.

33 Léon Séché, Études d'histoire romantique: A. de Musset, d'après des documents

inédits (Paris: Société du Mercure de France, 1907), p.213.

34 Scarfe, *André Chénier*, p.299.

35 Scarfe, *André Chénier*, p.330.

36 Scarfe, *André Chénier*, p.331.

37 Anne Brassie, *Robert Brasillach ou encore un instant de bonheur* (Paris: Editions Robert Laffont, 1987), p.320.

38 Brassie, *Robert Brasillach*, p.329.

CHAPTER XVI
Principal Published Sources

Hymnes adoptées par la Section du Panthéon Français pour être chantées au Temple de la Raison (Paris, 1792).

Le Grand Dictionnaire Universel du XIXe Siècle (Paris, 1875).

C.A.Sainte-Beuve, *'Causeries du Lundi' Tome Complémentaire comprenant les lettres, articles non encore receuillis avec une table lexique alphabétique des 11 volumes* (Paris, 1856).

Jean-François de La Harpe, 'Oeuvres', *Correspondance Littéraire*, Vol. 14, (Paris, 1820–1821).

Charles Marc des Granges, *Histoire Illustrée de la Littérature Française* (Paris: Hatier, 1917).

Antoine Guillois, *Pendant la Terreur: le Poète Roucher, 1745–1794* (Paris: Calmann Lévy, 1890).

Antoine Guillois, *Le Salon de Madame Helvétius: Cabanis et les Idéologues* (Paris: Calmann Lévy, 1894).

R. A. Leigh (ed.), *Correspondance Complète de Jean Jacques Rousseau, Tome 12* (Oxford: Voltaire Foundation, 1982).

Jean Lessay, *Rivarol: "le Français par excellence"* (Paris: Perrin, 1989).

Marie de Vichy Chamrond Du Deffand et al., *Lettres de la Marquise du Deffand à Horace Walpole (1766–1780). Première édition complète, augmentée d'environ 500 lettres inédites publiées d'après les originaux, avec une introduction, des notes, et une table des noms par Mrs. Paget Toynbee* (Londres: Methuen et Cie, 1912).

Jean-Antoine Roucher, *Les Mois: Poème en Douze Chants* (Liège, 1780).

Jean-Antoine Roucher, *Consolations de ma Captivité ou Correspondance de Roucher Mort Victime de la Tyrannie Décemvirale, le 7 Thermidor, an 2 de la République Française, Tome 1* (1797).

Christopher Todd, *Voltaire's Disciple Jean François de La Harpe* (London: Modern Humanities Research Association, 1972).

Notes (CH. XVI)

1 *Le Grand Dictionnaire Universel du XIXe Siècle* (Paris, 1875), p.1426.

2 Antoine Guillois, *Pendant la Terreur: le Poète Roucher, 1745–1794* (Paris: Calmann Lévy, 1890), p.15.

3 Guillois, *Pendant la Terreur*, p.15.

4 *Le Grand Dictionnaire*, p.1426.

5 R. A. Leigh (ed.), *Correspondance Complète de Jean Jacques Rousseau, Tome 12* (Oxford: Voltaire Foundation, 1982), p.36.

6 Guillois, *Pendant la Terreur*, p.71.

7 Antoine Guillois, *Le Salon de Madame Helvétius: Cabanis et les Idéologues* (Paris: Calmann Lévy, 1894), p.40.

8 Leigh (ed.), *Correspondance Complète de Jean Jacques Rousseau, Tome 12*, Lettre 7704 (Mai 1780).

9 Jean-François de La Harpe, 'Oeuvres', *Correspondance Littéraire*, Vol.14, (Paris, 1820–1821), 251.

10 Guillois, *Pendant la Terreur*, p.24.

11 Guillois, *Pendant la Terreur*, p.72.

12 Jean Antoine Roucher, *Les Mois: Poème en Douze Chants* (Liège, 1780), p.302.

13 Guillois, *Pendant la Terreur*, pp.74–77.

14 Jean Lessay, *Rivarol: "le Français par excellence"* (Paris: Perrin, 1989), p.216.

15 Guillois, *Pendant la Terreur*, p.166.

16 *Hymnes adoptées par la Section du Panthéon Français pour être chantées au Temple de la Raison* (Paris, 1792).

17 Guillois, *Pendant la Terreur*, p.150.

18 Guillois, *Pendant la Terreur*, p.169.

19 Jean-Antoine Roucher, *Consolations de ma Captivité ou Correspondance, Tome 1* (Paris, 1797), Lettre 18, p.48.

20 Roucher, *Consolations de ma Captivité ou Correspondance, Tome 1*, Lettre 80, p.256.

21 Roucher, *Consolations de ma Captivité ou Correspondance, Tome 1*, Lettre 69, p.223.

22 Roucher, *Consolations de ma Captivité ou Correspondance, Tome 1*, Lettre 13, p.36.

23 Roucher, *Consolations de ma Captivité ou Correspondance, Tome 1*, Lettre 15, p.40.

24 Roucher, *Consolations de ma Captivité ou Correspondance, Tome 1*, Lettre 73, p.233.

25 Roucher, *Consolations de ma Captivité ou Correspondance, Tome 1*, Lettre 83, p.271.

26 Roucher, *Consolations de ma Captivité ou Correspondance, Tome 1*, Lettre 36, p.91.

27 Roucher, *Consolations de ma Captivité ou Correspondance, Tome 2*, Lettre 132, p.178.

28 Roucher, *Consolations de ma Captivité ou Correspondance, Tome 2*, Lettre 108, p.58.

29 Roucher, *Consolations de ma Captivité ou Correspondance, Tome 1*, Lettre 42, p.112.

30 Roucher, *Consolations de ma Captivité ou Correspondance, Tome 1*, Lettre 75, pp.240–248.

31 Roucher, *Consolations de ma Captivité ou Correspondance, Tome 1*, Lettre 81, pp.257–270.

32 Roucher, *Consolations de ma Captivité ou Correspondance, Tome 1*, Lettre 75, pp.240–248.

33 Roucher, *Consolations de ma Captivité ou Correspondance, Tome 1*, Lettre 84, p.273.

34 Roucher, *Consolations de ma Captivité ou Correspondance, Tome 1*, Lettre 89, p.299.

35 Roucher, *Consolations de ma Captivité ou Correspondance, Tome 1*, Lettre 65, p.206.

36 Roucher, *Consolations de ma Captivité ou Correspondance, Tome 2*, Lettre 150, p.243.

37 Guillois, *Pendant la Terreur*, p.265.

38 Roucher, *Consolations de ma Captivité ou Correspondance, Tome 1*, Lettre 86, p.284.

39 Roucher, *Consolations de ma Captivité ou Correspondance, Tome 2*, Lettre 104, p.43.

40 Roucher, *Consolations de ma Captivité ou Correspondance, Tome 2*, Lettre 102, p.40.

41 Roucher, *Consolations de ma Captivité ou Correspondance, Tome 2*, Lettre 104, p.42.

42 Guillois, *Pendant la Terreur*, p.186.

43 Roucher, *Consolations de ma Captivité ou Correspondance, Tome 2*, Lettre 116, p.96.

44 Roucher, *Consolations de ma Captivité ou Correspondance, Tome 2*, Lettre 130, pp.163–166.

45 Roucher, *Consolations de ma Captivité ou Correspondance, Tome 2*, Lettre 130, p.163.

46 Matthiesson, Marking Time, p.170.

47 Gérard Walter, *André Chénier: Son Milieu et Son Temps* (Paris, 1947), p.323.

48 C. A. Sainte-Beuve, '*Causeries du Lundi' Tome Complémentaire comprenant les lettres, articles non encore receuillis avec une table lexique alphabétique des 11 volumes* (Paris, 1856), p.670.

49 Charles Marc des Granges, *Histoire Illustrée de la Littérature Française* (Paris: Hatier, 1917), p.670.

50 Auction held on 17 November 2015 at Maître Tajan, rue des Mathurins, Paris.

CHAPTER XVII

Principal Published Sources

Amnesty International 'Russian Women of Conscience. Report on the Small Zone' (July, 1985) reprinted in Irina Ratushinskaya, *No, I'm Not Afraid* (Newcastle upon Tyne: Bloodaxe Books, 1986).

Anne Applebaum, *Gulag: A History of the Soviet Camps* (London: Book Club Associates, 2003).

Orlando Figes, *Just Send Me Word: A True Story of Love and Survival in the Gulag* (London: Allen Lane, 2012).

Igor Gerashchenko, 'About the Arrest of Irina Ratushinskaya', in Irina Ratushinskaya, *No, I'm Not Afraid* (Newcastle upon Tyne: Bloodaxe Books, 1986).

Irina Ratushinskaya, *No, I'm Not Afraid* (Newcastle upon Tyne: Bloodaxe Books, 1986).

Irina Ratushinskaya, *Grey is the Colour of Hope* (London: Hodder and Stoughton, 1988).

Irina Ratushinskaya, *In the Beginning* (London: Hodder and Stoughton, 1990).

Irina Ratushinskaya, *Dance with a Shadow* (Newcastle Upon Tyne: Bloodaxe Books, 1992).

Peter Reddaway (ed.), *Uncensored Russia: The Human Rights Movement in the Soviet Union; The Annotated Text of the Unofficial Moscow Journal: A Chronicle of Current Events, Nos. 1–11* (London: Cape, 1972).

Michael Scammell, *Solzhenitsyn: A Biography* (New York: Norton, 1984).

Michael Scammell, 'Love Against All Odds', *New York Review of Books* (June 21, 2012).

Alexander Solzhenitsyn, *The Gulag Archipelago, 1918–56: An Experiment in Literary Investigation* (London: Harvill Press, 2003).

Yevgenia Semyonovna, *Into the Whirlwind* (Harmondsworth: Penguin Books, 1968).

Alexander Solzhenitsyn, *One Day in the Life of Ivan Denisovich* (New York: Dutton, 1963).

D. M. Thomas, *Alexander Solzhenitsyn: A Century in His Life* (London: Little, Brown, 1998).

Notes (CH. XVII)

1 Anne Applebaum, *Gulag: A History of the Soviet Camps* (London: Book Club Associates, 2003), p.3.

2 Applebaum, *Gulag*, p.517.

3 Applebaum, *Gulag*, p.4.

4 Applebaum, *Gulag*, p.64.

5 Applebaum, *Gulag*, p.106.

6 Applebaum, *Gulag*, p.63.

7 Yevgenia Semyonovna, *Into the Whirlwind* (Harmondsworth: Penguin Books, 1968), p.132.

8 Applebaum, *Gulag*, p.421.

9 Olga Cooke, 'Evgeniia Semenovna Ginzburg', in Neil Cornwall (ed.) *Reference Guide to Russian Literature* (London: Fitzroy Dearborn, 1998), p.321.

10 Allan Chappelow, *Shaw – 'the chucker-out': A Biographical Exposition and Critique, and*

a *Companion to and Commentary on 'Shaw
the Villager'* (London: Allen & Unwin,
1969), p.211.

11 Chappelow, *Shaw – 'the chucker-out'*, p.228.
12 Applebaum, *Gulag*, p.430.
13 Applebaum, *Gulag*, p.518.
14 Applebaum, *Gulag*, p.518.
15 Michael Scammell, *Solzhenitsyn: A
Biography* (New York: Norton, 1984), p.153.
16 Scammell, *Solzhenitsyn*, p.191.
17 Scammell, *Solzhenitsyn*, p.211.
18 Applebaum, *Gulag*, p.335.
19 Irina Ratushinskaya, *Grey is the Colour of
Hope* (London: Hodder and Stoughton,
1988), p.21.
20 Scammell, *Solzhenitsyn*, p.82.
21 Scammell, *Solzhenitsyn*, p.284.
22 Scammell, *Solzhenitsyn*, p.284.
23 Scammell, *Solzhenitsyn*, p.282.
24 Alexander Solzhenitsyn, *One Day in the
Life of Ivan Denisovich* (New York: Dutton,
1963), p.16.
25 Scammell, *Solzhenitsyn*, p.354.
26 Scammell, *Solzhenitsyn*, p.410.
27 Solzhenitsyn, *One Day in the Life*, p.191.
28 Scammell, *Solzhenitsyn*, p.448.
29 Scammell, *Solzhenitsyn*, p.840.
30 Orlando Figes, *Just Send Me Word: A True
Story of Love and Survival in the Gulag*
(London: Allen Lane, 2012), p.26.
31 Figes, *Just Send Me Word*, p.29.
32 Figes, *Just Send Me Word*, p.31.
33 Figes, *Just Send Me Word*, p.47.
34 Figes, *Just Send Me Word*, p.48.
35 Figes, *Just Send Me Word*, p.55.
36 Figes, *Just Send Me Word*, p.191.
37 Figes, *Just Send Me Word*, p.53.
38 Figes, *Just Send Me Word*, p.55.
39 Figes, *Just Send Me Word*, p.57.
40 Figes, *Just Send Me Word*, p.58.
41 Figes, *Just Send Me Word*, p.62.
42 Figes, *Just Send Me Word*, p.65.
43 Figes, *Just Send Me Word*, p.67.
44 Figes, *Just Send Me Word*, p.68.
45 Cooke, 'Evgeniia Semenovna Ginzburg', in
Cornwall (ed.) *Reference Guide to Russian*,
p.253.

46 Figes, *Just Send Me Word*, p.92.
47 Figes, *Just Send Me Word*, p.95.
48 Figes, *Just Send Me Word*, p.98.
49 Figes, *Just Send Me Word*, p.156.
50 Figes, *Just Send Me Word*, p.117.
51 Figes, *Just Send Me Word*, p.121.
52 Figes, *Just Send Me Word*, p.128.
53 Figes, *Just Send Me Word*, p.132.
54 Figes, *Just Send Me Word*, p.208.
55 Figes, *Just Send Me Word*, p.268.
56 Figes, *Just Send Me Word*, p.279.
57 Figes, *Just Send Me Word*, p.281.
58 Figes, *Just Send Me Word*, p.298.
59 Applebaum, *Gulag*, p.497.
60 Figes, *Just Send Me Word*, p.1.
61 Figes, *Just Send Me Word*, p.294.
62 Figes, *Just Send Me Word*, p.287.
63 Irina Ratushinskaya, *No, I'm Not Afraid*
(Newcastle Upon Tyne: Bloodaxe Books,
1986), p.10.
64 Ratushinskaya, *No, I'm Not Afraid*, p.10.
65 Ratushinskaya, *No, I'm Not Afraid*, p.11.
66 Irina Ratushinskaya, *In the Beginning*
(London: Hodder and Stoughton, 1990),
p.238.
67 Ratushinskaya, *In the Beginning*, p.241.
68 Ratushinskaya, *In the Beginning*, p.246.
69 Ratushinskaya, *In the Beginning*, p.274.
70 Irina Ratushinskaya, *Grey is the Colour of
Hope* (London: Hodder and Stoughton,
1988), p.38.
71 Ratushinskaya, *No, I'm Not Afraid*, p.34.
72 Ratushinskaya, *Grey is the Colour of Hope*,
p.165.
73 Ratushinskaya, *Grey is the Colour of Hope*,
p.170.
74 Ratushinskaya, *Grey is the Colour of Hope*,
p.39.
75 Applebaum, *Gulag*, p.479.
76 Applebaum, *Gulag*, p.474–476.
77 Ratushinskaya, *No, I'm Not Afraid*,
pp.31–44.
78 Scammell, *Solzhenitsyn*, p.636.
79 Peter Reddaway (ed.), *Uncensored Russia:
The Human Rights Movement in the Soviet
Union; The Annotated Text of the Unofficial
Moscow Journal: A Chronicle of Current*

Events, Nos. 1–11 (London: Cape, 1972),
p.20.

80 Applebaum, *Gulag*, p.478.

81 Reddaway (ed.), *Uncensored Russia*,
pp.25–26.

82 Reddaway (ed.), *Uncensored Russia*, p.27.

83 Reddaway (ed.), *Uncensored Russia*, p.23.

84 Ratushinskaya, *Grey is the Colour of Hope*,
p.236.

85 Ratushinskaya, *Grey is the Colour of Hope*,
p.44.

86 Ratushinskaya, *Grey is the Colour of Hope*,
pp.103–107.

87 Ratushinskaya, *No, I'm Not Afraid*, p.49.

88 Ratushinskaya, *Grey is the Colour of Hope*,
p.72.

89 Ratushinskaya, *Grey is the Colour of Hope*,
pp.165–166.

90 Ratushinskaya, *Grey is the Colour of Hope*,
p.67.

91 Ratushinskaya, *Grey is the Colour of Hope*,
p.69.

92 Ratushinskaya, *No, I'm not Afraid*, p.43.

93 Ratushinskaya, *Grey is the Colour of Hope*,
p.68.

94 Ratushinskaya, *Grey is the Colour of Hope*,
p.173.

95 Ratushinskaya, *Grey is the Colour of Hope*,
p.179.

96 Ratushinskaya, *Grey is the Colour of Hope*,
p.124.

97 Ratushinskaya, *No, I'm Not Afraid*, p.12.

98 Ratushinskaya, *In the Beginning*, p.122.

CHAPTER XVIII
Principal Published Sources

Benjamin Appert, *Bagnes, Prisons et Criminels,
Tome 4* (Paris, 1836).

André Castelot, *Louis-Philippe: Le Méconnu*
(Paris: Perrin, 1994).

Jacques Cellard, *Anthologie de la littérature
argotique: des origines à nos jours* (Paris:
Mazarine, 1985).

Cour des Pairs, *Attentat du 28 Juillet, 1835.
Procédure. Dépositions de Témoins*, No.290
(Paris, 1836).

Anne-Emmanuelle Demartini, *L'Affaire
Lacenaire* (Paris: Aubier, 2001).

Lisa Downing, *The Subject of Murder: Gender,
Exceptionality, and the Modern Killer*
(Chicago: University of Chicago Press,
2013).

François Foucart, *Lacenaire: L'Assassin
Démythifié* (Paris: Perrin, 1995).

Joseph Frank, *Dostoevsky* (London: Robson,
1995).

Pierre F. F. J. H. Giraud, *Histoire générale des
prisons sous le règne de Buonaparte* (Paris,
1814).

Stéphane Guégan, *Théophile Gautier* (Paris:
Éds. Gallimard, 2011).

Pierre François Lacenaire, *Mémoires,
Révélations et Poésies de Lacenaire, Tome 1*
(Paris: Marchands de nouveautés 1836).

Jacques Simonelli (ed.), *Mémoires et autres
écrits* (Paris: Librairie José Corti, 1991).

Philip John Stead (ed.), *The Memoirs of
Lacenaire* (London: Staples Press, 1952).

Edward Baron Turk, *Child of Paradise: Marcel
Carné and the Golden Age of French Cinema*
(Cambridge, Mass.: Harvard University
Press, 1989).

Notes (CH. XVIII)

1 Pierre François Lacenaire, *Mémoires,
Révélations et Poésies de Lacenaire, Tome 1*
(Paris: Marchands de nouveautés 1836),
p.205.

2 Lacenaire, *Mémoires, Révélations et Poésies
de Lacenaire, Tome 1*, pp.170–172.

3 Lacenaire, *Mémoires, Révélations et Poésies
de Lacenaire, Tome 2* (Paris: Marchands de
nouveautés 1836), p.213.

4 Lacenaire, *Mémoires, Révélations et Poésies
de Lacenaire, Tome 2*, p.172.

5 Lacenaire, *Mémoires, Révélations et Poésies
de Lacenaire, Tome 2*, pp.218–219.

6 P. F. F. J. Giraud, *Histoire Générale des
Prisons sous le Règne de Buonaparte* (Paris,
1814), p.53.

7 Giraud, *Histoire Générale*, p.53.

8 François Foucart, *Lacenaire: L'Assassin
Démythifié* (Paris: Perrin, 1995), p.263.

9 Lacenaire, *Mémoires, Révélations et Poésies de Lacenaire, Tome 1*, pp.127–129.

10 Lacenaire, *Mémoires, Révélations et Poésies de Lacenaire, Tome 2*, p.290.

11 Philip John Stead (ed.), *The Memoirs of Lacenaire* (London: Staples Press, 1952), p.19.

12 Lacenaire, *Mémoires, Révélations et Poésies de Lacenaire, Tome 2*, p.217.

13 Benjamin Appert, *Bagnes, Prisons et Criminels, Tome 4* (Paris, 1836), p.239.

14 Appert, *Bagnes*, p.367.

15 Anne-Emmanuelle Demartini, *L'Affaire Lacenaire* (Paris: Aubier, 2001), pp.318–323.

16 Lacenaire, *Mémoires, Révélations et Poésies de Lacenaire, Tome 1*, p.xxv.

17 Lacenaire, *Mémoires, Révélations et Poésies de Lacenaire, Tome 2*, p.112.

18 Demartini, *L'Affaire*, p.398.

19 André Castelot, *Louis-Philippe: Le Méconnu* (Paris: Perrin, 1994), p.279.

20 Cour des Pairs, *Attentat du 28 Juillet, 1835. Procédure. Dépositions de Témoins*, No.290 (Paris, 1836), pp.457–459.

21 Stéphane Guégan, *Théophile Gautier* (Paris: Éds. Gallimard, 2011), p.89.

22 Guégan, *Théophile*, p.90.

23 Appert, *Bagnes, Prisons et Criminels, Tome 4*, p.305.

24 Lacenaire, *Mémoires, Révélations et Poésies de Lacenaire, Tome 1*, p.113.

25 Lacenaire, *Mémoires, Révélations et Poésies de Lacenaire, Tome 1*, p.165.

26 Lacenaire, *Mémoires, Révélations et Poésies de Lacenaire, Tome 1*, p.199.

27 Lacenaire, *Mémoires, Révélations et Poésies de Lacenaire, Tome 1*, p.153.

28 Lacenaire, *Mémoires, Révélations et Poésies de Lacenaire, Tome 1*, p.150.

29 Lacenaire, *Mémoires, Révélations et Poésies de Lacenaire, Tome 2*, p.39.

30 Lacenaire, *Mémoires, Révélations et Poésies de Lacenaire, Tome 2*, p.198.

31 Jacques Simonelli (ed.), *Mémoires et autres écrits* (Paris: Librairie José Corti, 1991), p.287.

32 Foucart, *Lacenaire*, p.281.

33 Stendhal, *Lamiel* (Paris, 1899), p.302.

34 Guégan, *Théophile*, p.50.

35 Simonelli (ed.), *Mémoires*, p.17.

36 Joseph Frank, *Dostoevsky* (London: Robson, 1995), pp.66–67.

37 Edward Baron Turk, *Child of Paradise: Marcel Carné and the Golden Age of French Cinema* (Cambridge, Mass.: Harvard University Press, 1989), p.265.

38 Jacques Cellard (ed.), *Anthologie de la Littérature Argotique des Origines à Nos Jours* (Paris: Mazarine, 1985), p.135.

39 *Le Journal d'Adèle Hugo* (20 décembre 1853), p.439.

CHAPTER XIX
Principal Published Sources

Annual Report of the Curators of the Bodleian Library (1923).

Henry Steele Commager (ed.), *The Blue and the Grey: The Story of the Civil War as Told by Participants, Vol. 2* (Indianapolis: Bobbs-Merrill, 1950).

Peter Gilliver, *The Making of the Oxford English Dictionary* (Oxford: Oxford University Press, 2016).

'Dr. Murray's annual statements, Transactions of the Philological Society' (1883, 1887, 1888 and 1894).

James A. H. Murray (ed.), *A New English Dictionary on Historical Principles; Founded Mainly on the Materials Collected by the Philological Society, Volume V. H to K* (Oxford: Clarendon Press, 1901).

K. M. Elisabeth Murray, *Caught in the Web of Words: James A. H. Murray and the Oxford English Dictionary* (1977).

Simon Winchester, *The Surgeon of Crowthorne: A Tale of Murder, Madness and the Love of Words* (London: Viking, 1998).

Simon Winchester, 'Minor, William Chester (1834–1920)', *Oxford Dictionary of National Biography* (online ed.). Oxford University Press (2004).

Notes (CH. XIX)

1 Simon Winchester, *The Surgeon of Crowthorne: A Tale of Murder, Madness and the Love of Words* (London: Viking, 1998), p.122.

2 Winchester, *The Surgeon of Crowthorne*, p.52.

3 Henry Steele Commager (ed.), *The Blue and the Grey: The Story of the Civil War as Told by Participants, Vol. 2* (Indianapolis: Bobbs-Merrill, 1950), p.982.

4 Winchester, *The Surgeon of Crowthorne*, p.107.

5 Winchester, *The Surgeon of Crowthorne*, p.108.

6 Winchester, *The Surgeon of Crowthorne*, p.139.

7 Winchester, *The Surgeon of Crowthorne*, p.91.

8 Winchester, *The Surgeon of Crowthorne*, p.84.

9 Winchester, *The Surgeon of Crowthorne*, p.96.

10 K. M. Elisabeth Murray, *Caught in the Web of Words: James A. H. Murray and the Oxford English Dictionary* (1977), p.212.

11 Murray, *Caught in the Web of Words*, p.236.

12 Murray, *Caught in the Web of Words*, p.169.

13 Murray, *Caught in the Web of Words*, p.187.

14 Winchester, *The Surgeon of Crowthorne*, p.142.

15 *Transactions of the Philological Society* (1897 and 1899).

16 Winchester, *The Surgeon of Crowthorne*, p.160.

17 Winchester, *The Surgeon of Crowthorne*, p.154.

18 Winchester, *The Surgeon of Crowthorne*, p.155.

19 Peter Gilliver, *The Making of the Oxford English Dictionary* (Oxford: Oxford University Press, 2016), p.460.

Picture credits

Index